The Children of China's Great Migration

In China in 2018, there were over 280 million rural off-farm and migrant workers, approximately 173 million of whom moved beyond the borders of their registered hometowns, fuelling the country's rapid economic boom. In the 2010s over 61 million rural children had at least one parent who had migrated without them, while nearly half had been left behind by both parents. Rachel Murphy draws on her longitudinal fieldwork in two landlocked provinces to explore the experiences of these left-behind children and to examine the impact of this great migration on childhood and family relationships in China. Using children's voices, Murphy provides a multifaceted insight into experiences of parental migration, education, study pressures, poverty, institutional discrimination, patrilineal family culture and reconfigured gendered and intergenerational relationships.

RACHEL MURPHY is Professor of Chinese Development and Society and a fellow of St. Antony's College at the University of Oxford. She is President of the British Association of Chinese Studies and the author of *How Migrant Labor Is Changing Rural China* (Cambridge University Press, 2002).

The Children of China's Great Migration

Rachel Murphy
University of Oxford

CAMBRIDGE
UNIVERSITY PRESS

University Printing House, Cambridge CB2 8BS, United Kingdom

One Liberty Plaza, 20th Floor, New York, NY 10006, USA

477 Williamstown Road, Port Melbourne, VIC 3207, Australia

314–321, 3rd Floor, Plot 3, Splendor Forum, Jasola District Centre,
New Delhi – 110025, India

79 Anson Road, #06–04/06, Singapore 079906

Cambridge University Press is part of the University of Cambridge.

It furthers the University's mission by disseminating knowledge in the pursuit of
education, learning, and research at the highest international levels of excellence.

www.cambridge.org
Information on this title: www.cambridge.org/9781108834858
DOI: 10.1017/9781108877251

© Rachel Murphy 2020

This publication is in copyright. Subject to statutory exception
and to the provisions of relevant collective licensing agreements,
no reproduction of any part may take place without the written
permission of Cambridge University Press.

First published 2020

A catalogue record for this publication is available from the British Library.

Library of Congress Cataloging-in-Publication Data
Names: Murphy, Rachel, 1971– author.
Title: The children of China's great migration / Rachel Murphy.
Description: Cambridge, United Kingdom ; New York, NY : Cambridge
University Press, 2020. | Includes bibliographical references and index.
Identifiers: LCCN 2020013776 (print) | LCCN 2020013777 (ebook) | ISBN
9781108834858 (hardback) | ISBN 9781108877251 (ebook)
Subjects: LCSH: Children of internal migrants – China. | Rural children – China –
Social conditions. | Rural-urban migration – China. | Families – China.
Classification: LCC HQ792.C5 M87 2020 (print) | LCC HQ792.C5 (ebook) | DDC
306.850951–dc23
LC record available at https://lccn.loc.gov/2020013776
LC ebook record available at https://lccn.loc.gov/2020013777

ISBN 978-1-108-83485-8 Hardback

Cambridge University Press has no responsibility for the persistence or accuracy of
URLs for external or third-party internet websites referred to in this publication
and does not guarantee that any content on such websites is, or will remain,
accurate or appropriate.

Contents

List of Figures and Maps		*page* vi
List of Tables		viii
Acknowledgements		ix
1	Understanding the Lives of Left-Behind Children in Rural China	1
2	Migration, Education and Family Striving in Four Counties of Anhui and Jiangxi	39
3	Sacrifice and Study	66
4	Boys' and Girls' Experiences of Distribution in Striving Families	95
5	Children in 'Mother At-Home, Father Out' Families	132
6	Children of Lone-Migrant Mothers and At-Home Fathers	162
7	Children in Skipped Generation Families	181
8	Left-Behind Children in Striving Teams	215
Appendix: Field Research on Left-Behind Children in China		234
Bibliography		246
Index		282

v

Figures and Maps

Figures

1.1	The concept of 'striving'	*page* 6
1.2	'Care for left-behind children, build a harmonious school together: exercise for an hour a day and work healthily for fifty years, live happily for a lifetime'	25
2.1	Dormitory in a primary school in a rural township in Tranquil County, Jiangxi	54
2.2	Children looking in a child's storage chest in the dormitory	55
2.3	Children in a township in Eastern County, Anhui, boarding a van to go home for lunch	57
2.4	Dormitory block in a private boarding school in Eastern County, Anhui	58
3.1	Study well, advance upwards every day	76
3.2	Slogan at a primary school in Tranquil County, Jiangxi: 'Strive to improve and advance bravely'	76
3.3	'Care for left-behind children' activity room in a township in Eastern County, Anhui	78
3.4	Care for left-behind children room in Jade County – the plaque reads 'psychological advice'	79
3.5	Child's letter to migrant parents displayed in a junior high school activity room for left-behind children in Jade County, Jiangxi	80
3.6	A township junior high school in Tranquil County, Jiangxi – structure to life in school	81
3.7	Interaction among children at a primary school in Jade County, Jiangxi	82
4.1	New houses in a village in Tranquil County, Jiangxi	102
4.2	Typical village scene in Eastern County, Anhui, with no newly built houses	104
4.3	Xinhui's family's cottage in a village in Western County, Anhui	106
4.4	Lele's good student certificates in Western County, Anhui	109

4.5	Violin plot of the amount of pocket money received by boys and girls	113
4.6	Washing bowls at a primary school in Tranquil County, Jiangxi	124
4.7	Sweeping the playground in a junior high school in Jade County, Jiangxi	124
4.8	A 'steel cow' in a village in Tranquil County, Jiangxi	127
4.9	A girl in Tranquil County, Jiangxi, whose mother migrated, helps her grandmother	128
5.1	A family on a birth planning billboard in a township in Tranquil County, Jiangxi	136
5.2	Women transplanting rice seedlings in Jade County, Jiangxi	143
5.3	A mother in Eastern County, Anhui, preparing soil to plant cotton seedlings	144
7.1	Boy walking home with his grandmother after school on a Friday afternoon, Jade County, Jiangxi	199
7.2	Students buying snacks outside school	201
A.1	Children playing with an improvised slide at a township primary school in Jade County, Jiangxi	240
A.2	To the rural homes to interview caregivers	241

Maps

1	Map of China	xiv

Tables

2.1	Annual per capita disposable income of rural and urban residents (2015)	*page* 41
4.1	Sibling composition of the families of 109 child respondents (Number)	101
4.2	OLS regression of pocket money distribution to children by gender and parents' migration status	114
4.3	Logistic regression on children's receipt of gifts from migrant parents by child's gender	116
7.1	Count of children by care history and adult(s) to whom they felt closest	197
A.1	Distribution of 109 children interviewees by parents' migration status	237

Acknowledgements

I have accumulated many debts of gratitude in writing this book, and other debts of gratitude in the years before starting this project. The book was made possible by support from the British Academy and grants from the University of Oxford. In 2010 a British Academy Career Development Grant enabled Ran Tao, Professor of Economics at Renmin University, and me to carry out a joint survey-based project on the impact of parental migration on the educational well-being of children left behind in rural China. A John Fell Fund Grant from the University of Oxford also supported us in this project. Then in 2013 a British Academy Mid-Career Award enabled me to conduct fieldwork. This built on my two earlier rounds of qualitative fieldwork in 2010 and 2011, supported by my research allowance from the Oxford School of Global and Area Studies. The British Academy Mid-Career Award also gave me time to transcribe and analyse the interviews, and to write four draft chapters of this book, while a Returning Carer's grant from the Social Sciences Division at the University of Oxford permitted me to undertake two further rounds of field-work in 2014 and 2015.

The 2010 survey-based project with Ran Tao was carried out thanks to the efforts and skills of many scholars, notably Chunhui Ye, Professor of Economics at Zhejiang University, and Ran Tao's talented post-graduate students Minhui Zhou and Ernan Cui. Shuangxi Xiao Professor of Economics at Anhui Agricultural University, kindly arranged access to survey sites in Anhui. The survey generated data have permitted me to identify some aggregate trends and to contextualise aspects of the qualitative analysis in this book.

My research career more generally owes a long-standing debt of gratitude to Ran Tao. Our paths crossed when we were post-doctoral researchers in the Contemporary China Studies Programme at Oxford directed by Vivienne Shue in the 2000s. The programme hosted many exciting events on China's political economy and institutions, and I always gained new insights from Ran Tao's astute and knowledgeable observations and commentary. Ran Tao kindly made several valuable introductions that facilitated the fieldwork for this book. He is one of the most innovative and generous scholars I know.

Shuangxi Xiao made essential introductions for my interviews in Anhui. He also sought recommendations from his colleagues for superb research assistants, then graduate students at Anhui Agricultural University – Anqi Yang, Wenxian Chen and Sisi Wang, who turned out to be natural fieldworkers. Shangxi Xiao kindly arranged for me to present my research-in-progress to faculty and students in economics and in social policy at Anhui Agricultural University in September 2015. The feedback from this expert audience was immensely helpful, especially from Jingdong Luan, Professor of Economics, and from Shuanxi Xiao. I am also grateful to Guizhou Zhang and Bencheng Wu for their introductions to fieldwork sites and schools in Anhui and for sharing their deep insights about social change, family and education with me.

My research assistant for two fieldwork visits in Jiangxi was a student from a prefectural technical college located in one of the Jiangxi fieldwork counties. A native of a rural county in Gansu province, her perspectives enriched my understanding of what we heard in the field. I regret that I cannot trace her ten years on to seek her permission to name her here. In my visits in 2013, 2014 and 2015, Xiaoqian Kuang and Longfeng Tu from the Jiangxi Academy of Social Sciences were wonderful research assistants, and their insights and guidance helped me immensely. Shihong Yin, Wei Jiang and Yong Liang provided valuable support at different points. The Jiangxi Academy also warmly looked after my husband John and then eighteen-month-old daughter, Emily, who visited for part of the 2013 fieldwork trip. Additionally, Jennifer Holdaway kindly extended hospitality to John and Emily in Beijing during this visit while I was in Anhui.

I owe special thanks to King Lun Ngok, Professor of Social Policy, for hosting me in his department at Zhongshan University in 2013 and for inviting me to present my research, with the comments of the faculty and students shaping the later development of this project. King Lun Ngok introduced me to his then doctoral student, Yongxin Chen, who efficiently tracked down migrant parents in the Pearl River Delta, navigated the subway and bus system to get us to the relevant factory districts and urban villages, accompanied me on interviews, and contributed many helpful observations and suggestions. I also thank Bin Wu from Nottingham University for welcoming me to join him on a visit to a social work organisation that supported migrant children in an urban village in Guangzhou in August 2017.

I owe busy county and township education officials, principals and teachers in the fieldwork sites immense gratitude for arranging access to the schools, introducing research participants and for talking with me. Meanwhile, the research participants of all ages kindly shared their thoughts and experiences with me and my research assistants. I have used only pseudonyms for people and the fieldwork places in this book, so none of these people are identified. Nonetheless,

Acknowledgements xi

I hope that this book's pages do justice to their accounts and that they would recognise some of their lives in these pages.

At different stages of the research, including when applying for grants and later, in comments after my presentations or in conversations, many people gave valuable support, guidance and insights. It is perilous to name people for fear of missing anyone out, but to miss everyone out would be even worse. I am very grateful for support and/or for enlightening comments and conversations from Suzanne Choi, Harriet Evans, Arianne Gaetano, Charlotte Goodburn, Qin Gao, Susan Greenhalgh, Mette Halskov Hansen, Peter Ho, Jennifer Holdaway, Roy Huijsmans, Tamara Jacka, Jingchun Ji, Anita Koo, Pei Chia Lan, Junfu Li, Qiang Li, Catherine Locke, Jialing Luo, Yao Lu, Jillian Popkins, Nitya Rao, Dorothy Solinger, Stig Thøgersen, Jing Song, Zhuo Wang, Gerda Wielander, Qiaobing Wu, Biao Xiang, Lina Xiao, Zhenning Xu, Brenda Yeoh and Heather Zhang. I also learned much from the sociologist Qiang Li's richly researched monograph on China's left-behind people and am grateful that he gave me a copy.

In 2016 Dan Wang, Professor of the Sociology of Education, hosted me as a visiting professor at the Wah Ching Centre of Research on Chinese Education at Hong Kong University. I am grateful to her for this opportunity, for insightful conversations and for feedback from faculty and students after my seminar presentation, particularly from Ailei Xie, now Professor of the Sociology of Education at Guangzhou University. I am also grateful to Peter Robertson for arranging for me to hold an adjunct professorship at the University of Western Australia (UWA) during 2016–2019. This provided a wonderful environment for me to do writing during summers when visiting my family in Western Australia. He also arranged for me to present an early version of Chapter 4 to the economics department at UWA in 2016, and I benefited greatly from the generous comments of Peter, Anu Rammohan and their colleagues.

Audiences in departments and centres in other institutions also kindly gave their time to engage with my presentations of different parts of the manuscript. This includes presentations in Contemporary Chinese Studies at the University of Westminster, the School of Social Work at Columbia University, the Hong Kong Royal Geographical Society, the University of Oxford China Centre, the Departments of Sociology at Sichuan, Beijing City and Oxford universities, and the Department of Social Work and Social Policy at East China University of Science and Technology. I am also grateful to have participated in a 2013 workshop of migration and social reproduction organised by the School of International Development at the University of East Anglia. Additionally, in 2017 Jillian Popkins arranged for me to present at UNICEF in Beijing, which helped me in thinking through the significance of the research findings.

xii   Acknowledgements

The political scientist and sociologist Neil Ketchley ran the regressions and produced the violin plot and the tables in Chapter 4 and discussed the results with me. My own prior efforts with SPSS paled in comparison to his robust analysis. He kindly assured me that he loves playing with data so much that it was his pleasure to give up his time to this. I am indebted to him for his goodwill and for his cheerful and diligent help. Bo Aerelund, a brilliant sinologist at the University of Copenhagen, read and commented on the entire manuscript with a sharp eye. I cannot thank him enough for his careful and insightful suggestions throughout, and his many improvements to the manuscript. Both Neil Ketchley and Bo Aereland helped enormously in the realisation of this book project in its present form. I am also grateful to Sally Croft for her guidance on style and her proof-reading and checking of references.

Two anonymous readers for Cambridge University Press provided me with valuable and detailed comments for revision. I thank them for their serious engagement with the manuscript, for helping me to improve the presentation and argument and for saving me from errors and omissions. I am grateful to Lucy Rhymer, senior editor at Cambridge, for seeing the potential in this project, for guiding the manuscript through the review process and for helpful discussions of the reviewers' feedback, and to Emily Sharp, editorial assistant, and Natasha Whelan, senior content editor, for all their work in getting this book ready for publication. I also wish to thank Akash Datchinamurthy for efficiently steering the manuscript through production and Judieth Sheeja who carefully copy-edited and prepared the final manuscript.

Before this book research began former mentors brought me to the point where I had the luxury to embark on this project. During my undergraduate and honours years at Murdoch University in Western Australia, Tim Wright greatly inspired me to do research, and his meticulous approach to dissertation guidance has helped me throughout my career – to the extent that I can write critically, I learned this from his supervision and feedback. My research has also been inspired by other wonderful teachers of Chinese society, political economy and gender relations who were at Murdoch University in the early 1990s, including David Goodman, Beverley Hooper, Tamara Jacka and Sally Sargerson.

I received a life-changing scholarship from Trinity College, Cambridge, to study for a doctorate in Sociology, and I am always grateful to Tim Wright for encouraging me to apply. In my years as a doctoral student in Sociology and later as a post-doctoral researcher in Development Studies and at Jesus College at Cambridge, I encountered many perspectives that have stayed with me over the course of my research career. Peter Nolan, my doctoral supervisor, first told me that I should look at migration from the countryside rather than the cities, advice that set my research trajectory for the next three decades. The School of Social and Political Sciences, the Centre for Gender Studies and the Centre for

Acknowledgements

Development Studies at Cambridge held many seminars and reading groups on gender, exposing me to debates and literature. I benefited immensely from this inclusive and lively social sciences environment.

As Head of the Oxford School of Global and Area Studies (OSGA) from 2014 to 2018 at Oxford, I was fortunate to work with Erin Gordon, Head of Administration and Finance in OSGA, who along with the School Research Officer – Francesca Tucci – ensured fantastic support for research across the School, including for my own research. I am grateful for the fabulous colleagues and the lively intellectual environment of OSGA, the Oxford China Centre and St. Antony's College, where I am a fellow. It is a privilege to belong to these institutions that have provided so much flexibility and support, including the freedom to do slow research.

Over the past several years, fun, friendship and welcome breaks have been provided by Federica Felanti, Helen and John Heanue and their family, Neil Ketchley, Lamiaa Shehata Ketchley, Jenny Lunnon and Eileen Walsh. I also extend thanks for the same to my in-laws, Joan Harris, the late Ray Harris, Ruth Harris, and Jane and Rüdi Götschel and family.

I am grateful to my own family. My mother, the late Doris Murphy, spent many hours discussing practical criticism poems and assignments with me during my high school years, and devoted so much of her time to supporting my high school and university studies. It is only in hindsight that I see what a gift this was. My father, Patrick Murphy, himself a migrant from rural Ireland, inspired me with his home-spun philosophies about always giving things a go, never ruling oneself out and always picking oneself up. My parents both migrated far from their own families in search of a better life, so they always understood well my mix of feelings living at the other side of the world from them. My good-humoured brother Bill is also always in my thoughts and I miss him.

My husband John provides unstintingly excellent care for our daughter, Emily, which has enabled me to do fieldwork, though not without missing them. I am grateful to him for coming to China with Emily in 2013, so that I would not need to be separated from her for too long. Certainly, the flexibility and stability of our jobs cushion us from some of the difficulties that confront parents with less accommodating work, let alone migrant parents. I am deeply grateful to and for Emily. She has taught me so much and forever reminds me that time is indeed passing, and that time is all we have.

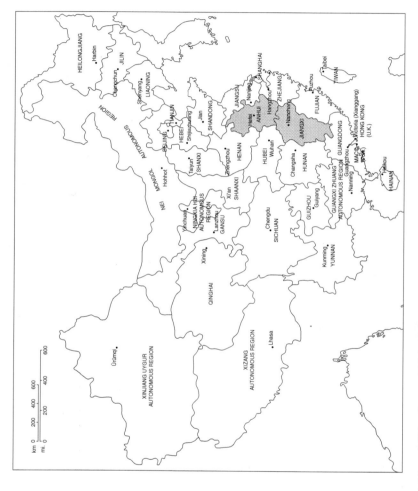

Map 1 Map of China Source: Hsieh, Chiao-min and Hsieh, Jean Kan. 1995. *China: A Provincial Atlas*. Macmillan Library Reference Publishers, map of China on the front inside cover, reproduced with kind permission from Cengage EMEA.

1 Understanding the Lives of Left-Behind Children in Rural China

Imagine as we live our comfortable lives in affluent societies that children elsewhere live separated from their parents because the parents feel compelled to migrate so that their children might live a decent life and 'get ahead' through education. In the 2010s, hundreds of millions of children from across developing countries – or the 'majority world' – and tens of millions of children in China lived separated from parents who worked in faraway places. Of course, non-migrant parents also worked long hours, locally in fields and factories or on construction sites, and they too wanted their children to thrive. But children whose parents had migrated without them were noteworthy because they only saw their parents once or twice a year, if that.

Zhangyong was one of these 'left-behind' children. I first met him in 2011 when he was eleven years old. He lived in one of a row of dilapidated single-storey red-brick houses in a village in Eastern County, Anhui province, in inland east China. Zhangyong was cared for by his *Yeye* or grandfather, a seventy-four-year-old with large gaps in his broad smile. At that time, Zhangyong and *Yeye* both complained that the roof of the house leaked when it rained, but they thought that life was otherwise 'okay'. During the week Zhangyong ate his meals with *Yeye*, cycling home from school for lunch at 11:20 a.m. and dinner at 4:20 p.m. *Yeye* would often ask Zhangyong whether he had done his homework, and Zhangyong would say 'yes' with such an impish grin that *Yeye* could never quite know if he was telling the truth or tricking him. In any event, they both knew that as an illiterate person, *Yeye* had no way of checking.

Zhangyong told me that as much as he liked to visit his parents in Kunshan during the summer holidays, he preferred to stay in the countryside. This was not only because he felt closer to *Yeye* who had 'raised' him since he was a baby but also because his mother would lose her temper at his incorrectly written characters and beat him. Even so, Zhangyong appreciated that she cared about his studies and that she entrusted migrant relatives to bring him presents such as pens and books on their visits back to the countryside. He was also grateful that his parents 'supported' him economically. Zhangyong expressed the idea of being 'raised' and 'supported' with the Chinese word '*yang*', which refers to one person's material and practical nurturing of another person.

I met Zhangyong and *Yeye* again two and a half years later. The day was hot. Grain, soya bean branches and corn dried in the sun while harvested fields smouldered. *Yeye* was wearing a blue Mao jacket and had just returned from a half-hour cycle ride to the township on his trailered tricycle to deliver his grain to the purchasing depot. Zhangyong now spent hardly any time at home with *Yeye*. The boy had just entered first grade at one of the several private boarding junior high schools that had sprung up in the county seat during the late 2000s. Zhangyong's school consisted of rows of red six-storey buildings. On Saturday mornings before 7:30 Zhangyong was met at the school gates by *Yeye* because the teachers allowed students to leave the premises only if an adult came to collect them. The pair took three buses to get back to the village. Zhangyong then returned to school by 4:00 p.m. on Sundays.

At this second visit, Zhangyong was wearing a fluorescent pink top with a silhouetted dance figure superimposed on the front, which contrasted with his quiet demeanour. He had chosen the top himself, buying it from a stall near to the school with money sent by his parents. When I asked him about his new school, he told us that he had implored his parents to come to this private school after hearing about it from others. His parents had agreed, telling him: 'We are seldom at home so we will feel more at ease with you at that school.' Just like at our meeting in 2011, Zhangyong again told us that his biggest wish in life was to get into university because that would help him to earn 'big money' by, for instance, becoming a company boss. Meanwhile, his second and third wishes in life were to live in a good house and to live happily with all his family, including his parents and *Yeye*.

On National Day 2013 I visited Zhangyong's parents in their sparse grey flat on the outskirts of Kunshan city. They were both aged in their late thirties. His mother worked in a seat belt factory and his father worked in a factory using a spanner to bolt on screws. They put in ten-hour shifts at least six days per week. His mother confessed that when her son was younger, he used to be afraid of her because she had been extremely strict with him. But now she recognised that putting too much pressure on him could be harmful. 'A boy in my sister's village jumped into the river because he had too much pressure to study', she explained. She also realised that if her son was to succeed in life he would need to exercise self-discipline, which she tried to foster in him. That summer Zhangyong visited Kunshan for two weeks. One morning before his mother went to work, she had left a note for him on the television set, which read: 'Your parents won't always be with you to *guan* you, so you need to proactively *guan* yourself.' *Guan* is a Chinese word that means 'to control', 'to govern' and 'to care for' and often refers to parents' or teachers' guidance of children. Zhangyong's mother was pleased to return home in the evening to find her son had drawn up a daily timetable that included study, limited television watching, housework and more study.

Zhangyong's days in the boarding school in the county seat – beginning at 6:00 in the morning and ending at 8:00 in the evening – reassured his parents that he would make the best use of his time while affording him little opportunity to 'waste' his life or literally 'turn fallow' (*huangdiao*) by playing games in internet bars, as so many 'left-behind' children reputedly did. At the same time, by paying 16,000 *yuan* per year in private boarding school fees, they demonstrated their fulfilment of their parental obligations to him and compelled him to be diligent. 'He can never say that we didn't give him every opportunity to study his way out', his mother claimed. For his part, Zhangyong understood that his parents were investing lots of money in his future.

This book explores the lives of children like Zhangyong, who lived in rural China separated from either one or both of their parents because of labour migration. It draws on the interviews I conducted in 2010 and 2011 in four counties located in Anhui and Jiangxi, two major labour-exporting provinces in China's east and southeast interior. I carried out interviews with 109 children alongside separate matching interviews with the children's at-home parents or grandparent caregivers. The children were aged nine to seventeen, with a median age of twelve. Seventy-nine of the children had at least one parent who was a migrant while ninety-three had at least one parent who was or who had been a migrant after they started school. The book also draws on my follow-up interviews with twenty-five of the children and their caregivers in 2013, 2014 and/or 2015. The first time I interviewed them, these children were in primary school (usually ages seven to eleven years), and by the time of my final interview with them they were in junior high school (usually by age fifteen) or else they had started senior high school or vocational school. My interviews with the migrant parents of twenty of the children and with twenty rural teachers provide further insights.

I conducted the interviews over the course of twenty-four weeks between 2010 and 2015. For all the interviews with the children and for most of the interviews with the adults, I was accompanied by a Chinese research assistant from a provincial tertiary institution. Different research assistants accompanied me to different interviews in different places at different points in time, with a total of seven people helping me over the course of five fieldwork trips. The purpose of the research assistants' presence in the interviews was to help put the children at ease; to follow good practice when interviewing children by having two adults present; to facilitate my integration into the fieldwork sites; to smooth my communications with local officials and school officials; and to help me understand what I heard in the interviews, especially when people spoke in local dialect. In this book, I mostly use plural pronouns such as 'we', 'our' and 'us' to signal the research assistants' presence and help in the interviews. I discuss details of the data collection and data analysis in the research methods appendix at the end of the book. In several places in this book I also refer to a survey conducted in two townships in each of the four fieldwork counties, two in Anhui and two in Jiangxi in 2010. Details of the stratified random sampling procedure and sample characteristics for this survey are available in Zhou, Murphy and Tao (2014). The survey, from hereon the '2010 Summer Survey', had a final sample of 1,010 children in grades 4, 6 and 8 (typically aged ten, twelve and fourteen years) and was matched by a survey of 1,000 caregivers.

This book uses the fieldwork material to address several gaps in the literature on children and migration. Notably, as several scholars observe, across the 'majority world' children sit at the heart of their parents' migration projects, but their viewpoints, experiences and agency – that is, their capacity to act and to make their own choices – have not been adequately researched (Dobson, 2009; Gardner, 2012; Zhang, 2015). The absence of children's voices in research on migration reflects a wider absence of children from sociological scholarship that persisted into the 1980s and 1990s (Thorne, 1987; Milkie, Simon and Powell, 1997; Qvertrop, 2009). After the 2000s, though, social scientists increasingly recognised that, just as gender is a social category, so is age too, with people's position in the life course influencing their viewpoints, aspirations and agency (Elder, Johnson and Crosnoe, 2003; Thorne, 2004).

In the late 1990s and 2000s, a 'new social studies of childhood' flourished. Drawing inspiration from Philippe Ariès's (1965) landmark argument that childhood is a historical creation of fifteenth-century Europe, interdisciplinary studies emerged illustrating the heterogeneity of childhoods across different historical periods and cultural contexts, and demonstrating that children are social actors rather than just pre-social adults-in-the-making (James, Jenks and Prout, 1998; Katz, 2004; Tisdall and Punch, 2012). Concurrently, a burgeoning stream of research examined the interconnections between mobility and children's everyday lives. In prioritising children's viewpoints rather than adults' viewpoints, these studies offer fresh perspectives on globalisation, migration and family reproduction (Katz, 2004; Dobson, 2009; Coe, 2012; Gardner, 2012; Punch, 2012; Tisdall and Punch, 2012; Coe, 2014).

Pioneering exceptions notwithstanding (e.g. Fog Olwig, 1999; Parreñas, 2005; Dreby, 2010; Ye, 2011; Ye and Pan, 2011; Coe, 2012; Coe, 2014; Hoang et al., 2015), though, most extant literature on children and migration focuses on the children who migrate, with few studies examining the experiences of left-behind children (Toyota, Yeoh and Nguyen, 2007; Nobles, 2011). When left-behind children do feature in migration studies research, they are seldom asked about their experiences (Graham and Jordan, 2011; Mazzucato and Schans, 2011). Moreover, research among children living in the 'majority world' concentrates on children in Latin America, Africa and Southeast Asia, while children in China are largely overlooked (Zhang, 2015). Meanwhile, the experiences of children left behind in circumstances of internal migration receive much less attention than children whose parents migrate transnationally, usually to more prosperous countries (Lu, 2012). China offers an especially illuminating case for studying children's experiences of migration because of the vast numbers of families affected, the pervasive influence of an authoritarian Party-state on capital owners and the market, a precipitous fall in family size over the past four decades and unique gender relations arising from the intersection of a patrilineal family system, the Party-state and the socialist market economy.

1.1 Striving in Context

In this book I use *striving* as the lens through which to interpret my observations about the lives of the left-behind children I met in four fieldwork counties in Anhui and Jiangxi. I view children who had at least one migrant parent as the members of *multilocal families*[1] – families with members split across two or more locations – with all the family members motivated by a *striving* ethos. I see the migrants' labour in the cities, the non-migrant family members' domestic chores in the village and the children's study all as types of *work* underpinned by *aspirations* to bring about a better life for the family members, with work plus aspiration constituting *striving*.

My approach heeds many scholars' stance that children's study constitutes 'work' in the sense of being purposeful activity that generates value (Field, 1995; Qvortrup, 1995; James, Jenks and Prout, 1998: 118; Mayall, 2000). Concurrently, I recognise that families' care practices – and the gendered and generational relations these practices express – are not just shaped by but also constitute wider political and economic forces (Katz, 2004). Indeed, it is through the different forms of work – labouring for income (production), domestic care work (social reproduction) and study – that different family members, including children, fulfil their relational obligations to each other. At the same time, I note that conventional boundaries between production and social reproduction dissolve because both types of work support the upbringing and education of children (Locke, Seeley and Rao, 2013). Striving thereby connects 'work' and 'aspiration' to family relationships.

In formulating a lens of 'striving' to orient the analysis, I knit together selected strands from different literatures. Specifically, I cull from literature on three broad topics, all of which highlight that human agency must be interpreted within its historical, institutional, and sociocultural *context*, and in relation to wider political and economic structures. I draw on subfields of

---

[1] 'Multilocal families' includes 'transnational families' with families split across two or more countries and 'translocal families' with families split across two or more locations within a country.

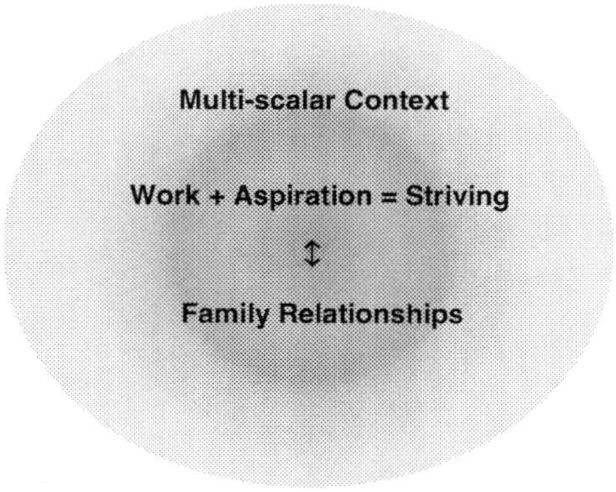

6   The Lives of Left-Behind Children in Rural China

Multi-scalar Context

Work + Aspiration = Striving

↕

Family Relationships

Figure 1.1 The concept of 'striving'

literatures that cover (1) adult–child relationships; (2) international and internal migration and multilocal families; and (3) Bourdieusian analyses of human struggle with special reference to child-raising, 'unequal childhoods' and education.

My understanding of *adult–child relationships* adopts the view from the life-course literature that lives are lived interdependently, and that children's agency and subjective well-being are relational – that is, they are realised through relationships. Meanwhile, adult–child 'linked lives' unfold within certain historical and institutional contexts, with subjective life accounts in turn elucidating these wider contexts (Elder, 1985, 1998; King and Elder, 1995; Punch, 2002a, 2002b; Locke and Lloyd-Sherlock, 2011). I also consult an ecological literature on child development, which overlaps with 'linked lives' research (also Elder, 1974, and Elder and Rockwell, 1978 cited in Bronfenbrenner, 1979: 226–291; Booth, 2003). An ecological approach situates dyadic or triadic adult–child relationship within a matrix of inter-relations that radiate outwards 'like a set of Russian dolls' (Bronfenbrenner, 1979: 3). These inter-relations extend from the dyads or triads out to ever looser institutional arenas including networks of kin, friendship groups, schools, hospitals and the media; outwards to macro-settings that a child may never enter but that may still influence their life; and outwards still to a 'macro-system', which is 'an overarching pattern of ideology or organisation of social institutions common to a particular culture or subculture' (Bronfenbrenner, 1979: 8). In this approach, the interplay between agency and structure/context involves a 'person's evolving conception of their . . . environment and their relationship to it as well as their growing capacity to discover, sustain or alter its properties' (Bronfenbrenner, 1979: 9). This resonates with some sociologists' observation

1.1 Striving in Context

that children's agency is 'thicker' in some arenas and 'thinner' in others (Klocker, 2007 and Robson, Bell and Klocker, 2007 cited in Tisdall and Punch, 2012: 255).

In understanding left-behind children's linked lives I also draw from scholarship on transnational and domestic migration and multilocal families. This literature demonstrates that people's migration projects are motivated largely by their aspirations for their families' reproduction. It further reveals that gendered and generational relations within families mediate different family members' 'work' contributions as they strive for a better life for the family (e.g. Hondagneu-Sotelo and Avila, 1997; Orellana, Thorne, and Chee et al., 2001; Schmalzbauer, 2004; Parreñas, 2005; Schamlzbauer, 2005; Schmalzbauer, 2008; Boehm, Hess and Coe et al., 2011; Fan, 2008; Dreby, 2010; Hoang and Yeoh, 2011; Nobels, 2011; Locke, Seeley and Rao, 2013; Montes, 2013; Choi and Peng, 2016; Jacka, 2018). Concurrently, this literature shows that social constructions of motherhood and fatherhood profoundly shape all family members' experiences of migration, including the children's experiences (Schamlzbauer, 2005: 3), but as mentioned, children's experiences await a fuller exploration in the literature.

A stream of this migration studies literature uses the sociologist Mike Douglass's concept of 'global house-holding'. Research applying this concept highlights how in different cultural, social and institutional contexts, households respond to structural pressures arising from globalisation by flexibly reconfiguring their members' different work and care contributions across space, adapting their gendered and generational relationships in the process (Douglass, 2006; Jacka, 2012; Douglass, 2014; Nguyen and Locke, 2014). Locke, Seeley and Rao (2013) recommend that researchers combine a house-holding approach with a life-course perspective, noting that the latter's attention to 'linked lives' fits well with the relational motivations of migrants and their families. Meanwhile, Jacka (2018) observes that along with changes in political economy and culture – including changes driven by migration and changes concurrent with but independent of migration – aspirations for family reproduction, mobility and 'distinction' change too, continually reconfiguring multilocal family relations and aspirations.

Bourdieu's analysis of human struggle and class reproduction proves instructive for understanding both migration and striving (Bourdieu and Passeron, 2000; Bourdieu, 2010). Bourdieu explains that what people *aspire* to most in life is *recognition*, so they struggle to be seen as more worthy *than others* by trying to obtain and command certain capacities and properties or 'capitals' (Atkinson, 2015). The struggle for recognition entails work. Meanwhile, reflecting influences from Marx, *work* is integral to Bourdieu's idea of capital in the sense that 'capital is labor accumulated', and when capital is possessed 'by . . . [private agents it] enables them to appropriate social energy in the form of reified or living labor' (Bourdieu, 1986: 241). In Bourdieu's framework, capital refers to: *economic capital* – money and property; *cultural capital* – including *embodied capital* such as knowledge and refinement, *cultural property* such as books and artefacts, and *institutionalised cultural capital* such as credentials; and *social capital* – or social contacts. Concurrently, Bourdieu notes that under certain conditions, one form of capital can be converted into another (Bourdieu, 1986; Atkinson, 2015).

A Bourdieusian approach sees people as struggling for recognition within overlapping 'social fields' of unequal power relations that include economic fields (e.g. labour markets), cultural fields (e.g. the education system) and local fields (e.g. dense intimate social networks such as families), all of which influence what forms of capital people deem to be valuable and desirable, as well as how these forms of capital are distributed. Meanwhile, different scales of value coalesce, with schools being an instance of an institution in which systems of value operating on global, national and family scales intersect (Kipnis, 2009). Bourdieu's concept of *habitus* offers particular insight into 'striving' by bridging agency and structure/context in understanding what individuals struggle for, why and how. Habitus refers to individuals' durable dispositions, inclinations, lifestyles and expectations arising from their adaptations to their circumstances, such that their social position within overlapping fields of unequal power relations become internalised and embodied, influencing how they perceive and act in and on the world (Bourdieu and Passeron, 2000; Bourdieu, 2010; Atkinson, 2015).

Some scholars use the idea of 'cultural repertoires' to reconcile structure/context and agency slightly differently (e.g. Lareau, 2003; Coe, 2014; Lan, 2018). Inspired by Swidler (1986) among others, Coe defines 'cultural repertoire' as 'a body or collection of practices, knowledges and beliefs that allows people to imagine what is possible, expect certain things and value certain goals' (Coe, 2014: 15–16). The idea of 'repertoires' resembles 'habitus' in that it refers to a set of perceptions, dispositions and actions that predisposes a person to act in certain ways. But 'repertoires' differs from 'habitus' in highlighting the multiple cultural resources and options that individuals can discuss and choose from as they pursue their 'strategies' (Coe, 2014: 36). Swidler defines 'strategies' as 'a general way of organising action' or as the 'larger assemblages' to which action belongs, referencing Bourdieu's observation that 'the habitus provides resources for constructing diverse lines of action' (Swidler, 1986: 276–277). Coe's (2014) use of 'repertoires' enables her to reveal the malleability of people's ideas about parental love and care in 'scattered' Ghanaian families.

Literature on child-raising, socialisation and education also uses Bourdieusian concepts of habitus, capital and social fields, as well as the idea of cultural repertoires, to cast light on class dynamics and on how people's

1.1 Striving in Context

struggle for intergenerational mobility is both stratified and stratifying. For instance, several studies reveal that adults' habitus or their 'innate feel' for how to raise their children and how to interact with school authorities on behalf of their children embodies and reproduces their learned class positions within given social fields (Reay, 1998; Reay, 2001; Lareau, 2003; Alanen, Brooker and Mayall, 2015; Lan, 2018), leading them to adopt distinct cultural repertoires of child-raising (Lareau, 2003: 4–8; Lan, 2018). Meanwhile, some research also observes that children are compelled to produce themselves as a form of capital, honouring their families' investments in them and realising their value over time, with their possibilities to do so influenced by their class background (James, Jenks and Prout, 1998: 118; Morrow and Vennam, 2015).

A further theme adapts Bourdieusian ideas to explore why individuals differ in their *aspirations* or their 'reference points for navigating life' (Appadurai, 2004; Hart, 2012). These scholars observe that different temporal influences are simultaneously manifest in individuals' aspirations (Hart, 2012; Barbalet, 2014; Lan, 2018). The past exists in individuals' habitus or dispositions, incorporating their capital endowments and their prior socialisation in their families (Hart, 2012). The present is manifest in individuals' class positions in a given structural context (Lan, 2018). The future is manifest in individuals' visions of their future selves, with these visions reflecting a habitus that is shaped and reshaped by the education system (Corbett, 2007), cultures of migration (Kandel and Massey, 2002; Coe, 2012; Gardner, 2012; Zeitlyn and Mand, 2012; Xiang, 2014), and the institutions of the market economy (Barbalet, 2014; Xiang, 2014). The market economy is especially significant because it is the 'social field' where future income, success and status may be obtained (Barbalet, 2014), but also where a person may fail or 'fall behind' – fear being the underbelly of aspiration.

The threads provided in these various literatures supplement each other well. Notably, the migration studies literature's analysis of intersecting gendered and generational relations redresses a neglect of gender and emotions in Bourdieusian analyses of human struggle and class reproduction (Atkinson, 2015). Admittedly, though, twenty-first-century research on child-raising and education has done much to remedy this neglect by investigating class-based differences in mothers' and fathers' contributions to their families' cultural capital accumulation strategies (Reay, 2001; Lareau, 2003; O'Brien, 2007; Lan, 2018). Meanwhile, Bourdieusian analyses of people's aspirations for their children's cultural capital accumulation and social mobility help in explaining the centrality of education in family migration projects.

In this book I offer fresh perspectives on families' capital accumulation strategies by exploring children's experiences of daily life and family relationships *when the children and parents do not live together* because of at least one parent's migration. In doing so, I adapt Norma Field's (1995) idea of 'parent–

child toiling teams' to see 'left-behind' children as the members of spatially dispersed *parent–child striving teams*. Field (1995) initially proposed her idea of 'parent–child toiling teams' to critique the ethos of ceaseless production, which she saw to be eroding the quality of childhood in urban middle-class Japan in the 1990s. She observed that owing to the intense normative pressure on parents to raise children who achieved upward social mobility through education, Japanese mothers toiled by supervising their children's homework, ferrying them to and from extracurricular activities, and taking care of all their needs so that they could concentrate on study. Sociologists describe similar repertoires of intensive child-raising among urban middle-class parents in twenty-first-century mainland China and Taiwan (e.g. Fong, 2004; Liu, 2015; Naftali, 2016; Lan, 2018), with their repertoires in turn resembling the 'concerted cultivation' that Lareau (2003) describes among middle-class parents in the United States. Indeed, in this book I see the work of China's rural families as analogous to the toil of the country's urban middle-class families because in both contexts, 'toil' gains meaning from powerful shared parent–child aspirations for the children's educational mobility and intergenerational socio-economic mobility.

While later chapters of this book draw on 'left-behind' children's voices to explore their agency, including the 'situated' (Choi, Yeoh and Lam, 2018) 'relational' (Locke and Lloyd-Sherlock, 2011) and multi-layered or multi-scalar 'contextualised' dimensions of this agency, in the next section I turn to discuss the *historical and institutional context* within which rural Chinese families strive in order to explain why so many children have been left behind. Thereafter, I review evidence and debates about the well-being of 'left-behind' children in twenty-first-century rural China. Then I position the children of *multilocal striving families* within the *sociocultural context of rural China*. Finally, I preview the book's chapters.

1.2   Historical and Institutional Context of Striving

To chart the historical and institutional context in which tens of millions of rural Chinese children live separated from at least one parent, below I discuss how rural–urban inequalities and regulatory mechanisms bequeathed by state socialism have compelled so many rural families to strive for intergenerational social mobility by means of migration. I show that even as rural–urban inequalities and regulatory mechanisms have morphed over time, they continue to impel rural people to live and work while separated from their family members.

1.2.1   *Parental Migration and Rural Children*

During China's state socialist period from the mid-1950s to the late 1970s, the macro-institutional configuration of the countryside and the national economy

1.2 Historical and Institutional Context of Striving

constrained people's possibilities for migrating. In the mid-1950s, the Communist Party-state implemented the *hukou*, or household registration system (Solinger, 1999: 42–44; Fan, 2008: 45–49). Under the *hukou* system, all households kept registration booklets that recorded the names and birthdates of their members, their 'non-agricultural' or 'agricultural' occupational designations and the location of each household's registration. Individuals' occupational designations and places of residence overlapped such that most rural residents were agricultural while most urban residents were non-agricultural (Fan, 2008: 45–49).

After 1957 rural people worked on collectively owned land and were remunerated in 'work points' that were redeemable as a share of the harvest. Meanwhile, the state used the price scissors – low prices for agricultural goods and high prices for industrial goods, alongside mandatory delivery quotas to siphon off agricultural surplus from the communes. The state used this surplus to fuel industrialisation and provide urban workers with cradle-to-grave benefits, and well-funded education and healthcare services (Oi, 1989; Chan, 1994; Solinger, 1999). In the absence of commodity markets, the *hukou* system and rural communes operated in tandem with a rationing system that distributed necessities such as oil, salt and matches to individuals at their registered place of residence (Oi, 1989; Chan, 1994; Mallee, 1995b; Solinger, 1999: 42–44). Although official pronouncements at the time lauded rural people for their ideological purity and endurance of class oppression, the policies of state socialism nevertheless turned them into second-class citizens tied to the land (Potter and Potter, 1990: 296–312).

In the early to mid-1980s, the dismantling of the communes, the allocation of farm land to households, and state retreat from welfare provisioning reinstated the household as the basic unit responsible for social provisioning (Croll, 1987; Potter and Potter, 1990; Croll, 1994; Cohen, 1993; Jacka, 1997; Lin, 1988). In rural China, a 'household' refers to a set of people who eat together and maintain a common budget. The household is often (though not always) synonymous with the nuclear family. Owing to shared patrilineal descent, even after a family has divided into at least two households, the boundaries between the different households usually remain porous with the members retaining 'close economic and socio-political ties' (Croll, 1987; Cohen, 1992). Even so, different households within a family mostly live in separate houses or aspire to earn enough money to do so.

In the1980s, the re-emergence of commodity markets, the expansion of township and village enterprises and the development of export-led manufacturing created new possibilities for rural families to incorporate off-farm income into their budgets (Croll, 1987; Croll, 1994; Jacka, 1997; Murphy, 2002; Day, 2013). Subsequently, in the 1990s, the rising costs of agricultural inputs, excessive fees and levies imposed by local governments, and an

12   The Lives of Left-Behind Children in Rural China

intensification of fee-based education and healthcare exacerbated rural families' need for cash, but the mass bankruptcies of township and village enterprises closed off many local opportunities to earn income (Croll and Huang, 1997; Day, 2013). Concurrently, rising intra-rural inequalities continually inflated the overall amount of resources that rural families needed to keep up with rising social standards (Murphy, 2002; Ye, 2011). Against the background of these changes, the number of migrants increased. The demographer Duan Chenrong and his team report that the numbers of rural migrants grew from approximately 6.7 million in 1982, to 21.3 million in 1990, to 70.7 million in 1990, to 102.3 million in 2000 (Duan, Yang, Zhang et al., 2008: 32; Duan, Yuan and Guo, 2013: 1). Their calculations use the census definition of a 'migrant' as someone who has lived outside their county of registered residence for at least a year without changing their *hukou* status.

But even as many rural people migrated during the 1980s and 1990s, the *hukou* or household registration system still limited their right to do so (Solinger, 1999; Fan, 2003, Chan, 2009). Individuals continued to inherit their *hukou* status: originally, inheritance was through the mother, though after 1998 it could be inherited from either parent (Chan and Buckingham, 2008). Rural migrants also had to obtain temporary urban residence permits that were costly and cumbersome to apply for, while those without the requisite documents could be harassed by the police (Chan, 1994; Solinger, 1999; Fan, 2003; Chan and Buckingham, 2008). It was only in 2003, after public outcry at the police's beating to death of Sun Zhigang – a university student who had been mistaken for a migrant worker – that the State Council declared it unconstitutional to fine, detain or repatriate rural people from the cities (Congressional-Executive Commission on China, 2005).

While in the state socialist era both men and women worked in agriculture, with the launch of the market reforms and the concomitant retreat of state feminism, traditional gender roles quickly re-emerged. In the early 1980s, men's 'outside' work occurred increasingly off the farm while women's 'inside' domestic work became redefined to encompass farming activities that had previously been designated as male tasks (Jacka, 1997). Although the gender balance of the rural migrant worker population has fluctuated over time and by region, at an aggregate level the proportion of male migrant workers has been higher than the proportion of female migrant workers. In the 1980s and early 1990s, various Chinese surveys reported proportions of male migrant workers that ranged from 70 to 84 per cent of migrant workers (Mallee, 1995a: 114). Meanwhile, in 2015, 68.8 per cent of rural migrant workers were males and 31.2 per cent were females (National Bureau of Statistics, 2016).

Nevertheless, in China rural women have always participated in migration. Initially, many rural women followed their migrant husbands (Duan, Yang and Zhang et al., 2008), but with the growth of the light manufacturing and service

1.2 Historical and Institutional Context of Striving

sectors, employers' demand for meticulous, docile and reliable female workers expanded. The image of the young, single 'factory daughter' and 'working sister' (*dagongmei*) soon came to represent the public face of China's labour migration and economic modernisation in both the Chinese and the global media. Meanwhile, several cutting-edge English-language ethnographies examined how *dagongmei* fared under the 'triple oppression' of family patriarchy, global capitalism and state socialism (Lee, 1998; Pun, 2005; Yan, 2008). But in the early 2000s, some scholars questioned whether the single *dagongmei* had ever really typified China's migrant workers. They pointed to data showing that in the 1990s and 2000s approximately two-thirds of migrants were married, and most had children under the age of sixteen (Lou et al., 2004; Roberts et al., 2004; Duan et al., 2008; Connelly, Roberts and Zheng, 2011). Village and county studies from the 1990s and 2000s also indicate that in many localities rural married women and mothers had migrated (Mallee, 1995a; Lou et al., 2004; Roberts et al., 2004; Murphy, 2004b; He and Ye, 2013). Nevertheless, an impression that rural Chinese mothers don't migrate has persisted (Fan, 2003; Liu, 2016).

Alongside a nationwide trend of fertility decline and population ageing, migrant workers' aggregate age has risen overtime. Between 2011 and 2015, the proportion of migrant workers aged sixteen to thirty years fell from 39 per cent to 32.9 per cent, while the proportion aged over forty years rose from 38.3 per cent to 44.8 per cent, with the thirty-one to forty age bracket remaining constant at 22 per cent (National Bureau of Statistics, 2016). As the numbers of migrants of 'parenting-age' grew so did the population of 'left-behind' children. Drawing on census data, Duan and Zhou (2005) report that in 2000 over nineteen million rural children aged nought to seventeen years had at least one parent who had migrated for six months or longer. Meanwhile, using the National Bureau of Statistics' 1 per cent population sample Duan, Yan and Gao (2013) calculate that in 2005 fifty-eight million rural children were left behind, though Chan and Ren caution that this 2005 figure could indicate an error in the children's sample (2018: 138, 157).

In their analysis of census data, the All-China Women's Federation Research Group (2013) and Duan, Yan and Guo (2013) each report that in 2010 the number of left-behind children in rural China exceeded sixty-one million, equivalent to the population of Great Britain. Of these sixty-one million, 46.74 per cent had two migrant parents, 36.39 per cent had a lone migrant father and 16.87 per cent had a lone migrant mother (ACWF, 2013; Duan, Yan and Guo, 2013). Meanwhile, using data from the 2010 census and a 2015 1 per cent population sample, Chan and Ren report that even though the number of *rural* 'left-behind children' fell from 61 million in 2010 to 41 million in 2015, the number of *urban* left-behind children increased from 7.7 million to 28.3 million (2018: 139). They explain that this fall mostly reflects a relabelling

14   The Lives of Left-Behind Children in Rural China

of districts from 'rural' to 'urban' without any real change in these children's circumstances (2018: 139).

In 2016, China's Ministry of Civil Affairs redefined the term 'left-behind children', ostensibly to focus greater policy attention on those children with the greatest need for care. Whereas previously the term 'left-behind' referred to any child aged under eighteen years with at least one parent who had migrated without them, the new definition of 'left-behind' referred to children aged between nought and fifteen years who either had both parents living away from them or else one parent who had migrated and the other parent unable to provide adequate guardianship. The same year the Ministry of Civil Affairs stated that more than nine million children in rural China counted as 'left behind'. Chan and Ren (2018) attribute most of the fall in the number of left-behind children to the ministry's narrowed definition. Meanwhile, some Chinese commentators cautioned that an official redefinition of 'left-behind child' should not substitute for making good-quality data available to researchers or for addressing the root cause of rural people's disadvantages (e.g. Duan, 2016; Han, 2016).

Further insight into the numbers of left-behind children living in rural China is provided by findings from a survey of over 7,000 children in fourteen provinces, carried out in 2017 by the Beijing-based NGO On the Road to School. The resulting White Paper estimates that in 2016, nationwide, twenty-three million students in grades 1 to 9 and aged under sixteen years were left behind by at least one migrant parent, while over ten million rural students in compulsory education were left behind by both their parents (On the Road to School, 2017). Differences in calculations notwithstanding, clearly, in the second decade of twenty-first-century China millions of children were living in families where at least one parent had migrated without them.

1.2.2   *Why Do the Parents Migrate without Their Children?*

To explain why parents in rural China migrate without their children, it is useful to distinguish between two forms of work, mentioned previously. *Production* refers to work that produces goods and services in the market place, usually for money (Katz, 2001). *Social reproduction* refers to 'daily and long-term' work in procuring and distributing the 'food, clothing, shelter and healthcare' needed for the biological reproduction of the family as well as of the labour force on which national and global economies depend (Katz, 2001: 711). Worldwide, within and across national borders, social reproduction has become ever more detached from economic production by state-endorsed structures that discourage poor people from ever *settling* in the places where they work (Katz, 2001; Katz, 2004; Pun and Chan, 2013). This detachment diverts the costs of social reproduction away from where the profits of economic production accrue

1.2 Historical and Institutional Context of Striving

(Katz, 2001; Pun and Chan, 2013). In China, the rural–urban labour migration system relies on and recreates family configurations whereby women and the elderly in the rural regions assume responsibility for social reproduction, including childcare, thereby underwriting a very cheap labour reserve in a globalising market (Day, 2013: 192; Chuang, 2016; Santos, 2017; Jacka, 2018).

Low wages is one institutional mechanism in China that precludes many rural migrants from settling with their families in the places where they work. Despite rises in the legal minimum wage in real terms, the proportion of GDP growth per capita claimed by China's workers fell over the course of the 'reform period' and remained low. In 1980, a peak of 16.99 per cent was reached; it then decreased to 10.74 per cent in 2000 before rising slightly to 11.21 per cent in 2008 (Chan, 2014). At the same time, migrant workers received lower pay than urban workers. In 2012, the average hourly wage of migrant workers was less than half that of urban residents (Chan, 2014). Moreover, approximately three-quarters of migrant workers failed to receive unemployment insurance, work injury insurance, and health insurance, while over two-thirds did not have a pension plan (Chan, 2014). Under such conditions, migrants have needed to work extra-long hours and to live austerely to save enough for their families' social reproduction (Chan, 2014). Hence, many migrants do not have the time, resources or living conditions necessary for raising their children in the cities.

The distribution of public goods and services through the *hukou* system further prevents most migrants from settling in the cities with their families (Chan, 2009; Tao, 2009). Although rural people have since 2003 enjoyed a legal right to be in China's cities, the *hukou* system has continued to determine who can enjoy the full benefits of urban citizenship (Chan, 2009; Tao, 2009). But the most pertinent reason why many rural family members live separated from each other remains the exclusion of migrants' children from urban schools. In 1998, the Ministry of Education's and the Public Security Bureau's 'Provincial Regulations on Schooling for Migrant Children' recognised migrant children's right to attend school in the place where they lived, rather than in their place of registered residence, but only a minority of children were able to claim this right. This is because the regulations stipulated that a city could be a child's domicile only if there was no suitable guardian in the countryside (Li, 2013). Most municipal authorities required migrants to produce several certificates to prove that their urban livelihoods were secure and that their children had no guardian in the countryside (Xiang, 2007; Goodburn, 2009; Ming, 2013). Few migrants could produce all these certificates.

China's authorities subsequently enacted policies to make education in the cities more available to migrants' children. In 2006, the State Council revised the Compulsory Education Law and appealed to municipal authorities to

16   The Lives of Left-Behind Children in Rural China

extend primary and junior high school education to migrants' children (Li, 2013; Ming, 2013). One reason was that the political elite wanted to address escalating socio-economic inequalities as part of rebranding the regime as 'people-centred' rather than GDP-centred (Murphy, 2009). Another reason was that provincial and municipal authorities realised that they could derive money for their coffers by supporting urbanisation. Specifically, urban officials saw that profits could be garnered by appropriating farmers' peri-urban land, converting it into industrial premises and real estate, and creaming off the increased land value. They also saw that profits could be generated by incorporating rural people into markets for low-end housing in smaller cities (Andreas and Zhan, 2015; Zhan, 2017).

Nevertheless, measures to make urban education available to migrants' children only went so far. Central authorities permitted municipal authorities to extend compulsory education to migrants' children at their own pace in accordance with local budgetary capacity (Murphy, 2009; Li, 2013; Ming, 2013). Meanwhile, authorities in cities such as Beijing, Shanghai, Suzhou, Wenzhou, Dongguan, Shenzhen and Guangzhou that attracted the most migrants continued to enact exclusionary measures to reserve educational resources for their own residents. Their measures included preventing migrants' children from attending urban public schools, permitting only the children of well-educated or highly skilled migrant parents to attend urban public schools, sequestering migrants' children into special buildings and classrooms within urban public schools, supporting second-rate migrant schools for migrants' children, or demolishing migrant schools (Goodburn, 2009; Woronov, 2009; Ming, 2013; Song, 2018). Furthermore, after 2014, many large cities adopted a *jiaoyu kongren*[2] policy, intensifying the exclusion of migrant children from urban schools in order to contain urban population growth (Chan and Ren, 2018). Simultaneously, these large cities also stringently adopted Ministry of Education regulations about giving priority in the allocation of school places to children whose parents owned housing in the school's catchment area, inflating the costs of housing in the catchment areas of good schools, and putting good urban schools even more beyond the reach of migrant children (Lu, 2019).

Even if a rural child could attend a decent urban public school from grades 1 to 9, he or she would still face hurdles later. In line with a place-based logic of public goods provisioning, the Ministry of Education decrees that students must sit their senior high school entrance examinations at their registered place of residence (Xiang, 2007). Although after 2014 some municipal authorities allocated a quota of places at urban vocational senior high schools to migrant children, these places were at lower-tier vocational schools (Song, 2018).

---

[2] This translates literally as 'use education to control population'.

1.2 Historical and Institutional Context of Striving

Moreover, if students without a local *hukou* wanted to continue along an academic-track after year 9 to prepare for the university entrance exam, they needed to go 'back home' (Koo, Ming and Tsang, 2014). At the same time, because of regional variations in curriculum, students who moved across school districts after year nine encountered such disadvantages in the examinations that their parents moved them to the rural hometown sooner so that they could acquaint themselves with the curriculum (Xiang, 2007; Koo, Ming and Tsang, 2014).

The option of having children study in the rural areas was also attractive to many rural parents because of the post-2006 'two exemptions and one subsidy' policy. This policy eliminated school fees for all rural students and textbook fees for students from poor rural families and provided a partial subsidy for rural students who boarded during the primary or junior high school stages (Hannum and Adams, 2009; Shi, 2016). The subsidy money is paid directly onto a canteen card given to the students. The free or low-cost compulsory education in the rural hometowns contrasts sharply with the miscellaneous fees that migrants need to pay for their children to attend either public schools or low-quality migrant schools in the cities.

Hukou and place-based public goods provisioning are not the only reasons that rural people experience ongoing discrimination in China's cities. A further reason is their lack of access to the money and education credentials – or the economic and cultural 'capitals' – that would enable them to obtain a local urban *hukou*. While *hukou* conversion has become easier in smaller and medium-sized cities, as noted earlier, barriers have intensified in the mega-cities: in the 2000s, some thirty-six of these mega-cities attracted over half of all China's rural migrants (Duan and Yang, 2009: 10). In the late 2000s and 2010s, these mega-cities even implemented points-based systems with educational attainment, secure employment, social insurance contributions, wealth and housing ownership all attracting high points, and indications of moral character such as being a Party member or donating blood earning bonus points (Zhang, 2012). When I visited a migrant children's outreach organisation in Guangdong in August 2017, a social worker told me that only the children of migrant parents with more than 500 points could attend the local public primary school. The stringent criteria for gaining access to urban public goods augments popular perceptions that movement to higher-order urban settlements corresponds with moving 'up' to a place where people are of greater value.

Rural migrants' aspirations have steadily urbanised within the context of institutional constraints. A so-called first generation of migrants born in the 1960s and early 1970s left their villages for the cities in the 1980s and 1990s to earn money to build a house, fund marriage and improve their families' economic security in the rural hometown (Murphy, 2002). But migrants who had left their villages in the late 1990s and 2000s had received more years of education than the previous generation and they had grown up witnessing rapid urbanisation and watching television programmes that depicted city life (Yan, 2011). These migrants increasingly aspired to a life free from manual work, and they also wanted more personal freedoms than rural family life permitted (Pun, 2005; Chan and Selden, 2014; Gaetano, 2015; Siu, 2015). They talked about having migrated to 'see the world' and to 'develop themselves' as much as to earn money (Pun, 2005; Chan and Selden, 2014; Gaetano, 2015). Nevertheless, in the 2010s migrants continued to find themselves stuck in precarious dead-end jobs while shouldering burdensome obligations to rural family members (Pun and Chan, 2013; Tang and Cheng, 2014; Siu, 2015; Choi and Peng, 2016).

In the light of persistent institutionalised discrimination against rural migrants and the difficulties that rural people experience in the cities, many rural parents aspire for their children to achieve the urban citizenship that has been beyond their own reach. Rural parents also perceive that their children's best chance for finding a 'way out' from economic insecurity and the drudgery of manual work is by studying in the rural hometown. The strategy of having at least one parent work in the city while a lone parent or grandparents care for an at-school child entails a time-discounting calculus across the generations. This calculus is manifest in three different Chinese words for 'work'. One word, *laodong*, or 'labour', refers to manual work including farm work (Huang, 2012). A second word, *dagong*, denotes paid labour and dirty, dangerous, demeaning and precarious work in manufacturing, construction and services. A third word is *gongzuo*. In the socialist era, *gongzuo* referred to jobs in state-owned enterprises and work units, while in the market economy era it refers to respectable, secure jobs in administrative bodies, schools, research institutes, hospitals, firms and banks (Murphy, 2002; 165; Huang, 2012). Adults repeatedly tell left-behind children: 'Your parents *dagong* now so that in the future you can study and find good *gongzuo*.' Indeed, as noted by the Chinese sociologist Jingzhong Ye and his colleagues, China's urban-biased development model has made migration a 'must' rather than an option for many rural families (Ye et al., 2013: 1124).

1.2.3 Care of Children When Parents Migrate Without Them

Although parents migrate to invest in their children's urban future, children such as Zhangyong (mentioned in the introduction) need to be cared for during the long intervening years while their parents are away toiling for this future. Some feminists explain that care can be distinguished from other forms of work by the emotional tie between the individuals involved. For instance, Ruddick (1998) observes that the actions and attentiveness involved in care are a response to a certain emotional relationship, such that when a father reads a book to his child, the activity carries a different meaning to when a teacher

1.2 Historical and Institutional Context of Striving 19

reads a book to the child (see also O'Brien, 2007). But Ruddick also highlights that caregivers need material resources to act on their feelings for those for whom they care. 'If caregivers do not have adequate material resources', she says, then 'the bodies and spirits of those for whom they care for are at risk' (Ruddick, 1998: 13).

Like migrant parents elsewhere, migrants from China's rural regions do not want to limit their care for their children to sending money and gifts. They also want to maintain an emotional connection with their children (Hondagneu-Sotelo and Avila, 1997; Schmalzbauer, 2004; Parreñas, 2005; Parreñas, 2008; Dreby, 2010; Nobles, 2011; Carling, Menjívar and Schmalzbauer, 2012; Locke, Hoa and Tam, 2012; Coe, 2014; Lam and Yeoh, 2015). A feature of migration globally is that migrants are helped in their efforts to 'do care across distance' by rapid developments in communication technologies (Dreby, 2010; Ye and Pan, 2011; Carling, Menjívar and Schmalzbauer, 2012; Peng and Wong, 2013). In China, the density rate of mobile phones increased from fewer than 2 per 100 rural households in 2000 to more than 100 per 100 households a decade later (Murphy, 2010). Moreover, in the mid-2010s many rural families obtained mobiles with video applications so that children could see their migrant parents as they talked with them – although, even as communication technologies expanded, migrants' work routines, children's school routines and cost typically limited calls to just a few minutes per week (Ye and Pan, 2011).

In China, visits are another way that migrant parents and children maintain contact with each other (Ye and Pan, 2011; Zhang, 2015). As Coe (2012) observes for Ghana, even as people's transnational migration often represents an extension of their domestic migration strategies, visits are easier to achieve in circumstances of domestic migration because transportation is cheaper and border controls need not be negotiated. In China, many migrants return home to see their family members at Chinese New Year and when pressing matters arise in the village. But the costs of travel and forfeited wages can be prohibitive even when the migrants live in a city only a few hours away from their village (Ye and Pan, 2011). As described in the vignette about Zhangyong and his mother at the start of this chapter, some children also visit their migrant parents in the cities during the summer holidays (Ye and Pan, 2011; Chan and Ren, 2018). Alternatively, a lack of contact can alienate children from their migrant parents, draining affection (Ye and Pan, 2011; Hansen, 2015) to such an extent that in 2017, 7.3 per cent of rural left-behind children surveyed by the NGO *On the Road to School* stated that the death of a migrant parent would not affect them (On the Road to School, 2017).

When parents migrate without their children, the work of daily child-care is entrusted to at-home adult family members. In China, these caregivers are supported materially in their care work by a socialist market land system. The socialist market land system distributes land

20   The Lives of Left-Behind Children in Rural China

usage rights – to be used for agricultural production – rather than land-ownership rights. The household land allocations seldom provide a basis for an adequate material life but contribute to the subsistence security of the at-home family members (Day, 2013: 192–194). Caregivers such as Zhangyong's grandfather use home-produced rice, vegetables, eggs and meat to feed the child or children in their care. Many caregivers also farm cash crops, generating income that helps with daily expenses such as the children's pocket money, snacks, or incidental school and medical expenses, thereby enabling more money to be saved for other purposes such as the children's school fees. Hence, social reproduction often involves labour-intensive agricultural work unique to a rural setting.

Who cares for the children depends on which parent(s) have migrated and which adults remain in the rural home. According to the breakdown from China's 2010 census, in families where one parent had migrated, over 90 per cent of children were cared for by an at-home parent, usually a mother, and in half of these families a grandparent was also co-resident. In families where both parents had migrated, 70 per cent of the children resembled Zhangyong in that they were looked after by at least one grandparent, while 23 per cent were looked after by other relatives (ACWF, 2013). Worryingly, though, in 2010 over two million children lived alone (ACWF, 2013), a number that decreased slightly by 2015, and may fall further after the State Council's 2016 prohibition against leaving children without an adult caregiver (Chan and Ren, 2018).

Schools also form part of the 'care mix' to which families such as Zhangyong's turn. As subsequent chapters of this book demonstrate, even though most school-age children spent much time at school, school assumed a special significance for those children whose parents had migrated without them (Murphy, 2014a). Additionally, as I discuss in Chapter 2, in some rural localities, an expansion in weekday boarding facilities in the late 2000s has meant that schools contribute even more to the care of some rural children (Murphy, 2014a). Consistent with insights from a literature on 'stratified reproduction' (Colen, 1995; Ginsburg and Rapp, 1995), schools also shape rural families' ideas about the types of caregivers and the types of care most suitable for equipping children to succeed in life. Pertinently, as scholars observe both for elsewhere in China (Hansen, 2015) and for other countries (Coe, 2013[3]), migrant parents often prefer for their children to board at school, especially if both parents have migrated, because the teachers are more educated than rural caregivers.

---

[3] Coe (2014) explains how in Ghana educational aspirations are such that international migrant parents prefer to use their money and entrust their children to boarding schools in cities rather than to family members, reflecting a devaluing of elderly and rural caregivers.

1.3 Representation of Left-Behind Children

1.3.1 Representation of Left-Behind Children in Academic and Policy Literature

English-language academic and policy publications commonly use the term 'left-behind' to refer to people with one or more family members who have migrated without them. The use of a 'left-behind' framework in academic, media or policy discussions tends to overlap with depictions of the at-home family members and the migrants as inhabiting the separate social worlds of 'origin' and 'destination', which in developing countries often correspond with a 'rural' and 'urban' binary (Archambault, 2010; Jacka, 2014; Murphy, 2014a). Authors assume that the migrants' actions generate various 'impacts' on 'origin' societies and left-behind populations, which can be measured quantitatively. This can create an unintentional impression that the identity of the non-movers exists because other people have migrated, and that the non-movers are therefore *passive* (Archambault, 2010; Jacka, 2014).

At the same time, a left-behind lens can imply that left-behind people do not move themselves, overlooking the fact that many 'left-behind' individuals have previously migrated or are contemplating future migration (Jacka, 2012; Thao, 2013; Nyugen, 2014; Xiang, 2014; Wu, Lu and Kang, 2015). The Chinese-language equivalent for the term 'left behind' is *liu shou*, meaning 'to hold the fort at home'. Its emphasis differs slightly from the English-language term because it conveys an expectation that the family members who stay in the countryside get on with their lives while awaiting the migrant's return (Xiang, 2007). In practical usage, though, both the English- and Chinese-language terms connote these people's vulnerability, poverty, backwardness and lack of agency (Xiang, 2007; Jacka, 2014).

Children whose parents migrate without them are especially prone to being portrayed as passive, for at least two reasons. Firstly, childhood is a stage of human development when an individual's competencies are viewed as still evolving,[4] and it is therefore a stage when many aspects of an individual's life are controlled by adults and when children depend on adults for much of their care and survival (Punch, 2002a; Ben-Porath, 2010: 66–88; Gibson, 2012; Tisdall and Punch, 2012). Secondly, sociologists and psychologists have long depicted adults as the active agents in child socialisation, thereby overlooking children's agency in adult–child bilateral interactions (Kuczynski, 2003; Kuczynski, 2003 cited in Goh, 2011). Certainly, children lack agency relative to adults; and when parents migrate, this lack manifests itself in particular ways. For instance, children are seldom consulted about their parents'

---

[4] Childhood studies scholars note that adults' competencies are also always evolving (e.g. Tisdall and Punch, 2012).

22 The Lives of Left-Behind Children in Rural China

migration decisions even as migration is ostensibly undertaken for their benefit (Ye and Pan, 2011: 373; Zhang, 2015: 390; Hoang and Yeoh, 2015). This recalls Katz's observation that childhood is a 'spectacle' *in whose name much is done*, with 'spectacle' referring to the 'accumulation of capital to the point of collapse' as adults try to alleviate their anxieties about the future (2008: 5, my emphasis).

The representation of left-behind children as passive and vulnerable is significant because it contributes to a discourse that may encourage left-behind children to internalise negative self-conceptions and a sense of fatalism, constituting a further kind of pressure on them (Graham and Jordan, 2011; Bi and Oyserman, 2015). In this book I try to avoid some of the pitfalls of a 'left-behind' paradigm by prioritising children's agency and viewpoints, and by situating their agency and viewpoints within a multi-scalar *context* that incorporates their relationships with parents and other caregivers, their families' different capital endowments, their families' gendered and generational configurations, the translocal social fields that the children inhabit (Levitt and Glick Schiller, 2004), and wider structural forces. After much deliberation, though, I retain the term 'left-behind' because it captures 'left-behind' as a structurally produced circumstance (Yeoh, 2019). Moreover, the term has wider currency in the migration studies literature, while alternatives such as 'stayers', 'at-homes' or 'children whose parents have migrated without them' also suffer from limitations or sound clumsy.

1.3.2   Left-Behind Children in China's Public Discourse

In China in the late 2000s and early 2010s, in the wake of a series of high-profile tragedies befalling left-behind children, this population began to gain prominence first in online posts and then in the state-controlled media (Li, 2015: 82–86). In one of the many tragedies involving left-behind children, a nine-year-old boy in Anhui province committed suicide after being told that his mother would not return home for Chinese New Year (China Labor Bulletin, 2008). Meanwhile, two tragedies that gained particular attention involved children from the impoverished county of Bijie in Guizhou province, southwest China: in 2012, four children who had set off to find their migrant parents suffocated while seeking warmth in a skip, and two years later three children died in a child's murder-suicide (China Development Brief, 2015b; Yin, 2016; Li, 2017). In the 2000s, multiple reports about the sexual abuse of left-behind children came to light. The sexual abuse cases filed at local police stations disproportionately pertained to left-behind children with the abusers including teachers, neighbours and relatives (Nie, Li and Li, 2008: 98–105; China Daily, 2013a; China Daily, 2013c; Li, 2015: 87–91). Media items about

1.3 Representation of Left-Behind Children

present and former left-behind children's delinquency and criminality also burgeoned (see Nie, Li and Li, 2008: 61–85; Du, 2012).

Reports of extreme neglect and abuse among left-behind children drew the public's attention not only to the plight of individual children but also simultaneously to the generalised vulnerability, suffering and potential ruin of this large population. China's media commentators increasingly asked: If rural parents earn money at the expense of the next generation, is it worth it? In a programme I watched on Guangdong Television Station in September 2015 called 'Forgotten Childhood', a teacher told the viewers: 'You are swapping a better quality of life for your children's emotional wellbeing.'[5] The anchor then advised migrant parents to take a hard look at their actions. Several teachers who I met in rural schools similarly criticised migrant parents. For instance, in 2011, a primary school teacher in Tranquil County, Jiangxi, explained:

All the children in grades 1 to 5 in our county have a test and the classes are ranked, which puts a lot of pressure on the teachers. When the kids are left behind, the grandparents don't know how to support their homework, so this burden comes to us. Many *dagong* parents earn more money than we do. Primary school teachers earn just over 2,000 *yuan* a month. I raised a son who got into a technical university. I put time into this. Even if a child is not quick, if the parents are there to help, the child does better than a quick child who is left with no support. The parents need to think.

Hansen (2015) and Kim (2018) likewise document teachers' perception that rural migrant parents do not supervise their children properly. But as sociologists observe for other countries (Parreñas, 2005; Boehm, 2008), a discourse that blames the migrants for their children's vulnerabilities renders invisible the policies and the institutional discrimination that compel the parents to live separated from their children.

To borrow Parreñas's (2005: 30–55) phrase, the 'dismal picture'[6] of left-behind children in China's public sphere captures many aspects of these children's real adversities. Nevertheless, resembling public discourses about parent–child separation because of migration in other countries (Parreñas, 2005: 30–55; Pissin, 2013; see also Lan, 2018 on the US discourse about 'satellite children'), the discourse in China reflects other dynamics too. Specifically, the intersection of class relations and gender beliefs within a unique historical, cultural and demographic context has produced the discourse about left-behind children in China.

---

[5] "Bei Yiwang de Tongnian" [Forgotten Childhood], *Guangdong Television Station*, 30 September 2015, 21.00 hrs.

[6] I borrow the term 'dismal' to describe the public discourse about left-behind children and migrant families from Parreñas, 2005: 30–55.

Recent demographic history has contributed to China's 'dismal' discourse on left-behind children partly through the uneven effects of fertility limitation policies across social classes. In 1979, China's government implemented a One Child policy that was later relaxed to a 1.5 or even a two-child policy in some rural regions, usually for families where the first child was a girl (Greenhalgh and Winkler, 2005). Urban middle-class parents were the first to embrace the fertility limitation policies, and in the process they avidly consumed expert parenting advice that stressed a mother's nurturing role in raising a high-quality child (Milwertz, 1997; Pissin, 2013; Naftalia, 2016). The discourse about left-behind children simultaneously reflected the urban middle-class's embrace of traditional familial gender ideologies as individuals sought sanctuary from the bewildering social transformations around them (Xiang, 2007). The Chinese educators and policymakers who wrote and talked about left-behind children thereby hailed from a class that took a dim view of the circumstances of children whose mothers lived apart from them (Pissin, 2013; Hansen, 2015: 166; Kim, 2018).

The 'dismal picture' of left-behind children in Chinese public discourse also reflected urban intellectuals' long-standing anxieties about the implications of rural 'underdevelopment' for the fate of the nation. As far back as imperial times, in their search to explain their country's weakness at the hands of foreign powers, China's urban intellectuals accepted the Western colonisers' evaluation of their country as backward but projected it on to the 'internal Other' of the peasantry (Jacka and Gaetano, 2004: 14). A refrain across both state socialist (1950s to late 1970s) and socialist market periods (early 1980s onwards) has been that China cannot be strong until the rural populace is 'lifted up'. But in the 2000s, more than fifty years after national 'liberation', urban intellectuals felt dismayed that the countryside had remained a bastion of deprivation (Day, 2013). In their eyes, millions of 'left-behind children' symbolised a wider malaise (Nie, Li and Li, 2008). Certainly, at conferences I spoke at in China in 2016 and 2017, impassioned Chinese intellectuals asked each other why China was putting so much money into the One Belt One Road initiative and overseas infrastructure aid when there was immense need among the country's rural children.

The discourse about left-behind children further encapsulated a tension between middle-class benevolence on the one hand and middle-class self-interest on the other. According to Wanning Sun (2009a), Chinese public discourse resolves this tension through 'an idiom of care'. Sun (2009a) observes that an idiom of care enables professionals to equate a given social problem with the characteristics of the afflicted individuals or social groups. Such a framing deflects attention away from the institutions that force rural families to split spatially, while maintaining the status differential between the middle-class audience that cares and the vulnerable 'other' who is cared about

Figure 1.2 'Care for left-behind children, build a harmonious school together: exercise for an hour a day and work healthily for fifty years, live happily for a lifetime'

(Sun, 2009a: 55–71). Reminiscent of Bourdieu's idea of 'symbolic dominance' (Bourdieu and Passerson, 2000), an idiom of care permits the urban middle class to be seen as more virtuous than other classes – even as its members resist opening up the urban education system to migrants' children (Cohen, 2012; Li, 2013; Ming, 2013). Sun argues that it is no coincidence that an idiom of care has become salient as China's socio-economic inequalities have soared (Sun, 2009a: 55–71). Certainly, since the early 2000s exhortations to 'Care for Left-Behind Children' have abounded in school yards, on billboards, as per Figure 1.2, in public squares and on television.

1.4 Research Findings on Left-Behind Children's Well-being

The topic of left-behind children first appeared in Chinese-language social science publications in the mid-1990s (Pissin, 2013), proliferating from 2000 onwards (Ye and Pan, 2011; Ye et al., 2013), while English-language academic studies on left-behind children in rural China emerged from the late 2000s onwards. In the following, I treat the Chinese- and English-language social science literatures as one body of scholarship because some researchers publish in both languages (see Ye, Wang, Wu et al., 2013), research in one language often references the other, and meta-analyses incorporate publications in both languages (e.g. Qin and Albin, 2010; Wang and Mesman, 2015).

Studies in both Chinese and English start from an assumption that children fare best when they live in 'intact' two-parent families. In the English-language literature, this assumption has been informed by findings from a parallel 'family structures' literature pertaining to children's development in circumstances of spousal separation in the United States (e.g. Kandel and Kao, 2001; Booth, 2003; Arguillas and Williams, 2010; Lu and Treiman, 2011; Lu, 2012; Wen and Lin, 2012; Zhou, Murphy and Tao, 2014; Chen, Liang and Ostertag, 2017). This literature reports that parental absence correlates with children's poorer educational and emotional outcomes (Garfinkel and McLanahan, 1986; Krein and Beller, 1988; Seltzer, 1994), while the presence of two parents correlates with children's better academic achievement and emotional well-being (Coleman, 1988; for a review, see Cunha, Heckman and Lochner et al., 2005; Heckman, Stixrud and Urzua, 2006). Importantly, though, this literature attributes the disadvantages of children who live in fragmented families to parent–child attachment disruption, the stress-related impairment of parenting quality and reduced parental input, rather than to an unconventional family configuration per se.

The literature on children who are affected by family dissolution in the West usefully analyses the implications of care input on the one hand and economic resources on the other for children's well-being. At the same time, though, this literature's findings are not wholly transferable to the circumstances of left-behind children. Firstly, unlike parental absence in circumstances of family dissolution, parental absence because of migration seldom signifies the adults' abandonment of family relationships but rather their commitment to them (Nobles, 2011). Secondly, parental migration seldom indicates that the family is economically disadvantaged vis-à-vis the community average (Bryant, 2005; Asis, 2006), whereas family fragmentation in the West often corresponds with economic disadvantage (Putnam, 2015).

The Chinese- and English-language literature on the well-being of left-behind children in China covers educational outcomes, emotional well-being and physical health. Several studies stand out in this voluminous literature in finding that left-behind children in rural China do not differ significantly from non-left-behind children for multiple aspects of their well-being, including for their educational outcomes, cognitive performance, psychological and emotional well-being, health, height, and nutrition (Xiang, 2007; Xu and Xie, 2013; Zhou et al., 2015; Yeung and Gu, 2016; Hu, 2019). Pertinently, though, many of these studies also find that children who live in China's rural areas fare worse than children who live in cities (Xiang, 2007; Xu and Xie, 2013; Zhou et al.,

1.4 Research Findings on Left-Behind Children   27

2015; Yeung and Gu, 2016), the latter including rural children who live in the cities with their migrant parents (Xu and Xie, 2013). The researchers therefore conclude that all children in China's rural areas count as 'left behind' by an exclusionary urbanisation process regardless of their parents' migration status.

But as mentioned, a far-greater number of studies reports at best neutral effects of parental migration on children's well-being. Findings for children's educational well-being are the most equivocal, while findings for children's psycho-emotional well-being and health are largely negative. To start with education, a few scholars find that parents' migration does not correlate with significant differences among children in terms of test scores. For instance, Yao Lu (2012) reports negligible difference in children's test scores by their parents' migration status, positing that the extended family members' care, the migrants' phone calls and the family's increased income compensated the children for deficits in parental care arising because of parental migration. But Lu further observes that children benefited from the migration of older siblings because the increases in family income did not come at the expense of reduced parental care. Scott Rozelle and his team likewise find no difference in the test scores of left-behind primary school children and children who lived with both their parents in rural Shaanxi, but they note higher scores for the children of lone-migrant fathers (Chen et al., 2009). Meanwhile, several other studies indicate that at an aggregate level there is little difference in the scores of left-behind children and the scores of children who lived with both their parents, but that a subset of children whose mothers had migrated without them fared less well than their peers (On the Road to School, 2015, 2016, 2017; Wu and Li, 2015).

Other studies reach more negative conclusions about left-behind children's educational well-being. Some studies observe lower test scores among left-behind children than other children. For instance, Wang and Mesman (2015) state that seven out of the eight Chinese-language papers they reviewed find that left-behind children performed worse on standardised tests than did children who lived with both their parents. Meanwhile, Zhou, Murphy and Tao (2014) discover lower test scores for boys with two migrant parents, which is consistent with other scholars' observations of the especially disruptive effects of parental migration on boys (Leng and Park, 2010; Jiang et al., 2015; Shen and Zhang, 2018; Lyu and Chen, 2019).

Outcomes for other measures of educational well-being are also negative. For instance, Rozelle and his team report that left-behind infants aged nought to five years raised by grandparents received less adult–child interaction, thus incurring lasting delays in their cognitive development from which they never recovered (Yue et al., 2017). Several studies also find that parental migration adversely affected children's progression rates in junior high school (Li, 2015: 55–75) and to senior high school (Li and Song, 2009; Hu, 2012; Lee, 2011;

ACWF, 2013; Li, 2015: 55–75), though Lee (2011) notes that children's prospects for progression to senior high school improved when only one parent had migrated. Yet other studies report that left-behind children received less homework supervision than children who lived with both parents (Li, 2009; Tao, 2009; Wang and Dai, 2009; Wan, 2009; Xie, 2009; Wu and Li, 2015). Furthermore, in their survey of young migrant workers, Lyu and Chen (2019) find that those young migrants whose fathers had been migrants during their childhoods received fewer years of education than those young migrants who had been raised by both their parents, while the former left-behind children of two migrant parents fared significantly worse than other young migrants for both years of education and wages.

Findings for left-behind children's psycho-emotional well-being are the most negative because this aspect of well-being depends very heavily on parents' guidance and involvement (Qin and Albin, 2010; Wang and Mesman, 2015). Several studies find that the children of two migrant parents exhibited lower life satisfaction, greater anxiety and depression (Chen and Chen, 2009; Liu, Li and Ge, 2009; Qin and Albin, 2010; Wu, Lu and Kang, 2015), more loneliness (Fan et al., 2010; Jia and Tian, 2010; Liu et al., 2012; Su et al., 2013) and more behavioural problems (Chen and Chen, 2009; Qin and Albin, 2010) than children left behind by one migrant parent, and that all left-behind children fared worse than children who lived with both parents (Chen and Chen, 2009; Liu, Li and Ge, 2009; Qin and Albin, 2010; Liu, Wang, Yang et al., 2012; Su, Li, Lin et al., 2013). Some authors report no difference among children by their parents' migration status for general happiness or satisfaction with life (Wen and Lin, 2012; Su, Li and Lin, 2013; Murphy, Zhou and Tao, 2016), but at least two studies observe adverse outcomes among left-behind children for these measures (On the Road to School, 2017; Shen and Zhang, 2018). Tan, Zhao and Liang (2009) report that left-behind children exhibited lower levels of interpersonal trust than children who lived with both parents. Li and Tao (2009) find that while left-behind children did not exhibit more anxiety or depression than children who lived with both parents, they exhibited more suicidal thoughts. Du (2012) and Wang and Dai (2009) observe more internet addiction among left-behind boys than children who lived with both parents, while Chen, Liang and Ostertag (2017) report more victimisation and bullying among children, especially boys, when their fathers had migrated alone, with the children's misbehaviour and perceived vulnerability identified as the likely causal mechanisms.

Other studies highlight that parent–child communication exerts independent and mediating influences on left-behind children's psycho-emotional well-being (Wen and Lin, 2012; Su et al., 2013; Wu, Lu and Kang, 2015), thereby mirroring international findings (Graham, Jordan, Yeoh et al., 2012). Many studies report that left-behind children felt emotionally estranged from their

1.4 Research Findings on Left-Behind Children

migrant parents because of a lack of communication (Ding and Sun, 2009; Liao, Song and Chen, 2009; Li and Tao, 2009; Li, 2009; Wang, 2009; Ye and Pan, 2011; On the Road to School, 2015, 2016 and 2017). Liu et al. (2010) report that compared with children who lived with both parents, left-behind children were more likely to dislike or to be uncertain if they liked their migrant parents, correlating with a lower self-concept – a cognitive aspect of self that is linked to self-esteem – and more loneliness. Meanwhile, some studies find that children whose mothers had migrated incurred the worst effects on their emotional well-being, with the harm being greater the younger their age at the time of the mothers' initial departure and the longer the mothers' duration of absence, reflecting migration's disturbance to mother–child attachment (Liu, Li and Ge, 2009; Fan et al., 2010).

Studies on left-behind children's health also yield mostly negative findings. Liu et al. (2012) find that children left behind with grandparents manifested more symptoms of illness than other children. Murphy, Zhou and Tao (2016) and Shen and Zhang (2018) find that lone-mother migration correlates with children's worse self-reported health. Studies also observe higher risks among left-behind children for smoking (Gao et al., 2010; Wen and Lin, 2012) and alcohol consumption (Jiang et al., 2015). Moreover, several studies discover that left-behind children incurred more injuries than children who lived with both parents (Li and Song, 2009; Shen et al., 2009; Li, 2015: 23–48; On the Road to School, 2015). Scholars also observe that the children of migrant mothers displayed worse health and nutrition – including an increased risk for anaemia – than children raised by both their parents (Lou, Zong and Yao et al., 2008; Li and Song, 2009; Wang and Dai, 2009; Li, 2015: 23–48;Wang and Wu, 2016; Wu and Li, 2015), with some scholars finding the effects to be the most deleterious if both parents had migrated (Lei, Liu and Hill, 2018), or if mothers had migrated alone (Wu and Li, 2015), though Wu, Luan and Lü (2009) note worse health for the children of lone-migrant fathers. Meanwhile, Zhang, Bécares and Chandola (2015) discover a 'gender paradox' of shorter height and lower weight among left-behind boys compared with boys in intact families but no significant difference among girls.

In summary, a wealth of quantitative studies provides multiple and some-times contradictory insights into the implications of parental migration for the well-being of children left behind in China's countryside. The mix in findings stems from diversity in different studies' survey sites, research designs, control groups, data sets, questionnaire respondents – whether the reports about the children's well-being were from children, caregivers or teachers (Jordan and Graham, 2012; Wen and Lin, 2012) – dimensions of well-being under inves-tigation, indicators for a given dimension of well-being (Jordan and Graham, 2012; Wen and Lin, 2012) and the analytical techniques. Nonetheless, these studies cumulatively demonstrate that rural children are profoundly affected by

30   The Lives of Left-Behind Children in Rural China

their parents' migration, or, at the very least, by the institutionalised discrimination of rural children and families in China's urbanisation process.

1.5   The Sociocultural Context of Striving, Family and Childhood in Rural China

The rich literature discussed earlier reveals much about family migration strategies, child-raising practices in multilocal families, and the impact of parental migration on different dimensions of children's well-being. But to reiterate, this literature still tells us little about left-behind children's experiences of their families' migration projects, their relationships with parents and grandparent caregivers, or the changing nature of rural childhood as China rapidly urbanises. As stated in the introduction to this chapter, in addressing these gaps this book sees the left-behind children as participants in multilocal *parent–child striving teams*. Next I turn to locate these multilocal parent–child striving teams within the distinctive sociocultural context of rural China.

1.5.1   Striving

In this book I use the term *striving* team rather than Norma Field's (1995) term of 'toiling' team not only because, as indicated previously, *striving* links 'work' to 'aspiration' and family relationships. I also use 'striving' because this word captures the significance of 'work' in a Chinese sociocultural context. Yan Yunxiang (2010; 2013) explains that economic restructuring in late twentieth-century China heralded the rise of a 'striving individual'. He further explains that the first stage of the individualisation process in China saw the individual become dis-embedded from traditional kinship networks or 'the ancestor's shadow' and re-embedded in the collective organisations of the socialist Party-state, for instance, in rural communes or in urban work units (Yan, 2010). Nevertheless, even as loyalty to socialist comrades displaced people's 'feudal' loyalties to kin during this phase of history, Chinese culture still retained an 'often hidden yet constant presence' (Yan, 2010: 494). Thereafter, economic reforms precipitated a second phase of individualisation whereby people became dis-embedded from collectives and were required to take responsibility for forging their own path in the wider market and society while remaining loyal to the nation incarnate in the Communist Party-state.

Yan (2013) contends that the striving individual in contemporary China resembles the 'enterprising individual' of Western neoliberal capitalism in many respects because the authoring of ones' own biography is a personal project (Yan, 2014: 283). However, Yan (2013) suggests that the word 'striving' is more apt than 'enterprising' because even though the subjectivity of an individual in China shares much in common with an

1.5 The Sociocultural Context

'enterprising' individual in the West, the resemblance is only partial (Yan, 2013: 283). Specifically, Yan notes that while China's Party-state adopted many development strategies initiated by liberal and neoliberal economic models, liberalism in China did not evolve from the same ancestry as Western European modernity. Chiefly, it does not share with Western liberalism a philosophy that an individual is the autonomous bearer of natural rights and it has not evolved in an environment where a welfare state provided individuals with security and support (Yan, 2010: 504). Rather, the striving individual connects to a long-held image of the *hard-working* person in traditional Chinese culture (Yan, 2014: 285, my emphasis).

Many of the parents my research assistants and I met in Anhui and Jiangxi villages said that they had to work hard to support their children's education because life is tough for a person if their *suzhi* is low or if they have no culture or education. *Suzhi*, meaning 'essentialised quality', refers to an individual's or a social group's overall level of quality as well as to specific dimensions of quality, for instance physical, intellectual, psychological or moral quality (Murphy, 2004a; Kipnis, 2006; Yan, 2008: 111–138; Kipnis, 2011). The concept of *suzhi* also resembles Bourdieu's notion of habitus in that both terms refer to individuals' 'disposition, ability and way of action' (Zhang, 2001:142–143).[7]

According to Ann Anagnost (2004), the term *suzhi* first appeared in policy documents in the 1980s following China's abandonment of class struggle in favour of increasing per capita GDP by reducing population size and accelerating economic growth, and thereafter the term circulated across all social classes. To explain how the concept of *suzhi* has been used to reconfigure human worth in China, Anagnost (2004) contrasts the 'two parallel poles' of *suzhi*: the urban middle-class child and the labouring rural migrant. She argues that urban middle-class parents invest in their children's education to increase the social and economic distance between themselves and the rural masses. The worth of urban middle-class children thereby takes the form of the competencies that they have accumulated and the potential that they have realised. By contrast, rural migrants are defined by a lack of worth, but it is this lack that permits surplus value to be extracted from their bodies through harsh labour discipline, low wages and exclusion from urban citizenship (Anagnost, 2004: 205).

Anagnost's (2004) analysis offers at least two insights instructive for understanding how hierarchies of human worth compel parents and children in

---

[7] Importantly, though, while Bourdieu proposed the term 'habitus' to critique inequality, the concept of *suzhi* invites an evaluation of people in ways that obscure the structural inequalities underpinning *suzhi* hierarchies.

multilocal families to work hard. Firstly, Anagnost highlights that migration and education are interlinked domains of endeavour whereby

suzhi works ideologically as a regime of representation through which subjects recognise their positions within the larger social order and thereby sets up the conditions for socio-economic *striving*. (Anagnost, 2004: 194, my emphasis)

Secondly, she explains that *suzhi* facilitates the transfer of value between the bodies of people from different social classes (Anagnost, 2004), which is pertinent to this book's exploration of families' pursuit of intergenerational class mobility by transferring value between the bodies of one generation to the bodies of the next generation. Indeed, many rural parents told my research assistants and me that owing to their low *suzhi* the best they could do for their children was to migrate.

Two pioneering books cast further light on why and how people in rural China strive for and through educational investment. In *Governing Educational Desire*, Andrew Kipnis (2011) explains that China's Party-state symbolically constructs social hierarchies and anxieties around 'lack' that devalue rurality as the nation rapidly urbanises (Kipnis, 2011: 144–145). He also argues that in schools, as in the wider society, elements of a historically constituted East Asian 'imperial governing complex' coalesce with other political, cultural and economic forces, such that 'education is as much a way to rule as to teach' (Kipnis, 2011: 91). Students thereby learn to self-govern in pursuing both local and translocal visions of human worth by following exemplary models of behaviour and by studying a set curriculum to pass exams.

In *Educating the Chinese Individual*, Mette Halskov Hansen (2015) examines how students in a senior high boarding school in a rural township in Zhejiang province were trained to experiment with making choices without having freedom, to take responsibility for success in their life without access to institutional rights and to strive for success without ever questioning authority or 'analysing [themselves] in a broader social context' (Hansen, 2015: 16). Hansen observes that the students she met – many of them left-behind children – wanted to achieve economic security for themselves and their families while also holding a concurrent but less pressing wish to help strengthen their nation. Hansen's ethnography confirms Yan's (2010; 2014) view that individualisation in China produces a different kind of citizen-subject than in the West (Hansen, 2015: 184). Specifically, she finds that even as China's 'neosocialist' education system is flawed, it resonates with individuals' perceptions of their own interests such that 'few see any need for collective action to change it.' Rather, they 'concentrate on their own social and economic investments in the private sphere' (Hansen, 2015: 184).

1.5 The Sociocultural Context

Kipnis and Hansen each offer fresh insights into how and why people from rural China work so hard for educational success and for success in life more generally, with 'success' construed inside and outside of the school gates as 'movement up' intertwined social and spatial hierarchies. Nevertheless, these authors also both mostly talk about 'students' rather than 'children', which is significant because the latter is a particular familial and relational category. Indeed, although Kipnis and Hansen explore the family changes that underpin 'educational desire' and 'individualization', respectively, family remains tangential to their analyses, with Hansen observing that owing to parental migration and boarding, the students in her fieldwork school were largely disconnected from their families. In this book, I differ from both Kipnis and Hansen in concentrating on left-behind children's experiences of migration and education as co-constituted domains of *family striving* and in prioritising children's voices – only faintly audible in Kipnis's book – in the analysis of family striving.

1.5.2   Family and Children

As noted previously, a lens on family brings to the fore how culturally specific social relations including gender structure people's participation in striving. In one essay, Brandtstädter (2009) examines how such social and gender relations play out in a Chinese sociocultural context. She begins by observing that work generates value – economic and social value, which in turn reproduces relatedness. She then explains that while

in a typical Western context, kinship and economic spheres are ideologically opposed as the separate domains of emotional states (love) and intentional agency (labour) in Chinese society *work* is the medium through which individuals express their emotions and sincerity to others. (Brandtstädter, 2009: 156)

Pertinently too, she demonstrates that different family members – each distinguished by their gender and generation – do work that produces different kinds of value, with women's work generating a certain kind of affective value that converts into other forms of value over time (Brandtstädter, 2009).

In Chinese culture, both individuals' work and 'child' as a relational category gain much of their meaning from the traditional familial ethic of filial piety (Chao and Tseng, 2002). Based in Confucian teachings, filial piety refers to the obligation on children to repay their parents for their lives with obedience and loyalty. It encapsulates a view that individuals exist not only to support their families but also to honour their ancestors and to secure a legacy for their descendants, with family continuity occurring patrilineally. This view of the individual's obligation to the family differs from an assumption in the West that

34   The Lives of Left-Behind Children in Rural China

the family should support the individual until they can fend for themselves (Baker, 1979: 26; Woon, 1983/84: 689; Yan, 2010). Attention to filial piety illuminates how Chinese family members interpret and give moral purpose to their 'linked lives' (Chen, Liu and Mair, 2011) and how adults foster a sense of intergenerational debt in their children. Brandtstädter offers an apposite example, explaining that in a Chinese cultural logic a studious child is praiseworthy not for her ambition but because she responds to her parents' work with meaningful effort of her own, thereby demonstrating her filial piety (Brandtstädter, 2009: 156).

Importantly, though, even as filial piety is an enduring ethic, Chinese families continually adapt their understandings and practices of it to changing institutional conditions (Chen, Liu and Mair, 2011; Tang and Cheng, 2014). The sociologist Yingchun Ji (2015; 2017) usefully elucidates such family adaptions by explaining that China's rapid social and institutional changes over the past seven decades have engendered 'mosaic familialism' whereby elements from different 'temporalities' such as resurgent Confucian patriarchal traditions, socialist vestiges, socialist modernity, early capitalist modernity and neoliberal marketisation – converge, conflict and synthesise. At least four adaptations of the ethic of filial piety stand out as pertinent for understanding family striving in twenty-first-century rural China.

Firstly, the rural Chinese family has become 'smaller and structurally simpler' (Yan, 2011: 211). One aspect of this arises from rapid fertility decline. The Total Fertility Rate in China's rural areas was approximately six births per woman from 1962 onwards, halving in the nine years from 1971 to 1980, falling yet further during the 1980s, and reaching 1.8 by 1992 (Ping, 2000: 23). This was accompanied by a growing emphasis on relationships within the nuclear family while interactions among extended kinship networks waned. Over the same time, relationships between parents and children became less hierarchical and more oriented towards mutual support (Croll, 2006). The status of sons and daughters also became more equal within the context of reconfigured repertoires of filiality, which I discuss in detail in Chapter 4.

Secondly, parents increasingly 'treat their children as "projects" whose achievements are their own rather than solely as sinks of reciprocal gift giving who repay parents with respect and old-age care' (Kipnis, 2011: 149). Ideally, the children participate in these projects (Kipnis, 2011: 145) through hard work, becoming more emotionally attached to their parents in the process (Brandtstädter, 2009: 156; Obendiek, 2017). Nevertheless, parents are still likely to hold some expectation of future support from their offspring (Ji, 2017: 9): according to Ji (2017), in 'mosaic familialism' filial piety 'is characterized by a sequential symbiosis between parents and children facing financial constraints and unforeseeable uncertainties with a lack of a social safety

1.5 The Sociocultural Context

net' (Ji, 2017: 1). Nevertheless, as Yan observes, rural elders still most hope for emotional attachment and respect from their adult children (2011: 217).

Thirdly, the power of ageing parents in daily life has eroded. During the 1960s, young couples were able to demand earlier division from the husband's parents because they had access to the collective's resources necessary for them to create their own families (Yan, 2011). In the 1980s and 1990s, the middle generation's capacity to obtain resources for themselves was strengthened by the rise of labour markets (Yan, 2011). By the turn of the twenty-first century, though, with the middle generations' autonomy to manage its own resources established, and mounting pressures on them to earn ever more money, couples increasingly saw advantages to retaining close ties with the husband's parents (Yan, 2011: 214–216). Indeed, in the 2000s, rural elders' access to material support from their children has come with a requirement that they help the middle generation with childcare and domestic chores (Croll, 2006; Chen, Liu and Mair, 2011; Harrell and Santos, 2017; Santos, 2017). Zhang (2017) calls this a shift in filial practice from traditional old-age dependence to intergenerational interdependence, with implications for how many children in rural China are raised.

Finally, families discharge parenting obligations across ever-widening distances. Families' adaptation to migration is significant not least because regular interaction was always integral to idealised practices of both child-raising and filial piety, epitomised in two words used by Zhangyong's mother and introduced at the start of this chapter: *yang*, which means 'to nourish', 'to support' and 'to raise', and *guan*, which means 'to govern' and 'to care for'. Stafford (2000) proposes the term a 'cycle of *yang*' to highlight the reciprocal intergenerational flows of support that an ethic of filial piety engenders. He explains that *yang* occurs through *mundane encounters in everyday life* whereby, simultaneously, food, household items and money are exchanged, emotion is expressed, and relatedness is maintained, an interpretation of family interactions that Brandtstädter (2009) echoes. Similarly, the Chinese sociologist Fei Xiaotong states:

Filial piety is simply a peaceful mind. Sons and daughters should become thoroughly familiar with their parents' personalities *in the course of daily contact*, and then should try to please them in order to achieve a peaceful mind. (Fei, 1992: 43–44, my emphasis)

Regular interaction likewise underpins the cultural ideal of *guan*. The child development scholar Ruth K. Chao (1994) explains that in their practice of *guan* Chinese mothers continually correct their children's behaviour, all the while staying *physically close* to them by, for instance, sleeping alongside them and meeting their every need. Thereafter, the mothers drive forward their children's academic success in school by means of close support and supervision (Chao, 1994). Chao observes that parents' *guan* practices centre on education because academic success reflects the quality of their sacrifice in raising a child who exhibits culturally approved and socially desirable behaviour. Paradoxically, though, in an environment of rising inequalities, reconfigured family repertoires of child-raising, filial piety and care have increasingly anchored educational and other investments at the heart of the parent–child relationship, such that millions of children must experience their parents' efforts to *yang* and *guan* them from afar.

Alongside these social and family transformations, perceptions of children's needs have also been changing. In traditional Chinese culture, parent–child relationships invested much authority and responsibility in parents to define their children's needs and interests (Chao and Tseng, 2002). This authority and responsibility co-existed with adults' perception that children did not understand adult matters, often leading them to couch their children's interests in terms of their survival and development. As sociologists observe of Chinese working-class immigrants in the United States, as well as of migrant parents in other Asian cultural contexts (Asis, 2006; Qin, 2009), and as Lareau (2003) also observes of poor and working-class parents in the United States, parents commonly express their love for their children through material provisioning. Certainly, many Chinese parents and grandparents see good childcare in terms of the provision of food and clothes, and – increasingly – the provision of money for education, with this provisioning demonstrating their love and concern for the children's welfare (Jiang et al., 2007). This is even though the children themselves may long for greater emotional engagement with their parents (Qin, 2009; Lan, 2018), especially if they have been left behind.

Even so, emotional intimacy is important to parent-child relationships in rural Chinese society (Liu, 2014; Shi, 2017a). During the 1960s, Wolf (1972) observed that rural Taiwanese mothers forged intimate bonds with their children, especially with their sons, partly to help them secure emotional belonging in their husbands' families where they were 'outsiders'. More recently, Jankowiak (2011) notes that at the time of his fieldwork in the 1980s and the 2000s even as women in families in urban China no longer needed to build alliances with their children to deal with a 'vengeful mother-in-law' or 'hostile spouse', mothers continued to have a deep emotional involvement with their children. Additionally, as mentioned previously, mirroring a global trend (Zelizer, 1994), given smaller family size, Chinese children have become ever more emotionally precious to their parents (Liu, 2015). Nonetheless, the flourishing of an awareness of children's desires, empowerment and rights that commentators observe in China's cities has appeared only dimly in the countryside (Naftali, 2016). Hence, although rural Chinese children are 'not just repositories of adults' desires and fantasies'

(Katz, 2008: 9), their perceptions and possibilities exist within a constrained familial context. As later chapters in this book demonstrate, multilocal striving simultaneously fortifies, expresses and strains emotional intimacy between children and their parents while aspirations for the future of the children give purpose to this toil and strain.

1.6   Organisation of the Book

This book comprises eight chapters. Following this introduction, Chapter 2 examines the characteristics of the four fieldwork counties in their provincial contexts and in relation to the national context. The discussion describes how each of the four counties' linkages to the 'outside' intersected with local histories, grandparents' and parents' personal biographies, gendered familial culture and school regime characteristics to shape the local geographic context of the children's care, daily routines, educational aspirations and family relationships. Chapter 3 explores how educational aspirations underpinned the migration projects of the children in the families I visited. Specifically, it teases out how different children responded to both family and school efforts to socialise them to be hardworking and filial and to prepare them for an urban future. Chapter 4 looks at boys' and girls' perceptions of how their gender affected what their migrant parents aspired to provide for them; the parents' decisions about which children migrated and which children stayed behind; and the allocation of investments, everyday resources and chores to different children by their gender.

Chapters 5 to 7 examine the experiences of children in differently configured families, thereby redressing a gap in the literature on the implications for children of who migrates and who cares for them (Mazzucato and Schans, 2001; Jordan and Graham, 2012). Chapter 5 examines children's relationships with their parents when their mothers stayed at home while their fathers migrated. It demonstrates that in poor rural regions, adults and children alike saw 'mother home, father out' to be the optimal family configuration for nurturing children's educational success. The chapter also describes how these children's relationships with their parents varied by their families' economic circumstances as well as by their mother's migration histories. Chapter 6 explores the children's relationships with their parents when their fathers stayed at home while their mothers migrated alone. It focuses on these children's strategies for coping with a family configuration that so defied customary gender norms that it signalled to other people their families' inherent vulnerability. Chapter 7 discusses how children in skipped-generation families navigated contradictory intergenerational dynamics arising from the middle generation's migration, revealing heterogeneity in different children's relationships with their migrant parents and grandparents. Chapter 8 reflects on what seeing children as participants in spatially dispersed 'parent-child striving teams' reveals about family adaptions to socio-economic transformation and how 'left-behind' children interpreted and influenced these adaptions.

2 Migration, Education and Family Striving in Four Counties of Anhui and Jiangxi

The left-behind children who my research assistants and I met in Eastern County and Western County in Anhui province and Jade County and Tranquil County in Jiangxi province lived in their caregivers' homes and studied in their rural schools while 'outside' or *waimian* loomed large in their imaginations, relationships and conversations. When I asked the children, 'Where are your parents?' many gave the one-word answer, '*waimian*'. They saw it as unremarkable that one or both of their parents worked 'outside'. 'How else could families in poor rural regions have enough money to live off?' The circumstances of the children in the four fieldwork counties were not exceptional within their provinces: in the early 2010s, over half of children in rural regions in Anhui and Jiangxi provinces had at least one parent working outside (Duan et al., 2013: 42). The normalisation of parents' labour migration could also be seen in the children's play. For instance, one Sunday morning in September 2013 in Tranquil County while my research assistant and I were waiting in a classroom for the primary school headteacher to arrive, we saw that the open compartments of the children's wooden desks contained paper wallets with the characters '*dagong* money' written on the front while the play money that they had made poked out of the tops. Clearly, children participated in sustaining wider material, conceptual and emotional linkages between their rural hometowns and 'outside'.

In migration studies, the concept of 'place' has been influenced by the ideas of the geographer Doreen Massey. For Massey (1994), as for most geographers, a place is space that people have invested with meaning through their routines, interactions, memories and stories. People move through space to get to places. But Massey (1993) asserts that boundaries are not essential to the idea of place. Rather, a place represents 'particular constellations of relations articulated together at a particular locus' with 'a large proportion of those relations, experiences and understandings ... constructed on a far larger scale than what we happen to define for that moment as the place itself' (Massey, 1993: 67). Pertinently, Massey (1993) notes that the conditions of modernity that generate time–space compression also confer on different people differential power over the flows and interconnections among places that constitute time–space

40   Migration and Education in Four Counties

compression. Some people can move wherever and whenever they wish; others have mobility for menial work or else immobility imposed on them.

Some sociologists take up Massey's insights into the idea of place and the attendant inequalities in peoples' agency. For instance, Mahler and Pessar (2001) propose that people's 'social locations' intersect with their geographic locations to affect their power over spatial flows. 'Social location' resembles Bourdieu's idea of 'social position' noted in Chapter 1, but rather than emphasising a person's position in overlapping fields in which different 'capitals' are unequally distributed – manifest in the habitus, social location highlights a person's position in intersecting multi-scalar power relations structured not only by class but also by gender, kinship, generation, ethnicity and other stratifiers. Dreby and Schmalzbauer (2013) extend Mahler and Pessar's (2001) approach to conceptualising people's agency in migratory contexts by referring to both their social locations *and* the dynamics of their family relationships within given geographic localities. Moreover, they explain that a crucial feature of geographic location is the social services infrastructure, which includes transportation and welfare services. Here, I likewise consider people's social locations and family relationships – with a focus on intergenerational relationships – while highlighting schools as a pivotal but often overlooked feature of the local social services infrastructure in migratory contexts.

This chapter introduces the characteristics of the four fieldwork counties in their provincial contexts while discussing the linkages to 'outside' that help to constitute each of these places (Massey, 1993: 67). The chapter addresses the questions: How do migration and local schools intertwine to shape the local geographic context in which rural families strive? And, how do families' actions to pursue migration, support their children's education and deliver childcare unfold in different places? The discussion proceeds as follows. Section 2.1 situates Anhui and Jiangxi provinces and the four fieldwork counties within a wider hierarchy of places in China. Section 2.2 examines how parents' aspirations for their children's education were forged partially through their personal experiences of having grown up in 'backward' places. Section 2.3 discusses the school regime characteristics of each fieldwork county. Section 2.4 charts how localised interactions among gendered familial culture, local school regimes and local migration histories shaped prevailing patterns of family striving in each county. Section 2.5 reflects on the implications of local geographic context for understanding children's aspirations, expectations, family relationships and daily lives.

2.1   A Hierarchy of Places

In China, hierarchies of places incorporate both regional and rural–urban dimensions. As landlocked provinces in China's southeast, Anhui and Jiangxi

2.1 A Hierarchy of Places

do not count as 'east' like the coastal provinces that have benefited from preferential economic policies and showcase the country's economic miracle. But nor are they among the Western provinces that in the 2000s received substantial central state investment for infrastructure and poverty alleviation projects to better integrate them into the national whole (Sun, 2002). Indeed, teachers, scholars and officials I met in Jiangxi sometimes joked that their province was 'not much of a thing', which translates to mean 'despicable'. 'Not much of a thing' is a pun because the Chinese word for 'thing' (*dongxi*) comprises the characters for 'east' (*dong*) and 'west' (*xi*).

The ranking of Anhui and Jiangxi vis-à-vis other provinces varies depending on the measure. If the measure is per capita GDP, then both provinces have languished in the bottom third of China's thirty-one provinces for decades. In 2000, Jiangxi and Anhui ranked twenty-fifth and twenty-sixth, respectively, while in 2015 they ranked twenty-second and twenty-third, respectively (Wikipedia, 2016). But if the annual per capita disposable income of rural residents is the measure, then in the mid-2010s the two provinces ranked only fractionally below the national average. Crucially, though, as indicated in Table 2.1, the income of rural residents still sits well below the income of urban residents, both within each province, nationally, and when compared to the income of urban residents in leading coastal cities such as Guangzhou in Guangdong province and Shanghai. Moreover, the rural–urban income gap appears even starker if we consider that rural income includes the value of in-kind farm produce.

Table 2.1 *Annual per capita disposable income of rural and urban residents (2015)*

	Rural (*yuan*)	Urban (*yuan*)
China	11,422	31,195
Anhui	10,821	26,936
Jiangxi	11,139	26,500
Guangdong	19,313	46,735
Shanghai	23,205	52,962
Eastern County, Anhui*	15,000	27,000
Western County, Anhui*	14,000	27,000
Jade County, Jiangxi*	14,000	30,000
Tranquil County, Jiangxi*	8,000	23,000

Source: National, provincial and city figures come from China Statistical Yearbooks CNKI.Net Online Data Set (2016). obtained the figures for the fieldwork counties from the relevant government statistical bureau websites.
* Figures for the fieldwork counties are rounded to the nearest thousand to prevent the fieldwork sites from being readily identifiable.

42   Migration and Education in Four Counties

Table 2.1 further indicates that in 2015 the rural regions of three of the four fieldwork counties – Eastern County, Western County and Jade County – were among the better-off rural regions in their provinces. Nevertheless, caution is needed because in China the reporting of economic statistics is inherently political, with officials over-reporting if wanting to demonstrate their career competence and under-reporting if wanting to benefit from the fiscal transfers that come with a formal 'poverty county' status. Counties' circumstances also change over time. For instance, Western County in Anhui was a state-designated national-level poverty county until the early 2010s, while Tranquil County in Jiangxi was a state-designated national-level poverty county until the late 2010s.

In each of the fieldwork counties, most households derived some form of income from farming, even if they transferred the usage of their farmland to other households and received rent in grain or cash. Eastern County and Western County both sit in central eastern Anhui, which borders Jiangxi and resembles Jiangxi in an emphasis on rice production (Sun, 2002). But whereas the Jiangxi fieldwork counties – Jade County in Jiangxi's central west and Tranquil County in Jiangxi's mountainous southwest – engage in double-rice cropping, Eastern County and Western County grow a second crop of cotton, maize or wheat. In 2006, China's central government abolished agricultural taxes and gave farming subsidies per mu[1] of cultivated land to improve farmers' livelihoods (Li, Sato and Sicular, 2019). But as in many parts of rural China, families in the fieldwork counties still struggled to make a decent living from agriculture because of the small land allocations, the high costs of farm inputs and low prices for farm produce (Luo and Sicular, 2019). Meanwhile, inadequate irrigation persisted as a hindrance to farming livelihoods in the two Anhui counties. Hence, in all four counties most rural families needed off-farm income.

The four fieldwork counties all had off-farm industrial sectors. Pre-empting the phasing out of agricultural taxes, during the early 2000s the counties set up economic and industrial development zones or else consolidated and expanded existing zones to boost the off-farm tax base for local coffers. The industrial zones in Eastern County, Western County and Jade County benefited from infrastructure construction during the 2010s, including work to build high-speed rail links. The industrial zone in Eastern County also benefited from its geographic location bordering Anhui's provincial capital of Hefei. In the 2010s, the zone in Eastern County produced items such as electronics, solar energy appliances, and construction and engineering machinery. The zone in Western County specialised in the production of cables and electronics. The zone in Jade County produced iron and steel goods, chemicals, rare earth

---

[1] 1 mu = 0.1647 acres = 0.0667 hectares.

minerals for mobile phones, solar energy equipment, batteries, shoes and clothes. Meanwhile, a modest zone in Tranquil County produced clothes and knitwear, packaging, and processed agricultural products. Villages and townships in all four counties also hosted some off-farm industries. Several townships had small factories and several villages had brick factories, stone quarries or logging businesses while one village I visited in Western County had four fireworks factories.

Despite the within-county industries, county-based off-farm jobs were not plentiful or attractive. In the early to mid-2010s, few people from the families I visited worked in the county economic and industrial zones. Jobs in these zones paid less than jobs in the manufacturing and service sectors in the coastal provinces. County-based off-farm jobs also entailed working long shifts, and, for many villagers, the travel time between the village and the industrial zone would still require them to live apart from their families for extended periods. Conditions in some county-based factories were also bad. For instance, respiratory illnesses afflicted workers in the cable factories of Western County, while workers in chemical and solar energy factories in Jade County were exposed to substances that reputedly impaired men's fertility so that locals said only people from extremely poor places – even poorer than Jade County – would work in them. Meanwhile, income from off-farm work in the village and township industries was mostly supplementary. Hence, in the late 2000s and early 2010s labour migration to places outside the county was still the most important source of off-farm income for most rural families: in the 2010 Summer Survey, reports of 992 families from each of the four counties indicated that in 2009 annual per capita income was 10,087 *yuan* in families with two migrant parents, 7,913 *yuan* in families with one migrant parent and 5,444 *yuan* in families with both parents at home.

2.2   Generations, Biography and Place

The representation of Anhui and Jiangxi within a wider 'geographical imagination' (Massey, 1994) reflects not just the image of each place at a given point in time but also the 'description and interpretation of a place which has lived through time' (Jess and Massey, 1995 cited by Sun, 2002). Concurrently, consistent with a view that historical processes are 'emplaced' (Kipnis, 2011) the grandparents and parents of the children my research assistants and I met had lived through local versions of national histories, which had in turn generated particular tropes about the natives of Anhui and Jiangxi. Moreover, people internalised aspects of these tropes, with 'underdevelopment' constituting a form of individualised identity (Escobar, 1995), often expressed in Chinese language with reference to the concept of *suzhi* (quality), discussed in Chapter 1 (Sun, 2009b). Indeed, when the grandparents and parents we met

44   Migration and Education in Four Counties

reflected on their own biographies in light of social and economic conditions in the 2010s, they recalled their past experiences of deprivation, especially of dropping out of school, which had left them without knowledge, ability or status in a world where education credentials and money – or 'numeric capital' (Woronov, 2016) – had become the prime objectives of striving and the prime measures of human worth.

Various historical vicissitudes of socialism contributed to the ongoing representation of people from both Anhui and Jiangxi as 'backward', 'poor', 'simple' and 'uneducated', albeit with some differences in the local manifestations of these histories. In both provinces, many rural adults had experienced China's Great Famine of 1959–1961, which followed the Great Leap Forward of 1958. The Great Leap was Mao's plan to transform China through accelerated collectivisation and industrialisation and entailed misguided efforts to boost farm output by unscientific production methods, for instance planting crops too close together and planting grain in unsuitable soils, and by channelling resources en masse to industrialisation (Meisner, 1986). Over the same period, severe weather conditions exacerbated the adverse impact of these policies on aggregate food yields (Meisner, 1986).

Anhui was one of the provinces hardest hit by the Great Famine, losing 18.37 per cent of its population (Chen, 2011). This was partly because the then provincial Communist Party leader Zeng Xisheng overzealously enforced high procurement quotas to support the construction of socialism (Chen, 2011). In subsequent years, people in rural Anhui continued to experience economic hardship, with natural disasters such as floods exacerbating their suffering. By the late 1970s, villagers in one region of Anhui, Fengyang prefecture, were pushed to such desperation that they experimented in secret with household farming, famously later paving the way for the nation's dismantling of the communes and adoption of the household responsibility farming system (Sun, 2002). Thereafter, during the 1970s and 1980s many Anhui natives combined farming with itinerant work in cities such that Anhui people became synonymous with beggars, paupers and tinkers (Sun, 2002).

Neighbouring Jiangxi was not as badly hit by the Great Famine as Anhui, losing 'only' 1.06 per cent of its population (Chen, 2011). The devastation was less severe because of the provinces' lower population density, larger water surfaces and a party leadership that avoided requisitioning excesses (Chen, 2011). Even so, Jiangxi was still poor, with one observer attributing this not only to civil conflict during the pre-PRC era but also to a revolutionary heritage that caused its provincial and local leaders to resist private commodity production and commercial activity even into the 1980s (Feng, 1999). Terms such as 'old revolutionary base area' have thereby gone hand in hand with 'hill country' (*qiuling didai*) and 'mountain region' (*shanqu*) to denote the province's relative underdevelopment. People from rural Jiangxi are often called

2.2 Generations, Biography and Place 45

'*laobiao*', or 'cousin', a term associated with stubbornness, a conservative outlook and simple tastes (Moser, 1985: 125).

In the fieldwork counties in both Anhui and Jiangxi, adults' aspirations for their children's education were forged partly through their personal experiences of having grown up in poor and 'backward' places and of later living with the consequences, which included constrained possibilities for spatial and socio-economic mobility. As sociologists observe of the rise of education fever in other East Asian countries, parents who were unable to obtain an education and socio-economic mobility in their own lives typically wanted their children to benefit, especially when they had only one or two children (Anderson and Kohler, 2013; Lan, 2018). This resonates with the sociologist Mayall's observation that children bear the 'sheer weight of history' because 'the structures that they need to work with and against' are formed by adults whose own 'past events, interactions and beliefs shaped their ideas of childhood, education and parent-child relationships' (2000: 252).

Rural adults' educational prospects reflected the wider conditions that prevailed while they were growing up, with education and fiscal policies both exerting effects. Some grandparents in their fifties and sixties benefited from the education policies of the Cultural Revolution years of 1966–1976 – the Cultural Revolution being Mao's attempt to use mass mobilisation to undermine his critics and distract from his earlier policy disasters (Meisner, 1986). During this decade of radicalism, education policies emphasised correct class consciousness and learning through labour, though teachers bore the brunt of violent and humiliating class struggle sessions for their supposed 'feudal' or 'bourgeois' thought. Even so, during these years many rural people obtained basic literacy alongside political indoctrination. After a decade of revolutionary education policies, though, China's educational agenda took a decidedly hierarchical turn (Pepper, 1996). In 1977, the national university entrance exam, or *gaokao*, was reinstituted, marking the end of correct class background as the criteria for university admissions (Hansen, 2015: 9), while in 1978 a two-tier education system was re-established (Pepper, 1996). Under this system urban schools were to prepare students for exams that would lead them to university while rural schools were to provide students with the rudimentary literacy and numeracy necessary for manual work (Pepper, 1996).

Subsequently, in the 1980s and 1990s, fiscal decentralisation transferred most responsibility for education funding to local governments. In poor rural places such as the fieldwork counties, this had three effects. Firstly, as teachers were underpaid, education quality suffered. Secondly, owing to a weak tax base in farming regions, the burden for school funding was shifted onto families through fees (Knight and Li, 1996; Hannum and Wang, 2006; Li, Park and Wang, 2007; Murphy, 2007). Thirdly, given the revival of household farming, keeping children at school for more than a few years meant forfeiting income

46   Migration and Education in Four Counties

that rural parents could otherwise obtain from their labour (Hannum, 2005), which did not seem worthwhile given their children's slim prospects for university entrance. So even as a national Compulsory Education Law had been promulgated in 1986, governments and schools in poor rural places were told to realise nine years of compulsory education at the pace permitted by their local fiscal resources, with 2000 becoming the revised deadline (Pepper, 1996; Hannum and Adams, 2009).

The parents of the 109 children we interviewed had all been born between 1967 and 1978, with their birth years bunched in the early 1970s. Few had completed junior high school. The 2010 Summer Survey data mirrors this picture: the parents of the surveyed children had an average of 6.15 years at school. As a six-year primary school system replaced a five-year system in China's interior provinces only after 2000, six years of education would have taken an individual born in the early 1970s through to what for that cohort was the first year of junior high school (Murphy, 2004a; Connelly and Zheng, 2007). Data on educational progression help to place the parents' average of 6.15 years at school in a provincial context. In 1990, 58 per cent of rural primary school children in Anhui and 60 per cent of rural primary school children in Jiangxi transitioned from primary school to junior high school (Connelly and Zheng, 2007: 70). By contrast, more than 95 per cent of urban children in both provinces transitioned from primary school to junior high school (Connelly and Zheng, 2007: 70). Parents in the fieldwork counties thereby belonged to a generation afflicted by a wider rural–urban educational lag.

When asked to compare their own childhoods and their children's childhoods, the parents of this generation noted that their children did not need to do manual work (*ganhuo*), whereas they had spent their time outside of school hours helping their families with domestic and farming chores. The parents further noted that their own children ate nutritious food such as eggs and meat and wore good-quality shoes and clothes, while they had eaten only vegetables and had worn old shoes and patched clothes. The parents additionally observed that their children received spending money, while they had never been given even one *mao* of spending money; and they also said that their children were not so easy to discipline (*haoguan*), while they themselves had been obedient children.

Several parents recalled their own departures from school with immense regret. The time when they dropped out of school overlapped with a burgeoning of migration as pioneer migrants introduced neighbours, relatives and former classmates to urban jobs. In many of the families that my research assistants and I visited, the parents had joined an early stream of migrants who went out from their villages in the late 1980s and early 1990s. A few years after working in the cities, they married, either someone they met while 'outside' or someone

2.2 Generations, Biography and Place

to whom they were introduced on a return visit home. Thereafter, following the birth of a child, some migrant women went to their husband's villages to raise their child; some migrant parents sent their baby or an older child from the city to the husbands' village to be looked after by grandparents; and yet others migrated only after parenthood, leaving their children behind with the husbands' parents in the village. For reasons I discuss in Chapter 7, placing children in the care of maternal grandparents was less common.

The influence of both 'emplaced' personal biographies and a growing awareness of 'outside' on rural adults' aspirations for children's education can be seen in the account of a seventy-nine-year-old grandfather from Western County, Anhui. The man, who looked after his twelve-year-old grandson, explained:

My own son only studied for four years in the countryside and has eaten much bitterness outside, but I want my grandson to at least graduate from senior high school. Once he [my grandson] came home and told me that he wanted to be a soldier. I said to him: 'Nowadays that requires a high school graduation certificate; it's not like in the past when an illiterate could join the army.' High school graduates talk differently from other people. They know what to say to any kind of person in any kind of situation.

Without recourse to the sociological language of *habitus*, this man expressed well his observation that in the contemporary world education enabled people to move within and upwards in both space and society in a way that he and his own children never could. Or, to use Massey's (1994) lens, this man recognised that he and his son had little power over the flows and interconnections among places that constitute time–space compression, and he saw education as the way to empower his grandson.

Gender also affected how people's emplaced experiences of educational and economic policies played out. In 2015, in Jiangxi province the illiteracy rate among rural people aged seventy to seventy-four was 29.02 per cent overall, 15.21 per cent for men and 42 per cent for women.[2] But later, rural people in general and rural females in particular benefited from the Mao-era education policies, as demonstrated in a drop in illiteracy rates: in 2015, in rural Jiangxi, the illiteracy rate among fifty- to fifty-four-year-olds was 4.5 per cent overall, 1.43 per cent for men and 7.51 per cent for women (Jiangxi Province Bureau of Statistics, 2016).

Nevertheless, a reintroduction of school fees in the early 1980s adversely affected the educational prospects of girls, especially those girls who had brothers. This is because rural parents allocated scarce family funds to boys who would stay in their families, while daughters would eventually marry into

---

[2] The Anhui Province 1 per cent Population Survey Sample Materials for 2015 were not available to me at the time of writing, but I imagine that the figures for Anhui would tell a similar story of the gender gap in illiteracy rates in rural regions as reported here for Jiangxi.

48 Migration and Education in Four Counties

their husband's family (Hannum, 2005; Lu and Treiman, 2008). A breakdown of the education levels of parents in the 2010 Summer Survey reveals a gender gap among adults in their late thirties and early forties[3] – and place-based variation in this gender gap: years at school for mothers versus fathers were 4.43 versus 7.3 in Eastern County; 4.58 versus 7.18 in Western County; 5.54 versus 7.03 in Jade County; and 5.06 versus 6.92 in Tranquil County. This regional variation in the gender gap most likely reflects the greater poverty that afflicted the Anhui counties in the 1970s and 1980s.

People's gender – a salient feature of their social locations – intersected with their past and present family relationships and their emplaced biographies, to shape their perceptions of their own educational deprivation and their aspirations for their children's education. The accumulated effects of social location, family relationships and the experiences of having lived in different geographic locations overtime could be seen in the account of a forty-year-old woman – the mother of fifteen-year-old Wang Delun – from Eastern County, Anhui. When I met her in a dilapidated rented room in Kunshan in 2013, she explained:

As a girl my mother could not bear to part with me. So, I stayed at home in the village and looked after the cow and the pigs. My elder sister went to live with my aunt who paid her school fees. My brothers also graduated from junior high school. But I was the second child and I never went to school. Now my mother feels that she short-changed me . . .. My mother said: 'You go "outside" and work and I'll look after your child. I barely spent a penny on you when you were a child, and you don't have a mother-in-law. So go outside and work.'

The woman had failed the basic literacy and numeracy recruitment tests of several factories, and at the time of our meeting she washed dishes in a restaurant for one-third the wage of a factory worker. Her husband had been orphaned as an infant and had dropped out of primary school after only two years. He worked lifting heavy boxes in an electronics factory. The couple lamented that when uneducated rural people go 'outside', no good employer wants them while others treat them with disdain. 'We will eat immeasurable bitterness to send our son to senior high school', the woman sighed.

2.3 Localised Migration Patterns

Labour migration from the four fieldwork counties mirrored nationwide patterns of migration in several respects. Firstly, much migration from the fieldwork counties fell under a wider pattern whereby people left their villages in the interior provinces to work in cities in the coastal provinces. In 2015,

---

[3] The mean age of the parents of the children sampled in the 2010 Summer Survey was: Eastern County – 39.2 years; Western County – 38.6 years; Jade County – 39.85 years; Tranquil County – 38.6 years.

2.3 Localised Migration Patterns

61.1 per cent of rural migrant workers from China's interior provinces crossed provincial boundaries with the majority working in coastal cities (National Bureau of Statistics, 2016). Even so, in the 2010s the percentage of migrants as a proportion of all migrants from Anhui and Jiangxi who crossed provincial boundaries was even greater than the aggregate percentage for China's interior provinces. The percentage of rural migrant workers from Anhui who crossed provincial boundaries was 70.04 in 2012, falling to 67.04 in 2015 (Anhui People's Government, 2017), while the percentage of rural migrant workers from Jiangxi who crossed provincial boundaries was 69.78 at the end of 2011, falling to 68.85 in 2016 (Jiangxi Province Bureau of Statistics, 2017). The slight decrease in the proportion of interprovincial migrants versus intraprovincial migrants from these two provinces can be attributed not only to more stringent *hukou* policies in major coastal cities but also to urbanisation in the interior and the relocation of some industries inland to take advantage of cheaper production costs (Anhui People's Government, 2017) and laxer environmental regulations: in 2010, the urbanisation rates for Anhui, Jiangxi and China were 43.2, 44.06 and 49.95 per cent, respectively, rising in 2015 to 50.5, 51.62, and 56.1 per cent, respectively (China Statistical Yearbook Database, 2019). Additionally, in 2017 some 40,000 rural migrants from Anhui province worked overseas, an increase of 22,000 on the previous year (Anhui Survey Group of National Statistical Bureau, 2018, cited in Dong, 2019).

Migration from Anhui and Jiangxi also mirrored a wider national pattern in that male migrant workers outnumbered female migrant workers. In the 1990s, 2000s and 2010s, at least two-thirds of Anhui's rural migrant workers were male (Mallee, 1995a; Sun, 2002; Dong, 2019): in 2017, 66.3 per cent were men (Anhui Survey Group of National Statistical Bureau, 2018, cited in Dong, 2019). Meanwhile, according to the Jiangxi Survey Group of the National Bureau of Statistics' Monitoring Survey of Rural Migrant Workers, in 2014 two-thirds of Jiangxi's rural workers (*nongmingong*) were male, though the term '*nongmingong*' includes both those who work within county boundaries and those who migrate across county boundaries (China News, 2014). The gender breakdown of migration streams partly reflects the proportions of migrants who were mothers or fathers. As noted in Chapter 1, in the 2010s most children left behind in rural China were left behind by two migrant parents, followed by lone-migrant fathers, while only a minority of children were left behind by lone-migrant mothers. Certainly, in the four fieldwork counties it was rare for mothers to migrate alone, with only 2.4 per cent of children in the 2010 Summer Survey sample having a lone-migrant mother. I discuss the reasons for this in Chapter 6.

Even as migration from the four fieldwork counties captured aspects of wider national and provincial patterns, there were also important differences among the counties. One difference was in the main destinations of the migrants. In

50 Migration and Education in Four Counties

2010–2015, most migrants from the two Anhui counties were concentrated in Yangtze River Delta cities including Shanghai, Kunshan, Wenzhou, Hangzhou and Suzhou. Meanwhile, some migrants from Eastern County went to the provincial capital of Hefei, which borders the county seat, as well as to nearby prefectural and provincial cities such as Bengbu, Chuzhou and Nanjing. Migrants from both the Anhui counties also went to more distant locations in Yunnan, Inner Mongolia and Western China. Additionally, in the 2000s men from Eastern County migrated to African countries such as Angola, Cameroon, Algeria and Namibia to work on two-year construction project contracts, while before 2010 Libya was another destination (Anon, 2008; Anon, 2016).[4] By contrast, most migrants from the Jiangxi counties concentrated in Pearl River Delta cities such as Guangzhou, Shenzhen, Dongguan and Nanhai, and in cities in Zhejiang and Fujian provinces such as Ningbo, Wenzhou, Wuxi and Xiamen. A minority migrated to border region towns in Yunnan and Guizhou provinces to do small-scale trading or drive taxis. Some migrants from each county also worked in northern cities such as Beijing, Dalian, Tianjin and Qingdao.

Alongside differences in the migrants' major destinations, the four counties differed by the migrants' principal occupations. As indicated earlier, many men from Eastern County worked in construction. An Eastern County government report states that in 2008 the county had 114 construction companies with projects located in twenty-one provinces; two-thirds of rural migrants from the county worked in construction; and the construction industry contributed to one-third of net per capita rural income in the county and to 30 per cent of the county government's fiscal revenue (Eastern County Government, 2009). Meanwhile, migrant men and women from Eastern County also worked in factories producing items such as cosmetics, clothing and electronics appliances, and service-sector jobs such as catering, cleaning and retail. A few men also worked cleaning or repairing cars.

Similar to Eastern County many migrant men from Western County were construction workers. Other migrant men from Western County were welders, chefs, security guards and taxi drivers, and some men ran stalls selling goods such as lettuce, fruit, salted preserved duck and breakfast snacks, while their wives sometimes helped them, shuttling to and fro between the village and the city. A few men and women also collected waste for recycling. Additionally, it was common for migrant women from Western County to do 'housekeeping' (*jiazheng*) jobs, such as cleaning in hotels, supermarkets and restaurants, catering, or working as domestic helpers and nannies. Unlike the two Anhui counties, hardly any men from the Jiangxi fieldwork counties worked in

---

[4] A local newspaper article from 2008 states that over 60 per cent of rural labour from Anhui working overseas came from Eastern County with over 7,000 construction workers from the county working abroad.

2.3 Localised Migration Patterns

construction. Rather, men and women from the two Jiangxi counties most commonly worked in manufacturing and services. This included working in factories that produced items such as clothes, shoes, handbags, toys, electronics, computer chips, machine parts and plastics. Meanwhile, common service-sector jobs included driving taxis, working as security guards, repairing vehicles, cleaning, giving massages, and working in hotels and restaurants.

In the 2000s and into the mid-2010s, Anhui and Jiangxi consistently ranked among the top five of China's labour exporting provinces such that – as mentioned previously – by the early 2010s parent–child separation had become an established fact of life in most villages. Census data show that in 2000 in Anhui 11.55 per cent of rural children aged nought to fourteen years had been left behind by at least one parent, while in Jiangxi the proportion was 9.38 per cent (Duan and Zhou, 2005: 33). In 2005, a mid-decade 1 per cent population sample survey indicated that the proportion of rural children aged nought to fourteen years left behind by at least one migrant parent was 33 per cent in Anhui and 34.7 per cent in Jiangxi, higher than in other provinces (Duan and Wu, 2009: 27), though, as noted in Chapter 1, the sample for 2005 may contain errors. Subsequently, 2010 census data revealed that in six provinces including Anhui and Jiangxi, over 50 per cent of rural children aged nought to seventeen years had been left behind by at least one parent, with the proportions for Anhui and Jiangxi standing at 53.49 per cent and 51.47 per cent, respectively, approximately fifteen percentage points higher than the national rural average (Duan et al., 2013: 42). A later report from the Jiangxi Province Ministry of Education offers a more modest picture stating that in 2018 10 per cent of children of compulsory school age in the province were left behind, with 'left-behind' adhering to the Ministry of Civil Affairs's revised 2016 definition of children fifteen years and less with two parents working away or one parent working away and the other unable to provide care (Jiangxi Provincial Government Education Supervision Office, 2018).

The four fieldwork counties I visited all appeared to have extremely high proportions of children affected by parental migration. In the 2010 Summer Survey sample – conducted in two townships in each county – 69.9 per cent of the surveyed children had at least one parent who had migrated without them while 30.1 per cent had both parents living at home with them. In sampling, the survey team initially aimed to ensure that half the children in the sample had at least one migrant parent and that the other half lived with both parents. Based on information from the homeroom teachers (i.e. the teachers with particular responsibilities for a class), the survey team divided the children in each year-grade into the categories of 'left-behind' and 'not-left-behind' from which the team drew the samples. However, we later discovered that many children who had been allocated to the 'not-left behind' category had at least one migrant parent. The presence of 'left-behind' children among the children who we initially classified as 'not-left-behind' most likely reflects the fluid situation of migration or the exceptionally high rates of outmigration in the sampled townships, though it could possibly also indicate sampling distortions.

There were also differences among the counties' subsamples for the percentages of children who had at least one migrant parent. The breakdown is as follows: Eastern County – 79 per cent, Western County – 61 per cent, Jade County – 73 per cent, and Tranquil County – 68 per cent. The proportions broadly resonate with headmasters' estimates for their schools and teachers' accounts of their own classrooms.[5] Even so, the percentage of left-behind children in the Eastern County subsample is higher than the teachers' estimates, which was generally at 'over two-thirds'. Meanwhile, in Western County the headmasters' and teachers' estimates of 35 per cent to one half of their student-body counting as 'left-behind' fell below the percentage in the survey subsample. Conversely, though, a government report states that in 2017 over half of all children in Western County were left behind, with 'left-behind' children defined as children under sixteen years of age with two parents living away from them, as per the Ministry of Civil Affairs's revised 2016 definition (Prefectural People's Government Website, 2017).

The fieldwork counties – or at least the two rural townships we sampled in each county – also differed by whether two-parent migration or lone-father migration dominated. In the Eastern County subsample and in the Western County subsample, approximately one-third of the children had two migrant parents.[6] Moreover, the percentage of children with a lone migrant father was especially high in the Eastern County subsample at 45.6 per cent, while the proportion of children with a lone-migrant father was higher in the Western County subsample (25.9 per cent) than in the two Jiangxi county subsamples. In the Jade County subsample, 61.3 per cent of children had two migrant

---

[5] In Eastern County, the junior high school headteachers in the two sampled townships estimated that over two-thirds of the students had at least one migrant parent. In Western County, the primary and junior high school headteachers' estimates ranged from 35 per cent to over one-half of the students, with variations by village and by township. In Jade County, estimates also varied depending on the township as well as by the students' year grade. In one township the numbers reported by homeroom teachers in grades 4 and 6 equalled 70 and 75 per cent, respectively, but 56 per cent for year 8, year 8 being a stage when many parents return for several months in advance of their child's preparations for the *zhongkao* exam, which determines if they can enter a senior high school, and, if so, which one. In another township in Jade County, the headteachers in the primary and junior high schools estimated that over half of the students had at least one migrant parent. In Tranquil County, the junior school headteacher in one township estimated that one half of children had both parents out while in another township the primary and junior high school headteachers said they knew that 70 per cent of the children were 'left behind' because they had done their own survey the previous year in order to prepare for a Jiangxi Television Station team that came to report on their 'older child cares for a younger child' initiative in the school dormitories.

[6] The percentages of surveyed children in two-parent migrant families were 32.8 in Eastern County and 34 per cent in Western County.

2.4 Local School Regimes

parents and 9.2 per cent had a lone-migrant father, while in the Tranquil County subsample 47.4 per cent of the children had two migrant parents and 15 per cent had a lone-migrant father.

2.4 Local School Regimes

As noted previously, schools were an important feature of each county that interacted with local linkages to 'outside' places to shape families' strategies in pursuing migration, delivering childcare and supporting children's educational progress. The school regimes in each of the fieldwork counties incorporated features of the national education system while manifesting their own distinct features. Like children elsewhere in China, children in the fieldwork counties attended six years of primary school and three years of junior high school, constituting the compulsory stage of their education. Students then sat a standardised prefecture-wide senior high school entrance exam known as the *zhongkao*. Students with sufficiently high *zhongkao* scores could then attend an academic-track senior high school or a vocational high school where they studied for a further three years. The academic-track senior high schools were divided into two tiers: key-point senior high schools, which admit students with high grades, and 'ordinary' high schools, which admit students with lower grades (Hansen, 2013; Hansen, 2015). Then, after three years, the senior high school students could sit the university entrance exam, the *gaokao*.

Many of the differences among the counties' school regimes stemmed from the local implementation of a national programme of rural school mergers and consolidation undertaken from 2001 to 2012 (Mei et al., 2015). Under this nationwide programme, between 1998 and 2010 the number of primary schools decreased by 57.8 per cent to 257, 410 while the number of teaching posts fell by 66.46 per cent to 66,941 (Mei et al., 2015: 140). The closure of village-based schools occurred because of: fewer in-coming students attributable to falling birth rates and urbanisation; pressures on county governments to fund education with limited fiscal resources; and planners' desires to consolidate educational resources to improve educational quality. Students in grade 4 or 5 and above were directed to well-equipped consolidated schools in rural townships, widening the travel distance between home and school for many rural families (Mei et al., 2015). Importantly, families' care routines in and around school were also affected by school responses to these distances including whether the schools provided meals, the midday supervision of children and boarding facilities.

In the two Jiangxi counties, many rural families relied on schools to provide lunch, midday supervision and board. In these counties, the children ate lunch in the school's canteen, washed their utensils and bowls in communal outdoor sinks and then napped with their heads on their desks under the watch of a teacher. Children could board at school from Sunday night through to Friday afternoon, with boarders eating breakfast and dinner as well as lunch at school. Figures 2.1 and 2.2 both show a dormitory in a primary school in a mountainous township in Tranquil County, Jiangxi. After dinner, the primary school boarders did activities and read, participated in revision sessions, and could watch television one evening a week, while the junior high school boarders spent till 8:00 p.m. in the classroom doing self-study or revision classes with teachers. They then went to bed. Although fees for the compulsory education years were eliminated in 2006, in 2010 rural families in the Jiangxi counties still had to pay between 900 and 1,500 *yuan* per term, for two terms per year, to enrol their child in school, with this money covering food, board and incidental expenses. Nevertheless, as mentioned in Chapter 1, boarders received a subsidy which in 2010 was approximately 500 *yuan* per term.

Rates of boarding were extremely high in the Jiangxi fieldwork counties. In a breakdown of the Jade County 2010 Summer Survey subsample, two-thirds

Figure 2.1 Dormitory in a primary school in a rural township in Tranquil County, Jiangxi

2.4 Local School Regimes

Figure 2.2 Children looking in a child's storage chest in the dormitory

of children boarded and nearly three-quarters of these boarders had at least one migrant parent. Furthermore, boarding occurred in all the sampled year-grades with percentages in the Jade County subsample for years 4, 6 and 8 standing at 52.5 per cent, 72.5 per cent and 70 per cent. respectively. In the Tranquil County subsample, the proportion of boarders was even higher at 85.9 per cent. This is because in one of the two townships where the team implemented the survey the headteachers had ruled that all children from grade 4 onwards had to board. The headteachers justified this rule on the grounds that the children faced risks walking to and from school along winding mountainous roads, especially when attending the extra evening classes to prepare them for milestone exams, including an exam held at the end of year 6. In the Tranquil County subsample, the percentage of boarders in years 4, 6 and 8 were 69.2, 92.4 and 96.1, respectively while nearly 70 per cent of boarders had a least one migrant parent.

By contrast, schools in the Anhui fieldwork counties contributed much less to the rural families' overall daily work of social reproduction. Schools we visited in rural townships in the Anhui counties did not provide meals or supervise the children at midday, while boarding facilities were scarce. The children arrived at school at 8:00 a.m., and most of them returned home at 11:20 a.m. before going back to school at 2:30 p.m. and then returning home again at 4:20 p.m. The only school that I encountered which provided lunches was a village-based school in Western County. Although in Western County some school consolidation had occurred and many children attended schools in the townships, the consolidation had been much less than in some other areas and a number of larger villages had managed to retain their own primary schools. It was one of these village schools that provided lunch.

As noted previously, the rural schools in the Anhui counties offered very limited boarding. In the 2010 Summer Survey, less than 1 per cent of children from the Anhui county subsamples boarded: eighteen children in the Eastern County subsample and two children in the Western County subsample, all but one of them in year 8, which is the first year of junior high school. Children who lived near to the school could walk or cycle home. However, when children lived farther away from school, the caregivers dealt with the distance either by transporting the children on bikes or mopeds or by paying for a seat for the child on a village-hired van. In 2013, the cost of a seat on the village van, such as that depicted in Figure 2.3, was approximately 30 *yuan* per month per child for two daily return trips. Meanwhile, some other families rented small rooms in the township near to the school. The grandmothers lived there during the week with one or more grandchildren, returning to the village on the weekends. Importantly, though, in the Anhui counties, at lunchtime and at the end of each school day too, children usually returned home to be with their caregivers.

When compared to the percentage of students who boarded in China's interior provinces, the Jiangxi fieldwork counties had above-average rates of boarding at both primary and junior high school stages, while the Anhui counties had below-average rates of boarding for both stages. For reference, China's Ministry of Education reported that in 2011 in the interior provinces 14.2 per cent of primary school students boarded and 54.1 per cent of junior high school students boarded. Meanwhile, in 2011, nationwide, 10.89 per cent of primary school students boarded and 43.34 per cent of junior high school students boarded (Ministry of Education, 2012). Du (2009) identifies Jiangxi, Inner Mongolia, Sichuan, Shanxi and Henan as provinces where many county-level governments were especially active in promoting the construction of rural boarding schools.

Partly reflecting local variation in the prevalence of boarding in township-based schools, out of the 109 children we interviewed, 37 out of 50 children in the Jiangxi subset of cases boarded, but only 3 out of the 59 children in the Anhui subset of cases boarded. Yet even as the low number of boarders in the Anhui subset of interviewees reflected aspects of the local school regime, it also reflects a bias arising from how I recruited the research participants. Chiefly, many boarders in Eastern County attended private high schools in the county

2.4 Local School Regimes

Figure 2.3 Children in a township in Eastern County, Anhui, boarding a van to go home for lunch

seat rather than public high schools in the rural townships, but as I conducted the research through the rural schools, I mostly missed out on talking with children who boarded in the county seat.

Indeed, Eastern County stood out because its county seat hosted at least five private boarding schools, such as the one shown in Figure 2.4. These private schools reflected a local manifestation of a wider national development that unfolded unevenly. Whereas private schools had barely existed in China in the late 1980s, more than a hundred thousand such schools at all levels of education existed by 2008 (Hansen, 2015: 9). Private boarding schools in Eastern County had been established and burgeoned during the late 2000s. They combined junior and senior high levels with several thousand students in each school. Most students came from rural families, both within Eastern County and from neighbouring counties. These schools were renowned locally for their strict supervision of the students and for the credible possibilities that they offered for educational progression. Importantly, though, headteachers in the township-based public schools complained that these private schools creamed off the best

Figure 2.4 Dormitory block in a private boarding school in Eastern County, Anhui

teachers as well as the better-performing students, depleting the rural schools. There were also some private boarding schools in Western County and its vicinity, but not on the same scale as in Eastern County. Indeed, I did not meet any children in Western County whose parents actively considered sending them to private boarding schools. Rather, a couple of better-off families in Western County mentioned that they would send their children to board at the houses of retired teachers who lived near to good junior high schools.

Private senior high schools also existed in two of the other fieldwork counties. Western County and Tranquil County each had two 'ordinary' senior high schools which were previously 'public' or 'state sector-run' (*gongban*), but which had converted to *minban* ('people-run', meaning non-state or 'private') status in the early 2000s. These schools were owned by entrepreneurs. Nevertheless, the admissions and curriculum of these schools were subject to the county education bureau's 'integrated management' alongside its management of state-run ordinary senior high schools: there were two ordinary senior high schools in Western County and one in Tranquil County. The *minban* schools had lower entrance requirements than the state-run senior high schools. Over 80 per cent of students at the ordinary senior high schools came from rural

2.4 Local School Regimes

families. The private ordinary senior high schools ran their own exams at the start of each May to allocate scholarships to high-scoring students, with the aim of improving their rankings in the *gaokao* to attract more good students. Even so, most rural families' hopes were fixed on the key-point state-run senior high schools – between one to three such schools in each county. This meant that academically talented rural children would only take up scholarship places at these private 'ordinary' schools if their families were too poor to send them to a key-point state-run senior high school. Jade County had several public ordinary high schools, while its only *minban* school was a vocational school.

All the senior high schools in Eastern County and in the two Jiangxi counties were situated in the county seat, while all township-based senior high schools had closed by 2011: 'Everyone wants to go to the city', explained the county education bureau officials. Only Western County had retained a township-based senior high school, which took in students from poorer rural families.

Alongside the shift in educational resources to the cities, a trend in all the counties was for rural families with the requisite resources to try to get their children into a good urban-based school, before the senior high school stage if possible. However, according to county education bureau officials, by 2014 this had become harder because of wider shifts in school admissions regulations, mentioned in Chapter 1, requiring children to attend their nearby school and giving priority in the allocation of school places to children whose parents owned a house in the school catchment area.[7] These changes made it more difficult for a rural family to rent a room in the county seat and pay a high 'crossing the boundary study fee' (*jiedufei*) in order to get their child into a good urban primary or junior high school. The new admissions practices also meant that a change in the family's *hukou* status was not enough for a child to be given priority in the allocation of a place, such that they could still need to attend a poorer-quality school. Although buying an apartment in the county seat was beyond the reach of most farmer-migrant families, it remained an aspiration for some families, especially for rural families in Eastern County. I discuss the reasons in Chapter 4. Even so, in all four counties teachers told me that in visiting their rural schools I was only meeting left-behind children who came from the poorest families: many left-behind children came from much more prosperous families, they said, but these better-off children had relocated to schools in the county seat. Certainly, children in the rural schools I visited felt that they lived and studied in places that were lagging behind and becoming depleted, reinforcing their aspirations for migration and an urban life.

---

[7] The shift was partly in response to Ministry of Education caps on the numbers of children in a class to fifty students because it has been common for classes to have over sixty students. The cap on class sizes reduces the capacity of urban schools to supply student places.

2.5　Intersections of Local School Regime and Migration

In each of the four fieldwork counties, the characteristics of the local school regimes interacted with locally prevalent migration patterns to affect how rural families reconciled their need to earn money with their need to deliver childcare and support their children's education. The interaction between migration patterns and school regimes was bidirectional. On the one hand, school characteristics fed into families' deliberations about who should or could migrate and who should or could provide childcare. On the other hand, the care implications of the families' post-migration configurations were mediated by the local school regime because families' changing care routines occurred in and around school, while families' aspirations for their children's education were realised through schools.

In the two Jiangxi counties, the schools' provision of meals, midday supervision and boarding facilities alleviated some families' care and work burdens to the extent that they felt they could manage a two-parent migration strategy even if the elderly caregivers were frail or widowed or were already looking after several grandchildren. An emphasis on education in the family's striving project also led some parents to think that by sending their children to board during the week they could mitigate the adverse effects of leaving them with semi-literate grandparents because for five days a week the children were supervised by educated teachers (see also Hansen, 2015).

By comparison, in the two Anhui counties, rural families had to factor in a weekday 'care void' at lunchtimes and a scarcity of rural-based boarding facilities when thinking about migration and childcare arrangements. The dilemma of how to ensure adequate childcare if both parents migrated could be seen in an exchange I saw between a migrant woman and a teacher in a township-based primary school in Western County. The woman had just returned from Shanghai with her eleven-year-old son to arrange for him to start at the school. The matronly homeroom teacher told the much younger woman:

I can see that you're in a difficult situation. Leave your son in the countryside and you worry. Leave your husband in the city and you worry. But there is midday from 11 to 2 when your son needs to have lunch and when he is not supervised. Girls are more sensible, but boys run here and there. You need to think this through.

Many mothers in the Anhui counties accounted for their non-migration with the statement, 'I need to cook lunch for the child.' Moreover, in Western County, in a few families, owing to the caregivers' need to prepare lunches and transport children between home and school, the migration of two parents led to the children being transferred from the township-based primary school to the village school.

2.5 Intersections of Local School Regime and Migration

In Eastern County, some rural parents' deliberations about migration were also affected by the buoyant private boarding school sector. Indeed, the burgeoning of the private schools had led to the emergence of new norms about standards of good parenthood, reinforcing the impetus for some men to migrate to African countries. For instance, a forty-five-year-old woman whose husband worked in Angola expressed a wider sentiment among the wives of overseas construction workers when she said that she had urged her husband to 'go out' so that they could send their thirteen-year-old son and fifteen-year-old daughter to a private school. She explained:

I've heard others say that the enclosed schools are good. You need ten thousand a year, so that is twenty thousand for the two of them. In our village everyone else's child goes, so if one's own children don't go it is not so good. If my children's studies fall behind that of others, they will laugh at me and look down on me.

Meanwhile, some other rural parents from Eastern County thought that sending their children to a private boarding school would make two-parent migration especially worthwhile and would at the same time compensate the children for the parents' absence. For instance, the forty-year-old migrant father of a thirteen-year-old girl and a seven-year-old boy said that he planned to send his children to one of the enclosed private schools in the county seat because he and his wife could not look after their children or tutor them. Moreover, even if he and his wife were to stay at home, as it was over twenty years since they had last been at school, they would still not be able to tutor their children. The man explained:

Other parents have sent their children to a private school, so we need to let them try. Even if they fail, if they do not pass the future exams, they cannot have an opinion against us. We've got to let them try.

In a similar vein, Zhangyong's mother – mentioned in Chapter 1 – also indicated that sending a child to a private school insulated the parents against any future blame from a child because they had demonstrated optimal support for the child's education.

Geographic location – including the local school regime – clearly shaped the immediate context of striving that the children negotiated. At the same time, though, consistent with some sociologists' observations, the children's everyday lives occurred in several different significant places (James, Jenks and Prout, 1998: 37–58). Specifically, the children my research assistants and I met experienced their rural hometowns not as one single place that existed in opposition to 'outside' but as various places such as school, their caregivers' house and sites of play. Moreover, each of these places derived some of their meaning for the children from their families' striving project and from the emotional relationships that connected them to 'outside'. The following two vignettes assembled from my field notes illustrate the significance of local geographic context for the children's everyday lives, routines, relationships, and expectations of family support.

Vignette 1

When I first met Wenwen in 2011 in Tranquil County, she was eleven years old. Her eyes welled up during our conversation because her parents had recently remigrated after her mother had given birth to a baby boy, taking the baby with them. Wenwen also had two younger sisters. Her parents worked in a small handbag factory in Shenzhen run by her eldest uncle. Wenwen told my research assistant and me that she walked home from her boarding school every Friday afternoon, and the walk took her two hours. The scenery was stunning, with pine trees in a clear blue sky above and lush paddy in the gullies below. But she had also become accustomed to seeing the mountains such that it was all too familiar (*kanguan le*) while the uphill walk was tiring. I visited Wenwen and her family again in September 2013. At this time, her parents had returned to the village to entrust her younger brother to her grandfather. When we met her father, who was visiting his village for a short period, he told us that he had recently fetched Wenwen from school on his motorbike but that his wife had later said to him: 'It is good for her to walk. It trains her independence. The other children must walk. She will get arrogant if you pick her up.' He had not realised how much it had meant to Wenwen to see him waiting for her at the school gates.

In April 2014, on a third visit to her family, my research assistant and I saw Wenwen's seventy-year-old grandfather, a dark muscular man with twinkling eyes and a wide smile. He had lost his wife thirty years previously and had won the admiration of all the villagers and of his six adult sons for his years of industriousness and care of his children and grandchildren, and for his calm temperament and wisdom, which had kept the relationships between the six brothers' families harmonious. The grandfather told us that looking after his grandchildren tired him out but that he missed them when they were away at school. After our catch-up with the grandfather, my research assistant and I turned back to see him holding the hand of his toddler grandson as they walked slowly to buy snacks from the village store. Wenwen loved her grandfather, siblings and cousins but she still felt lonely without her parents. Now in her final year of junior high, she was trying to produce scores that would be high enough for her to attend the key-point public senior high school in the county seat where her eldest male cousin now boarded.

2.5 Intersections of Local School Regime and Migration 63

That afternoon I taught several English classes in Wenwen's school before staying overnight in the room of Ms Dong, a twenty-year-old newly graduated English teacher. At 8 p.m., the lights in the classrooms of this mountain school still shone. In some classrooms, students read aloud from textbooks while in other classrooms teachers addressed the students. As I sat writing field notes, Ms Dong returned to the room, had a shower, and changed into her pyjamas. Then at 8:30 p.m. she visited the dormitories to check on her homeroom students. By 5:40 the next morning, everyone, including Ms Dong, was up and about in the playground for morning exercise. Like many teachers I met in rural boarding schools, Ms Dong told me that she was like the children's mother and father. Her burden was heavy, and if she ever phoned the parents of students who had behavioural or learning problems, they invariably entreated her to discipline and care for the child more (*duo guan*). Wenwen did not display any problems to her teachers. Nonetheless, she struggled emotionally. Even as most of her classmates were in the same situation as her in that they also lived separated from their parents, this did not ease her daily pain at missing her own parents.

Vignette 2

When I met up with fifteen-year-old Wang Delun in September 2013, he gallantly held up his umbrella for my research assistant and me as we walked along the muddy road to his maternal grandparents' house. In a dark front room stood a shiny white fridge bought with the money that his parents had sent home. Wang Delun's two young cousins sat at a wooden table, sword fighting with chopsticks. His grandparents warmly welcomed us. They told us that they liked looking after their grandchildren and watching them grow, but poverty was their biggest headache.

Wang Delun was class monitor, a role that required him to liaise closely with the homeroom teacher and to help ensure that the students behaved well by, for instance, admonishing over the loudspeaker system students who dropped litter. Wang Delun's teacher said that the boy showed much promise but like many children from poor families he shouldered mental burdens. Wang Delun studied the best he could. On weekday evenings, after helping his grandparents to clear up the dinner table he walked half an hour to reach his school for evening revision classes. His grandparents worried all the while on these evenings until he returned home safely through the door at around 9.15 p.m. He also attended a few weeks of revision sessions each holiday break, run in the rural township by teachers from his school at an additional cost to his parents, and he planned to do so again over the winter break.

These efforts at study notwithstanding, Wang Delun's most earnest wish was to transfer to a good-quality urban school. Several students from his class and several children from his village had transferred to one of the private junior high boarding schools in the county seat. One of the children who had transferred was his cousin. The cousin's father was a migrant worker, but his mother had died, so everyone in the family had chipped in to support the cousin's school fees, including Wang Delun's parents. The cousin showed academic promise, and the family wanted to compensate him for the loss of his mother. And, as mentioned earlier, it was unusual for maternal grandparents to provide childcare, so contributing to their nephew's fees was also how Wang Delun's parents demonstrated reciprocity within the wider family network.

Wang Delun had asked his parents repeatedly to send him to a private school in the county seat, but he now realised that this would not happen. When I met his parents in Kunshan City later that year, his mother said:

Some people criticise me for helping my nephew. They say I should send my son . . . If we had better conditions, we'd send our son to study in the county seat, but we don't have the county *hukou* and they won't let you study there. We don't have enough money so there is no choice but for him to study in the rural hometown (*laojia*) . . . He refuses to talk with me these days. It is so different to how we were before when he would tell me everything. I have told him that no matter what I will try to find a way for him to study at the private senior high school . . . He sees that other parents send their children to the boarding school in the county seat, but it is not so easy for us. You can see our situation with your own eyes.

Wang Delun felt frustrated, stuck and let down by his parents for failing to meet the new localised standards of good parenthood, even as he also missed them.

Conclusion

Situated in the landlocked provinces of Anhui and Jiangxi, the four fieldwork counties of Eastern County, Western County, Tranquil County and Jade County shared many characteristics. These characteristics included the following: a devalued 'rural' status; the dominance of low-quality and low-paying local off-farm jobs; localised histories of economic and educational deprivation manifest in the grandparents' and parents' personal biographies; a patriarchal family culture apparent in customary gendered divisions of parenting, patri-local marriage patterns and long-standing preferential treatment for boys; a within-county rural–urban gap in the quality of the schools; histories of rural–urban labour migration that commenced on a noteworthy scale in the late 1980s; over half of rural children affected by the migration of at least one parent; the prevalence of two-parent migration and lone-father migration and the rarity of lone-mother migration; the long distances travelled by many migrants; and a shared belief among rural children and adults that hope, opportunity and success lay in the cities.

Conclusion 65

At the same time, though, distinctive characteristics of each of the counties also impacted on the children's lives. As discussed, each county had its own migration linkages to 'outside' that intersected with other aspects of local geographic context, including physical location, school regime features and gendered family culture, shaping prevailing patterns of family striving. These various factors affected the immediate institutional and normative setting within which rural families deliberated about who should and could migrate and who should and could deliver childcare, which in turn impacted on the children's experiences of daily care and of school, including the frequency and length of their journeys to and from school, how much time they spent at school, how much time they spent with different caregivers, the educational trajectories to which they aspired, and their expectations of support from their parents for their education. Place was therefore an important contextual variable that interacted with the children's social locations to impact on their socialisation, education, aspirations and agency and their experience of family relationships.

3 Sacrifice and Study

The children and adults my research assistants and I met in Anhui and Jiangxi held very high educational aspirations, especially given the obstacles that rural children faced. In the 2010 Summer Survey covering 1,010 children in the four fieldwork counties, over three-quarters said that they wanted to obtain at least an undergraduate degree and over three-quarters said that their parents worked hard for their education, with no significant difference in their responses by the parents' migration status or by the children's gender. But while the majority of rural children cherished high aspirations for their education, study took on added significance for them if their parents had migrated without them (Murphy, 2014a). Indeed, a survey-based White Paper finds that even though there was no difference between left-behind children and children living with both their parents in their self-evaluation of their grades, left-behind children expressed significantly less satisfaction with their grades, indicating their heightened desire for winning parental recognition by means of academic attainment (On the Road to School, 2016).

Some Chinese social work post-graduate students who had spent much time working with left-behind families likewise observed rural families' high aspirations for their children's education. After I presented my research on left-behind children to social work and economics students at Anhui Agricultural University in September 2015, a student who hailed from Jiangxi stood up and said that when she had gone to the countryside to do parenting interventions in the summer holidays, the caregivers were only interested in whether or not the social workers could give the children extra tutoring. Clearly, education caused immense pressure in rural families, while working to support the children's educational success and requiring the children to study was how they dealt with this pressure.

The remainder of this chapter examines how and why in the 2010s the 'parent-child striving team' was a potent social institution that propelled people of all generations to toil ceaselessly, reproducing and legitimating wider inequalities in the process. Section 3.1 discusses why rural people cherished such high educational aspirations despite the huge obstacles that rural children faced in pursuing educational progression. Section 3.2 examines how the

3.1 Getting Ahead Through Education

children were socialised both at home and in school into accepting values supportive of multilocal family striving. Thereafter, Sections 3.3 and 3.4 explore how children's educational aspirations changed over time, with attention to the experiences of children who had to reconcile themselves to 'learning a skill' rather than pursuing an academic-track education.

3.1 Getting Ahead Through Education

Even as the parents and grandparents we met in Anhui and Jiangxi wanted the children in their families to escape economic insecurity and drudgery through education, rural children encountered immense obstacles in progressing along an academic track. One study estimates that in 2006 the rural progression rate from junior high school to an academic-track senior high school was 20–30 per cent (Liu et al., 2009: 508). The study further notes that in 2008, even in the developed coastal province of Guangdong, fewer than half of rural students scored highly enough on the *zhongkao* exam to gain a place at an academic-track senior high school (Liu et al., 2009: 508). Meanwhile, data for 2010 indicate that less than half of rural students stayed in school until age eighteen (Huang, 2012). Furthermore, rural students have consistently been under-represented in first tier tertiary institutions but over-represented in lowly ones (Wang, 2014).

Many factors underpin rural students' disadvantages in the nationwide competition for education. Firstly, rural students typically grow up in family and school environments less conducive to cultural capital accumulation than those of their urban counterparts (Hannum and Adams, 2009; Hao, Hu and Lo, 2014; Koo, Ming and Tsang, 2014). In 2010, compared to rural residents 'urban residents spent four times more on education, culture and recreational services' (Jacka, Kipnis and Sargeson, 2013: 225). Indeed, the students we met in township junior high schools in Anhui and Jiangxi listed their weekend hobbies as watching television, singing, playing ball and talking with friends. By contrast, in schools based in the county seats – where I taught English to reciprocate the county education officials' kind help of my research – students listed their weekend hobbies as playing the flute, violin and piano, calligraphy, painting, reading novels and watching English-language films. Additionally, as I discuss in Chapter 1, parents' migration further diminished many children's family environments by impairing the quantity and quality of daily guidance and support that they received.

Rural and urban children also experienced disparities in teaching styles at school (Hao, Hu and Lo, 2014; Koo, Ming and Tsang, 2014). Usually rural children are drilled in examination subjects, which can make the material dull and difficult to master. By contrast, urban children benefit from a fuller implementation of the so-called *suzhi* education reforms launched in the late 1990s:

68 Sacrifice and Study

these reforms entail less emphasis on rote learning, more use of didactic teaching methods and exposure to a wider range of subjects, which enhance students' engagement with learning (Koo, Ming and Tsang, 2014: 800).

Fees for non-compulsory education after year 9 also discouraged some children from poor families from thinking that educational progression was possible for them (Liu et al., 2009). One author calculates that in 2012 the national cost of high school tuition was approximately 23 per cent of an average rural Chinese person's annual net income, while the costs of miscellaneous fees, textbooks and board were extra (Hu, 2019: 644). Moreover, as noted in Chapter 4, nearly three-quarters of the children I interviewed had at least one sibling, thereby doubling the families' overall burden of high school costs if two children progressed to senior high school. During the 2000s and early 2010s, the costs of senior high school could be inflated further because the top academic-track senior high schools offered a quota of places to those students whose *zhongkao* scores fell just below the cut-off, for which the family needed to pay high tariffs. Some poor parents used these thresholds to motivate their children. They said: 'Just so long as you are not one point short of the cut-off line, I will find a way to give you an education.' But some of these children felt that it was not reasonable for them to expect their parents to support their post-compulsory stage studies given their families' economic burdens.

Rural students were further impeded in pursuing education by discrimination in China's tertiary admissions process. In coastal provinces and municipalities that host the largest number of tertiary institutions per capita, admissions officials require applicants from other provinces to attain higher scores than locals. They justify their biased admissions criteria partly on *suzhi* grounds, claiming that a good rural student from an interior province will only be able to memorise material for exams, whereas a local student with a comparable score will have a wider range of competencies needed for successful learning (Zhang, 2007).

During the late 2010s, some public intellectuals and media outlets in China reported that rural people had increasingly adopted a 'study is useless' mentality [*dushu wuyong lun*]. They attributed this mentality to a rise in graduate numbers, the phasing out in the 1990s of the old socialist graduate job assignment system, and a fall in starting salaries (e.g. Yu, 2015; see also Hansen, 2015: 66). But this narrative overlooks the vehement fight of urbanites against any proposals to open up rural children's access to urban senior high schools or universities (Ming, 2013), as well as an intensified internal stratification of higher education that disadvantages rural students, which I discuss further in the following text.

Why did high educational aspirations persist among rural families given the immense obstacles that rural children face in getting into reputable tertiary institutions? There are at least four reasons. Firstly, in the reform era China

3.1 Getting Ahead Through Education

witnessed a steady expansion in educational provisioning (Kipnis, 2011). From the mid-1980s, the state expended much effort to realise the 'two basics' of 'nine years of compulsory education and the eradication of illiteracy among the younger part of the population' (Ministry of Education, 2011: 1 cited in Hansen, 2015: 16–17). The 2006 policy of eliminating school fees and providing a boarding subsidy to rural students helped these efforts, especially by boosting the school attendance of girls from poor families (Chyi and Zhou, 2014) and teenagers (Shi, 2016). The increasing preciousness of children to their parents also reinforced parents' desires to invest in their children's education (Liu, 2015; Murphy, 2004a). At the same time, falling birth rates made it easier for planners and educators to improve rates of transition from junior to senior high school (Hansen, 2015: 17). Furthermore, the rapid expansion in the number of university places since the late 1999s was such that 'a desire to attend some sort of tertiary institution ... spread from an elite to the masses' (Kipnis, 2011: 88).

Next, rural people see attending university as the only alternative to *dagong* or farming (Kipnis, 2011; Huang, 2012; Hansen, 2015). This view partly reflects the paucity of decent vocational training options for people from rural families. Indeed, rural students are not eligible to attend most top-tier vocational schools in the cities while in 2012, 82 per cent of students in China's medium-ranking vocational schools were of rural origins (Huang, 2012). Moreover, many unregulated vocational schools charge high fees while offering substandard instruction (Kipnis, 2011; Hansen, 2013; Ling, 2015; Koo, 2016; Yi et al., 2018). They also exploit the students' labour through compulsory internships on assembly lines (Smith and Chan, 2015; Koo, 2016), a practice that I discuss later. But even respectable vocational schools are looked down on. As Hansen explains: 'The [resulting] job would be less secure than the jobs one could get with an academic education; it would probably pay less; and it would not bring "face" or social status to the family' (Hansen, 2013: 172).

Thirdly, rural people perceive that individuals with more education enjoy higher living standards and more opportunities in life, and as noted in Chapter 2, their exposure to urban labour markets has strengthened this perception. For instance, the mother of Zhangyong, mentioned in Chapter 1, quit school in her mid-teens to find work. Over the course of twenty years, she worked in more than ten factories in the Yangtze River Delta. By the time I met her, she had reached the rank of production line manager on the night shift, a feat she attributed to her tenacity and boldness. Even so, she noted that some of her co-workers who had senior high school certificates and technical diplomas had fared better than her. Hence, when her son visited Kunshan during the holidays, she would tell him: 'So and so in our factory makes 3,000 *yuan* per month with a technical diploma. Imagine what you could earn with a college degree.'

70   Sacrifice and Study

Rural people's view that individuals with more education enjoy a better standard of living is supported by evidence. Hannum and her colleagues report that by 2000, one additional year of education resulted in an average wage increase of 6.4 per cent (Hannum, Wang and Adams 2010, cited in Hansen, 2013), while a 2009 World Bank study for China states that having a senior high school graduate in a family virtually guaranteed its escape from poverty (World Bank, 2009). At the same time, though, as mentioned before, China's higher education sector not only expanded but also became more internally stratified, replicating a pattern observed in earlier decades in the United Kingdom and France (Bourdieu and Passeron, 1979; Reay, David and Ball, 2005). As the numbers of tertiary graduates rose from three million in 1996 to twenty-six million in 2016, a college degree itself no longer guaranteed higher earnings. Even so, graduates who obtained higher *gaokao* scores and went to higher-tier tertiary colleges still earned significantly more in the labour market than did graduates with lower scores who went to lower-tier tertiary colleges (Knight, Deng and Li, 2017; Awaworyi Churchill and Mishra, 2018).

Finally, owing to 'the idealisation of a merit-based stratification process', people in China widely believe that power, status and opportunity are allocated to individuals based on their hard work and educational accomplishments. 'Evidence' to support this belief is the overall package of stability, perks, favourable working conditions and prestige that educated government and state sector employees enjoy even though their salaries are often less than some private sector employees' salaries (Jacka, Kipnis and Sargeson, 2013: 162). A belief in meritocracy fuels rural parents' hopes that their children can progress to such a reputable job by means of education (Kipnis, 2011). Indeed, several rural parents said that they hoped that their child could go to university and then find a job in a *danwei*, the term for 'work unit': in the socialist era, most urban workers belonged to a *danwei*, while in the socialist market economy era the term is often used to refer to any institution or company that offers the workers secure employment, decent benefits and a respectable social identity.

When children were still in primary school or even in the first year of junior high school, their educational 'potential' had yet to reveal itself, thereby sustaining both the children's and the parents' hopes that a child would be able to study his or her 'way out' (*chulu*) of a lowly rural status and economic insecurity. Certainly, most children I met in Anhui and Jiangxi could name someone from their village, their extended family, their primary school or their junior high school alumni, or even a rural person from a television programme, who had made it to a teachers' college or even to a good university, making the dream of tertiary education seem within the realm of the possible.

3.2 Family Socialisation of Children in Striving Teams

Although the rural parents we met held high aspirations for their children's education, as sociologists observe in relation to a US context, parents need to *transmit* these aspirations to their children, with the number of parents in a household and the strength of parent–child attachment both constituting aspects of the 'social capital' conducive to the intergenerational transmission of aspiration (Astone and McLanahan, 1991). Specifically, sociologists argue that parents need to maintain emotional closeness with their children to influence them positively (Coleman, 1988). However, parental migration impedes children's possibilities for benefiting from this parental influence because of the physical separation (Booth, 2003). Worldwide, therefore, migrants try to stay close to their children and to encourage them in their studies by casting their migration as sacrifice (Dreby, 2010: 1–54; Carling, Menjívar and Schmalzbauer, 2012). In rural China, family members routinely invoke filial piety to cast parental migration as a sacrifice (Hu, 2019; Murphy, 2014a). Certainly, the children we met in Anhui and Jiangxi were socialised in daily life to see their parents' migration as a sacrifice, while most children wanted to honour this sacrifice through study.

3.2.1 The Purpose of the Parents' Migration

The initial separation of children from their parents was the first time that many children we met were told that their studies were of such consequence that at least one parent had to migrate.[1] Thirty-eight out of the ninety-one currently and previously left-behind children we interviewed reported that they could recall their initial separation from their parents. Of the children who recalled this event, twenty-six said that their parents had mentioned study to them in their parting words. For instance, a twelve-year-old boy in Tranquil County, Jiangxi, said:

I was in first grade and getting ready to go to school. I saw that they were packing things and asked them what they were doing. They said that they were preparing to *dagong*. I asked them, 'What about me when you are gone?' They said: 'We will send you to your *waipo*'s [maternal grandmother's] house to study.' I was very sad and said, 'Don't go.' They said: 'We are going out to earn money for you to let you study.' I thought: 'They are doing this all for me.' I cried.

Ten other children said that their parents had left home without telling them in advance, but they nevertheless inferred that their parents' migration was motivated by a wish to support their education. For instance, when we first met thirteen-year-old Shenyi in 2010 in his primary school in Tranquil County,

---

[1] Subsections 3.2.1 and 3.2.2 in this chapter rework and extend material from Murphy (2014a).

72   Sacrifice and Study

Jiangxi, he explained that at the time of his widowed mother's first departure, she had tricked him by saying that she was going to his maternal grandmother's, a memory that several years later still caused him to cry. However, Shenyi consoled himself that his mother sent money for his school fees and that his diligence at school made her happy.

The children were also reminded about their parents' aspirations for their studies when the parents prepared to return to the city after their visits home, usually at Chinese New Year. Children said that their parents mentioned study in their parting words, promising to return home again only if the children studied hard. Further reminders about study came when family members consoled the children. Some children reported that if their grandparents saw them cry, they would say something like: 'Your parents are out earning money for your education. There is nothing for you to cry about.' Children similarly mentioned study when they comforted their younger siblings. For example, a twelve-year-old girl from Jade County, Jiangxi, explained:

It is not good at all that my parents are outside because there is no one to take care of me. Sometimes I say to my older sister: 'Why have they still not returned? I really miss them'. Then my sister says: 'Don't worry. Study hard. They are earning money. Don't disappoint them'. My parents really endure hardship. I will study hard.

Children also heard about the need to study in the weekly or fortnightly phone calls with their migrant parents. In the 2010 Summer survey, 579 (82 per cent) of the 706 'left-behind' children who gave a response about phone calls listed 'study' as the main topic that they talked about with their parents, outranking all other topics.[2] In the interviews, some children offered further explanation about how their migrant parents used phone conversations to encourage their studies. For example, a thirteen-year-old girl in Jade County, Jiangxi, said:

When my parents were at home, they could help me with washing clothes and homework. I was happy when they were with me. They cared for me every day. Now they care for me by telephone. They tell me to study hard. They say study hard and find a good job, and in the future look after *baba* and *mama*.

Her classmate similarly explained:

Now they only call me. They ask about exams and tell me to be sure not to catch cold, study hard and do not miss us all the time when you are at school. They fear this will influence my studies.

Study likewise featured in text exchanges between children and their migrant parents. A thirteen-year-old boy from Western County, Anhui, said:

---

[2] The breakdown of children's responses for other phone topics was: health – 359; other family members – 227; parents' life outside – 109; feelings – 78; local happenings and gossip – 57; future plans – 23 and other – 10. Multiple responses were permitted.

3.2 Family Socialisation of Children in Striving Teams 73

'When I miss them, I send them text messages saying, ". miss you". I use *yeye*'s mobile. They reply saying "study hard"'.

Children were also frequently coaxed by at-home mothers or grandparents to talk with their migrant parents on the phone, with their coaxing again referring to the migrants' support for the children's education. A fifty-eight-year-old grandmother in Tranquil County, Jiangxi, said of her ten-year-old grandson:

When he was little, he was unfamiliar with them and was unwilling to talk with them on the phone. But now that he is older and a little more obedient, I told him that when his parents phone he is to receive the call. I told him that if he doesn't receive the call then they won't give him the money that they earn outside. Then when he is older, he won't have money to study ... Now he understands and will receive their calls ... Now he asks, '*Baba*, when will you return? Will you buy me this or that?'

Sometimes, though, an emphasis on study in phone conversations could prove counterproductive, especially when children felt that their grades were inadequate or had deteriorated. For instance, in 2011, a twelve-year-old boy from Western County, Anhui, whose parents peddled lettuce in Kunshan, told us:

Only grandfather and elder sister talk with them [my parents] on the phone. I don't take their calls because they only ever ask me, 'Are your grades good or not?' which makes me feel under pressure ... ... When my grades are good *baba* says, 'I'll buy you whatever you want.' I asked for a bike. When my grades are poor *baba* says, 'I'm not going to buy you anything.'

Several at-home mothers and grandparents also recounted how children would hide when asked to take a call from a migrant parent, partly because they knew that the conversation would turn to study.

3.2.2   Children's Understanding of Dagong

Children's views of their parents' experiences of *dagong* further influenced their aspirations for educational mobility. The children we met learned from listening to adults, seeing their parents on return visits and observing their parents' lives when they visited them in the cities during the summer holidays, that *dagong* was 'bitter' and that they needed to study to avoid this fate themselves. They thus differed from some children in other low-income countries whose parents had migrated across national borders to prosperous countries. Specifically, Dreby and Schmalzbauer observe that children living in transnational families often thought that their migrant parents' working and living conditions were comfortable (Dreby, 2010: 11, 156) or even luxurious, a misapprehension that could exacerbate their sense of abandonment (Schmalzbauer, 2008).

74   Sacrifice and Study

The children we met in multilocal families in Anhui and Jiangxi did not want to *dagong* partly because they realised that their migrant parents' lives were extremely difficult. For instance, in 2011, a twelve-year-old from Tranquil County, Jiangxi, explained that he did not want to be like his father who made baseball bats or like his mother who made water bottles. He said: '[*Dagong*] ... is bitterly exhausting. I want to be a software engineer. There is a computer at home. Uncle arranged it when he returned last year.'

Several other children gleaned that *dagong* was bitter from observing their parents' physical frailty. They described hearing tiredness in their parents' voices on the phone. Or else they learned about their parents' poor health from incidents recounted to them. A fourteen-year-old girl called Heqin from Tranquil County, Jiangxi, explained:

When *baba* was working he had to be rushed to the hospital and they found that his kidneys were not good ... Keeping working makes it worse. [Her eyes fill with tears.] This summer my older cousin will take me to visit them. I will take stinky tofu, peanuts and medicine for kidney stones.

RACHEL : What do you think *dagong* is like?
HEQIN : I think a boss is there, dry, while *baba* and *mama*'s sweat drips non-stop.

Some children also noticed the physical deterioration of their migrant parents on their return visits. In 2010, Shenyi, the boy from Tranquil County whose father had died, said: '*Dagong* is bitterly exhausting. The last time my mother returned she was very thin, and her complexion was dark and rough. She didn't look well. Her appearance had changed a lot.' Similarly, some children from the Anhui fieldwork counties whose fathers worked in the construction industry noted that on their return visits home these men had 'changed form' for the worse (*bian le yang*).

Visits to see parents during the summer holidays provided further occasions for children to glean impressions of their parents' *dagong* lives. In 2011, a twelve-year-old girl from Jade County, Jiangxi, told us:

Their life out is not good ... I know this because the last time I visited, each time my mother would not take much food herself and would give extra to us. ... I will not *dagong* because I've already told my parents that I will pass the exam for university. They told me: 'Your study is not for us, it is for you. You do not want to be like us. *Dagong* is tiring. *Dagong* is exhausting.'

Indeed, fifteen children talked with us about how on visits to see their migrant parents they saw the frugality of their lives. They said that when their parents returned to the room after their work shifts, they could see symptoms of their fatigue such as red eyes, sore fingers or aching backs.

3.3 Schools' Socialisation of Children in Striving Teams

3.3.1 School and Striving Values

Children were socialised into multilocal striving teams not only through their interactions with their migrant parents and at-home family members, but also in school. School guided children on how to interpret and respond to parental migration in two ways. Firstly, school reinforced core values that informed the logic of parent–child striving, notably urban superiority, meritocracy and filial piety. Secondly, school provided an institutional and physical space where the children engaged in their own daily striving activity. As mentioned, school influenced all children's aspirations and structured their daily lives regardless of their parents' migration status, but when their parents had migrated without them, the values promoted through school held special resonance for them (Murphy, 2014a).

Children learned about urban superiority because the curriculum presented an urban future as desirable and inevitable. In the early 2000s, pedagogues redesigned the curriculum for rural primary schools: whereas during the 1990s the curriculum aimed to prepare rural children for their future lives either on the farm or in other manual work, in the mid-2000s a revised curriculum aimed to prepare them for urban work (Ross, 2006). In 2003–2004, in interior provinces such as Anhui and Jiangxi, the weekly labour class (*laodong ke*) was dropped from the primary school timetable: this class had previously taught practical skills such as how to make a broom with straw, how to tie knots for hanging meat cuts or how to feed chickens. Space was thereby freed up for weekly computer and English classes (Murphy, 2004a).

Schools also exposed children to meritocracy. In the schools we visited, notices and slogans abounded in classrooms, playgrounds and at school gates, such as those depicted in Figures 3.1 and 3.2, urging children to 'move up a step at a time', 'keep up with others', 'keep up with the times' and have 'a progressive heart' (*shangjinxin*). Furthermore, every June large red and yellow posters adorned the outside walls of junior high schools listing the names of students who had achieved more than 600 points in the *zhongkao*, while posters outside senior high schools listed those who had made it to first and second tier universities. In China, the examination system has long served as an instrument of meritocracy because people see it as impartial and free from corrupting influences (Kipnis, 2011: 123–124). Indeed, people widely regard exam scores as an indication of students' 'promise' (*chuxi*), 'talent' (*caineng*), 'ability' (*benshi*) and 'quality' (*suzhi*) and even their morality (Kipnis, 2011: 123–124). In the 2000s and 2010s, the examination system also generated intense pressure

Figure 3.1 Slogan at a primary school in Tranquil County, Jiangxi: 'Strive to improve and advance bravely.'

Figure 3.2 Study well, advance upwards every day

for striving partly because it evaluated the worth not only of students but also of the teachers, headteachers and local education officials, with implications for how different children were treated (Murphy, 2004a; Kipnis, 2011). For instance, despite the Ministry of Education's repeated proscriptions against the practice, in Anhui and Jiangxi in the early 2010s children were often seated in rows in their classroom according to their grades. I could see the effects when teaching English because it was always the students seated in the back rows who averted their eyes when I asked a question and looked to find someone to answer.

Schools also urged children to adopt the value of filial piety. In schools across China, teachers commonly encourage children to see their teachers as parent-like and to work hard to repay both parents' and teachers' efforts to educate them (Kipnis, 2011: 144–145). Like Ms Dong, who I mentioned in Chapter 2, many teachers in the Jiangxi boarding schools said that they were like 'mother and father' to left-behind children. Moreover, schools in regions of high out-migration even held dedicated lessons in filial piety to meet the perceived needs of left-behind students. For instance, in 2013 in Jade County, Jiangxi, in a local television news item, an education bureau official explained that rural students especially needed lessons in filial piety. With echoes of Fei

3.3 Schools' Socialisation of Children in Striving Teams

Xiaotong (Fei, 1992: 42–43) noted in Chapter 1, the official said that this was because left-behind children were not able to interact regularly with their parents, so they did not always fully understand the requirements of filial piety. Hence, in the lesson, the students were invited to discuss questions such as: How old are your parents? Where do they *dagong*? Why do they *dagong*? How should children express appreciation for their parents? But several children told us that some classmates cried at these questions.

In Eastern County, Anhui, schools also undertook activities to teach left-behind children about filial piety. The teachers contributed lesson plans to a resource catalogue to support the moral education of left-behind children. A portion of the activities in this catalogue aimed to help left-behind children foster greater self-reliance and resilience (*ziqiang*) by telling them that if they demonstrated these qualities, they would free their migrant parents from worrying about them, enabling the parents to better concentrate on working for the family. In one of the lesson plans, the children launch their thoughts to their migrant parents by flying kites and shouting out sentiments such as '*Ma Ba*, your son has grown into a man', and 'Mother I promise you, I will score 90 points in the exam and I will look after myself' (Eastern County Education Bureau, 2008). Paradoxically, these lessons advocated self-reliance as the way for the children to fulfil their *relational* obligations to their parents.

3.3.2   School Support for Left-Behind Children

Besides exposing children to the values of urban superiority, meritocracy and filial piety, schools also provided support for left-behind children in daily life. Schools provided this support both formally and informally. In the wake of successive media reports about millions of vulnerable children left behind in China's countryside, in 2004 China's Ministry of Education convened a national summit on the topic, which was followed by other high-level meetings and the publication of a series of landmark official documents. For instance, in May 2007 a much-publicised document initiated by the All-China Women's Federation and involving thirteen ministries and organisations, called for all children to 'share the same blue sky'. Then in July 2007, the Organisation Bureau and six ministries, including the Ministry of Education, issued a joint 'work notice' requiring schools in regions with high rates of out-migration to adopt specific measures to 'care for left-behind children' (Wang and Wu, 2016). In the 2010s, following more tragedies involving left-behind children, especially the deaths of the children in Bijie county, Guizhou province, still further documents were issued including a 'work suggestions' document of January 2013 by the Ministry of Education requiring a strengthening of work to care for left-behind children in grades 1–9 (Wang

78 Sacrifice and Study

and Wu, 2016), and a State Council decree of February 2016 – mentioned in Chapter 1 – requiring local officials to ensure left-behind children's safety and prohibiting parents from leaving their children behind without an adult guardian (Wang and Wu, 2016).

In line with the Ministry of Education's requirements for formal actions to 'care for left-behind children', the primary schools and junior high schools I visited in townships in each of the fieldwork counties had all set up programmes. These programmes comprised two core elements. Firstly, the schools maintained annually updated registers of the mobile phone numbers and addresses of all migrant parents, and each teacher was allocated between six and eight left-behind children to 'help and support' (*bangfu*). Secondly, in response to official requirements on schools to run enrichment activities to support left-behind children, all the township-based primary schools and junior high schools I visited had designated a special activity room for left-behind children. These rooms were called a 'home for left-behind children' (*liushou haizi zhi jia*), with two such rooms shown in Figures 3.3 and 3.4. Importantly, though, these rooms were seldom used. An excerpt from my 2011 field notes

Figure 3.3 'Care for left-behind children' activity room in a township in Eastern County, Anhui

3.3 Schools' Socialisation of Children in Striving Teams 79

Figure 3.4 Care for left-behind children room in Jade County – the plaque reads 'psychological advice'

describes my visit to one of these rooms in a township-based junior high school in Eastern County, Anhui:

A faded sign outside the door shows that this room was previously a 'young pioneers' room, but it has since been renamed. Inside the room is a flat t.v. screen with a plaque on the frame stating: 'television designated for use by left-behind children'. There is also a small library in the corner. Mr Liu, the teacher responsible for maintaining the left-behind children's register, tells me that all the equipment and books in the room were bought in 2009 with a grant from the central government's 'people's welfare programme'. (*minsheng gongcheng*)

The walls of the room are decorated with children's colourful artwork and with photos of activities held in the school over the past five years, for instance, drawing, speech and singing competitions and a 'popularising legal knowledge activity' whereby a policeman came to talk to the students. When I asked Mr Liu if these activities had been just for left-behind children or for all students, he confirmed the latter. There are, though, some exhibits from activities solely for 'left-behind children', namely letters and poems that the children had written to their migrant parents. In these letters and poems, the children tell their parents to take care of their health and they promise to study hard (see Figure 3.5 for such a letter in a Jiangxi school).

Figure 3.5 Child's letter to migrant parents displayed in a junior high school activity room for left-behind children in Jade County, Jiangxi. Sentences include: 'I would prefer to be cursed and hit with a stick without reason than to be left alone to cry under my quilt in an empty house', and 'When I ask *yeye* when my parents will return he says, 'They are out enduring hardship to earn money for your studies, they will come back when you are in university.''

As my research assistant, Mr Liu and I look around the room, groups of students curious to see a foreign visitor crowd in behind us, peering through the partially open door and windows. They exclaim to each other with delight at how beautiful the room is! Obviously, it is the first time they have ever seen inside the room.

When we asked children about their experience of school-run activities for 'left-behind' children, several recalled isolated activities from two or three years earlier, such as visiting the county martyrs' museum or university students coming to read poems to them. One girl in Jade County, Jiangxi, even recalled an activity to post a card to her migrant mother for Mothers' Day. In general,

3.3 Schools' Socialisation of Children in Striving Teams

Figure 3.6 A township junior high school in Tranquil County, Jiangxi – structure to life in school

though, as many teachers also told us, there was a gap between the upper levels' formal requirements and what schools could realistically do to support left-behind children in daily life. The teachers had to look after all students regardless of the parents' migration status, and they also had to meet teaching objectives handed down to them by their superiors. If any child's grades fell suddenly or if

82 Sacrifice and Study

Figure 3.7 Interaction among children at a primary school in Jade County, Jiangxi

any child displayed behavioural problems or played truant or became ill, the teachers would try to contact the parents. But it was often difficult for teachers to get immediate support from parents who had migrated or from some elderly caregivers. Schools' financial resources to support left-behind children were also limited. For instance, a primary school headteacher in Eastern County explained that in order to improve communication between children and their migrant parents, 'we had a school scheme to encourage phone calls, but it was too expensive, so we had to stop it'.

3.3.3 School and Daily Life

Although schools struggled to sustain formal regularised programmes to care for left-behind children and to enrich their lives, schools still helped many children in less direct ways to cope with difficult circumstances created by their parents' migration. Specifically, as Figures 3.6 and 3.7 indicate, school gave all

3.3 Schools' Socialisation of Children in Striving Teams

children structure to their time as well as interaction with teachers and class-mates, with these aspects of school holding special significance for those children whose parents had migrated without them.

School also offered some children relief from challenging home situations that had arisen because of their parents' migration. For instance, attending school gave a few children reprieve from living with an elderly person who needed help with daily life. As a fourteen-year-old girl from Tranquil County, Jiangxi, explained:

Living with *yeye* I am independent and look after myself. *Yeye* is in poor health, he is eighty-eight. My parents are not here to look after me. I cook, wash clothes, clean and buy medicine for *yeye*. I have lived at school for two years. In the beginning it was unfamiliar. I like living at school, but I also like to return home. *Yeye* loves me and I like to see what he is doing. But then I like to go back to school again. I miss my classmates and games, especially jump rope.

Two children who lived alone found particular relief in school. In 2010, a fifteen-year-old boy from Tranquil County, Jiangxi, talked to us about how after the death of his grandfather his life at the weekends had no pattern but on school days there was a timetable of activities. Meanwhile, an eleven-year-old girl from Jade County, Jiangxi, liked school for similar reasons. According to her homeroom teacher, she lived in a mud adobe room next door to her aunt and when at home she washed her own clothes, and cooked and ate alone. The girl refused to talk with us about her life at home, but she told us that she looked forward to going to school because she liked the lessons and her teachers sometimes praised her.

Several children said that they received guidance and support from a teacher with whom they felt a special connection. For example, a twelve-year-old girl from Western County, Anhui, said that she had once written in her school diary that her parents did not love her as much as they loved her little sister (*meimei*) because they spent more time with *meimei* than with her. Moreover, the parents planned to take *meimei* with them to Guangdong when they remigrated, leaving her behind with her grandfather and a younger sister. Subsequently, the girl received a written reply from her homeroom teacher, a woman in her mid-fifties, which she found comforting. It read:

Your parents love you as much as your sister. But your sister is younger than you, so she needs more care. Your parents cared for you in this way when you were young. Do not feel sad. They are migrating to earn money for both you and your sister. Study hard.

Children also derived comfort from the familiarity of the schools' physical and social environment. For instance, several children told us that although their migrant parents had suggested to them that they study in the city, they wanted to

84   Sacrifice and Study

stay in the countryside. A twelve-year-old girl from Jade County, Jiangxi, reflected wider sentiments among these children when she explained:

I visited my parents' place when I was in fourth grade . . . and went last year for one month. My parents worked all day and they came back when I was already asleep. I was in the room by myself watching television, reading and sleeping. Sometimes they took me to the supermarket . . . I didn't want to leave them because we had some happy times together. But I am unfamiliar with that place. It is better for me to study here so that I am freer. I can play with my classmates and hang out with family members. My parents asked me if I wanted to study in the city. I said that I didn't because my parents are at work all day and also the city school fees are expensive. I cried when my parents went out again after Spring Festival, I was broken-hearted. My grandparents comforted me saying: 'Study hard, your parents have to go out for your future studies.'

3.4   Inner Conflict

Even as most children accepted the work–study logic of the parent–child striving team, some children nevertheless felt conflicted about what their migrant parents' sacrifice required of them. Several children indicated that they felt torn between recognising their migrant parents' contribution to their futures on the one hand and missing them on the other. For instance, a thirteen-year-old boy from Jade County, Jiangxi, said that he missed his parents and wanted them to return home but then in the next breath added that he would prefer them to stay out because he was better able to concentrate on his studies when they were not around. Similarly, an eleven-year-old boy from Jade County, Jiangxi, said that he felt sad when his parents returned to the city after their visits home and he would often ask them on the phone to return. But once they returned, he told them to go out again to continue earning for his university fees.

For some teenagers, inner conflict about the work–study bargain of the parent–child striving team stemmed from a different source. Specifically, these teenagers had reached a stage in their education where they increasingly doubted that their own grades would be good enough for them to progress further along an academic path. Certainly, in Western contexts sociologists identify academic motivation as an important source of resilience that can help emotionally troubled youth and youth who face adversity to function well at school and get good grades (Roeser, Eccles and Sameroff, 2000; Schoon, 2006: 6), with Schoon stating that 'cultural and group values are crucial to the study of resilience' (Schoon, 2006: 152). Meanwhile, Hu (2019) observes that in a Chinese cultural context, rural adolescents' perception of migrant parents' support for their education is particularly influential in sustaining their resilience in the face of long-term parental absence.

3.4 Inner Conflict

Importantly, though, if a child's academic performance is weak or declines then their academic motivation can crumble and fail to be a source of resilience. Indeed, a survey-based study finds that as children in rural China grow older, they become less satisfied with their grades (On the Road to School, 2016). It is at this point that the inner conflicts of children n parent–child striving teams become the most acute. Based on her interviews with migrant adolescents in Beijing, sociologist Anita Koo (2012) proposes that individuals' inner conflicts over education can be explained with reference to a gap that class-based disadvantage generates between 'aspirations' on the one hand and 'expectations' on the other. In the following longitudinal case study of a girl called Jingjing from Tranquil County, Jiangxi, I extend Koo's (2012) analysis to explore how the gap between children's aspirations and expectations evolve over time. Specifically, I demonstrate how the gap emerges because of the cumulative interactions among a child's family-class background, experiences at school and the immanent end of the compulsory period of schooling.

Jingjing

I first met Jingjing in Tranquil County in Spr ng 2011 when she was twelve years old. At the time, her mother worked as a masseur in Wenzhou city, Zhejiang, and her father worked as a security guard in Dongguan city in the Pearl River Delta. At this meeting, Jingjing explained to my research assistant and me that she wanted to go to university. Like many children we met, she did not know why she wanted to go university or what she wanted to study. She told us that she hoped one day to tell stories on television, but her dream did not appear to be connected to her desire to get into university. When I asked Jingjing about her grades, she lowered her head and whispered: 'My grades are "really poor"' (*hen cha*). I immediately felt bad for having asked her this question.

The next day we visited Jingjing's grandparents in their dilapidated house on the corner of a dusty road that cut through their village. They told me that they wanted Jingjing to study. Their own five children – two daughters and three sons – had never finished primary school so they had endured much hardship in life. The grandfather had lost his own father when he was only two years old and his mother had remarried into another family where educating him was not the priority. Like the grandfather I mentioned in Chapter 2, Jingjing's grandparents did not want their grandchildren to repeat their own children's hardships. Jingjing's grandfather explained: 'I tell my grandchildren, if you have studied then even *dagong* is okay, but if you have not studied then the only *gong* you will ever *da* is bitter *gong*.'

On a Sunday afternoon in Autumn 2013 when I visited Jingjing's grandparents for a second time, accompanied by a different research assistant,

86   Sacrifice and Study

Jingjing sat next to her younger brother, his arm tightly interlocked in hers as he played a game on a mobile phone. On seeing me at the front door, the grandfather must have recalled our conversation from three years ago because after my greeting he immediately launched into a monologue about how unlike some children cared for by their grandparents, his grandchildren never did bad things. Of course, he wanted them to study and get into university, but even if their grades were poor, at least they never ran around like hooligans.

I pointed to a yellow and orange certificate stuck on a wall in their reception room on which black ink characters stated: 'Awarded to Jingjing for her work in the tuition class, 2012'. Jingjing screwed up her nose at my gesture but stayed silent. However, her grandmother spoke up: 'We want her to study but she is not diligent, so what can we do? The sooner she goes out to *dagong* the better.' Jingjing stared expressionlessly at the screen of the mobile phone her brother was holding.

When we went to find Jingjing at her junior high school the next day, I saw recruitment advertisements from several prefectural vocational training schools displayed on boards inside the entrance. It was the post-lunch rest period. My research assistant went for a walk while Jingjing sat with me on a sun-drenched bench in the playground. Jingjing knew that I planned to visit her father in Dongguan, which made her cheerful: she asked me a few times, 'Are you really going to see my father?' and she smiled each time I confirmed this was so.

She told me that she felt sad because her father had returned to Dongguan without telling her beforehand. The purpose of his return visit to the village had been to take the enrolment money for boarding to the school at the start of the new academic year. She explained that her father seldom told her when he was leaving because he could not bear to see her cry. As we talked it transpired that she had been thinking hard about her future. As per our conversation nearly three years earlier, she still wanted to do post-compulsory stage study before starting work. Now, though, she hoped to attend a vocational school because one of the advertisements at her school entrance displayed information about a course to become a railway hostess, accompanied by pictures of young attractive women in smart stewardess uniforms. She said that she wanted to work as a railway stewardess because she would be able to see other places and while away time looking out of the window at the scenery.

A few weeks later I went to visit Jingjing's father in Dongguan city. He had just quit his job as a security guard because of a kidney infection. When he was not resting on the sofa in the foyer of the middle-class apartment complex where he had previously worked, he earned tips from the apartment residents for helping them to carry objects, run errands and call taxis. Of his then fourteen-year-old daughter, he explained:

3.4 Inner Conflict 87

She doesn't really know what she wants to do. I told her at the very least you need to graduate from senior high school. She said, "I can't get the material into my head (*du bu jin qu*)." I said, "But you must study." I want them to study more. I don't want them to be like us. If I'd studied more, I would be able to find a job in a company.

He went on to say that he and his wife had tried to support their daughter's education. Specifically, in 2012, his wife had arranged for her to attend a fortnight of summer tuition classes held in the county seat. He also said that he had urged her to attend the classes again the following summer, but she did not want to because she could not keep up. At that point I realised that the certificate I had seen at Jingjing's grandparents' house had been given to her for participating in the tutoring class rather than for meeting any academic standard.

In Spring 2014, I visited Jingjing at her school again. She told me that she felt happy because her father had been at home for over six months. But she also felt vexed. She wanted to study at the vocational school because at least this was 'study' rather than *dagong* though she had not told her parents about this wish for fear they would not agree. Tearfully she said that her parents and grandparents had said to her that she would need to *dagong* because she was 'useless' at studies (*du shu mei yong*). She added: 'They might be joking about sending me out to *dagong*, I don't know.'

When we visited Jingjing's grandparents' house, her father was there. He showed us the scar from his operation across the top of his stomach. It had cost over 7,000 *yuan*, and this was even after he had received medical insurance reimbursement. He also showed us the concrete foundations of where he was preparing to build a separate house of his own. He told us that his daughter had talked to him about a railway service course. But he was convinced that these vocational schools were schemes to trick people. He said that he had met his share of tricksters in his life and that even though he did not have much education, his time 'outside' had taught him how to spot dodgy situations. In his view, given his family's financial burdens and the poor prospects offered by vocational education, it would be better if his daughter went to *dagong* directly. At this point, Jingjing's grandmother piped up saying: 'There's no point in her studying. Now we only hope that our grandson can get to university, we have only that wish.'

On a fourth visit to Jingjing's family home in 2015, her father was still in the village. He showed us around the family's newly built house. He explained that he was still looking for a way to earn money in the rural hometown that was not strenuous because his body had not fully healed. He also told us that Jingjing now boarded at a military-style vocational school in Jian city, Jiangxi, which was run by a former army officer from Shanxi province. He showed my research assistant and me a short clip on his mobile phone of her class doing military drills inside the school grounds during induction. He said that the fees cost ten thousand *yuan* per year and that even though she did not learn much, the headmaster had promised that after two years she would be allocated a job working for the railways, with the language of 'job allocation' (*gongzuo fenpei*) holding special appeal to rural people who had been mostly excluded from job allocations under the previous socialist system of ensuring employment for graduates. I felt pleased for Jingjing that her wish to train as railway hostess had come true and asked her father if we could go to visit her.

Jingjing's father rang up the headmaster of the vocational school to tell him that he would visit his daughter and that he would bring a foreign teacher who had known his daughter for several years, a university teacher from Nanchang (my research assistant), as well as a teacher from Tranquil County. At that point, the voice of the headmaster exploded down the phone. He bellowed that he forbade a visit. Fifteen minutes later, a tearful Jingjing phoned her father. As the call was on loudspeaker, we could hear what transpired. We heard the headmaster berating Jingjing in the background as she told her father that she did not want the foreign teacher to visit. Jingjing also said something which my research assistant heard as 'she would die' (*fanzheng yao si*) but which a teacher visitor to the family heard as her saying 'she was fed up' (*fan si*).

I later learned from various sources that students at this vocational school had to do four months of factory work per year as 'interns', ten hours per day for six days a week for one to two hundred *yuan* per month, and also that there were open sewers in the dormitory areas and caterpillars in the meals. Jingjing's father knew she worked in a factory with only a basic allowance and that her living conditions were abysmal, but he clung on to the hope that she would be allocated a coveted railway service job. After the awful phone call, I looked for more information about the school on the internet. Its advertising webpages displayed the same pictures of smart uniformed railway hostesses I had seen on the advertising board in the school. But there was also a clip made by hand-held camera of some teenage girls doing racy modern dancing for a male audience, including for the school headmaster. I also found blogs posted by some former students complaining that the few railway jobs available were allocated to those individuals who paid the teachers money.

Jingjing's experience of low-quality instruction at her vocational school and her experience of labour exploitation as an intern in factories were not exceptional. Sociologists report that in China the state has targeted poor rural youth as a new source of students for vocational schools and capital has targeted poor rural youth as a source of cheap and disciplined labour for factories (Smith and Chan, 2015; Koo, 2016) and the service sector (Woronov, 2016), thereby helping to sustain labour supply in the face of demographically and structurally induced labour shortages and evolving labour needs. In the vocational schools that Koo (2016) visited, in the first two years of study, students with financial

3.5 Alternative Educational Aspirations

hardship were urged to join internships organised during the summer and winter holidays to earn their spending money. Meanwhile, the students had to work as unpaid interns in their third year to pay off school and accommodation fees (Koo, 2016). To their dismay these interns found themselves on assembly lines carrying out repetitive tasks, with the internships having no link to their course of study (Smith and Chan, 2015; Koo, 2016; Pun and Koo, 2019). Like Koo (2016), I found that the young people I met in Jiangxi had high aspirations for social mobility through education, which fed into their despair once it became clear that their post-compulsory 'education' was unlikely to translate into better life prospects.

The longitudinal case study of Jingjing demonstrates that some rural children were forced to revise their educational aspirations over time in light of unfolding circumstances and their dawning realisation of these circumstances. By the final year in junior high school, when Jingjing had to face the reality that she would never go to university, she tried to find an alternative way to continue studying. With its attractive photos, a vocational course to become a railway hostess had captured her imagination and seemed to offer her a 'way out' of drudgery and economic insecurity. She negotiated with her parents to support her financially to attend the vocational school. But even though she managed to convince them to support her, complex power structures and vested interests involving rural schools, Pearl River Delta factories and the vocational school combined to extract money, labour and hope from a fragile girl and her struggling family. Meanwhile, the vocational school's website legitimated this exploitation with reference to rural youth's need for discipline, cultivation and *suzhi* enhancement.

3.5   **Alternative Educational Aspirations**

Although most rural parents did not aspire for their children to take a vocational education route – and even as most children did not wish to take this route themselves – some families believed that 'learning a skill' (*xue yi men jishu*) was an option that they would need to consider if a child's academic prospects looked uncertain (Hansen and Woronov, 2013). When I first started carrying out fieldwork in Jiangxi, I asked some adults and children about their view of vocational education. However, my research assistant at that time advised me to stop asking this question, saying: 'I can see that your question makes them feel uncomfortable. In asking them about vocational education it is like you're cursing the children's fate.' I then changed to ask a more general question about what the children and the family members had discussed with each other as possibilities for the future.

Fourteen children volunteered that they and their parents had at one point discussed the possibility of them learning a skill or going to vocational school.

90   Sacrifice and Study

There were, though, differences between the two Anhui counties and the two Jiangxi counties with respect to when and how the children and adults had discussed this topic. Eight of the children in the Anhui counties who indicated that they had ever discussed vocational training with their parents had done so when they were aged fifteen years or older, so at an age when they had given an academic-track enough of a chance but had conceded a need to consider other routes. These children also all had tangible ideas about regionally based possibilities for attending vocational school, which they viewed somewhat positively.

By contrast, the six children in the Jiangxi counties who said that they had talked with their parents about learning a skill did not see training in a regionally based vocational school as an option. Two boys from non-migrant families who were still in primary school told us that they had contemplated 'learning a skill' rather than attending a vocational school in response to their families' poverty and their own poor grades. Two other children, one of whom was Jingjing, had turned to vocational school in the hope of a job allocation while the two Jiangxi children who had a positive view of vocational training had heard from their parents about possibilities in coastal cities.

Why did children and families in the Anhui counties feel positive about regionally based vocational training opportunities while children and families in the Jiangxi counties did not? The differences partly reflect the provinces' and counties' different geographical locations. In the 2010s, Hefei City in Anhui hosted a number of reputable vocational schools. Additionally, as noted in Chapter 2, the county seats in the two Anhui counties had recently enhanced transport connections to Hefei. When I met Xinhui from Western County in 2015 after she had transferred from a township junior high school to a specialist nursing school in Hefei, she said: 'Several of my classmates have gone to different vocational schools in Hefei including clothes design and advertising and they seem mostly satisfied.' Furthermore, she enthused about her own course, saying: 'Our teacher said that most people begin and end life in hospital, so this is worthwhile.' Likewise, when I visited Wang Delun at his vocational school in Hefei, he appeared satisfied with his course in computing and graphic design – even though he was still bitterly disappointed at missing out on going to university. Indeed, he planned to set up an e-commerce business with some 'brothers' from the school.

By contrast, the adults and teenagers in the Jiangxi counties all said that there were no decent vocational schools available. This may have been because the two Jiangxi fieldwork counties were situated far from the provincial capital while the vocational schools publicised in the township junior high schools were based in third- or fourth-tier cities, away from the main hubs of educational investment and regulatory oversight. The Jiangxi counties were also

3.5 Alternative Educational Aspirations

linked to the Pearl River Delta manufacturing sector by migration and sub-contracting networks in a way that the Anhui counties were not. Several sociologists document the systematic use of unpaid student interns in Pearl River Delta factories (Chan, Pun and Selden, 2015; Smith and Chan, 2015; Koo, 2016; Chan, 2017), while one sociologist discusses the use of underage workers in the prefectural city of Jian, Jiangxi, where Jingjing's dismal vocational school was based (Han, 2016). Rural parents and teenagers in the Jiangxi counties therefore had good reason to be wary of vocational schools in their region.

Children's views about learning a skill were also affected by their parents' occupational backgrounds. The two primary school boys from non-migrant families in Jiangxi I mentioned earlier echoed their parents' view that they should learn a skill to ensure a full stomach in life. One boy's parents 'got by' by doing cotton threshing in the township, while the other boy's mother had died, and his returned migrant father had told him that he needed to learn a skill to 'get by'. Several other children's parents' migration experiences fed directly into their family conversations about learning a skill. In Jiangxi, the two children I mentioned previously who talked about possibly attending vocational schools in coastal cities – to learn accountancy or computing – came from returnee trader families. Three boys – two in Anhui and one in Jiangxi – wanted to be cooks like their migrant fathers. A girl in Anhui planned to learn computing in Hefei so that she could get an office job: her brother was training to be an electrician; her father had worked as a carpenter in African countries and later in Singapore, and their mother raised and traded a few hundred pigs in the village. Meanwhile, two teenage boys wanted to become mechanics: one boy's father was a long-distance truck driver while the other boys' migrant parents ran a tailoring stall and thought that he could run his own repair business if he could not get into university.

Teenagers whose grades were weak but whose families contemplated vocational school as a viable back-up option for them seemed to feel more positive about their left-behind pasts and more hopeful about their futures than did other teenagers whose grades were weak. For instance, at our first meeting in 2010 in Eastern County, Anhui, a twelve-year-old girl told us that her father sometimes hit her on his return visits home because he wanted her to work harder to pass the *zhongkao* and get into a key-point senior high school. She herself admitted to being lazy and to frequenting internet bars in the township. However, when we met her again in Autumn 2013, she told us that her parents had noticed the proliferation of kindergartens on their travels and they had learned about a good vocational course in Hefei that would let her train to be a kindergarten teacher, a prospect that excited her. Unlike at our first meeting, she now said that her parents' migration had been 'worth it' because there was money for her to study a course that would enable her to find a good job.

92   Sacrifice and Study

Teenagers who struggled academically but whose families saw vocational training as a possible path for them also seemed to see themselves more positively than did teenagers who struggled academically but whose families saw academic study as the only way out. In the former cases, grandparents and parents stressed a need for the child to be happy, of good character and self-reliant rather than necessarily academically successful. Like the working-class mothers Reay (2000) met in London, these parents and caregivers separated out the children's worth and well-being from their educational success, enabling them to deal with their anxieties about their child's prospects in life. These teenagers still felt obligated by their parents' sacrifice to work hard, behave well and be filial, but unlike their peers who had only *dagong* before them, they did not describe themselves as 'low *suzhi*', 'useless' or 'without promise'.

Conclusion

In low-income countries, children's education underpins both the parents' migration and the children's obligations to their families. However, how this plays out varies across countries, sociocultural, economic and local geographic contexts, families and individuals. This chapter has shown that in rural regions in Anhui and Jiangxi, a combination of influences including falling family size, migrant parents' experiences of life at the bottom rungs of urban society and shifting parenthood norms intensified parents' aspirations for their children's education as well as the children's aspirations for their own education. As discussed in Chapter 1, the rural parents' work in urban labour markets – and the at-home parents' and grandparent caregivers' work in social reproduction – approximated urban middle-class parents' more personalised use of time and money to invest in their children's education. This was even as the rural adults' child-raising efforts were seldom recognised by urbanised middle-class profes-sionals – including teachers – as demonstrating the families' commitment to the children's education (Kim, 2018).

The children whom my research assistants and I met in Anhui and Jiangxi learned through interactions with family members that they were obligated to honour their parents' sacrifice of *dagong* by studying hard, behaving well and being filial. The children frequently heard from their at-home parents, grand-parents, migrant parents and siblings that their education was the main reason for their parents' migration. Meanwhile, the advice to study hard was the usual comfort that caregivers and siblings offered to the children whenever they expressed sadness because they missed their parents. Moreover, the children were repeatedly reminded of the importance of study in phone conversations with their migrant parents.

In the logic of the parent–child striving teams, the more bitter the parents' experience of *dagong*, the greater is their sacrifice, and the deeper the children's

3.5 Alternative Educational Aspirations

awareness of their parents' sacrifice, the greater is their obligation to demonstrate filial piety through obedience and hard work. Conversely, children's awareness of the bitterness of *dagong* fed into their own aspirations to escape the drudgery of being a migrant worker – a desire that in turn enhanced their appreciation of their parents' sacrifice and intensified their unwillingness to disappoint their parents. Both parents and children therefore internalised and reproduced the aspirations that bound them together in toiling teams and gave meaning to their daily work, while distracting them from class injustices.

Schools supported the striving logic of the multilocal parent–child teams formally and informally. Schools socialised children in values such as urban superiority, meritocracy and filial piety, encouraging their acceptance of their parents' migration and impelling them to study hard. Many schools provided boarding facilities that made it easier for both parents to migrate, even as school consolidation was the initial reason for establishing the public boarding schools. School also provided some children with ways to cope with the pressures that parental migration and academic expectations placed on them. For instance, some children used their study to maintain an emotional connection with their migrant parents whilst distracting themselves from their feelings of loss at their parents' absence, at least temporarily. Additionally, school life and interactions with school friends and teachers gave some children reprieve from difficult home situations that had arisen because of their parents' migration, for instance, living with infirm grandparents or feeling lonely.

However, when children's grades appeared unlikely to get them to university, study and the anticipation of academic success did not help them in giving meaning to their daily lives or in coping with long-term separation from their parents. Some teenagers who had begun to realise that they would not get into an academic-track senior high school thought that they were failures. They therefore avoided communication with their parents, disengaged from study and reconciled themselves to a future of *dagong*. While a sociological literature finds that high parental aspirations benefit children's educational engagement (Booth, 2003; Hannum, Kong and Zhang, 2009), the experiences of the children I met in Anhui and Jiangxi also reveal that exceedingly high expectations can demotivate children and strain a parent–child bond already weakened by protracted spatial separation. However, some children's parents saw vocational training as a possible fallback option for them and had identified viable courses. These children appeared to feel better about themselves than did their peers who struggled academically while having no 'way out' in life.

This chapter confirms earlier migration studies research in finding that implicit family bargains mediate how migrants and at-home family members practise reciprocity across distance. Pioneering in its time, this earlier research overturned a previous view of migrants as lone individuals (Lucas and Stark, 1985; Stark and Lucas, 1988; Stark, 1991). At the same time, this chapter joins

94 Sacrifice and Study

more recent research – notably the research into transnational and translocal families discussed in Chapter 1 – in moving away from economistic explanations of migration as a family strategy. Through an emphasis on relationships and attention to situated context, this chapter casts light on how 'parental migration as sacrifice' draws on and reworks local cultural logics and repertoires; how different family members invoke 'parental migration as sacrifice' as they make sense of reconfigured intergenerational relationships and the obligations that these relationships engender; migration's role in obligating the children to honour their side of intergenerational obligations by studying hard; and the impact of study obligations on the children's views about their self-worth, their relationships with their parents, and daily life.

4 Boys' and Girls' Experiences of Distribution in Striving Families

Does it matter whether a left-behind child is a boy or a girl? In addressing this question, I adopt sociologist Barbara J. Risman's (2004) view of gender as a feature of individuals' identity and as institutional and interactional in nature. This view of gender recognises that even as individuals claim their belonging to a sex category, usually on the basis of biology, gender gains its meaning in relation to wider social, cultural and political structures, in an institutional context, and as West and Zimmerman (1987) famously highlight, in interaction with others (Risman, 2004).

In China, the patrilineal family is the most basic institution through which children acquire and develop their gendered identities (Hu, 2015). Simultaneously, children's gender intersects with their family's social position and 'geographical location' (Mahler and Pessar, 2001; Dreby and Schmalzbauer, 2013) to impact on their gendered socialisation, gendered habitus, gendered expectations and gendered pathways for attaining recognition (Atkinson, 2015: 88–90; Lan, 2018). Meanwhile, schools, labour markets, media, welfare systems and other institutional domains also influence gendered beliefs, gendered social relations and gendered distributional practices within and beyond the family.

Gender could affect children's lives in their multilocal families in a number of ways. For example, parents' striving goals for a given child may vary by his or her gender. Parental migration reconfigures gendered and generational relationships within families, with potentially different implications for boys and girls. Certain striving imperatives and the long-term migration of parents may influence the *accountability* that children feel towards their parents in doing what is necessary to be recognised as filial *sons* or *daughters* (West and Zimmerman, 1987). Influences from institutional domains outside the family, including those domains most pertinent to multilocal striving (for instance, schools and labour markets) may also assume special significance for children whose parents have migrated without them, influencing how they 'do gender' (West and Zimmerman, 1987).

This chapter concentrates on the *distribution* of resources and chores to boys and girls in multilocal families because respondents readily talked with us about these topics. Distribution is integral to children's gendered experiences

96   Boys, Girls and Distribution in Striving Families

of family life. As Risman (2004) explains, gender beliefs and resource distribution are the 'twin pillars' of a holistic gender structure that incorporates institutions, culture, everyday interaction and individual identity. Indeed, gender as a structure comprises gender beliefs in the sense of the cultural repertoires that individuals use to enact and interpret gender, and the distribution of resources that result (Risman, 2004). Hence, distribution is a core activity through which individuals and families both reproduce and change gender relations (Risman, 2004).

4.1   Distributional Differences

In this chapter, two different bodies of literature to help me think about gendered distributional differences among children in multilocal families. One body of literature from development studies measures gender disparities in the allocation of household resources and work burdens to children. Some of this literature finds that in patrilineal sociocultural contexts including in China, South Asia, North Africa and Latin America, household economic hardship correlates with disadvantages for girls in nutrition, health and education investments (Obermeyer and Cardenas, 1997; Pande, 2003; Oster, 2009; Song and Burgard, 2008; Goodburn, 2014). Research also finds that across the global South, girls spend significantly more time on household chores than do boys (UNICEF, 2016), with a parallel family sociology literature documenting this phenomenon for Western countries (Hu, 2015), particularly in low-income families (Dodson and Dicket, 2004).

Only a few studies explore the influence of parental migration on the intrafamily distribution of resources to boys and girls. In a study using data from rural Mexico, McKenzie and Rapoport (2006) find that all children were disadvantaged by their parents' migration to the United States with teenage boys dropping out of school to migrate and teenage girls dropping out of school to do housework. But they also find that the migrants' remittances mitigated poor girls' disadvantages by alleviating household credit constraints. Two studies based on nationwide survey data for China from 2005 and 2006 likewise highlight the ameliorating influences of remittances on gender inequality among children. Firstly, Duan and Yang (2008) find that parental migration corresponds with a smaller proportion of children aged thirteen to seventeen years who had not received the years of compulsory education appropriate for their age. Of children who had enrolled in school late or dropped out of school prematurely, the proportions were highest among girls with at-home parents, followed by boys with at-home parents, then left-behind girls and lowest among left-behind boys: by age seventeen, 15 per cent of girls who lived with both their parents had not attended the mandated number of years at school versus 10 per cent of left-behind girls. Similarly, Hu (2012) finds that

4.1 Distributional Differences

even though parental migration negatively affected rural Chinese children's progression to high school, the effect on girls in poor families was partially offset by remittances. By contrast, other research finds that parental migration most adversely affected boys' access to nutrition (Zhang, Bécares and Chandola, 2015) and to other family resources because the parents had migrated to save for the boys' future (Zhang et al., 2016). It remains unclear, though, why girls who had brothers were not also adversely affected by the migrant parents' focus on accumulating resources for the boys' future.

A second body of literature, from child psychology, draws on US and European data to investigate children's perceptions of Parents' Differential Treatment (PDT) of siblings in the allocation of resources and chores, as well as parental time, affection and discipline. This literature finds that children have a strong sense of fairness in how they are treated vis-à-vis siblings, with their perceptions varying by the meanings that they bring to interpreting these differences. For instance, some research finds that children were more likely to accept PDT if they saw fairness in terms of each child's needs rather than in terms of equality per se, but when a merit lens was used to judge fairness, a disfavoured child experienced less close family relationships and lower self-esteem (Lerner, 1974; McHale and Pawletko, 1992; Kowal and Kramer, 1997; Kowal et al., 2002; Feinberg et al., 2003). This literature further finds children's interpretations of PDT varied by their age, the quality of family relationships and the dimension of PDT in question.

Hardly any studies have examined the influence of family gender beliefs on children's experiences of PDT. An exception is a study conducted among Mexican American families (McHale et al., 2005). It finds that gender beliefs embedded in family culture affected distributional practices such that when parents held more traditional gender beliefs, older brothers with younger sisters performed fewer chores while older sisters with younger brothers enjoyed fewer privileges. It further finds that in families with a strong culture of *familialism* children were more likely to interpret distributional differences in terms of parental benevolence or the needs of the favoured child rather than parental favouritism. This finding is instructive for understanding children's views of distributional differences in rural China because cultural values articulated through a lens of filial piety likewise stress family members' obligations, interests and needs.

In this chapter, I draw on the aforementioned insights from these literatures to explore two interlinked topics. Firstly, I examine *why* family-based responsibilities, needs and interests are *gendered* in the sociocultural context of rural China, and of Anhui and Jiangxi in particular, and how they become reconfigured by wider demographic, cultural and institutional changes, including migration. Secondly, I look at children's *everyday* experiences of gendered distributional differences in *multilocal* families. This entails exploring

98   Boys, Girls and Distribution in Striving Families

children's responses to gendered distributional differences, and the implications of their responses for the families' distributional practices.

The remainder of the discussion proceeds as follows. Section 4.1 probes why parents strive to provide sons with money for education and housing while usually only supporting daughters economically up until the point of their graduation, and how children perceive these differences. Section 4.2 discusses the influence of children's gender on their actual and perceived access to everyday items and the effects of parental migration on the children's perceptions of these daily distributional practices. Section 4.3 examines changes in boys' and girls' involvement in household and farming chores arising from parental migration alongside the influences of other concurrent changes such as rising educational competition, an expansion in rural boarding schools, and agricultural mechanisation. I reveal that even as gender beliefs affected families' distributional practices, the significance of children's gender for the parent–child relationship was nevertheless changing as part of a wider shift towards gender equality in child-raising practices (Hannum, Kong and Zhang, 2009; Huang, 2012; Shi, 2017a). At the same time, though, because of variations in how these changes played out across individuals, families and geographic localities, there was no singular experience of being a 'left-behind' boy or girl.

4.2   Children's Gender and the Family Migration Project

4.2.1   Sons and Daughters in the Rural Chinese Family

In the rural Chinese family system, males and females occupy distinct positions linked to their gendered obligations. Chiefly, a male is connected to his family vertically, and grows up knowing that he must continue his descent line by having a son and looking after his parents in their old age (Baker, 1979; Fang, 2015). To prepare for these responsibilities, he is raised to forge an independent path beyond the home (Chen and Liu, 2012). By contrast, a female is connected to her family horizontally as a daughter who will marry out and later as a wife who has married in (Wolf, 1972; Fang, 2015). She grows up learning to depend on family relationships, to help her mother in the home, and to anticipate carrying out caring duties in her future roles as wife, mother and daughter-in-law (Bond cited in Chen and Liu, 2012: 487). A married woman may provide elder care to her parents if her circumstances permit, but her support to her parents is a private matter rather than a public moral obligation as is the case for sons (Miller, 2004; Hu, 2017).

Owing to males' pivotal role in family reproduction, even as rural parents love their sons and daughters, they place more *value* on sons (Yan, 2003) and have often felt obligated to raise at least one son (Greenhalgh and Li, 1995;

4.2 Children's Gender and the Family Migration Project

Choi and Peng, 2016: 71).[1] The starkest indication of parents' need to have a son is distorted sex ratios at birth (SRB). Nationwide in 1990 there were 111 boys for every 100 girls, while during the early 2000s the SRB hovered at around 120. In the 1990s, China's SRBs were the most distorted in Anhui and Jiangxi provinces, exceeding 130 boys for every hundred girls (Attané, 2009). In 2010, the national SRB fell to 118. While the effectiveness of a Care for Girls public education campaign in reducing son preference, sex-selective abortions and SRBs was uncertain (Murphy, 2014b), socio-economic changes such as rising levels of education, agricultural mechanisation, industrialisation and increased labour force opportunities for women all contributed significantly to mitigating son preference (Murphy, Tao and Lu, 2011). Nevertheless, in 2010 SRBs remained high at 129 in Anhui and 123 in Jiangxi (Basten, 2012), though such high imbalances may omit a substantial number of unregistered female births (Kennedy and Shi, 2019). The SRB statistics also belie complexity in how rural parents treat their children. Specifically, low fertility increases the preciousness of all children such that once a girl joins her family, her parents invariably treat her well (Yan, 2003; Hannum, Kong and Zhang, 2009; Shi, 2017a).

Greater gender equality in child-raising practices notwithstanding, rural parents continue to expect to invest more overall in sons than in daughters across their lifetime (Gruijters, 2017; Hu, 2017). One reason is that in the absence of a robust welfare system, even as rural parents work for as long as they can to avoid burdening the middle generation (Pang, de Brauw and Rozelle, 2004), most rural parents still feel that ultimately they will need to rely on a son for their old-age livelihood. This perception of a need to rely on a son for elder care has persisted despite the fact that the gap between sons and daughters in the actual delivery of elder care has narrowed over time (Cong and Silverstein, 2008b; Hu, 2017). Indeed, many rural parents think that they must ensure that a son has resources *for which* and *with which* to show them gratitude in later years.

A further reason that rural Chinese parents expect to invest more in sons than daughters is that they need to help their sons marry. In the twenty-first century, this parental duty has become especially onerous because of inflation in the amount of money and the educational credentials that men need to attract a bride (Shi, 2017b): indeed, in Chinese popular culture, ideal grooms are wealthy and educated while ideal brides are beautiful (Jacka, Kipnis and Sargeson, 2013: 172). The inflation in the value of the economic and cultural 'capital' men need to be 'eligible' as grooms has been driven by a squeeze in

---

[1] Choi and Peng (2016) refer to an 'obligation to have sons.' Greenhalgh and Li (1995) explain that in the 1990s many rural parents desired to have a daughter and a son, though they needed to have at least one son. Meanwhile, research indicates that in the 2010s son preference was waning, albeit unevenly, across rural regions (Shi, 2017a; Shi, 2017b).

the marriage market exacerbated by three decades of SRB imbalances along-side economic marketisation. Demographers calculate that in 2020, among China's 'never-married population' – which they define as those aged fourteen to forty-nine years who have never been married – China will have 150 males for every 100 females. So, three never-married males will compete for two never-married females, a ratio projected to rise to 180 males for 100 females in 2030 and to reach nearly 200 males for 100 females by 2045 (Jiang, Feldman and Li, 2014).

Consistent with demographers' analyses (Jiang, Feldman and Li, 2014), the people we met in the fieldwork counties knew that the men most at risk of a lifetime of bachelorhood were rural, poor and uneducated. For instance, a sixty-six-year-old woman in Eastern County, Anhui, told us in the presence of her twelve-year-old grandson:

In our village, peoples' brains are stupid, and people are without ability, so we are poor, and that is why my [thirty-four-year-old] son is unmarried. Outside people look down on us (*kan bu guan*). Everyone now wants to live in the city and that needs a lot of money.

The pressure on rural Chinese parents to accumulate resources so that their son would be able to marry affected their migration strategies (see also Zhang, Chandola, Bécares et al., 2016). One study finds that in counties with high sex ratio imbalances, the parents of sons were more likely to engage in off-farm work including jobs for which they migrated, and to do riskier but more lucrative jobs, for instance jobs in construction and jobs involving exposure to hazardous materials (Wei and Zhang, 2011b). Another study reports that in rural households, the presence of one or two sons versus only one daughter increased the number of hours the adults worked in the off-farm sector, raising the household income (Knight, Li and Deng, 2010). A further study reveals that in counties with high sex ratio imbalances, parents of sons migrated to improve the next generation's marriage prospects while sex-ratio-induced migration spilled over to sonless families by other channels, thereby increasing aggregate migration rates (Sun, 2012).

4.3 Parents' Views on Children's Gender and Family Striving Goals

Parents we met from Anhui and Jiangxi all wanted to ensure that their children would be *recognised* as individuals of worth within the education system, job markets and marriage markets. But even as the parents wanted to invest in their sons and daughters, they also perceived that boys and girls needed different overall investments, with implications for their striving goals and for how the children understood their parents' migration. In the following, I discuss firstly how parents in the fieldwork counties and in different families viewed the help

4.3 Parents' Views on Children's Gender and Family Striving Goals   101

that they needed to give their sons and daughters with housing and education. I then examine the children's perceptions of how their gender affected their parents' striving goals. For reference, Table 4.1 indicates the numbers of children and their gender in the families of the 109 children we interviewed. It shows that most families had no more than two children while just over half the families had a child of each gender.

4.3.1 Parents' Views about Housing for Sons

The parents we met all felt obligated to assist their sons with housing costs to help them attract a bride and to give them a foundation for their future marriage. Across China, this social obligation on the parents of sons has underpinned a correlation between sex ratio distortions and a high domestic savings rate as well as inflation in the real estate market (Wei and Zhang, 2011a). Nevertheless, there were differences in families' approaches to helping their sons with housing. Chiefly, the adults in the families we visited varied in their thoughts about *where* and *when* to invest in housing for sons, reflecting a combination of local and family conditions. In general, rural adults differed in their views about whether to prioritise building a new house in the village or even in the township versus buying an apartment in the county seat, and they also differed about whether they thought that the family needed to build a new house in the village at all.

Table 4.1 *Sibling composition of the families of 109 child respondents (Number)*

Family composition	At least one parent has migrated	Both parents at home	One parent has died	Total
One boy	15	6		21
Two boys	5	3		8
One girl	8	0		8
Two girls	7	3		10
Three girls	1	0		1
One boy and one girl	37	15	2^+	54
3–4 Children of mixed genders	4	2	1^*	7
Total	77	29	3	109

[*] Mother was a migrant

[+] In one case, the father had died, and the mother was a migrant with no family contact. In the other case, the mother had died, and the father was a returned migrant.

In the two Jiangxi counties, adults mostly thought that they needed to build a new house in their village even if they were also saving to buy an apartment in a township or in the county seat. This was because they saw a house in the village as anchoring the patrilineal family to the ancestral land, and as a source of practical and emotional reassurance for the future: it was a place to which migrants could return in the event of illness, injury, tiredness and pregnancy, in the early years of parenting and in old age. During the betrothal process young women and their families would usually visit their fiancés' villages to 'look at the house' (*kan fangzi*) to see their future in-laws' economic conditions and the quality of the house where they would stay at some points in the lifecycle, for instance after giving birth. A new house also gave status to families when migrants returned to their villages for Chinese New Year, and it was additionally a way for the middle generation to reassure their elders that they were progressing. In the Jiangxi fieldwork counties, patrilineal 'clan consciousness' was especially strong, evidenced in the physical presence of village ancestral halls. In Tranquil County, the significance of a village house to a family's status within and beyond the patrilineal network even fuelled a local fashion of building a third storey that stayed empty, referred to colloquially as a *dianzhui ceng*, or 'display floor', as shown in Figure 4.1.

Figure 4.1 New houses in a village in Tranquil County, Jiangxi

4.3 Parents' Views on Children's Gender and Family Striving Goals   103

People in the Anhui counties were much less concerned than people in the Jiangxi counties about building new houses in their villages. Even as clan identification was strong in the Anhui counties, it did not have the same intensity or visual expression in villages in central eastern Anhui as it did in the villages of the Jiangxi counties (Tang and Cheng, 2014). I saw some newly constructed houses in villages in Western County, but they were not as numerous or as big as in the Jiangxi villages. In one village I visited in Western County, house-building was also not possible because the houses shared the same traditional style and neighboured each other within a single compound. Several people in Western County villages said that their family planned to buy an apartment in the county seat when a child reached junior high or senior high school. Mostly, though, people from Western County were content to make modest improvements to their existing houses in the village by, for instance, buying water heaters, electric showers and solar panels, as shown in Figure 4.3, and building kitchen extensions with tiled floors and gas stoves. Some left-behind teenagers and elderly people even said that living in a big new house would make them feel even lonelier and that their existing houses were comfortable enough.

People in Eastern County stood out, though, for seldom building new houses in their villages or investing substantially in improvements to their village houses because their eyes were fixed firmly on the county seat or even on the neighbouring provincial capital of Hefei. A man who had returned temporarily to Eastern County with an injured leg explained:

Now in our village many people have bought a new house in the county seat. We Chinese are like that. We want to make sure our sons are doing great … I feel great pressure when I see what others have done for their sons … Our burden is so heavy. We've seen others buy houses. Our son will need to find a wife and we still haven't bought a house for him.

The ubiquity of this man's view in his county was reflected in the rural landscape: I saw hardly any of the partially and newly constructed two- and three-storey houses in Eastern County villages that dotted villages in the other fieldwork counties, especially the two Jiangxi counties. Figure 4.2 shows a typical village scene in Eastern County with old houses dominating the landscape.

The trend of rural people buying apartments in the county seat of Eastern County or even in the neighbouring city of Hefei was underpinned by a mix of particular regional geographic, real estate market and economic conditions. Hefei was one of only three inland cities in China that managed to sustain double-digit GDP growth during 2005–2015, achieved through an ambitious industrial development strategy. This strategy incorporated real estate development as a core component, supported by an increase in housing stock, an

Figure 4.2 Typical village scene in Eastern County, Anhui, with no newly built houses

easing of down payments, reduced mortgage interest rates and *hukou* conversion criteria more favourable than in other Chinese cities (Liu, 2017).

Local real estate prices were another influence on family deliberations about housing, with people feeling greater urgency to buy an apartment in the county seat if they sensed that prices were rising and that it was 'now or never', as was the case in Eastern County. In 2015, the average cost of an apartment in the county seat of Eastern County was 5,850 *yuan* per square metre, rising to over 11,000 *yuan* per square metre by 2018. Prices in the other three counties were lower and flatter. In 2015 the average cost of an apartment in the county seat of Western County was 5,100 *yuan* per square metre, rising to 7000 *yuan* by 2018, with demand over the later 2010s increasing in response to regional economic development and the high-speed rail links mentioned in Chapter 2. By contrast, in the Jiangxi fieldwork counties, the cost of an apartment in the county seat in 2015 was approximately 4000 *yuan* per square metre, stagnating at that level throughout the 2010s. An oversupply of housing stock and economic malaise, as well as severe air and water pollution in Jade County and the geographic remoteness of Tranquil County had kept the prices low relative to the two Anhui counties.

4.3 Parents' Views on Children's Gender and Family Striving Goals   105

Migrant parents of sons also varied in their thoughts about *if* and *when* to buy an urban property, with the local housing culture, the local real estate market and family economic status intersecting to inform their thoughts. In Western County, Anhui, and in the two Jiangxi counties many parents in farmer-migrant families thought that they would make do with a house in the village because the cost of just one square metre of urban housing was more than an average migrant worker earned in a month. By contrast, in Eastern County, people did not usually build in the village even if it was doubtful that they could ever buy an apartment in the county seat. Some rural families turned to the private boarding schools in the county seat to give their children an urban-based education, and designated the purchase of an apartment in the county seat as a longer-term aspiration. Meanwhile, poor families in Eastern County either stayed in their old village houses with no intention to buy an urban property or else they incurred severe debts in order to buy in the county seat, with the members sometimes going hungry, a circumstance that resonates with a finding of poorer nutrition among left-behind boys compared with boys raised by both parents (Zhang, Chandola and Bécares, 2015) Additionally, in all four field-work counties, people in villages within easy commuting distance of a county seat felt a less-pressing need to buy an urban property than did people from more remote villages.

Parents' decisions about if and when to purchase an urban apartment could be further influenced by their return migration intentions. Some parents viewed an apartment in the county seat as an asset that could help them to establish an off-farm base for their post-migration livelihoods, while at the same time underwriting a son's life chances in the event that he failed to progress up the urban hierarchy through his own efforts. Additionally, a few parents' decisions about if and when to purchase property in the county seat signalled their intention to transfer a child from a rural school to a school in the county seat and for at least one migrant parent to return to 'accompany the studies' of the child (*peidu*). As mentioned in Chapter 2, though, the plans of some better-off rural families to buy an urban apartment were also partly in response to the priority given in the allocation of school places to children from families that owned property in the catchment area.

Parents' deliberations about buying an apartment in the county seat were further influenced by their sons' academic potential. As the academic potential of a child had often not become apparent at the primary school stage, parents usually thought that it was premature for them to buy an urban apartment on his behalf. But by the time a son had passed the first year of junior high school, parents could usually speculate with greater confidence about his chances for future success in milestone exams. Most parents who thought that their son could not make it to an academic-track senior high school or to university aspired to accumulate enough money to help him buy an apartment in a county seat, though some less well-off parents also thought to build a house in a local rural township with space below for a small business. By contrast, parents who thought that their son stood a chance of getting into university prioritised saving money for his future tuition, assuming that on graduation he would be able to find a good job and earn money to buy a house close to his workplace.

4.3.2 Parents' Views about Housing for Daughters

While parents wanted both their sons and daughters to live economically secure lives in the cities, parents did not feel the same obligation to help their daughters with housing that they did for sons. Some sonless parents said that not being obligated to provide housing for a son offered them consolation for the fact that they would need to rely on themselves for their future old-age economic support, with the long-term burdens that sons presented to rural parents causing some of them to increasingly see advantages in having just daughters (Shi, 2017b). For instance, in 2011, in Western County, the returnee father of an only daughter, then twelve-year-old Xinhui, told us that he would not build a new house because the family's cottage, shown in Figure 4.3, could

Figure 4.3 Xinhui's family's cottage in a village in Western County, Anhui

4.3 Parents' Views on Children's Gender and Family Striving Goals   107

adequately accommodate him and his wife in their old age. He later added: 'If I had to work hard for a son's house and marriage, wouldn't that be the same as having a daughter: no money for my old age?'

Nevertheless, parents' views about helping their daughters with housing were neither uniform nor immutable. During my return visits to the fieldwork counties in 2014 and 2015, I learned that some teenage girls' parents were thinking of helping them to buy an apartment. For instance, in September 2015, shortly after Xinhui, then sixteen years old, had transferred from junior high school to a nursing vocational school, she told me that her father had returned from Qingdao to accompany her when she had enrolled at her new school, and that he had promised to help her buy an apartment. He had also said that he hoped that as his only child, she would find stable work in a nearby city such as Hefei or Nanjing so that the family could finally live in closer proximity after years of separation. Parents with children of both genders likewise often wanted to help their daughters with the costs of housing.

A wish on the part of some rural parents to help their daughters with housing can be attributed to several factors. Firstly, as noted previously, falling family size increased the preciousness of all children to their parents, including girls. Next, owing to the socialisation of girls to be emotionally expressive, many parents felt closer to them than to their sons, such that they wanted to look after them (Chen and Liu, 2012; Shi, 2017a). Thirdly, parents knew that young women who entered marriage with some of their own property enjoyed higher status among their in-laws, and they wanted their often only daughters to be treated well. Fourthly, as the village houses of sonless parents are customarily inherited by nephews, the parents of only daughters had further incentive to help their own offspring with urban housing rather than invest in a village house.

Importantly too, when parents were or had been migrants, their migration histories affected their wishes to help their daughters with housing in two ways. Firstly, some migrants such as Xinhui's father regretted not having spent more time with their child or children when they were younger, and they wanted to compensate them – a form of reasoning that applied to children of both genders, but girls benefited too. Secondly, migrants who had worked for many years had often accumulated savings, giving them a means to act on their wish to help their daughters. Even so, parents' wish to help their daughters with housing did not drive their migration in the same way it did for sons.

4.3.3   Parents' Views of Educational Investment

Whereas parents said explicitly that they would contribute different amounts of money to sons' and daughters' housing, the parents we met insisted that they practised gender equality when it came to their children's education. Certainly, in the twenty-first century, rural parents' have favoured the academically strongest children with educational investment regardless of their gender: these are the children most likely to provide greater future financial support (Huang, 2012; Pei and Cong, 2020). Even so, the picture is complex, with parents' calculus for investing in their children's education also reflecting gender differences embedded in the patrilineal family system. Specifically, parents realise that if a daughter migrates for work, she may meet a migrant man from a distant province and marry far away from them. But if a daughter obtains a good education, she will have both greater inclination and greater means to keep in close contact with her parents, including ideally the ability to find decent *gongzuo* and a good husband in the county seat or a nearby city (Gruijters, 2017; Obendiek, 2017).

The interviews we conducted in rural Anhui and Jiangxi offer a different but compatible set of insights into the complexity of rural parents' attitudes to investing in boys' and girls' education. Specifically, parents' attitudes to investing in their children's education varied not just by the children's gender but also by the number, gender composition and birth order of their children. Parents we met who had a 'singleton son' or 'two sons' at school usually held very high aspirations for their education, while parents' expectations of older sons could sometimes be the most exacting. The exception was if an older boy's grades were obviously dire. Likewise, though, parents with a 'singleton daughter' or two daughters hoped that their children would excel at school. Indeed, the parents from six daughter-only families we visited expressed views such as: 'I have no sons so I just hope my daughter can study' and 'A daughter who can study is better than several useless sons'.

Parents of 'an older daughter and a younger son' also wanted their children to succeed in education regardless of their gender. Owing to the effects of the birth planning policies of previous years, the older daughter and younger son configuration appeared most often in our set of cases (forty-two out of the fifty-four mixed-gender two-child families). Some parents and caregivers in these families told us that if their eldest daughter could study well and then find a stable job (*gongzuo*) suitable for a young woman, for instance a teacher, a nurse, or an accountant, she would attract a higher *suzhi* husband and would be better able to help her brother with education and housing in the future. Conversely, six mothers with two or more children of different genders told us that they felt guilty that an eldest daughter had grown up when they had not been able to support her studies. These eldest daughters had migrated after dropping out of junior high school. Parents used the hardships experienced by their older daughters to remind their younger children about the preciousness of education.

Many parents of an 'older boy and a younger girl' configuration – twelve out of the fifty-four mixed-gender two-child families in our set of cases – likewise wanted both their children to obtain as much education as possible. Short et al. (2001) report that the parents of an older son and a younger daughter typically invested even more time and resources in their daughters than other parents because they had wanted a daughter so much that they had incurred a birth planning fine and the costs of raising her despite having a son. But even as the adults we met treasured their daughters, neither the adults nor the children ever mentioned an older brother helping to pay for his younger sister's education.

Parents with three or more children also wanted all their children to study. With one exception where the children were all girls, these families comprised children of both genders. In four families where at least one child had reached adulthood, the fathers had migrated to help the younger children stay in school for longer than the eldest child had done. But these parents also had to adapt their support for their children to their strained economic circumstances. For instance, in 2011, a mother of four children in Western County, Anhui, tearfully told us that the grades of her fourteen-year-old daughter, Lele, had fallen after she had realised it would be difficult for her migrant father to pay her fees. Even so, when we visited her family again in 2015, Lele's good student certificates decorated the reception room wall (shown in Figure 4.4). At this time, her

Figure 4.4 Lele's good student certificates in Western County, Anhui

father worked as a security guard. This job was less strenuous than his previous job as a decorator but paid less. Lele attended the only township-based senior high school I encountered, which charged lower fees than schools in the county seat. Her parents hoped that she would make it to a teachers' training college where the programme of study was shorter while she herself wanted to become an art teacher.

4.4   Children's Views of Their Parents' Striving Goals

Families' beliefs about the roles and attributes of males and females affected the family's gender-based expectations of the children, as well as the parents' views about what their children needed. Certainly, many children in Anhui and Jiangxi could glean that their gender affected what their parents intended to invest in them. Meanwhile, as predicted by a sociological PDT approach (McHale et al., 2005), gendered familial beliefs about the needs and roles of males and females also affected how the children interpreted their parents' intentions to invest in them, with these interpretations varying by individual and family factors. Children's age mattered in that it was mostly teenagers who mentioned to us gender differences in their parents' intentions for the support of children. Meanwhile, children's school grades, birth order and family income also affected how some children perceived their parents' intentions to support them.

Nearly all the teenage boys whom we met thought that their parents should support them economically, but as just noted, their grades and their families' income influenced their views. Academically high-performing boys from poorer families said that their parents' hard work for their studies was all they needed. For instance, when we interviewed one fifteen-year-old boy in Jade County, Jiangxi, after he had secured a place in the most prestigious senior high school, he stated:

I think my parents should not help me with a mortgage. They've supported me so much at school. I need to pay my own way as an adult – it would be shameful.

A few academically promising boys also said that they had explicitly told their parents not to save money for a house because education was their priority. By contrast, boys with no university prospects talked about the need to prepare a car and a house (*bei chefang*) to meet the expectations of modern young women. But their view about the extent to which their parents would be able to help them similarly varied by their families' circumstances.

Singleton girls and girls with sisters also perceived that their gender affected their parents' intentions to support them. For some girls, the absence of a boy in their family intensified their feeling of needing to excel academically: four teenage girls told us that they had overheard either a parent or a grandparent say

4.5 The Gendered Distribution of Everyday Resources to Children 111

that their family's prospects had been ruined by having neither a son nor a daughter who could study. These comments could be especially devastating for those girls whose migrant parents had been absent for long periods. Conversely, some girls such as Xinhui at age sixteen years noted that her parents had only her to invest their savings in. When I expressed surprise to Xinhui that her father planned to help her buy a house, she asked: 'Who else could he give his money to?'

In families with a child of each gender, children's perceptions of their parents' investments in them depended on circumstances. Some teenagers who had a sibling of the opposite gender told us that their parents invested in their own and their siblings' education equally. But usually the children in these families displayed similar levels of academic promise. Even so, several children noted that the parents planned to allocate additional money to the boy for housing and marriage. Most boys in these families thought that the parents' larger overall intended investment in them was justified because the parents wanted to give each sibling what they needed in life. They further noted that boys had a greater obligation than girls to support their parents in old age. By contrast, three teenage girls felt that their parents' intention to invest more in their brothers was unfair and 'out-dated'. They told us that they had learned about gender equality from television and school politics lessons. So, when conversations with parents turned to housing, they had jokingly asked about their share.

Some other children with a sibling of the opposite gender thought that their parents' overall investment in them and their sibling was equal. Some boys in these families did not seem to do as well at school as their sisters: five boys with an older sister talked about the sister's strong performance in senior high school. The additional funds that the parents planned to invest in these boys' housing and marriage were counterbalanced by their ongoing investment in the girls' education. For example, we met a fifteen-year-old boy in Eastern County, Anhui, whose parents were saving to build a house and premises for a small mechanics shop for him in the township. He did not want to endure the boot camp regime of a private boarding senior high school. Meanwhile, his elder sister attended a private senior high school in the county seat and his parents would pay her fees if she got a place at university. The boy said that his father had told him outright that he and his sister were equal in his eyes. Girls with two or three siblings similarly felt that their parents supported the children equally, though they too expected to help their brothers in the future.

4.5 The Gendered Distribution of Everyday Resources to Children

Children's gender not only affected their parents' intentions to invest in them, it could also affect the actual and perceived distribution of resources to them in

112   Boys, Girls and Distribution in Striving Families

everyday life. Admittedly, children's gender could influence both the actual and perceived distribution of resources to them, regardless of their parents' migration status. However, parental migration could complicate the picture. Specifically, parental migration could influence: the amount of resources available for distribution; intra-family distributional practices; and how the children 'did gender' in daily life – for instance, some girls studied extra hard or did more chores – with implications for adult–child relationships and families' distributional practices. Moreover, some children's experiences of multilocal striving family could affect if or how they perceived a link between their gender and distributional practices within their families.

4.5.1   Distribution of Pocket Money and Gifts

Before looking at children's own accounts of how they perceived and responded to the distribution of everyday resources along gendered lines, I first contextualise the children's perceptions by mapping the *actual* distribution of two items for which I had data from the 2010 Summer Survey: pocket money and gifts. Admittedly, cross-sectional data fails to capture boys' and girls' receipt of pocket money *before* and *after* their parents' migration and so does not indicate the effects of parental migration per se.[2] But it can still flag up whether gender differences existed among children in families differently configured by migration.

In the Summer 2010 survey, the sample median for children's reports of the monthly amount of pocket money they received was 15 *yuan*, while 26 per cent of the sample of 1,000 children received no pocket money. Figure 4.5 presents a violin plot showing the distribution of pocket money to the children by their gender.[3] The white circles on the figure mark the median. The median marks show that children's receipt of pocket money barely differs by their gender. Moreover, a two-sample t-test of means reveals that any difference between the genders is not statistically different from zero ($p = 0.36$).

The pocket money distribution can be investigated further in a multivariate setting. The dependent variable is a child's reported pocket money per month. The distribution is highly skewed, so each pocket money report has been transformed by taking its logarithm to the base ten plus one.[4] The unit of analysis is a child in the Summer 2010 survey. We estimated the distribution of pocket money using ordinary least squares regression. We entered a dummy

---

[2] Neil Ketchley ran the regressions and produced the violin plot and the tables. I am deeply grateful to him. In this subsection, 'we' refers to Neil Ketchley and me.

[3] As the distribution is highly skewed, the y-axis is transformed by taking its logarithm to the base ten plus one.

[4] These results are robust to alternative transformations including taking its quintiles, as well as taking its deciles and estimating it using an ordinal logit model.

4.5 The Gendered Distribution of Everyday Resources to Children

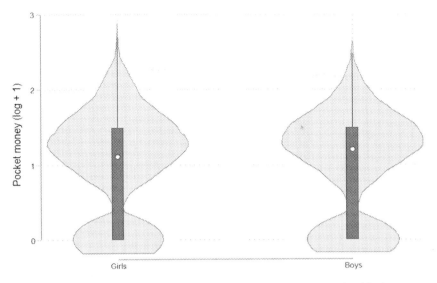

Figure 4.5 Violin plot of the amount of pocket money received by boys and girls

variable for a child's gender (males are coded as '1'), a categorical variable for which parent is a migrant (the reference category is 'both parents at home'), and a dummy variable for whether a child has siblings (children with siblings are coded as '1'). We also entered a series of control variables that could confound the amount of pocket money a child received. We entered a variable measuring the number of years of education received by both parents transformed to the square root, and variables recording a child's age and age squared. A core control variable is household income as reported by the caregiver, transformed by taking its logarithm to the base ten. Robust standard errors account for heteroskedasticity.

Table 4.2 shows the results. Boys received on average slightly less pocket money than girls, but this is not statistically significant ($p = 0.22$). Compared to a family where both parents were at home, children of lone migrant fathers received less pocket money than did other children, which may be because the at-home mothers used remittances to buy what their children needed in daily life such as snacks or study items. Meanwhile, children with one or more siblings received, on average, less pocket money compared to singleton children. Turning to the control variables, a child's age seems to have no effect, while children of more educated parents received more pocket money, though this is not quite statistically significant ($p = 0.14$). As expected,

114 Boys, Girls and Distribution in Striving Families

Table 4.2 *OLS regression of pocket money distribution to children by gender and parents' migration status*

	(OLS) DV: Pocket money
Sex	−0.0552 (0.0450)
Which parent has migrated: Lone father	−0.210[**] (0.0687)
Lone mother	0.0983 (0.135)
Both out	−0.0171 (0.0596)
Divorced/widowed	0.0145 (0.0827)
Child's age	0.0267 (0.140)
Child's age squared	0.00179 (0.00551)
Child has siblings	−0.151[**] (0.0478)
Parents' years of education (sqrt)	0.0526 (0.0362)
Household income (Log 10)	0.240[***] (0.0718)
Constant	−0.584 (0.924)
Observations	831
R-squared	0.088

Robust standard errors in parentheses
P-values: *** $p<0.001$, ** $p<0.01$, * $p<0.05$

4.5 The Gendered Distribution of Everyday Resources to Children 115

children from households with more income received more pocket money. Overall, these results confirm for rural China a trend observed in China's cities, namely that fertility decline increases parents' investment in their children irrespective of their gender (Fong, 2002), but it contrasts with an observation in the United Kingdom of a pocket money premium favouring boys (Weale, 2017).

Qualitative data and survey data on gifts present a picture similar to that of pocket money. The left-behind children we met were not showered with gifts. Rather, they received gifts for special occasions such as Chinese New Year or birthdays, parents' return visits or the achievement of good grades. Usually the gifts were modest items such as clothes, shoes, watches, toys and sweets, and items to support study such as books, stationery and study machines. In the quantitative analysis of children's receipt of gifts by their gender, the unit of analysis is a child surveyed in 2010, but we confine attention to children with at least one parent who had migrated without them. After taking into account missing data for independent variables, the sample reduces to 553. The dependent variable is whether a child has received a gift. As this is a dummy variable, we used logistic regression. We entered the same variables as tested in the above analysis. Table 4.3 shows the results. Again, children's gender has no discernible effect: boys are slightly more likely to receive a gift, but this does not approach statistical significance ($p=0.73$). Again too, children whose fathers had migrated alone were less likely to receive gifts compared to children where both parents had migrated. Meanwhile, children with siblings were less likely to receive gifts, though this is not statistically significant at $p<0.05$.

4.5.2 Perceived Distribution of Everyday Resources

Even as the aforementioned quantitative analysis indicates that rural Chinese parents practised gender equality in the allocation of pocket money and gifts to their children, many children whom my research assistants and I interviewed nevertheless *perceived* gender-based differences in the distribution of everyday items among the children in their family, with these items including food, treats, and the use of the television remote control. Children's views about the distribution of these items reveal aspects of gender difference not captured by data on pocket money and gifts, while also offering a unique lens into children's subjective experiences of daily life and gendered relationships in their families.

In the following, I draw on the accounts of children who lived in the same household as an opposite-gender sibling, because these children had the strongest basis for drawing gendered comparisons of differential treatment. Out of the forty-three left-behind children who had at least one opposite-gender

116   Boys, Girls and Distribution in Striving Families

Table 4.3 *Logistic regression on children's receipt of gifts from migrant parents by child's gender*

	(Logistic regression) DV: Child receives gift
Sex	0.0689 (0.196)
Which parent has migrated: Lone father	−0.716[***] (0.199)
Lone mother	−0.0182 (0.529)
Child's age	0.243 (0.614)
Child's age squared	−0.00494 (0.0246)
Child has siblings	−0.259 (0.205)
Parents' years of education (sqrt)	0.240 (0.164)
Household income (Log 10)	−0.0270 (0.374)
Constant	−1.588 (4.054)
Observations	553

Robust standard errors in parentheses
P-values: *** $p<0.001$, ** $p<0.01$, * $p<0.05$

sibling, nearly half of them ($n = 21$) talked about parental gender bias in the distribution of everyday items. Importantly, though, it was not only left-behind children who perceived gendered distributional inequality between them and a sibling: out of seventeen children who lived with both their parents *and* had an opposite-gender sibling, five of these children mentioned gendered distributional inequalities.

4.5 The Gendered Distribution of Everyday Resources to Children   117

Crucially, though, the migration of parents inflected the significance of gendered distributional practices for the children. The accounts of the subset of forty-three left-behind children indicates that if and how they perceived gender differences in their treatment vis-à-vis their siblings reflected not only actual distributional practices but also how they felt about their parents' migration, their relationships with at-home caregivers, and their school grades. Conversely, children's feelings about these aspects of their multilocal striving lives could affect if or how they perceived gendered differences in resource distribution among siblings.

A fourteen-year-old boy from Tranquil County, Jiangxi, who we met in 2011, was one of seven boys who told us that a parent favoured him over a sister because of his gender. At the time of our interview, his fifteen-year-old sister attended a vocational school in a nearby prefectural capital. Meanwhile, his parents had worked for ten years in a shoe factory in Fujian province but had recently returned home to care for him while he prepared for the *zhongkao* exam. The boy explained:

My parents love me more than *jiejie* (older sister). They get me whatever I want, but with *jiejie* there is always some reservation. I will need to look after my parents because when *jiejie* is older she will have her own life. Plus her studies are not very good, so my parents depend on me to do well in my studies and get a good job.

Another boy, a twelve-year-old from Western County, Anhui, likewise felt favoured over his sister. When we met him in 2011 he and his eighteen-year-old sister lived with their seventy-four-year-old grandfather while their parents sold lettuce in Kunshan. He explained:

My parents favour me because I am a boy. They buy me more things than *jiejie*. I am happy to see that I get more things. *Yeye* likes me best too. He hides the good things and gives them to me when I come home at lunchtime because *jiejie* is still at school.

However, when we visited him again in 2015, his circumstances had changed. He lived in a spartan room in his maternal aunts' house because his grandfather was too ill to look after him. Subdued, he no longer felt that anyone particularly cared for him.

While some children felt favoured, other children felt disfavoured. Eight left-behind girls said that their parents preferred a brother to them: in two cases the brother was older and in six cases he was younger. Moreover, three girls who lived with two returnee parents said that their parents favoured their younger brother, the birth of whom had prompted the parents' return. Six girls thought that their parents' favouritism of their brother was unfair. They described incidents that had occurred when their parents had visited or when they had visited their parents, for instance when a parent had hit or scolded them because they had protested at their brother's monopoly of an electric fan or television remote control, or at his snatching of items from them. Such incidents could cause the girls to feel deep despair if they occurred after long periods of parent–child separation. Nevertheless, in explaining such differential treatment some girls referred to their brother's younger age either concurrently with or as an alternative to an explanation that referenced parents' son preference. The girls thereby resembled some other children we met who talked about a younger sibling's greater 'need' for care to explain differential treatment, including one boy with an infant sister and several children who had same-gender siblings.

It was not only girls but also boys who identified themselves as the disfavoured party. Specifically, three boys said that an at-home mother favoured their sisters over them, and in two of these cases the sisters were older. When we met one of the boys, twelve-year-old Xinhao from Jade County, Jiangxi, in 2011, he lived with his farmer mother while his father worked on construction sites in Beijing. At the time, his sixteen-year-old sister boarded at a key-point senior high school in the county seat and returned home fortnightly. Xinhao, as well as the other boy with an older sister, explained his parents' high regard for his sister in terms of her attributes of studiousness, thoughtfulness, sensitivity, warmth and a love of conversation. Xinhao said:

My mother cooks good food when *jiejie* comes home. Last time she killed a chicken. My sister and I will both look after my parents when they are old because my sister is filial and thoughtful. She's good at cheering *mama* up.

These two boys also resembled some other boys who explained their parents' high regard for their sisters with reference to their sisters' gendered attributes even as these other boys thought that their parents treated the siblings equally.

Some girls had clearly internalised social expectations of their gendered attributes in ways that affected their claim on family resources and their parents' regard for them, with the girls taking it on themselves to be frugal. For instance, four mothers particularly talked about how their daughters understood the hardship of home in a way that their younger sons did not, with their daughters proactively economising on food. This dynamic could be seen in a text message that Xinhao's mother received from her daughter, which read:

'Mama, I got my hardship student subsidy of 350 *yuan* today. I used it to buy milk. I'm sending you 85 *yuan* for vegetables. Pay attention to your health and get nourishment. Don't work too hard.'

Similarly, a mother from Western County, Anhui, whose migrant husband gambled, told us that her sixteen-year-old daughter only ate noodles soaked in an old plastic cola bottle because she was unwilling to spend four *yuan* on a meal at school. The mother wept, saying:

4.5 The Gendered Distribution of Everyday Resources to Children   119

I told her that she suffers because her mum and dad have no ability, and she replied: 'Mother, don't worry, I will work hard.' My son [aged twelve] does not understand things in the way my daughter does.

However, our interviewees also included two girls and one boy who thought that the opposite-gender parent favoured them while the same-gender parent favoured their younger sibling. One of these girls was Jingjing, discussed in Chapters 3 and 6. Jingjing told us that whenever her father visited home, he brought back treats for both her and her brother. However, he talked to her on the phone for longer and he spent more time playing cards and chatting with her on his return visits. He also put more credit on her mobile phone than on her brother's. Jingjing's awareness of her father's affection for her made her miss him even more while consoling her in the face of loneliness, poverty and low school grades. Additionally, another girl said that her at-home mother gave more attention to her younger brother, but that her migrant father talked with her more and brought back more treats for her, while a boy felt that his at-home mother favoured him but on return visits his migrant father gave more treats and attention to his younger sister.

As mentioned though, the other half of the left-behind children with an opposite-gender sibling mentioned no PDT of the siblings. Several children observed that whenever they visited their parents or whenever their parents visited them, they gave good food to both (or all) the siblings. These parents' egalitarian treatment of the siblings affirmed to the children that 'we each belong to our parents' even as migration had forced the family members to live apart. Three girls who had two or more siblings including a younger brother also observed that the treats the migrant parents brought back were always apportioned equally in the family, while two of the girls, including Lele mentioned earlier, noted that their mothers especially appreciated their companionship in their fathers' absence. Conversely, a few children came from families where parental migration and sometimes also the loss of a parent had generated such strain that they felt as though they and their siblings were equally lacking in support and care, regardless of their gender.

In addition, several children mentioned that they were disfavoured vis-à-vis a co-resident cousin. Two girls complained that their grandparents favoured a male cousin in the distribution of treats and the arbitration of fights because he was a boy. However, three girls noted that their grandmothers had raised their younger cousins – two male cousins and one female cousin – since their birth, while the girls themselves had arrived to live with their grandmothers at a later age, so that the grandmothers felt closer to the younger child. In two further cases, differences in the treatment of the children stemmed from the caregivers' preference for an adult in the middle generation. For instance, at age fifteen, one boy said that his paternal grandmother used to favour his uncle's children in the

120   Boys, Girls and Distribution in Striving Families

allocation of food while his own father – a younger middle son – had been crippled by polio, so both he and his father were less favoured. Furthermore, one girl thought that her grandmother gave the best food to her younger male cousin. For her part, the indignant grandmother complained that her oldest daughter-in-law had accused her of favouring her younger daughter-in-law and grandson.

4.5.3   Parental Favouritism When Siblings Live Apart

Some children's experience of differential treatment in their families arose from their parents' decisions about which sibling to take with them to the city and which sibling to leave behind. According to the All-China Women's Federation report based on census data, in 2010 the ratio of boys to girls in the 'left behind' population aged nought to fourteen years was lower than for the overall rural population despite an underlying masculinisation of this cohort (ACWF, 2013). This finding is consistent with other analyses of data for 2010 indicating that migrant parents were more likely to take sons with them to the city (Connelly, Roberts and Zheng, 2011; Duan, Lü, Guo et al., 2013). A similar dynamic existed in the fieldwork counties: in the 2010 Summer Survey, out of 1,010 children, 109 or 11 per cent had once accompanied their parents to the city and attended school there, and of these 58.7 per cent were boys. Nevertheless, reflecting a wider trend towards gender equality in rural child-raising practices, national data indicates that by 2015 the gender gap among school-age migrant children had nearly closed (Chan and Ren, 2018).

In explaining the sex ratio imbalance among school-age migrant children in the late 2000s and into the early 2010s, some commentators refer to the likely effects of parental son preference (ACWF, 2013). This explanation is convincing. But several left-behind children we met also offered other explanations, providing a more nuanced picture of families' deliberations around the migration of some children and the non-migration of others. In the following, I refer to the insights of three girls and two boys who each had a younger brother living in the city; one boy and one girl who each had a younger sister living in the city; three girls whose younger brothers were imminently about to move to the city; and several children whose siblings had previously lived with their parents in the city before returning to the countryside.

When explaining their parents' decisions about sibling migration, the six girls we met whose brothers lived in the city or whose brothers were imminently moving to the city all referred to their younger siblings' greater need for parental care concurrently with or as an alternative to the explanation of parental son preference. In highlighting sibling need alongside or instead of parental gender bias, these girls echoed some girls' explanations of gender differences in the distribution of everyday items within their families, as

4.5 The Gendered Distribution of Everyday Resources to Children   121

discussed previously. For instance, in 2011, a twelve-year-old girl from Jade County, Jiangxi, explained that her parents had worked in Shenzhen since she was a few months old, leaving her with her grandmother. Then three years ago, her mother returned home to give birth to *didi* (a younger brother). The girl said:

> Of course *mama* prefers *didi*. '*Favour males, overlook females*' (*zhongnan qingnü*) is typical in the countryside. They give good things to *didi* but I don't mind because he's younger so he needs more care. They've said that they'll take *didi* out with them, one working the day shift and one working the night shift. They'll take *didi* because he's younger than me and so he needs more care than me.

Importantly, though, four of these girls did not refer to parents' son preference when explaining their parents' decision about sibling migration and referred only to their younger brother's need.

A couple of the girls also noted that their parents had taken or would take their younger brother to the city with them because he was too naughty for *nainai* (grandmother) to *guan*. A view that young boys are naughty resonates with survey research showing that in rural China boys misbehave more than girls, and that children misbehave more when their parents or fathers have migrated without them (Leng and Park, 2010; Murphy, Zhou and Tao, 2016; Chen, Liang and Ostertag, 2017). Again, these girls highlighted their brothers' need when explaining the PDT of them and their sibling.

In 2013, a fifteen-year-old girl from Eastern County offered yet another explanation for parents' decisions about sibling migration. She said that in Shanghai the policies limiting migrant children's access to public schools had changed in time for her seven-year-old brother but not for her. If her brother enrolled in a Shanghai public school that year, he would have spent seven years in the urban education system by the time he turned fifteen, enough for him to attend an urban public senior high school. Owing to the large number of rural families consisting of older sisters and younger brothers, this aspect of municipal policy could over time become an unintentional source of gendered educational inequalities among some rural-origin children.

Differences in the amount of time that siblings spent with their migrant parents could also produce differential treatment. Specifically, the close relationship that a migrant child could build with migrant parents could override a child's gender as the basis for favouritism. This dynamic could be seen in Fangfang's family. A few months after his birth, Fangfang's parents migrated to Guangzhou leaving him with his grandmother. Then, when he was ten years old, his father returned home but as Fangfang felt estranged from him, he ran to his grandmothers' house. Two years later, Fangfang's mother also returned, commuting from the village to work long days in Jade County's manufacturing zone. After a year, though, Fangfang still barely said a word to either parent.

122 Boys, Girls and Distribution in Striving Families

The father described the relationship between him and his son as 'indifferent' (*wusuowei*) and 'without feeling' (*meiyou ganqing*). By contrast, he chuckled when explaining that his six-year-old daughter talked to him incessantly and followed him everywhere. He attributed the closer bond between him and his daughter to the fact that she had lived with him and his wife in Guangzhou from her birth till she was eighteen months old, and then she had lived with him again after his return to the village, by which time she was four years old.

4.6 Gender and Children's Work

4.6.1 Gender Variation in Children's Workloads

A final topic to be explored in this chapter is gender variation in the distribution of household and farming chores to children, and the implications of parental migration for this. In their analysis of data from a survey conducted in 2004 covering 4,400 households in six provinces in China, Chang, Dong and MacFail (2011) report that owing to a 'gender substitution effect' when parents migrated, girls performed disproportionately more chores than boys to alleviate the strain on household labour supply. Specifically, the authors observe that for children aged seven to fourteen years, when one parent migrated, girls' extra contribution to domestic chores equalled 5.3 hours per week, and when two parents migrated, this rose to an extra 10.6 hours per week. The authors also report that although children's overall rate of participation in farming was low, parental migration increased both boys' and girls' involvement. In a similar vein, Hu (2015) finds that in rural China a gendered substitution effect underpinned girls' greater work burdens even in families where both parents lived at home because the mothers' earning activities decreased their share of housework time. Hu (2015) therefore argues that girls compensate for, rather than model, their mother's decreased share of housework time.

My fieldwork data from Anhui and Jiangxi was collected more than a decade after Chang, Dong and MacFail's (2011) survey was conducted, and offers some different insights that can be interpreted in the light of their and Hu's (2015) 'gendered substitution effect' thesis. Chiefly, my data support the view that a gendered division of household labour shapes children's involvement in chores, but I also find that parental migration and structural changes operating concurrently with parental migration *diluted* gender differences in *some* children's involvement in chores. There are two counter-directional dimensions to how a dilution in gender differences in chores played out. Firstly, parental migration created conditions that required *increasing* numbers of both girls *and boys* to perform self-care and family-care tasks. Secondly, a rise in educational aspirations, the expansion of rural boarding schools and accelerated agricultural mechanisation,

4.6 Gender and Children's Work

combined to *mitigate* the impact of parental migration on the work burdens of some *boys and girls*. In the following, I examine these two broad trends in turn while qualifying that my aim is not to celebrate these shifts as signs of gender equality, but to tease out substantive changes in the children's lives.

4.6.2   Living Conditions Requiring Boys and Girls to Do Chores

In the 2010s, large-scale parental migration created conditions that required many *boys* as well as girls to undertake self-care and family-care tasks. Whenever children talked to my research assistants and me about how their daily life differed from that of their classmates who lived with both parents, they referred to chores. A response from a sixteen-year-old boy in Eastern County, Anhui, echoed a wider sentiment:

Other children's mothers cook and wash clothes for them, but I must do it all myself. I am more independent than others. I did not know how to cook before, but now I can cook simple things.

Similarly, when some children compared their life before and after their mothers' migration or their life before and after their mothers' return home, they referred to chores.

We also met several children who said that when they visited their migrant parents in the city during the summer holidays, from mid-July to mid-September, they did chores. In 2013, fifteen-year-old Wang Delun told us that when he went to Kunshan city, he cooked for his parents and washed their clothes because they did not return from work until after 9 p.m. He explained that doing chores helped him to dispel his boredom and made a change from watching television. Boys' involvement in housework may signal a relaxation in the gendered division of labour because they did chores that men in their home villages usually shunned. However, these boys also saw having to do chores as symptomatic of their mothers' unavailability, indicating that their involvement in domestic chores either preceded a change in gender beliefs or else was temporary.

Twenty-six out of the 109 children were socialised into doing chores not only by their parents' migration but also by boarding at school on weekdays, while a further fourteen children whose parents were both at home also boarded on weekdays. As discussed in Chapter 2, most boarders were in the Jiangxi subsample. Figures 4.6 and 4.7 show boys washing dishes and sweeping in shared school space. Many caregivers and teachers thought that children's involvement in such chores helped them to develop personal qualities such as self-reliance, orderliness, industriousness and cooperativeness that would help to prepare them for their future lives 'outside'. For instance, in 2010, a woman

Figure 4.6 Washing bowls at a primary school in Tranquil County, Jiangxi

Figure 4.7 Sweeping the playground in a junior high school in Jade County, Jiangxi

who had returned from Shenzhen to enrol her twelve-year-old son in a township primary school in Jade County, Jiangxi, explained:

I've told him that it is good that he lives at school. He can improve his living habits. He can improve his *suzhi*. When we work outside, the boss teaches us in the same way. For instance, the boss teaches those without *suzhi*. In the past, when we were in a large company, the boss would tell us to wash our things and tidy up. Like being in the army ... The school is also that way. I think it is good to teach children to do things. Then later when you go out, for instance to study, or wherever you go, even to work, no-one will say anything.

In seeing chores as facilitating children's personal development, these adults resembled many parents in Western countries (Goh and Kuczynski, 2014), the vastly different cultural and socio-economic context notwithstanding. For their

4.6 Gender and Children's Work

part, children accepted that looking after themselves and helping out were essential to 'being a person', regardless of their gender.

4.6.3   Constraints on Children's Work Burdens

While parental migration *increased some boys'* as well as girls' involvement in chores, other parallel influences also *limited* the extent to which *some girls* as well as boys participated in chores. Extrapolating from the 'gendered substitution effect' thesis mentioned earlier, one can infer that some girls may have benefited more than boys from influences limiting their availability for domestic chores. Meanwhile, both boys and girls would be likely to benefit from reductions to farming workloads. However, it is also possible that reduced farm workloads may have especially benefited some girls given that a 2011 survey of young migrant workers finds that females from families with larger land allocations obtained less education than other young migrant workers (Lyu and Chen, 2019). In the following, I discuss how the influences of rising educational aspirations, the expansion of boarding schools and agricultural mechanisation buffered *some* children against increases in domestic and farming chores when their parents had migrated without them.

Firstly, rising educational aspirations limited some children's participation in chores by informing their caregivers' ideas about what help they could ask for from the children. Support for this contention comes from survey-based White Papers showing that at an aggregate level left-behind children did only slightly more housework than children who lived with both their parents (On the Road to School, 2015), while a greater frequency in migrant parents' contact with their children by means of phone calls and visits significantly protected left-behind children from doing more housework (On the Road to School, 2017). Indeed, many grandparents stressed to us that they only ever asked their grandchildren for help with small chores because if the children's grades deteriorated, the middle generation would curse them.

The children's accounts of their involvement in housework corresponded with the claim of many caregivers: the children mostly reported doing 'minor' chores such as wiping the table, sweeping the floor, washing dishes, lighting the fire for cooking or heating water, as well as feeding chickens or pigs or weeding. Nevertheless, in the 2010 Summer Survey, approximately a quarter of boys and a third of girls reported regularly helping at home with the more substantial chores of cooking meals and washing clothes, but with no difference among the children by their parents' migration status. Admittedly, though, the survey did not record how much time children spent doing these chores so it may not have been sufficiently sensitive to detect differences among children. Additionally, of the 109 child interviewees, as the oldest sibling was often a girl it was common for them to look after younger siblings.

Boarding at school was yet another factor that reduced some children's availability for household chores on weekdays and during term-time. This effect of boarding can be seen in the changing household contributions of Puhua from Eastern County, Anhui. When we first met her in 2011, she was eleven years old. Her mother was blind, and her father worked on construction sites in northern cities but remitted little. Puhua told us that every morning she woke up at five, and in the dim light she cooked porridge for her family, taking care not to add too much salt. Next, she got her younger sister washed and dressed. When she returned home from school at 11:20 a.m. she helped to pick, wash and peel vegetables and light the fire for cooking, then after lunch she washed the dishes and wiped the table. She returned to school at 2:00 p.m., coming back home at 4:30 p.m. Once home, she helped with making cow pat fuel discs, weeding, preparing dinner, tidying and entertaining her younger sister. When we met Puhua again in 2013, she boarded at the township junior high school. Like other children whose caregiver had health problems, at this second meeting, Puhua lamented that she was only able to help her mother at the weekends.

Some children's work burdens were also mitigated by agricultural mechanisation. During 2006–2008, with the help of state subsidies, combine harvester contractors and tractor ploughs, known colloquially as 'steel cows' (*tieniu*), such as the one shown in Figure 4.8, became common in all the fieldwork counties, reducing the labour intensity of farming. Mechanisation notwithstanding, many rural children we met in the early 2010s still spent part of the summer holidays helping their families with the 'double snatch' (*shuangqiang*) when one crop is harvested, and another crop is planted in quick succession. Some children also helped their families with farming on the weekends. Children's help was especially valuable in the Jiangxi counties, where double-rice cropping generated a more critical timing pressure than a second crop of wheat, maize or cotton, as was common in the Anhui counties. However, consistent with Chang, Dong and MacFail's (2011) findings, only a minority of children in the fieldwork counties regularly farmed: in the 2010 Summer Survey, 9.1 per cent of left-behind boys, 8.2 per cent of boys living with both parents, 6.6 per cent of left-behind girls and 7.8 per cent of girls living with both parents said that they regularly farmed. Conversely, farming burdens could be heavy for children in families where at-home parents had taken on land vacated by migrant families, as Fangfang's returnee father had done: he farmed over 20 *mu*[5] with Fangfang helping him.

---

[5] *Mu* is a unit for the measure of land: 1 *mu* = 0.1647 acres = 0.0667 hectares.

4.6 Gender and Children's Work

Figure 4.8 A 'steel cow' in a village in Tranquil County, Jiangxi

4.6.4 Boys' and Girls' Interpretation of Doing Chores

Irrespective of gender differences in the chores that children did, boys and girls differed subtly in how they gave meaning to their contributions, reflecting the *gendered nature of familialism*. Broadly, when boys talked about chores, they often linked their parents' migration to their character development as young men, emphasising their independence and industriousness. At age thirteen, Zhangyong told us that he felt happy when once during the summer holidays his mother had remarked that he was now a 'grown-up young man' because of his efforts to wash his parents' clothes while they were at work. Meanwhile, a fifteen-year-old boy from Jade County noted that in the absence of another man in the family it had been up to him carry water for his grandmother and that his mother had praised him for his helpfulness. Both these boys felt valued by significant adults' recognition of the attributes that their help demonstrated. Many boys also dreamed about relieving their parents' and grandparents' work burdens in the future by ensuring that they would have enough money so that they would not need to work hard.

Girls similarly talked about self-reliance in relation to doing chores, but unlike the boys, they additionally emphasised intimacy. Specifically, several girls told us that they did household chores because they had an aptitude for looking after home (*gujia*) and caring for others (*zhaoguren*), and that they were more sensitive to the situation around them (*geng dongshi*) and to their family members' hardships than their brothers or male cousins (*geng liaojie jiali de kunnan*). As Oxfeld observes in a village in South China, because of mothers' migration, girls often learned how to cook from their grandmothers rather than from their mothers (Oxfeld, 2017: 61). Meanwhile, several girls, such as the girl pictured in Figure 4.9, also described the feeling of companionship that came when chopping vegetables or hanging out laundry alongside their mothers or grandmothers. Even so, girls resembled boys in dreaming about earning enough money to ensure that their parents and grandparents would not need to work hard, but some girls also talked about caring for at-home parents or migrant parents directly, for instance, by preparing tea for them or massaging their aching shoulders.

Figure 4.9 A girl in Tranquil County, Jiangxi, whose mother migrated, helps her grandmother

Conclusion

Conclusion

Rural Chinese families' *gendered culture of familialism* affected what parents in migrant families wanted to provide for their children. In rural regions in Anhui and Jiangxi, the gendered family obligations of children and parents' perceptions of the distinct needs of boys and girls informed the parents' striving goals. In the families we visited, parents felt obligated to support a son's education and to help him with housing and marriage costs while they felt that their economic obligations to a daughter ended after she finished her education. Meanwhile, children's perceptions of the connection between their gender and the allocation of resources and chores to them affected their experiences of being left behind.

Owing to institutional constraints, migration was one of only a few routes available for many parents from rural places to help their children with housing and education expenses. The teenagers we met understood that their gender affected what their parents hoped to provide for them. Teenage boys mostly appreciated their parents' work for them and believed that it was justified for them to receive a larger overall share of family investment than their sisters. Girls likewise appreciated their parents' efforts on their behalf even as they knew that their parents did not feel the same obligation to provide for them as for boys.

Children's awareness of the significance of their gender for their position in their families influenced their view of the distribution of everyday resources to them. While all children with opposite-gender siblings could potentially perceive gender-based differential treatment of them and their siblings regardless of their parents' migration status, differential treatment assumed special significance for those children whose parents had migrated without them. If and how left-behind children perceived gender-based distributional inequalities reflected not only the actual distribution of these items, it also reflected how the children felt about other aspects of their multilocal striving lives, including parental absence, their relationship with their at-home caregivers and their school performance. Conversely, how children felt about these aspects of their lives indicated how conducive their home environment was to them developing sources of resilience, such as positive family relationships and good school grades, which could help them to feel happy.

While some children talked about differential treatment vis-à-vis co-resident children, other children experienced differential treatment because of their parents' decisions about the migration and non-migration of siblings. The separation of siblings through migration was significant not only because it further fragmented the left-behind children's experience of family, but also because it impacted on different children's possibilities for spending time with

130   Boys, Girls and Distribution in Striving Families

their parents. Additionally, the spatial separation of siblings could generate further intra-family inequalities. For instance, as noted in Chapter 1, Xu and Xie (2013) found that children who accompanied their migrant parents to the city exhibited significantly better cognitive and emotional outcomes than children who stayed behind in the countryside.

Nevertheless, when left-behind girls' brothers migrated with their parents to the city, the girls explained the family arrangement mostly in terms of their siblings' greater need for care rather than their parents' gender bias. Their emphasis on siblings' needs reflected aspects of the parents' actual deliberations. At the same time, though, reference to familial norms enabled the girls to feel more included in their spatially dispersed and patrilineal families.

Even as gendered distributional practices affected children, these practices were mutable. Sociologists demonstrate that in rural China the significance of children's gender in the parent–child relationship has shifted in response to falling fertility, educational expansion, urbanisation, rising marriage costs for sons and increased possibilities for women to earn money to support their parents in later life (Yan, 2003; Zhang, 2007; Kipnis, 2011; Murphy, Tao and Lu, 2011; Huang, 2012; Gruijters, 2017; Hu, 2017; Shi, 2017a, 2017b). This chapter augments this wider picture. In Anhui and Jiangxi, gender equality was evident in a number of distributional practices even as patrilinealism still informed how parents invested in certain children, and if or how the children perceived inequalities in gendered terms.

Education stands out as the area of investment where rural parents were committed to gender equality, mirroring findings in the sociological literature on education in rural China (Hannum, Kong and Zhang, 2009; Huang, 2012; Shi, 2017a). Simultaneously, though, education provided a space where some rural girls could demonstrate their 'worth' to others, securing parental recognition through their studiousness. The opportunity for some girls to win recognition from their parents through study could be particularly important to them in circumstances where their parents had migrated. But, as discussed in Chapter 3, even as studiousness enabled some children to win recognition, a preoccupation with attainment could also reinforce insecurities arising from study pressures and protracted parental absence.

Striving pressures – pressures arising from both parental absence and study – could also become manifest among children in gendered ways. Research indicates that in rural China at an aggregate level, girls report worse subjective well-being than boys (On the Road to School, 2017). Studies also find that when parents migrate, the behaviour of all children is adversely affected, but boys exhibit worse behaviour overall (Leng and Park, 2010; Murphy, Zhou and Tao, 2016) and have a higher risk of drinking and smoking (Jiang et al., 2015). This resonates with findings for the United States that boys are not as endowed

Conclusion

as girls with the protective psychosocial qualities that enhance resilience in the face of reduced parental input (Bertrand and Pan, 2013).

Aside from education, gender equality was also evident in other areas of resource distribution. For instance, pocket money and gifts were distributed to boys and girls equally, with the presence of siblings correlating negatively with the amount of pocket money that children of both genders received. Chores were also an aspect of everyday life where even as gender beliefs and gendered divisions of labour shaped children's burders, parallel structural changes mitigated or altered the influence of gender for some children. Specifically, changes operating in tandem with parental migration including falling family size, rising educational aspirations and farm mechanisation exerted effects that (1) *increased* some *boys'* and girls' involvement in chores and (2) *limited* some boys' *and girls'* involvement in chores.

In summary, in twenty-first-century rural China even as gendered distributional differences influenced many left-behind children's lives, their lives were also affected by parallel currents favouring gender equality in the treatment of all children. But these currents played out unevenly, with variations between boys and girls arising from the intersecting influences of their age and academic performance; their families' income, demographic composition and internal relationships; as well as local migration patterns, local school regime characteristics and local farming practices. Hence, boys' and girls' experiences of being 'left behind' were heterogeneous.

5   Children in 'Mother At-Home, Father Out' Families

In the villages of Anhui and Jiangxi, where local off-farm earning opportunities were few, 'mother at home, father outside' sat at the top of a notional hierarchy of parenting configurations. Adults and children alike told my research assistants and me that owing to the lack of money in the countryside the 'mother at home and father out' arrangement was best for improving the children's living conditions and life prospects. This view was grounded in traditional cultural models of parenting captured in the adage 'stern father, nurturing mother' (*yan fu ci mu*) (Qin, 2009: 469) and in assumptions that in the natural order mothers work inside the home to *yang* and *guan* their children while fathers work outside the home to *yang* the family.

Since the 1980s, the rising 'scarcity value' of children, family nuclearisation and state-endorsed market discourses feminising intimacy have cumulatively reinforced rural Chinese mothers' tendency to develop an emotionally intense relationship with their children (Wolf, 1972; Evans, 2010; Jankowiak, 2011; Song, 2018). At the same time, in rural China, rising economic competition, divestment from collective welfare provisioning, and eroding livelihood security, have accentuated the importance of mothering in families' strategies to support their children's 'cultural capital' accumulation (Chuang, 2016), a trend also observed elsewhere in the world (Reay, 2000; Katz, 2004; O'Brien, 2007; Lan, 2018).

Motherhood is pivotal in defining a woman's status in any society, but it takes on added meaning in the context of migration (Orellana et al., 2001). The sociologists Menjívar and Agadjanian use the term 'intensive mothering'[1] to describe how left-behind women in rural regions in Armenia and Guatemala devoted their resources, time and emotional energies to child-raising (2007: 1254). They explain that the women attributed special significance to their child-raising activities because this was how they demonstrated their fulfilment of their family obligations and their judicious use of their husbands' remittances (Menjívar and Agadjanian, 2007: 1254). But even as these sociologists' usage of the term 'intensive mothering' directs academic attention to the left-

---

[1] The term 'intensive mothering' was coined by Hays (1996).

Children in 'Mother At-Home, Father Out' Families   133

behind women's preoccupation with child-raising activities, in my view this term still does not translate easily to the caregiving practices of left-behind mothers in low-income rural areas.

Because of a lack of social infrastructure, hired help, labour-saving technologies and pre-prepared food, most of women's caring activities in low-income contexts takes the form of chores (Razavi, 2011), with the volume and intensity of these chores exacerbated by the husbands' migration (Wu and Ye, 2016). In China, the possibilities for farming mothers to personally invest time and effort in their children's education are also limited by their educational disadvantages (Ye and Pan, 2011). The women we met in rural Anhui and Jiangxi therefore did not think in terms of pursuing the 'intensive mothering' practised by their urban middle-class counterparts even as they shared a hegemonic view that mothers should do their best to nurture their children's education. Rather, as Christopher (2013) observes of African American and Latina women in the United States, women have their own repertoires of motherhood, grounded in their cultural norms and reflective of their social and geographic locations.

In China in the 2010s, societal and family expectations of fatherhood were also complex, reflecting the influences of both hegemonic and local class-specific expectations of men, and the influences of migration. When discussing fatherhood, some sociologists use Connell and Messerschmidt's (2005: 840) term 'hegemonic masculinity', which refers to 'the most honoured way of being a man'. They note that in many patriarchal societies – and rural Chinese society qualifies as such, fatherhood is one of the most common ways for men to acquire a masculine identity (Connell and Messerschmidt, 2005: 840; Montes, 2013). Meanwhile, *work* is another hegemonically prescribed way for men to demonstrate their masculinity, though this work needs to occur outside the home and generate money (West and Zimmerman, 1987; Connell and Messerschmidt, 2005: 840; Lam and Yeoh, 2015; Lam and Yeoh, 2018).

In rural and urban China, men certainly define their worth and are evaluated by others according to the status of their work and how much they earn (Choi and Peng, 2016; Liu, 2019). At the same time, rural migrant men are highly invested in helping their children to progress. As Choi and Peng observe of male migrants in the Pearl River Delta, 'their children's success, no matter in what form, helps . . . [them] to regain their dignity as a man and a father in the cities in which they are treated as second class citizens, [and] defined as economically unsuccessful because of their unusually low-paid jobs' (2016: 122). Noticeably, though, the lone-migrant fathers of the children we met in Anhui and Jiangxi varied in their contributions to their families, reflecting differences in their capital endowments, dispositions and luck.

Men's migration intertwined with culturally hegemonic expectations of fatherhood. In Chinese culture, fathers' customary responsibility for discipline, instruction and provisioning in child-raising co-exists with their detachment from daily childcare (Ho, 1987; Li and Jankowiak, 2016: 189–190). Meanwhile, as Parreñas (2008) observes of Filipino fathers, such a detachment coheres with and is often compounded by migration's removal of these men from the home. Indeed, Parreñas (2008) observes that migrant men tend to narrow their fathering practices to focus on breadwinning and discipline, thereby exacerbating a gap in their emotional intimacy with their children. In China, state-sanctioned public discourses have since the 1990s urged fathers to become more emotionally involved in parenting for the benefit of their children's cognitive and non-cognitive development. Nevertheless, sociologists note that whereas urban and well-educated men in China embrace this tender and expressive approach towards fathering, rural and uneducated men mostly reject it (Jankowiak, 2011; Li and Jankowiak, 2016: 198).

On the flipside, though, some recent studies from China (Peng and Choi, 2016) as well as from Guatemala (Montes, 2013), Indonesia (Lam and Yeoh, 2015) and Mexico (Dreby, 2010) offer a different perspective on migrant fathers. These studies indicate that migrant men feel deep affection, longing and fears for their children, and these emotions shape their interactions with them. Research also demonstrates that migrant fathers are diligent in phoning their left-behind children. One study finds that rural Chinese fathers who had migrated alone phoned their left-behind children significantly more frequently than either two-parent migrants or mothers who had migrated alone (On the Road to School, 2016). Research among transnational migrant fathers from Mexico and Indonesia similarly finds that they frequently phoned their left-behind children (Nobles, 2011; Lam and Yeoh, 2015). Hence, many migrant men try to sustain an emotional relationship with their children even as these efforts remain subordinate to their financial contributions.

Although a wider literature offers rich insights into the perceptions and practices of left-behind mothers and migrant fathers, mostly in Latin American and Southeast Asian countries (e.g. Parreñas, 2005; Parreñas, 2008; Dreby, 2010; Nobles, 2011; Montes, 2013; Lam and Yeoh, 2015), at least three questions remain underexplored, especially of farmer-migrant families in China. Firstly, how do *children* in sending regions perceive the 'mother at home, father out' family configuration in light of their own parents' migration statuses? Secondly, how do *children* perceive, influence and experience their relationships with their mothers and fathers when fathers have migrated alone? Thirdly, how do *children's* relationships with their at-home mothers and migrant fathers vary by their families' economic circumstances?

This chapter addresses these questions in three sections. Section 5.1 examines why most children and adults we met in the Anhui and Jiangxi fieldwork counties deemed the 'mother home, father out' configuration to be optimal. The remainder of the discussion draws on the twenty-eight cases of children we met

5.1 The Mother at Home and Father Out Ideal

who lived with their mothers while their fathers worked away. Section 5.2 explores the children's relationship with their at-home mothers, including their appreciation of their mother's care, as well as their mother's emotional sacrifices and support for their studies. It also teases out differences among the children by their families' economic circumstances and by their mothers' recent migration histories. Section 5.3 examines the children's relationship with their migrant fathers, highlighting the children's expectations of their fathers as breadwinners alongside the children's constrained possibilities for interacting with their migrant fathers.

5.1 The Mother at Home and Father Out Ideal

In rural China, children were exposed through multiple channels to the idea that children fare best when their mother is by their side. Schools, popular culture, the media and official policy discourse all transmit this idea. School children in China – as in many countries – read textbooks that depict women rather than men as homemakers (Li, X., 2016), with connections often made between the mother's domestic work and the children's education. For instance, Kipnis (2011: 145) explains that in the 2000s all sixth-grade students in Shandong province had to memorise a Tang dynasty poem about an elderly mother who darned her son's socks by candlelight so he could spend all his time studying to become an official.

Many popular songs performed on television variety shows likewise extol mothers' devotion to their children (Pissin, 2013). A famous lullaby, sung on Mother's Day, 'Mother is the Best in the World', contains the lyrics:

Mama is the best in the world; with *mama* you have most treasure; jump into your *mama's* heart and you will find happiness ... away from your *mama's* heart where will you find happiness?

Other songs include: 'Dote on Mother' (*Tengai mama*) sung by Geng Weihua, 'Dear Mother' (*Qinai de mama*) sung by Andy Lau, 'Mother, I love you' (*Mama, wo ai ni*) sung by Ren Juntai and 'Mother in the candlelight' (*Du guang li de mama*) sung by Zhang Qiang. Television commercials for commodities such as soap, soya milk, yoghurt drinks, laundry detergent and medicine often likewise feature mothers doting on their children.

The idea that a mother's love (*mu'ai*) has an essential quality to it also pervades Chinese official and policy discourses about child-raising in general as well as the care of 'left-behind' children. Since coming to power, President Xi Jinping has repeatedly asserted that women in China have a duty to provide affection in their families and that mothers should educate their children, nurture the young and old and promote both family and societal harmony (Fincher, 2018: 168–169). It is therefore not surprising that in response to the

State Council decree of 2016 calling on at least one migrant parent to return home to look after unaccompanied children, the notices issued through schools and in the media often called on *mothers* to return home if parents could not take their children with them to the city.

Even so, the idea that mothers are the most responsible for ensuring their children's healthy development is not unique to Chinese society. A view that children are naturally attached to their mothers has long underlain heated debates about the implications of maternal employment and non-parental care for children's development in Western countries (Silverstein, 1991; Brooks-Gunn, Han and Waldfogel, 2002; Ruhm, 2008). In both Chinese and Western contexts, feminists observe that debates about the implications of women's labour force participation for children's well-being often emphasise mothers' responsibilities while side-stepping unequal gender relations, institutionalised gender discrimination and inadequate welfare and employment policies. Indeed, the eminent Stanford economist Scott Rozelle caused a stir among some Chinese feminists with his recommendation that rural Chinese women ought to return home from the cities to provide good quality maternal care for their young children (China Development Brief, 2017).

Attention to the mother as the primary caregiver is not to deny that Chinese society values a father's presence: the ideal family consists of parents and children living together, as Figure 5.1 shows. Increasingly

Figure 5.1 A family on a birth planning billboard in a township in Tranquil County, Jiangxi

5.1 The Mother at Home and Father Out Ideal

Chinese media depicts fathers interacting warmly with their children, especially as ideas about emotionally engaged fathering have taken hold among the urban middle class, with the reality television programme, '*Father Where Are We Going?*' being an example (Li, Xuan, 2016). Nevertheless, as discussed in Chapter 1 and mirroring scholars' observations in other low-income countries (Parreñas, 2005), in China too commentators still accept paternal migration more than maternal migration. Indeed, as scholars report for patrilineal Mexican society, a 'culture of migration' reinforces the gendering of family roles such that in villages with few local off-farm jobs, people think that responsible, capable and industrious men must migrate (Kandel and Massey, 2002).

As mentioned previously, many children and adults who we met in Anhui and Jiangxi felt that given the lack of money in the countryside, 'mother at home and father out' was the best option for their family. Seven children from poor non-migrant families we visited told us that they wanted 'one side' (*yifang*) to go out. When we asked them which side, they replied matter-of-factly that men migrate to *yangjia* (support the family) while women stay at home to *dai* or 'bring up' the children. When we asked them why this was so, their answers included: 'It is easier for men to earn money', 'It is easier for men to be outside', 'Mother is closer' (*genqin*) and 'Mother needs to look after the home'.

The children's perception that men earn more than women is supported by data showing that in China's male-dominated transport and construction sectors wages are higher than in the manufacturing and services sectors (China Labor Bulletin, 2018), while even controlling for education and sector differences, rural migrant women incur significant gender-based wage discrimination (Magnani and Zhu, 2012). Similarly, data on young migrants from a 2011 Chinese Migrant Dynamics Monitoring Survey demonstrate that the wage return for education was lower for females than for males: for one year's increase in education female respondents received a wage increase of 6.33 per cent compared to 8.82 per cent for male respondents (Lyu and Chen, 2019). If we recall the educational disadvantages incurred by the children's mothers, discussed in Chapter 2, then the gender differential in migrant earnings becomes even more pronounced.

Among the poor families we visited where an able-bodied man had never migrated (*n*=3) or where a returnee man had been at home for several months (*n*=4), the children and wives both wanted him to migrate. This was so in the family of a twelve-year-old girl from Tranquil County, Jiangxi, who we met in May 2010. At the time of our interview, both her parents had been at home since their return at Chinese New Year. The girl explained that 'one side' (*yifang*), her father, needed to go 'outside'. Later, her mother elaborated:

138   Children in 'Mother At-Home, Father Out' Families

There is no money for the family to use . . . We often discuss which one of us should go out. He can go and I can go. But usually it is better if the woman is at home, it is better for the children, especially from a hygiene point of view. A man won't do washing for the children.

In April 2011 a twelve-year-old boy in Western County described a similar circumstance in his family, saying:

Dad [a construction worker] returned at Spring Festival but he hasn't found work yet. Now Dad is at home life is more frugal. For the past few months Mum has not wanted to spend money. Now we buy only necessities like study items. It is not economical (*huasuan*) for father to be at home.

Conversely, in families where both parents had migrated, many children and some grandmothers told us that they wanted 'one side' (*yifang*) to return home, and on probing, they clarified that it was '*mama*' who should return. The children said that a mother's care is 'more attentive' (*geng xixin*)' or 'on the mark' (*daowei*) while grandmothers said that the children's mothers were better able to *guan* the children and to monitor their studies than they were. For their part, children in 'mother home, father out' families – the focus of the following discussion – appreciated their mother's at-home presence and thought that she should stay by their side, while also recognising that rural mothers could and often did migrate. Moreover, even as the children of lone migrant fathers often missed their fathers, they accepted that their migration was necessary for the family, as I discuss later.

5.2   Children with an At-Home Mother and Migrant Father

In Anhui and Jiangxi, children's views of at-home mothers and migrant fathers were influenced by people's beliefs about the appropriate gendered divisions of parenting labour, such as the beliefs discussed earlier. Like the children Coe (2011; 2014) met in Ghana, the children we met in Anhui and Jiangxi saw each of their parents' contributions to them as evidence that they were trying their best, with evidence of parental commitment being as important to the children as the parents' actual material provisioning. Meanwhile, family income, the extent of the local schools' contributions to the families' social reproduction, and the possibilities that local school regimes offered to families to support their children's educational progression, combined to further shape the micro-worlds within which families' gendered beliefs and relational obligations played out.

The economic circumstances of the 'migrant father, at-home mother' families we visited could be seen as sitting along a continuum. At one end were families where the fathers remitted reliably such that the mothers could devote more time to accompanying the children. The richest of these families were in Eastern County, Anhui, with the fathers working in construction in African countries. We met eight children whose fathers worked in African countries including Algeria, Angola, Namibia and Libya, with one of these fathers later going to work in Singapore. In 2010, a construction worker in Angola could earn 60,000 *yuan* per year with food and accommodation provided by the employer, which was more than double the average wage of an internal migrant worker. These men worked on two-year contracts, with one rest day per month, and they typically interspersed overseas sojourns with periods of work in the construction industry in China. They signed up to *maiming* or to 'sell their lives', a reference to the harsh employment and living conditions overseas. As noted in Chapter 2, many of the men migrated overseas to send their children to a private boarding school in the county seat. The men's high earnings, long-distance migration and long-term absence, all confirmed to their family members and to the wider society their status as breadwinners while enabling their wives to be homemakers.

At the other end of the continuum, though, were poor families. This included three families where the fathers seldom remitted: in two of these families the fathers gambled, while in yet another family the father gambled though he still sent money. In several poorer families, especially where the men gambled, it was the man's perceived failure to do his best to *yangjia* that underlined to the children that their mother was the one at home who cared for them. In some of these families, the mothers remained in the village because they would have struggled to find even low-end work in the cities. Indeed, four at-home mothers from poorer families did little farming or other chores because of disabilities or ill health – two of these women's husbands seldom made financial contributions while the husbands of another two women remitted as best they could.

5.2.1   Children's Relationship with Their At-Home Mothers

Regardless of their families' economic circumstances, most children in farmer-migrant families appreciated the comforts bestowed by their mother's presence. These comforts included regular meals, clean clothes and bedding, and heated water for washing, as well as the sense of reassurance that a mother's presence gave and the structure that a mother's presence imposed on the days. Indeed, the children all mentioned in one way or another that their mother's provision of conveniences, security and routine helped them to concentrate on their studies.

Crucially, too, the children knew that rural mothers could and often did migrate, heightening their appreciation of their own at-home mother's contributions. Children we met from 'at home mother and migrant father' families often used the word *diu* meaning 'to throw' or 'to put aside' to imply that in staying with them, their own mother had not put them aside like so many of their classmates' mothers or neighbours' mothers had done. In using the word *diu* the children implicitly echoed a societal judgement that mothers *ought* to stay with their children even as maternal migration to earn money had become widespread in the fieldwork counties.

Some grandmothers' verbal interventions also reinforced to children a sense that their mother's at-home presence made them fortunate. Specifically, five children had overheard their grandmothers compare the children of migrant mothers with the children of at-home mothers when encouraging their daughters-in-law to stay at home rather than migrate. Significantly, children echoed these comparisons when lobbying their own mothers to stay at home. For instance, a twelve-year-old boy from Western County, Anhui, explained:

I don't want my mother to go out because I love her. She was talking about going out with *nainai* and I told her I loved her so she decided to work locally [she works six days per week for twelve hours per day in a local fireworks factory]. When a mother is at home children feel very peaceful and warm but without mother at home their lives are terrible (*zaogao*) and they don't study as well. Grandparents can't *guan* them properly because they have to farm.

5.2.1.1   Heterogeneity in Children's Experiences of Maternal Care   Although children who lived in regions of high out-migration appreciated their at-home mothers' contributions to their well-being, children differed in their experiences of maternal care, reflecting each family's particular economic and relational micro-world. The accounts of Yulin and Puhua, two girls who I first met in March 2011 in Eastern County, Anhui, cast light on how family circumstances impacted on children's experiences of maternal care while also demonstrating that, disparities in their family's circumstances notwithstanding, these children both felt reassured by their mother's presence.

In 2011, Yulin was twelve years old. If benchmarked against other rural families in Eastern County, Anhui, or against the families of the other 108 children we interviewed, Yulin's family was of above-average socio-economic standing. During the 1990s and early 2000s, her father worked in China and then in the 2010s worked in North and sub-Saharan Africa. His above-average salary enabled Yulin's mother to devote much of her time to child-raising without needing to earn a wage herself, though in the early 2010s she did some piece-rate work in a township clothing workshop to fit around school hours. Yulin told us:

I don't consider myself 'left-behind' because I have my mother. In our village there are many children whose mothers are outside. Their homes are not swept clean, and their days do not have structure to them. They have to wash their clothes in the village pond. At the weekend, they might eat lunch as late as 3pm. With mother by my side in daily life, my brother and I have love and care.

5.2 Children with an At-Home Mother and Migrant Father 141

Yulin's two paternal uncles also worked overseas, interspersed with migrant sojourns in China, so she, her brother, and three cousins often ate with their grandparents, especially if their mothers had to work. Yulin enjoyed a close bond with both her grandparents and cousins, who all lived in neighbouring houses.

In 2011, Puhua was eleven years old. Puhua's family was among the poorest out of the families of the 109 children we interviewed. When we first met Puhua's mother, she was pumping water, dressed in dusty clothes, her hair pulled back in a bun and her skin tanned and sweaty. We were surprised to learn that she was only thirty-four years old as she looked at least a decade older. She told us that her husband had many brothers and that:

> They have all done better than us. They went to Shanxi to *dagong*. It is only us who have fallen behind because we have no 'ability' (*benshi*).

She revealed that her sight had nearly gone and that her grandmother and father had similarly lost their sight:

> Like me they were born in the year of the horse. I heard this only affects people born in the year of the horse, while my daughters were born in the year of the dragon and the chicken.

She continued:

> I keep worrying about whether or not [my husband] will return to help with planting the rice crop (*chayang*) because I can't see properly. I have no way to phone him and he only phones me now and then.

Puhua told us:

> I overheard my mother tell my Dad that he only works sixteen days a month and the rest of the days he gambles so she wants him to come home, but he doesn't want to. When he comes back they fight about gambling.

Puhua's mother bore many work pressures and mental pressures but with little support in the village. She lamented:

> The only households [in our village] where all the younger adults have not gone is a family where the husband has a muscle-wasting disease and the wife needs to care for him, and a man with a brain tumour. Everyone else has gone.

Her parents-in-law did not help her either because 'there are too many sons for them to start helping anyone'. To make matters worse, as of 2013, her parents-in-law had sided with her brothers-in-law in trying to take farmland off her, arguing that her nuclear family did not have a right to the land because she and her husband were sonless. When we visited Puhua in 2013 she told us that she felt alone because her mother always seemed to be worried and distracted. 'She only ever talks to me to tell me to be quiet or to hurry up', Puhua said. Puhua

142   Children in 'Mother At-Home, Father Out' Families

also worried about her poor grades and about being bullied at school. My research assistant and I noted that Puhua often shifted into talking in a rapid stream of consciousness in dialect, her eyes cast down. We thought that she retreated into her own head at such times.

Despite the inattention of Puhua's mother, Puhua still found her mother's presence reassuring. For example, in 2011 Puhua said:

Sometimes in the morning I can hear the person next door crying and then I feel too afraid to get out of bed. My mother turns the light on and tells me that there is nothing to be afraid of.

Given her worries and loneliness, Puhua treasured any of her mother's obvious gestures of care for her: for instance, she told us that she felt happy whenever her mother reminded her to take an umbrella to school or to wrap up warm. Furthermore, when we met Puhua again in 2015, she said that if on the weekends a television programme was ever broadcast about girls being tricked by men, her mother would use the story to warn her. She added that her mother had recently entrusted a visiting maternal aunt to buy a sex education book for her. Puhua appreciated her mother's expression of concern for her, noting that many girls in her class did not have a mother near them to explain such things.

5.2.2   Awareness of the Mothers' Sacrifices and Burdens

Children not only recognised that their mothers contributed to their well-being, they also realised that in staying at home while their fathers worked elsewhere their mothers incurred sacrifices and inconveniences. Mirroring research findings for some other countries (Chant and Radcliffe, 1992; Nelson, 1992), field studies in various rice-farming and double-cropping regions in China likewise indicate that left-behind women incur longer working hours, carry out more physically demanding work and shoulder increased emotional burdens because of their husbands' migration (Murphy, 2004b; Wu and Ye, 2016). My research in Anhui and Jiangxi extends these findings by highlighting that the *children bore witness* to their at-home mothers' work burdens and emotional burdens, influencing their appreciation of their mothers.

Most children we met from 'mother home, father out' families said that their mothers worked very long hours. The exceptions were the few children whose mothers were afflicted by ill-health or disability. Mothers' heavy physical work burdens and long working hours were especially visible to the children in their mothers' farming activities. These at-home women grew vegetables on the family garden plot and cultivated rice in the paddy fields, both for home consumption and for market. As Figure 5.2 demonstrates, cultivating rice is '*backbreaking work*'. Cultivating rice is 'not the end goal of any parent for their children or grandchildren. *Yet it is . . .a way of enacting a commitment to the*

5.2 Children with an At-Home Mother and Migrant Father

Figure 5.2 Women transplanting rice seedlings in Jade County, Jiangxi

family' (Oxfeld, 2017: 52, my emphasis). At the same time, these mothers also farmed cash crops, such as soya bean or cotton, as shown in Figure 5.3. Furthermore, on top of their own household's land, these women farmed land transferred to them by migrated family members, while some women additionally worked as casual wage labourers on other migrant families' land. In 2013, a fourteen-year-old girl in Eastern County, Anhui, reflected a common sentiment among the children of 'left-behind' farming mothers, saying:

My mother has to look after us. She is in the fields and among the crops without rest. Whereas father can rest and play when he is not working my mother can never rest. I see her so tired and sweaty every day, so I can't let her down.

In 2013, a twelve-year-old boy from Jade County, Jiangxi, similarly told us that if it rained when the grain was spread outside his mother could barely manage to sweep it up and carry the load inside in time, even if he tried to help her. He therefore resolved to make her work burden worthwhile by being obedient and hardworking, and by looking after her in the future.

Several children noted that their mothers had to endure greater mental burdens on account of their father's migration. The children mentioned a number of different worries occupying their mothers including the safety of their migrant fathers, especially if they worked on construction sites or overseas; the health problems of certain family members; conflicts with in-laws; financial pressures; and fathers' gambling habits, with the exact mix of worries depending on their families' unique circumstances. A few children also overheard their mothers talking about their worries to other family members, such

Figure 5.3 A mother in Eastern County, Anhui, preparing soil to plant cotton seedlings

as grandmothers or aunts. However, it was mostly teenagers who understood the details of what they had heard.

Children's awareness of their mothers' worries could influence what they talked about with them, though here again children varied by their age. Some younger children told us that they shared all the 'words in their heart' (*xinlihua*) with their mothers. This was the case for twelve-year-old Xinhao from Jade County, Jiangxi, who in 2011 said that when he told his mother about being bullied at school for being poor, she would comfort him by hugging him, and saying: 'Once you're at university, you won't fear their bullying.' By contrast, some teenagers told us that they never told their *xinlihua* to their mother because they did not want to increase her mental burden. Meanwhile, for their part, five mothers said that they attributed their teenagers' growing reticence to talk with them to the onset of adolescence, while two of these mothers added emphatically that the growing distance between them and their teenager was not because they had ever 'put them to one side' (*diu*).

5.2.3 Children's Experience of Their Mother's Educational Support

The pivotal position of education in the mother–child relationship in farmer-migrant families in Anhui and Jiangxi mirrored an aspect of the relationship between left-behind women and their children documented in other country contexts (Menjívar and Agadjanian, 2007). Education was of such significance

5.2 Children with an At-Home Mother and Migrant Father   145

to the mother–child relationship because, consistent with Chuang's (2016) observation for farmer-migrant families in Sichuan province, a gendered bargain operated whereby the husbands remitted in exchange for their wives' domesticity. Wu and Ye (2016) likewise note that women in rural China experienced even greater pressure for their children to do well at school when their husbands migrated. As Xinhao's mother once asked me rhetorically, 'If the child grows up to have promise, isn't *dai haizi* (bringing up children) the same as me earning money?'

But as mentioned previously, even though the mothers felt under pressure to ensure that their children studied hard, children from farmer-migrant families rarely received direct tutoring from or arranged by their mothers. At twelve years of age, Xinhao explained to us that his mother could not tutor him because 'she doesn't recognise characters', a refrain we heard from many children. Hiring regular tutors was also not an option for these families because they had neither the money nor the access to tutors, with some mothers remarking wryly that even if they could find the money, most teachers headed to their county seat residences on Friday afternoons. Some rural parents sent their children to two or three weeks of summer holiday revision classes after they had entered junior high school, but this tutoring was qualitatively and quantitatively different from the tutoring that urban *hukou* children received. Maternal support for most of these children's studies instead took the form of repeated reminders to them that they needed to do their homework to avoid disappointing their migrant fathers or causing his efforts 'outside' to be in vain. Furthermore, like some poor and working-class parents in the United States discussed by Lareau (2003), rural mothers we met in China saw the teachers as responsible for and as the best able to support their children's studies so they urged their children to listen to and obey their teachers.

The children experienced various degrees of strictness in their mother's monitoring of their studies. However, overall, in our set of cases, fewer children of at-home mothers and migrant fathers experienced corporal punishment when compared to children in other family configurations: only two out of the twenty-eight children who were looked after by their home-alone mothers said that a parent sometimes hit them, compared with a fifth of the children of two at-home parents and over a quarter of the children of two migrant parents, though this breakdown does not necessarily indicate any wider pattern.[2] Nevertheless, most of the children of lone migrant fathers complained that their at-home mothers often nagged them about study, especially if their grades fell, saying things like, 'If so and so can get a high score then so can you, he or

---

[2] Twelve out of forty-three children with two migrant parents reported being hit. This does not include the fifteen-year-old boy who lived alone; otherwise the number for the children of two migrant parents would be forty-four. Meanwhile six out of twenty-nine children with both parents at home said they were sometimes hit.

146   Children in 'Mother At-Home, Father Out' Families

she is also just a human being'. But several children stressed that their at-home mothers only ever encouraged them and never scolded them about study, with a few teenagers saying that even though their mothers cared about their studies, they were far more concerned about their happiness. In such cases, deep mother–child bonds had developed over time such that the at-home mothers did not want to threaten the intimacy of their 'uterine family' (Wolf, 1972) with harshness much as they wanted their children to do well.

5.2.4   Children's Relationship with Their Returnee Mothers

Children's relationship with their at-home mothers could be further influenced by the mothers' recent history of migration. I explained above that some children compared their own circumstances to the circumstances of their peers whose mothers had migrated without them. However, when children's mothers had been migrants for a significant stretch of time before returning home, the children could also directly compare their own circumstances and feelings with and without their mother by their side. Indeed, while some researchers observe that many 'left-behind women' in rural China are former migrants (Jacka, 2012; Zhang, 2013; Chuang, 2016; Wu and Ye, 2016), I extend scholarly understanding by examining the implications of children's awareness of their mothers' previous sojourns for their relationship with them.

In 2010–2011, nine children from the Anhui subset of respondents lived with returnee mothers, two of whom had returned home while the children were still in first grade and three of whom had returned home more recently. These nine also included the mothers of four children from Western County, Anhui, who had replaced their previous extended stays in the city with short periodic shuttles between their husbands' stalls in the city and the village, where they spent approximately three-quarters of the year. Meanwhile, five children from the Jiangxi counties whose fathers were lone migrants also lived with returnee mothers. Additionally, in two non-migrant families we visited in the Jiangxi counties, the children's mothers and fathers had both returned home within a couple of years of the interview, with the mothers having returned home first, and in each case it was assumed that the fathers would remigrate. Furthermore, six children in the Jiangxi counties lived with parents who had both returned home because the mother had given birth to another child. At the time of interview in 2010–2011, in five of these cases, the parents intended for one or both parents to remigrate when the youngest child was slightly older, and in my follow-up interviews with two of these children two years later, I learned that two girls' fathers had remigrated and that the mothers were thinking about remigrating. In total, therefore, I met eighteen village-based children who had at some point lived in a family consisting of a returnee mother and a migrant father.

5.2 Children with an At-Home Mother and Migrant Father   147

Children's relationship with their mothers inevitably unfolded within the micro-worlds of their own families regardless of their parents' migration histories. But when mothers were returnees, the factors that had prompted their return to the village both reflected and shaped other aspects of these families' micro-worlds. Two dimensions of a mother's return migration stood out as especially noteworthy in shaping the family context in which these mother–child relationships unfolded. Firstly, whether the family members understood the mother to have returned home on a 'temporary' or a 'permanent' basis could influence how securely the children felt that she would stay with them and be there for them. Secondly, the importance of the child's education in motivating a mother's return could signal to the child and more generally the amount of time and money that both the mother and the family were willing or able to invest in a child

5.2.4.1   When Mothers were Compelled to Return for Family Reasons   Children's relationship with their returnee mothers was partly affected by whether the family saw the mother's return as temporary or permanent. Four out of the eighteen children mentioned earlier had lived with their returnee mother knowing that before long, she would migrate again for at least several months. Specifically, she would depart when a younger sibling was old enough to attend an urban or rural kindergarten or school or when a grandparent had recovered sufficiently from an illness or injury to resume childcare duties. These children tearfully told us that they secretly wished that their mother would stay at home with them forever because this would give them a sense of security (*anquangan*). They also said that even though they loved their grandparent(s), they enjoyed more interaction, liveliness (*huoli*) and warmth (*wennuan*) when their mothers were at home, and they dreaded the coldness, lonely coldness or cold boredom (*lengqi/lengmo/lengdan*) when their mothers went away.

By contrast, the fourteen children whose mothers had returned home on a more 'permanent' basis felt reassured by their return, with the change in the families' circumstances that had precipitated the mother's return also largely precluding her long-term re-migration. Typical changes in the family's circumstances included a grandparent becoming unavailable for childcare because of illness or death or, less commonly, a grandparent deciding to not look after a certain grandchild any more – in one case, the grandmother became unavailable after she migrated to look after her son s child in the city. The length of time that the four shuttling mothers from Western County could spend on city visits was also curtailed by the declining health of grandparents and the difficulties in securing alternative childcare from other family members. In all these cases, mothers and children both de-emphasised the involuntary nature of the mother's return and highlighted that the mother needed to stay at home to 'bring up the studying children' (*dai haizi dushu*), a phrase that

148   Children in 'Mother At-Home, Father Out' Families

encapsulated both the mother's function in remedying a childcare deficit at home and her support for her children's education.

Children seldom felt close to their returnee mother in the initial period after her return home, even in situations where the mother's return was understood to be long-term. For instance, a thirty-six-year-old returnee from Western County, Anhui, said of her ten-year-old daughter, Tianming:

When I first returned home there was a distance. She didn't want to talk to me and I didn't know how to talk to her except to ask her about study. I've been back nearly a year and it is much better now. My daughter once said to me: 'In the past, you weren't good to me, you didn't *guan* me, you "put me aside" (*diu*) with granddad and grandma.' That's what she said. Those words hurt. A neighbour had teased her by saying, 'Your parents don't like you, so they've gone' . . . I'm here to bring her up (*dai*). I want her to study hard and to learn more knowledge . . . Her grades are good now. . . . I tell her: 'If you don't listen to me, *mama* will not *guan* you. I'll go out to *dagong*.' Then she says: 'Mum, don't go. I'll be obedient. I won't make you angry.'

But even as children initially felt distanced from or reproachful of their returnee mothers, they also told us that they felt more cheerful, ate better and concentrated more on their studies after their mothers had come home. Tianming, just mentioned, said that her grades had stabilised after her mother's return because she felt happier and because her mother paid more attention to her homework than her grandparents had done. Similarly, a thirteen-year-old boy in Western County, Anhui, whose mother had previously lived in Inner Mongolia for two years selling lettuce alongside his father and was now mostly at home, said:

When mother was over there my grades and health were worse because I'd miss my parents so much I couldn't concentrate in class, and my health was worse because I'd cry so couldn't eat. Now mother is by my side.

There were at least three likely factors that caused the children to emphasise improvements in their well-being after their mother's return home. Firstly, the children were treated very well by their returnee mothers, especially during the early period after their return home. For instance, several children said that after their return home, their mothers spent more time talking with them, cooked good food for them and gave them treats. Next, children felt happier with their mothers at home because, in general, after a period of unfamiliarity, the interaction with their mother was more stimulating than the interaction with grandparents. Finally, some children may have wanted to communicate to any adults who would listen that they wanted their mother to stay at home with them.

5.2.4.2   Life with a Returnee Peidu *Mother*   Although most returnee mothers thought that their children's education benefited from their presence, a minority of returnee mothers stood out from the others because they had returned home *primarily* to support their children's education *and* they had accompanied their

5.2 Children with an At-Home Mother and Migrant Father 149

children as they moved from a school near to the village to a school in the county seat. This kind of *peidu* or 'accompanying studies' – whereby some returnee mothers followed their children from the village to the county seat – differed from another practice also referred to as *peidu* whereby mothers (or more usually grandmothers) move with children from a village to a township or even to a county seat in response to a lack of schools in or near to the home village coupled with a lack of suitable boarding facilities in the township or the county seat schools. Whereas in the first situation *peidu* represents the nuclear family's strategic investment in a child's urban education, in the second situation *peidu* occurs more in response to the spatial consequences of the rural school consolidation programme. Here I concentrate on the children of returnee mothers who participated in the first *peidu* situation.

While many people we met in Anhui and Jiangxi believed that the return of a mother to *peidu* was an optimal strategy for families to secure intergenerational mobility, in our interviews with 109 children and my follow-up interviews with twenty-five children intermittently over five years, I met only two children whose mothers did actually return to *peidu*. There were four reasons why I encountered so few cases of children whose mothers had returned to *peidu*. Firstly, *peidu* in the county seats of interior provinces is mostly undertaken by members of the rural elite, including township cadres, and rural professionals, entrepreneurs and industrialists (Xie, 2016: 93–98), while my child respondents were from farmer and farmer-migrant families. Secondly, at the time of the initial round of interviews, the children were in primary or junior high school, which meant that they had not yet reached a stage where they needed to relocate to progress with their education. Thirdly, as mentioned in Chapter 2, I recruited the children for interview from rural schools, so I missed *peidu* children who were based in schools in the county seat. Finally, in Eastern County, Anhui, rural parents aspired to send their children to private boarding schools at the junior high school level, or else at the senior high school level, if the children could not make it to a public senior high school, while a few rural parents we met in Western County wanted to send their children to board with current or retired teachers who lived near to good high schools. These parents opted for boarding arrangements over *peidu* partly because they thought that teachers in the private boarding schools or in boarding houses were better able than rural caregivers – including rural parents – to prepare their children for educational advancement.

The two children I followed over five years whose mothers did eventually return to *peidu* included a boy called Hanhan from Jade County, Jiangxi, and a girl called Fengmian from Tranquil County, Jiangxi. I interviewed Hanhan in 2010, 2013 and 2015 and Fengmian in 2011, 2013 and 2014. In 2013, Hanhan was fifteen years old while Fengmian was fourteen years old. Hanhan had been raised by his paternal grandparents since he was seven years old, before which time he had lived in Guangzhou with his migrant parents, with his grandmother looking after him during the day. Fengmian had been raised by her widowed paternal grandfather since she was three years old. Hanhan's and Fengmian's mothers had each returned home a few months before their children sat the *zhongkao* exam for entry into senior high school to support them during this crucial revision period – a stage in children's education when many rural parents try to return home for a few months.

At the time of our second meeting, Hanhan had won a place at the second-ranked academic-track public senior high school in Jade County, where over two-thirds of the students were urban *hukou* holders. He had benefited from a provincial scheme that added points to the *zhongkao* scores of students from rural junior high schools to encourage rural parents to keep them in the rural schools rather than transfer them to urban schools. Even so, Hanhan's parents still had to pay an admissions tariff, which they believed that they owed to their son because they thought that his lower *zhongkao* score was partly their fault for not having raised him themselves. In the fifteen years before Hanhan's mother returned to Jade County, she had worked in Guangzhou, first in a clothing factory and later running a shop that supplied needles and bobbins to the factory, while his father worked as a machine repairer. When I met Hanhan's mother in 2013 and 2015, she lived in a sparsely furnished rental apartment in the county seat and worked part-time in a shop. She cooked three meals a day and ate each meal with her son and her younger daughter, and she supervised her son in the evenings while he did his homework.

In 2014, at the time of our second interview, Fengmian studied in the art stream in an 'ordinary' *minban* ('people-run' or private) senior high school where 80 per cent of the 1,100 students were from the countryside and 10 per cent were in the art stream, which has slightly lower entrance score requirements. The same year, her returnee mother worked in a factory that manufactured parts for remote controls, established by a migrant who had returned from Guangdong province. Fengmian and her mother shared an apartment that the family had bought, which was situated near to the county industrial zone. The mother worked night shifts so that she could spend more time with her daughter and the two of them hung out together on Sunday afternoons. The mother explained that she was one of more than twenty returnee *peidu mama* in her factory, all of whom had children in kindergarten or in the final year of junior high school or else in senior high school.

Hanhan's and Fengmian's mothers had both returned to *peidu* because they wanted to compensate their children for their past years of absence. They also wanted to protect themselves from being held responsible for any

5.2 Children with an At-Home Mother and Migrant Father 151

disappointments in their children's futures. In 2013, Hanhan's mother, a fashionable woman aged forty, told us:

I fear he is too wild and that he could turn bad. I cook food for him because the food at school is not good. Also, it is quieter here than in the school dormitories so it is better for his sleep. I plan to stay here for three years. I need to see if he is obedient. This is the rebellious period. If you talk too much they get fed up . . . This child does not have much self-control. I fear he'll just spend all his time playing internet games. In the beginning he'd talk on the phone and later he did not take the initiative to speak with us. At this age there is a gap with parents. I think it could have been better if he'd always been with us. We feel very guilty because we did not bring him up. At this time if you mix with those who've turned bad, for example, take drugs, then everything is lost regardless of how much money you earn . . . I asked my son if he was willing for me to come back and look after him and he said 'yes'. I thought to myself if I don't come back and something goes wrong, he can blame me. This way there is nothing he can blame me for because I'll have done my best.

In 2014, Fengmian's mother, a stout practically dressed woman in her forties, echoed some of the same reasons in explaining her return, saying:

I came back at my husband's suggestion when my daughter was in the final year of junior high school. Our daughter is at an age where she could go astray, and she needs support for her studies. Other people also told me that I should come back home now my daughter is at this age.

Hanhan and Fengmian both recognised that their mothers wanted to compensate them for their past absence by means of two or three years of time-compressed intensive mothering before they reached full adulthood. They also appreciated their mother's gestures of love, but they both still regretted that they had grown up without their parents. An extract from one of my conversations with Fengmian is as follows:

FENGMIAN: My life would have been much better with my parents, with my mother especially. There were times when I needed her.
RACHEL: Like when?
FENGMIAN: Well, when, with the changes of growing up . . . with the start of female . . . I wanted to talk to her.

[] . . . *Yeye* was often too strict so now our relationship is not close . . . Classmates talk about their parents returning home. One girl said to me: 'You are so lucky your mother has returned'. Children really want their mothers with them.

Hanhan and Fengmian also differed in their relationships with their *peidu* mothers, which partly reflected differences in their respective study pressures. In 2015, Hanhan explained:

I feel so lost. I have exams every Sunday morning and every day I get up at 6 and go to bed at 11. I appreciate my mother's hard work in returning home. Her return is beneficial for me because my ability to restrain myself is poor. But all she ever talks about is study, which is not helpful. I already know this, and it creates a distance.

Hanhan was also one of only three teenagers we met, all boys, who said that they had ever had a girlfriend. Hanhan never told his mother about the girlfriend, a former classmate, or his feelings after she broke up with him – she dropped out of an ordinary senior high school to work in a nail bar in Shenzhen. His mother would only have criticised him for having jeopardised his studies, firstly by becoming distracted by a girl, and, secondly, because students who court face expulsion from school. Hanhan's inability to concentrate in a demanding and repetitive study regime and his lack of focus in life strained the relationship between him and his mother during the *peidu* period. By contrast, Fengmian had not made it to an academic-track school so her parents had already adjusted their expectations of her. Meanwhile, she had a sense of purpose – she wanted to get into an art college, and her mother wanted to support her by cooking and washing for her so that she would have more time for drawing practice. *Peidu* therefore helped Fengmian and her mother to rebuild intimacy.

While most adults we met came from families that could not support a returnee *peidu mama* strategy, they still often cited instances of children who had relocated from their village to the county seat accompanied by a *peidu* mother or *peidu* parents, and they had also seen stories on television about *peidu*, such that *peidu* influenced their perceptions about optimal family support for children's education. Many people said that rural migrants could only *peidu* if they had 'necessary conditions' (*yiding de tiaojian*) (Xie, 2016: 94–96), or to use Bourdieu's language, certain 'capital' endowments, with these endowments including education, income, contacts and information. Indeed, in 2013, while lamenting her daughter's poor grades, Puhua's mother said: 'It is our fault. We don't have any ability.' Poignantly, she then told us that other villagers sometimes ridiculed her by asking her if she was at home to *peidu*, thereby insinuating that *peidu* was above her station in life. The *peidu mama* phenomenon as an ideal rather than as necessarily a widespread practice, confirmed to rural people the centrality of educational aspiration in the moral purpose of motherhood (O'Brien, 2007). More generally, *peidu* as an ideal also casts light on how stratified social reproduction intersects with migration to reflect and reproduce hierarchies of human worth that are subject to gendered evaluation.

5.3 Children's Relationship with Their Migrant Fathers

The children's relationship with their migrant fathers was likewise affected by gendered expectations. As mentioned earlier, children's expectations of their migrant fathers hinged on economic provisioning. But even as children expected their fathers to provide for the family, they also wanted to interact with their fathers and to develop the same tacit understanding of their fathers as they had of their mothers. The interplay between these two axes of migrant fatherhood – expectations around economic provisioning on the one hand and possibilities for interaction and intimacy on the other – underpinned the variation in different children's relationship with their fathers. Broadly, when children could recall positive interactions with their father and had a sense of his character, his sacrifices to provide for the family moved them emotionally: they felt *close* (*qin*) to their father rather than just knew that he loved them.[3] By contrast, when children barely interacted with their fathers, the two parties could be emotionally distant even as the children recognised that their fathers loved them and even as they did not blame their fathers for their absence.

Importantly too, the physical distance and the emotional distance between fathers and children were not always commensurate. It was easier for domestic migrant fathers to phone their children weekly, while most fathers working in African countries usually only talked with their children two or three times a month. For example, a woman whose husband worked in Angola explained: 'It costs twenty *yuan* for about two phone calls, eight or nine minutes per call – just enough time to ask him how he is.' Moreover, internal migrant fathers could return home regularly, whereas their overseas counterparts couldn't. Twelve children's fathers returned home at least twice a year to help during the busy farming periods. However, as I show in the following, some children felt emotionally close to their overseas migrant fathers, while others felt emotionally estranged from their internal migrant fathers who returned to the village a few times a year.

5.3.1 Children's Experiences of Paternal Provision and Closeness

A mix of family and individual factors influenced (1) children's impressions of their migrant fathers' commitment to them and (2) the children's interactions with their migrant fathers. These factors included: the family's economic circumstances; whether the children thought that their father was *trying* to *yangjia*; the children's age at the time of interview and the children's age at the time of the father's initial departure; the father's duration of absence; the

---

[3] Xiao (2014) explores the concept of *qin* with reference to how some left-behind children express ambivalence towards their migrant parents. They say that they love their migrant parents, but they are not *qin*.

154   Children in 'Mother At-Home, Father Out' Families

frequency of the father's return visits and phone calls; and the personalities of the children and the fathers. To explore the variation in the children's relationship with their migrant fathers with reference to these factors, I grouped the twenty-eight children of lone migrant fathers into four ideal types: children whose migrant fathers provided for them economically and interacted with them ($n = 10$); children whose fathers provided only a small amount for them economically but who interacted with them ($n = 9$); children whose fathers provided for them economically but did not interact with them ($n = 6$); and children whose fathers neither provided for them economically nor interacted with them ($n = 3$).

Yulin, discussed earlier, belonged to the first group: her father provided for the family and interacted with Yulin, though the frequency of these interactions varied. During her early childhood up until she was ten years old, Yulin's father had worked on construction sites in the Yangtze River Delta, returning home five times a year for festivals and to help with farming. In 2011, she described her father to us as introverted, thoughtful and kind and said that after each of his departures she felt as though a part of her family and herself was missing. She recalled that in 2009, as he was preparing to leave for Libya, she could not bear to see him go (*shebude*) and told him to come home if he felt homesick. On the phone, conversations between Yulin and her father were short, and she felt too awkward to use the few minutes available to ask him about his life because she knew it was not good. In June 2010, his sojourn in Libya was cut short when he and other Chinese workers were repatriated back to China by the Chinese government. A tearful Yulin reported that, now at home, her father frequently woke in the night screaming 'Don't kill me' and that he had lost much weight.

When we met again in 2013, Yulin's father had migrated to Cameroon after a year's interlude working on a construction site in Bengbu city, Anhui. Because of his previous brush with death, Yulin worried constantly about her father. Then at our third meeting in 2015, she explained that her parents now rented a small flat in Eastern County's county seat and they all lived together during the week, though she returned to the village some weekends to stay with her grandparents. Her father operated a digger in Hefei eleven hours per day six days per week for the construction of a high-speed rail link while her mother worked in a restaurant in the county seat. Yulin said that she knew that her father was cheered on during his long working hours because she had made it to the 'top talent class' or *yingcai ban* – higher than the 'key class' or '*zhongdian ban*' and the ordinary class or '*putong ban*' – in the top public senior high school in Eastern County. Yulin explained that her father would not migrate overseas again because his left leg was limp and owing to long periods of sitting in a confined space in the digger machine he suffered from haemorrhoids. Furthermore, she told us that in the past few months she had appreciated being

5.3 Children's Relationships with Their Migrant Fathers 155

able to sit down beside her father. She could discern his affection for her through his gestures such as adding food to her bowl at mealtimes – food is often used in Chinese culture to symbolise care for a person's welfare (Jiang et al., 2007; Jankowiak, 2011). This resonates with the observations of Lam and Yeoh (2015) for Indonesia and the Philippines that on their return visits many transnational migrant fathers made extra efforts to reconnect emotionally with their children. Yulin's father's expressions of care assumed extra poignancy for her because of the earlier years of separation from him.

The second group of children felt emotionally close to their migrant fathers despite their fathers' poor economic provisioning. Their fathers were seldom overly disciplinarian even if they did ask the children about their grades, though one man sometimes hit his son for poor grades, but he also spent much time with his son on return visits, telling him stories and playing chess with him. These children cherished warm memories of their migrant fathers based on their interactions with them during their early childhood as well as when the fathers visited home. These children also felt that although their fathers did not earn much money, they were trying their best to *yangjia*. One such child was Lele from Western County, Anhui, the eldest of four children who I mentioned in Chapter 4. In 2011, at fourteen years of age, she said of her Guangdong-based security guard father:

Father first went out when I was six years old, and I remember I couldn't bear for him to go (*shebude*). When he visits home, I feel that we're not used to each other, but we get closer during his stays because he is after all my father. He's out to support so many people. . . . Once he rushed home for Chinese New Year and we went to meet him on the roadside, and we were really excited . . . Sometimes he'll bring things home. Surplus things from the company, not what he has bought, like curtains and quilts . . . He's really busy. He must cook for himself and he doesn't permit himself to eat good food . . . He looks different each time we see him, thinner. If I say anything, he'll tell me to study hard and get into university.

Similarly, Xinhao (mentioned previously in this chapter and in Chapter 4) felt close to his migrant father even though his father did not earn much money for the family. According to the boy's mother, during his preschool years, Xinhao used to follow his father everywhere including to the hills when he went to chop wood. Xinhao also recalled that during his first and second years of primary school, his father used to help him with homework. Xinhao's mother gave us further insight into the boy's relationship with his father, saying:

Whenever he gets good grades, he texts his father. He says, Old Dad (*laoba*) I got however many points. His father replies: 'I'm so happy to have a son like you, not stupid like me.' His Dad returns home only once a year for Spring Festival. He can't return mid-year because he earns 60 *yuan* per day, so if he came back for ten days that would be 600 *yuan* plus travel costs. Some people say that my husband is stupid, but

I think he's just honest and quiet. When my husband first said he would go out, my son trembled and cried. I said: 'Don't cry, he's got to go out, he'll come back at Chinese New Year'.

The third group consisted of children whose fathers provided for them economically but seldom interacted with them. These fathers were what the sociologist Sarah Swider (2015) calls 'permanently temporary' migrants. At-home women sometimes talked about their husbands bringing back sweets for their children because they had no idea about what their children needed or were interested in or what size shoes or clothes they wore. These women also observed that their husbands had little idea of how to interact with their children on the phone or during return visits and that their efforts seemed awkward.

In 2011, in Eastern County, Anhui, we met a ten-year-old boy whose 'permanently temporary' migrant father had worked on construction sites in the United Arab Emirates, Shanghai and Shenzhen, and, at the time of our interview with the boy and his mother, the father was in Angola. The boy's mother told us:

My son likes to chat with me. But even if his Dad is at home he does not talk with him. There is a big distance between them when his Dad returns, then as soon as they are a little bit more familiar with each other, his Dad needs to go again ... When he was younger he didn't want his father at all, but now that he is older he understands things better and he is used to his father being out. He doesn't care anymore.

Like the Filipino migrant fathers Parreñas (2005) discusses, some of these 'permanently temporary' migrants tried to fulfil their conventional fathering duties by admonishing their children over the phone for not working hard enough or for misbehaviour reported by the mothers. Indeed, several at-home mothers we met explained that their husbands worried that the children did not fear their mother enough, so they felt a need to instruct their children from afar.

Echoing an international literature about how children deal with the 'ambiguous loss' of a parent because of migration or divorce (Suárez-Orozco, Todorova and Louie, 2002; Pottinger, 2005; Dreby, 2010; Nobles, 2011), many of these children felt a degree of ambivalence towards their 'permanently temporary' migrant fathers. They told us that they did not miss their fathers because their fathers had always been 'outside' so they had hardly any memories of them. Indeed, the ten-year-old boy mentioned earlier said that the few times he had met his father he felt uneasy. He said that it was the same to him if his father was away or visiting home.

The fourth group of children experienced a strained relationship with their migrant fathers because the fathers did not *try* to provide for them economically and seldom interacted with them. We met three such children, though another child who I placed in aforementioned group three also partially fit the criteria for inclusion in this last group: the boy and his mother both noted that the father

5.3 Children's Relationships with Their Migrant Fathers

wasted lots of money 'outside' but he still remitted some money to the family. The children and fathers in this fourth group were distanced from each other, not only because the father did not appear to be doing his best to provide economically, but also because of a lack of interaction. The fathers were all internal migrants who returned home a few times a year to help with farming, so the children and fathers had more possibilities for interacting with each other than did the members of some other father–child dyads. Nevertheless, the father–child interactions were few and were rarely positive. For instance, in 2011, a twelve-year-old boy in Western County, Anhui, told us that his construction worker father returned home five times a year to farm and at Qing Ming festival, but the two rarely communicated because the father was extremely fierce. The father also gambled. The boy sighed: 'I only wish that my father would earn money to repair the house.'

The relationship between Puhua – discussed earlier – and her migrant father was similarly undermined by his unreliability as a provider and by his unwillingness to interact with her. In 2011, Puhua recalled how during one of his visits home he had blamed her for the disappearance of some money. But a few days later, following her repeated denials, he confessed that he had taken the money to repay a mahjong debt. When we visited Puhua's family again in September 2013, cotton was drying in the sun outside the house. Her mother opened the door and told us that a teacher had just phoned to tell her to stay at home because there would be a visitor, and she had assumed that a teacher was coming to tell her that her daughter would be expelled. However, to her relief she discovered it was only me and my research assistant. Puhua's father was also at home to help with the harvest. Of Puhua, he said: 'That child only watches television. She can watch all day, through the night and into the next day.' The parents' despair about their daughter's lack of prospects for upward mobility evidently impaired the quality of their engagement with her.

The estrangement between Puhua and her father clearly upset her. She told us that when she was little she used to run after him as he departed and he would turn to wave at her, but these days he never said goodbye before leaving the village. Her mother also said that when Puhua and her sister were little, their father used to let them tweak his ears and nose but these days he ignored them. To my immense surprise, though, at the time of our third visit in 2015, the father had re-engaged with his family. It transpired that the previous year Puhua's mother had walked into the village pond threatening suicide. She had told him that all she asked was that he try to *yangjia*. She would feel satisfied with even only a few *yuan*, if it came from his genuine effort to *yangjia*. He had retrieved her and promised not to gamble again, and since then he had phoned home at least twice a week. Puhua felt happy because of the greater warmth in her family, which she said was much more precious to her than money.

158   Children in 'Mother At-Home, Father Out' Families

5.3.2 Mothers' Influence on the Relationship between Children and Migrant Fathers

The relationship between children and their migrant fathers was further affected by the mothers' signals to them about their fathers, both intentional and unintentional. This resonates with research in other countries indicating that when a father is non-residential because of either divorce or migration, the at-home mother – often described as a 'gatekeeper' – mediates his involvement with his child or children (Parreñas, 2005; Dreby, 2010; Carlson, McLanahan and Brooks-Gunn, 2008, cited in Nobles, 2011: 732). Studies in other countries, notably in Mexico, also demonstrate that at-home mothers try to recreate the presence of the migrated fathers in the lives of their children by referencing them throughout the day (Kanaiaupuni, 2000 cited in Nobles, 2011: 733). This was similarly the case in Anhui and Jiangxi. At-home mothers often told the children that their migrant fathers did 'bitter work' (*da ku gong*) for them. Additionally, the mothers regularly prompted the children to talk with their fathers on the phone or when they visited, and if a child said that he or she did not know what to say, the mother would suggest topics or advise, 'talk to him just like you talk to me'.

Several children were urged by their mothers to be lenient or understanding in their judgement of their migrant fathers if they felt that he had disappointed them through his absence or through not understanding them. For instance, in 2011, a woman from Eastern County, Anhui, with a husband in Namibia and two at-school sons aged sixteen and eighteen, explained:

My boys said 'Father hasn't returned this year for Chinese New Year' ... and I said 'He's out doing bitter work (*da ku gong*) for your school fees .... Aren't you grown up now? Can't you tie up the decoration couplets and open the front door of the house yourselves?'

Another mother told her son not to blame his father for bringing home a plastic action toy that was too babyish for him. By encouraging the children to engage with their fathers and to see them favourably, the mothers worked to sustain the emotional tie between the breadwinner and the rural-based members of the multilocal family.

Mothers' inadvertent signals could also influence the children's views about their migrant fathers. A few children noted that their mother's mood improved when their migrant father visited home. For instance, Tianming said that her father usually returned home with a bag full of dirty laundry, but that her mother was still extra smiley while he was around. Some children mentioned that their mothers prepared special dishes for their visiting fathers to boost their health, such as egg or chicken soup. Meanwhile, six children of

Conclusion 159

construction workers remarked that their mothers were very pleased when their fathers came home with money: labour sociologists document that the wages of China's construction workers are routinely delayed and paid after several months, typically at Chinese New Year (Pun and Lu, 2010; Swider, 2015; Chuang, 2016). Less positively, though, four children reported that when their fathers returned home, their parents fought, usually over money or over their fathers' gambling.

Conversely, a mother could exacerbate estrangement between a child and a migrant father. I encountered only one such case but include it to illustrate holistically the influence of at-home mothers. In Eastern County, Anhui, in 2013 a fifty-six-year-old grandmother explained that her son had married a mute (*yaba*) woman because the family was too poor to attract any other bride. To the woman's annoyance, her husband would never walk beside her. At the time of our interview, he had been selling snacks in Jiangsu for nine years. The grandmother explained that owing to her daughter-in-law's anger about her husband's failure to acknowledge her or to remit money, the few times he phoned, she refused to let their eleven-year-old son talk with him. The grandmother added that morning, noon and afternoon, rain or shine, her daughter-in-law ferried the boy to and from school on her bicycle. For his part, the boy said that his mother had migrated to the city with his father. My research assistant and I thought that the boy must have misled us about his mother's whereabouts because disability carries immense stigma in Chinese society and he did not want us to ask to interview her, which we did not. Even so, the boy also told us that he only felt close (*qin*) to his mother because she was the one who raised him while he did not miss his father at all.

Conclusion

During the early 2010s in rural regions in Anhui and Jiangxi, growing aspirations for children's educational success reinforced gendered ideas about the best way for families to arrange their earning activities and social reproduction work. In villages with few opportunities for off-farm employment, people saw 'mother home and father out' to be the family configuration most conducive to investing in the future of the next generation. Nevertheless, actually-existing versions of this family configuration were varied and stratified. Specifically, families where a father worked overseas or where a mother had returned to *peidu* in the county seat gave children greater investments of parental money and time. But only parents with 'certain' capital endowments could pursue these more esteemed reproduction strategies, for instance fathers who were healthy enough and had the necessary 'skills' and contacts to migrate overseas, or parents who had enough money to sustain the costs of *peidu*. By contrast, at the other end of the spectrum were children whose mothers had no choice but to stay at home – because of the lack of an alternative source of childcare and their own unsuitability for urban labour markets – while their fathers remitted little money.

When people in rural China said that children benefited educationally from mothers' at-home presence, they expressed their own localised understanding of good mothering rather than aspirations to emulate the hegemonic 'intensive mothering' script or the 'concerted cultivation' repertoire (Lareau, 2003) adopted by urban middle-class families. Specifically, even though family members often said that a mother's at-home care of the children would ensure that the migrant father's toil was not in vain, nobody expected farming mothers to directly tutor their children or to arrange tutoring or extracurricular activities for them. Instead, children and adults in these families thought that the most important contribution of a mother to her children's educational prospects was looking after 'life' (*shenghuo*) matters (food, clothing, hygiene, warmth), imposing routine and stability on their daily life, and nurturing them emotionally, thereby creating the conditions for them to concentrate on their studies. For their part, the children recognised that owing to their fathers' migration, their mothers incurred greater work and mental burdens. They therefore aspired to repay their mothers for their sacrifices through diligence at school and through their future educational and economic achievement. The children's awareness of their mothers' contributions to their comfort and prospects was also heightened because they knew that it was not inevitable for rural mothers to stay at home with them rather than migrate and leave them behind.

But even though idealised gendered models of the family emphasised mothers' domesticity and fathers' economic provisioning, children from farmer-migrant families still valued interaction and intimacy with both of their parents, including with their fathers. The children's emotional closeness to their fathers was affected by several intersecting individual- and family-level factors including the children's age at the time of the father's initial migration, the father's migration history and frequency of return, and the children's and fathers' attributes and personalities. Conversely, the degree of emotional closeness between children and their migrant fathers also moderated how the children viewed their father's economic provisioning. Indeed, while most children saw their migrant father's economic support as evidence of his commitment to them, a father's success as an economic provider did not necessarily guarantee emotional closeness between him and his child. As Coe (2014) observes of children in Ghana, children in rural China valued closeness with their migrant fathers more than they valued their fathers' material provisioning only if they also perceived that their fathers were trying their best to support them. In other words, it did not matter to children if fathers provided only a little material support so long as he interacted warmly with his children and so long as the children thought that he was doing his best to provide.

Conversely, if a father provided a lot of material support but did not interact with his children, the father–child relationship would still not be close. Children's relationship with their migrant fathers was therefore influenced not only by gender beliefs about male breadwinning but also by a fundamental human need for emotional intimacy, which expectations of hegemonic masculinity and gendered migration regimes both suppress (Montes, 2013).

In summary, across 'mother home, father out' families, the family's income, the parents' migration histories and intra-family relationships affected the care and economic investment that different children received. However, the heterogeneity across these families notwithstanding, children mostly just wanted to feel that their mothers and their migrant fathers were committed to them and were trying their best for them. Indeed, closeness (*qin*) between children and their parents mediated how the children perceived their at-home mothers' and their migrant fathers' support for them, affecting their relationship with each. These children's relationship with their mothers and migrant fathers thereby revealed that the gendering of families' multilocal striving strategies both expressed and reproduced socio-economic inequalities, while influencing different children's possibilities for receiving affection and support from each of their parents.

6 Children of Lone-Migrant Mothers and At-Home Fathers

Whenever I asked teachers in the two Anhui fieldwork counties for introductions to children from families with lone-migrant mothers and at-home fathers, they laughed and said that there were no such families. When I asked rural residents in the Anhui fieldwork counties for introductions to friends' or neighbours' families where mothers had migrated alone, they responded similarly: 'A man would never let his wife go out while he stayed at home. What kind of man would do that?' I partly wondered if given their busy lives, my generous hosts had tired of my repeated requests for interview introductions – they thought that my fieldwork was nearly finished and here I was asking for further introductions to the children of lone-migrant mothers. But even as my hosts may have understandably become tired, I think that the main reason I met hardly any children of lone-migrant mothers in Eastern County and Western County was because there were not many. This impression was supported by the small proportion of left-behind children in the Anhui subsample of the 2010 Summer Survey that had a lone-migrant mother – less than 1 per cent.

While teachers and villagers in the Jiangxi fieldwork counties greeted my requests to interview children whose mothers had migrated alone with less incredulity than did teachers and villagers in the Anhui fieldwork counties, they nevertheless said that this family arrangement was rare. Again, the local people's impression was consistent with the breakdown of data from the 2010 Summer Survey. In the Jiangxi subsample, 4.59 per cent of left-behind children had a lone-migrant mother, which, even though higher than the proportion in the Anhui subsample, fell well below the 2010 national average of 16.87 per cent of 'left-behind' children. Research conducted in different parts of China's rural interior in the 1990s, the 2000s and 2010s likewise indicate that families with lone-migrant mothers and at-home fathers were far fewer than other family configurations (Wen and Lin, 2012; ACWF, 2013; Duan et al., 2013; On the Road to School, 2015, 2016 and 2017).

In the Jiangxi fieldwork counties, officials, teachers and farmers frequently said that rural families would only ever adopt a 'mother out, father home' arrangement in two circumstances. One was if the family was very poor and a man's physical or mental impairment prevented him from migrating.

Children of Lone-Migrant Mothers and At-Home Fathers 163

A second circumstance was if the relationship between the couple was discordant. 'Why else would a man risk his wife finding a more capable man outside?' they asked. In 2014, to help me understand why so few mothers had migrated alone relative to other family configurations, the principal of a township junior high school in Tranquil County told me about his own family, explaining:

I am the eldest of four brothers. One of my brothers was born in 1977 and he and his wife migrated to Guangdong. This was when their son was in third grade. My sister-in-law found work in a computer factory and earned good money, several thousand *yuan* per month. But my younger brother could not endure *dagong* life. So he returned home and did some transportation work and lives in the village. I told my brother: 'Money is something you can accumulate slowly, but if you lose your wife it is not easy to find another one, and the child will suffer. You should call your wife back. The wife was reluctant to return because she earned good money ... Women usually only migrate alone if the relationship is broken otherwise the husbands will worry.

The extant literature confirms a view that in China's rural interior provinces the lone migration of a mother indicates inherent strain in the family. Fan reports that in her fieldwork sites – which included localities in Anhui and Sichuan – men opposed the lone migration of their wives (Fan, 2003: 42). Lou (2004; cited in Xiang, 2007) observes that when rural married women migrated leaving their husbands behind, they did so in special circumstances that created immense psychological pressure for the husbands. Murphy, Zhou and Tao (2016) find that nearly two-thirds of the mother-only migrant families sampled in the 2010 Summer Survey had a member who had incurred a major illness after 2005 compared with 40 per cent of other families, and their debt from medical costs since 2005 was 16,000 *yuan*, about a third more than for other families. Meanwhile Duan and Wu's (2009) analysis of a national data set and Wen and Lin's (2012) analysis of a local data set indicate that the families of lone-migrant mothers were characterised by inherent vulnerability including a lack of external support and weak internal coherence. Finally, a survey-based White Paper reports that lone-migrant mother families contained more girls than boys, with the authors positing that given a patrilineal family culture, couples with only daughters may experience greater marital pressure than other couples (On the Road to School, 2015).

The migration studies literature richly documents the experiences of transnational migrant mothers who hail from Ghana, the Philippines, Indonesia, Latin American countries and Caribbean countries, and who, because of an increasing global demand for female labour in the service sector, have assumed family providership roles (e.g. Chant and Radcliffe, 1992; Colen, 1995; Hondagneu-Sotelo and Avila, 1997; Hochschild, 2002; Schmalzbauer, 2004; Parreñas, 2005; Dreby, 2010; Carling, Menjívar and Schmalzbauer, 2012; Gardner, 2012; Peng and Wong, 2013; Coe, 2014; Lam and Yeoh, 2018).

164 Children of Lone-Migrant Mothers and At-Home Fathers

Similarly, research from rural Vietnam casts light on the parenting practices of migrant mothers and the lives of their left-behind families, rural Vietnam being another context where the lone migration of mothers is common (Hoang and Yeoh, 2011; Locke, Hoa and Tam, 2012; Thao, 2015). By contrast, with only a handful of exceptions (e.g. Parreñas, 2005; Dreby, 2010; Hoang and Yeoh, 2011; Hoang, Yeoh and Wattie, 2012; Lam and Yeoh, 2015; Hoang et al., 2015; Thao, 2015; Lam and Yeoh, 2018), few studies examine the childcare practices of left-behind men or children's relationships with their left-behind fathers. Meanwhile, still fewer studies explore children's relationships with their lone-migrant mothers and at-home fathers in contexts where the lone migration of mothers is a social anomaly.

This chapter draws on the cases of eight children and their families in the two Jiangxi fieldwork counties, where lone-mother migration was extremely rare, in order to probe the following questions: How did the children of lone-migrant mothers perceive their mothers, grandparents and at-home fathers in the light of gendered expectations about family and striving? How did different family members participate in or support the parent–child striving team when a mother had migrated alone, and how did the children respond to this support? And what were the implications of a migrant mother and at-home father family configuration for parent–child relationships?

The cases on which this chapter is based include three girls (Lanlan, Caihong and Mingming) and two boys (Taihe and Fangfang). We interviewed the girls when they were aged twelve, fourteen and fifteen. We interviewed one boy, Taihe, when he was ten, and another boy, Fangfang when he was ten and twelve years old and again when he was thirteen years old after his mother had returned home. The return migration of another child's father also added a sixth case. Specifically, when we met Jingjing at ages twelve and fourteen, she belonged to a 'two-parent migrant family' but when we revisited her at age fifteen, she lived with her father while her mother continued to work in Wenzhou City, Zhejiang province. This chapter additionally refers to two other children whose migrant mothers were widowed: a boy called Shenyi, who I mentioned in Chapter 3 and who we interviewed at ages thirteen and seventeen, and a girl called Kaili, who we interviewed at age fifteen.

6.1 Women, Men and Children in Lone-Migrant Mother Families

6.1.1 Gender Roles in Lone-Migrant Mother Families

As I discussed in Chapter 5, school textbooks, television programmes and the comments of adults exposed children to conventional expectations about femininity and masculinity. These expectations were also manifest in a customary division of household labour whereby women assume responsibility for 'inside

6.1 Women, Men, Children in Lone-Migrant Mother Families 165

domestic' work including food preparation, housecleaning, laundry, shopping for food, tending domestic livestock, childcare and repairing clothes, while men do the 'outside work' that earns money (Jacka, 1997). Even though in the 1950s to late 1970s China's socialist state made women's involvement in 'outside' and 'productive' work the lynchpin of its strategy for promoting female emancipation and economic modernisation, efforts to involve men in domestic chores were half-hearted (Croll, 1983). Ethnographers who conducted fieldwork in different villages in the 1990s observed that most housework was done by women (Jacka, 1997; Yan, 2003). Meanwhile, Liu (2017) reports that in the 2010s upper-second-year boys in a Beijing senior high school thought that domestic chores should be done *mainly* by women. Women's responsibility for domestic chores has thereby persisted as a cornerstone of Chinese patriarchy (Jacka, 1997; Song, 2017; Liu, 2019).

In rural Chinese society, people commonly perceive that men and women need each other's unique work contributions to manage daily family life (Liu, 2000:77). Furthermore, in the market economy era, they see women's care work as necessary for optimising men's well-being. Meanwhile, disruptions that leave a man without a wife are thought to harm his physical and psychological health and to distract him from building a career and supporting a family. As I discussed in Chapters 1 and 5, in a Chinese sociocultural context, people also think that the absence of a mother leaves a child in a very pitiful situation and disadvantages the child. Indeed, the neologism *peidu* mama ('accompanying studies mother') was ubiquitous in Anhui and Jiangxi, while I never heard anyone talk about a '*peidu* baba'.

Mirroring scholars' observations for Latin American and Southeast Asian countries (Hondagneu-Sotelo and Avila, 1997; Parreñas, 2005; Dreby, 2010; Lam and Yeoh, 2018), in the Jiangxi fieldwork counties I observed that a woman-as-homemaker model informed family expectations about who would do the domestic work vacated by the migrant mother. In the families we visited where a mother had migrated while the father remained at home, the influence of the woman-as-carer model was evident in two respects. Firstly, the family arranged for a grandmother to do much of the domestic work. In four of the six families, either one or both paternal grandparents co-resided with the at-home fathers and children. Meanwhile, in the other two families, the children – Fangfang and Jingjing – lived with their father and a sibling, but they still lived nearby or next to their grandparents. The involvement of grandparents in these families reflects a nationwide pattern: according to a breakdown of 2010 census data, approximately half the children of lone-migrant mothers resided with fathers and grandparents, while half lived just with their fathers (Duan et al., 2013). Nevertheless, many children who did not live in the same household as their grandparents still had a grandparent living nearby because of patrilocal marriage patterns.

Next, and as a corollary of the aforementioned text, the children were mostly cared for in daily life by grandmothers. In the four families where grandmothers co-resided, grandmothers cooked and washed for the children, while in the other two families, the fathers did some household chores, but the grandmothers helped them substantially. This differs from researchers' observations in some Southeast Asian countries where left-behind fathers cooked for, fed and bathed their children, and oversaw their children's studies alongside earning money, shopping, attending school functions and administering discipline, all with minimal help from female relatives (Hoang and Yeoh, 2011; Hoang, Yeoh and Wattie, 2012; Thao, 2015; Lam and Yeoh, 2018). Lam and Yeoh (2018: 115) explain that in these countries owing to an intensification of female labour migration over several decades, fathering practices had changed gradually such that the 'mothering father' was no longer a 'social oddity'.

When left-behind fathers in the Jiangxi counties performed domestic chores, like the migrant men that Choi and Peng (2016) observed in the Pearl River Delta, they tried to make these tasks look less like women's work. For instance, Fangfang's father cooked meals, but he thought that this was acceptable because, as Choi and Peng also note, men customarily cook at village ceremonies while some migrant men work as chefs (2016: 96). Caihong's father sometimes cooked rice or warmed up leftovers that his elderly mother had prepared, and he helped his mother and daughter with tidying the house. Meanwhile, Jingjing's and Fangfang's fathers escorted them to and from school, which was acceptable because riding a motorbike was a masculine activity. In the Jiangxi fieldwork counties, as Thao (2015) observes for some left-behind men in rural regions in Vietnam, some men also bought domestic appliances to alleviate their chore burdens. For instance, two households used remittances to buy water pumps. Meanwhile, Fangfang's father had bought a washing machine, the only one in his village. Nevertheless, the water pressure was not powerful enough for the machine to work, so he washed small items in the sink, his mother helped with washing larger items, and he used the machine to spin clothes dry. These men's involvement in domestic work notwithstanding, attending to children's daily care needs was not integral to their fathering identities.

The other aspect of fatherhood to influence children's perceptions of their fathers was how their fathers measured up as breadwinners. The children knew that men needed to earn money to be seen as competent. They also knew that men with more education obtained more desirable jobs. Indeed, education was widely associated with societal perceptions of successful men (Jacka, Kipnis and Sargeson, 2013: 173). Some children in Anhui and Jiangxi mentioned that richer classmates and children in the cities had fathers with 'ability' (*benshi*). Meanwhile, poorer children were sometimes told by a parent, 'We are sorry that *ma* and *ba* have no ability'. The at-home fathers of five of the children we met,

6.1 Women, Men, Children in Lone-Migrant Mother Families

whose mothers had migrated alone earned little money, had little education, and suffered from a disability or else they had been pushed back from the city by ill-health and fatigue. Kohrman (2005) argues that in China the idea of 'ability' (*nengli*) 'has become coterminous with mobility and national development and has 'deeply informed gender'. He further argues that physically impaired men are seen by others as incompetent because they do not drive forward development outside the home (Kohrman, 2005: 185). This was the case in Anhui and Jiangxi, where, as I show later, some children's awareness of their fathers' poor performance as providers made them feel extra protective towards them.

6.1.2 Lone-Mother Migration and Children's Well-being

Extant studies on international migration and on China's internal migration both suggest that when mothers migrate alone, left-behind children's well-being is adversely affected. Research in Southeast Asian countries finds that left-behind children fare better than children who live with both parents because international migration generates large remittances to compensate for deficits in parental care, but the children of migrant mothers fare worse than the children of migrant fathers (Yeoh and Lam, 2006). Some of this research observes that in comparison with children whose mothers are at home, the children of migrant mothers display more emotional difficulties, lower levels of happiness, a higher incidence of common illness (Battistella and Conaco, 1998; Asis, 2006; Jordan and Graham, 2012) and reduced rates of school enrolment (Jampaklay, 2006). The research in Southeast Asian countries and some research in Mexico and Eurasia also suggest that maternal migration is most disadvantageous to children because it unsettles established gendered roles, generates stress within families, and reduces the children's access to attentive care (Kandel and Kao, 2001; Luecke and Stoehr, 2012).

Studies from rural China similarly find that maternal migration correlates with worse outcomes for left-behind children. Duan and Wu's study (2009), based on data from a 2006 nationally representative population and birth planning survey, finds that compared with other left-behind children and children who lived with both their parents, a higher proportion of children whose mothers had migrated alone did not receive the mandatory years of compulsory education. Meng and Yamauchi's (2015) analysis of data from nine provinces discovers that the children of lone-migrant mothers exhibited significantly worse health than the children of lone-migrant fathers. Murphy, Zhou and Tao's (2016) analysis of the 2010 Summer Survey data finds that the children of lone-migrant mothers fared worse for self-reported health and confidence in the future than other left-behind children or children who lived with both parents. Wen and Lin's (2012) survey in a county in Hunan province finds that children whose mothers migrated alone were more likely to drink and

168   Children of Lone-Migrant Mothers and At-Home Fathers

smoke and were less engaged at school than the children of two migrant parents or the children of lone migrant fathers. Meanwhile, a White Paper based on a survey of over seven thousand children in six provinces finds that the children of lone-migrant mothers reported lower self-evaluations of their grades than other left-behind children and children who lived with both their parents (On the Road to School, 2015).

6.2   Children's Perceptions of Family Life When Only Mothers Have Migrated

In many countries, including in Western industrialised countries, families that violate gendered expectations in their parenting arrangements often incur social and emotional costs in the form of other people's disapproval (Kramer and Kramer, 2016). Scholars also observe for several countries, for instance Indonesia, Philippines and Vietnam, that when mothers migrate alone, the left-behind family members try to present their families as conforming to prevailing gender norms, even as these norms are mutable (Lam and Yeoh, 2015; Thao, 2015; Lam and Yeoh, 2018). Similarly, the children and adults in the six lone-migrant mother families we visited in Jiangxi knew that their configuration deviated from the norm. The remaining discussion turns to explore how the children dealt with their families' unconventional arrangement and how they responded to their mothers' and fathers' efforts to be *accountable* to their gendered identities as they tried to fulfil their family responsibilities (West and Zimmerman, 1987). In the following sections, I examine how the children dealt with their mothers' migration, how they perceived their fathers' contributions to the family and how two children experienced living in a family where a mother's capacity to participate in the striving team had waned because of challenging circumstances.

6.2.1   Children's Responses to the Lone Migration of Mothers

Children's responses to their mothers' lone migration included: keeping silent about their mothers' absence; trying to understand their mothers better; relying on grandmothers as mother substitutes both practically and emotionally; and cherishing any affection from their fathers. At the same time, each child's mix of responses varied by family and individual level factors. Specifically, the quality of the parents' marital relationship stood out as a salient family-level factor while the children's school grades and age were noteworthy individual-level factors.

6.2.1.1 Children in Harmonious Families   My research assistant and I first met Caihong in 2010, and, like some other children whose mothers had

6.2 Perceptions When Only Mothers Have Migrated

migrated without them, she did not want to talk about her mother, so we let the conversation move to other topics. On meeting her again five years later, Caihong explained that when she was in primary school, if ever a teacher asked her a question, she would automatically think of her mother, seize up and try not to cry. Then when she returned home, she used to console herself by drawing pictures of her parents together and hiding them in her bedside drawer.

By her teenage years, Caihong's aspirations for her studies and her parents' aspirations for her education aligned ever more closely, and she found herself increasingly wanting to talk with her mother because she could better appreciate her mother's reasons for being outside and her mother's hopes for her. Her mother worked in an electronics factory in Dongguan to earn money for the education fees for both Caihong and her elder sister, with Caihong's sister having already made it to a decent university. Echoing Fei Xiaotong's explanation of filial piety discussed in Chapter 1, Caihong said that as she grew to better understand her mother's reasons for having migrated, she felt closer to her. Once when she was in junior high school, her Dad had told her that her mother would visit home in a few days' time, so she wrote a letter to her mother. She had wanted to show her mother that she was now mature enough to understand (*dongshi*) why she was 'outside'.

Another girl, Lanlan, resembled Caihong in her family circumstances, educational aspirations and the evolution of her relationship with her migrant mother. Lanlan's mother worked two jobs in Jiangsu, as a factory cook and as a cleaner, to pay the fees of Lanlan and her older sister who, like Caihong's older sister, attended university. One day in spring 2014, while my research assistant and I were waiting in Lanlan's village for her father to return from buying a tool in the county seat, the then fourteen-year-old took us to a stream at the foot of a hill. She told us that she visited the stream whenever she felt vexed. As we sat listening to cicadas, Lanlan sighed apologetically for our wait, saying: 'This village is really boring, there is nothing to do.' She told us that she had always felt 'left-behind' as a child because owing to her mother's absence, her sister's transfer to board at the senior high school and her father's taciturn temperament, she had spent many hours sitting alone watching the water shrimps on the rocks. In the past she had refused to talk with her mother because she blamed her for her loneliness. But as her visions for her future became clearer, she started to want to talk more with her mother. Consistent with Obendiek's (2017) analysis, parents' educational support increased both Lanlan's and Caihong's sense of debt to their migrant mothers, deepening their emotional attachment to them.

But even as both girls grew to better understand their mothers, they had also become accustomed to relying on their grandmothers. One Friday afternoon as Lanlan and her grandmother shelled beans on the front porch, the phone rang. Lanlan looked at the number display, smiled, said it was her mother, and took the phone inside. Half an hour later the phone rang again, and the mother asked to talk with me. Her animated voice explained:

I have no other way. My husband's eye is damaged, and he is handicapped so I must work outside for my children's studies. *Nainai* is so old and she must replace me in cooking and washing clothes. There is no other way . . . Tell her to study hard. Tell her how to study.

Caihong similarly relied on her grandmother. Caihong's mother had first migrated when Caihong was a few months old and had returned home when Caihong was in second grade but then had remigrated when Caihong was in fourth grade. Caihong's father stayed at home because his leg had been permanently injured in a farming accident. Caihong recalled that for several weeks after her mother had left the village in a bread-loaf-shaped van (*mianbao che*), she had felt helpless. Shortly after, though, her grandmother began to help her with cooking, cleaning, washing and making the bed. Caihong and Lanlan said that they *loved* their mothers and grandmothers, but they felt *closer* (*qin*) to their grandmothers, echoing Xiao's (2014) observation, noted in Chapter 5, that children sometimes distinguished between *ai* (love) and *qin* to articulate their feeling of distance from or ambivalence towards migrant parents.

The children of lone-migrant mothers also dealt with their mother's absence by turning to their fathers for affection. Although the fathers generally avoided domestic work, maternal migration still created space for them to adopt more flexible fathering practices, which the children appreciated. For instance, Caihong said that she did not feel 'left-behind' because her father always looked after her carefully and gave her a mother's love as well as a father's love. When I asked her for an example, she replied:

When my mum was at home, she'd always make sure I was properly covered by the quilt at night and when she's not here my dad always makes sure that I'm properly tucked in.

Caihong also recalled that as a young child whenever she cried after her mother's departures, her father hugged her until she stopped crying. Jingjing – discussed in Chapters 3 and 4 – similarly valued her father's gestures of affection towards her. When we met in 2014, she said that she was happy for her mother to stay outside so long as her father stayed at home, and that the best thing about her father being at home was that: 'He's always there to pick me up from school.' Lanlan did not enjoy the same intimacy with her father that Caihong and Jingjing shared with theirs because of his reserved nature, but as I discuss in the following, she still felt consoled by knowing that he cared about her.

6.2.1.2 Children in Discordant Families When parents' marital relationships were discordant, children dealt with the circumstance of maternal

6.2 Perceptions When Only Mothers Have Migrated

migration in ways that resembled the responses of the children discussed earlier: they preferred not to mention their migrant mothers, especially when they were younger, and they relied on their grandmothers. A crucial difference, though, was that the children of estranged parents did not have the same opportunities to maintain a close relationship with their migrant mothers as did children such as Lanlan and Caihong. The patrilineal family system meant that the children of discordant parents belonged to striving teams in which the mother's membership was insecure or had even been revoked. This compromised the mothers' opportunities to care for their children from a distance, while fathers or grandparents sidelined or replaced the mothers.

Given the patrilocal family culture, maternal migration and marital discord compounded each other in distancing the children and their migrant mothers from each other. On the one hand, in an environment where taboos against divorce remained strong, marital discord could precipitate a mother's lone migration. A saying I sometimes heard in villages in Jiangxi was, 'If you marry a chicken follow the chicken and if you marry a dog follow a dog' (Murphy, 2004b). Migration offered women a less radical alternative to divorce but a married woman's lone migration was still a serious step. Conversely, a migrant woman's decision to remain 'outside' while her husband had failed to earn money could exacerbate existing marital tensions or generate new ones.

The children of discordant parents faced specific challenges in maintaining relationships with their migrant mothers. The distance between the children and their migrant mothers could be exacerbated because – as noted in Chapter 5 – the at-home parent mediated the child's relationship with the migrant parent. In circumstances of marital discord, it was also less feasible for the parents to cast the mother's migration as a sacrifice undertaken on behalf of the child. The children of discordant parents often thought about their mothers and wanted to retain contact with them, but they did not seek to 'understand' them in the same way that children did when they and their mothers unambiguously belonged to the same striving team.

When we met fourteen-year-old Mingming in 2013, her parents had separated. Her father was unusual amongst the fathers discussed in this chapter because his masculine identity as a breadwinner was secure. He did not work in the devalued agricultural sector and he earned a decent income: four years prior to our meeting he had returned from working in Shenzhen and had established a cardboard box factory in the Tranquil County industrial zone. His factory employed fifteen returnee workers. Meanwhile, Mingming's mother remained working in a factory in Shenzhen. During their early childhoods, Mingming and her younger brother had been raised by their grandmother. Mingming told us that she preferred her father to her mother because her mother had a fierce and unpredictable temper and because she had spent more time with her father. Nevertheless, of all the adults in her life she felt closest to her grandmother.

When we revisited Mingming in 2015, her parents had divorced. Mingming said that while she enjoyed living with her father, grandmother and younger brother, she often worried about her mother who sometimes phoned her and had not taken the divorce well.

Another child who had to cope with maternal migration in the context of his parents' marital discord was Taihe from Tranquil County. His father had returned after several years of working in a shoe factory in Zhejiang and now worked in a nearby township making aluminium frames for doors and windows for newly constructed houses. His mother lived in a city three hours away by bus, where she worked as a seamstress. A source of tension between Taihe's parents was his father's gambling. For over six years, Taihe's mother returned home once every two months to see her son but she never stayed overnight. Taihe explained to us that all matters in his life were decided by *Yeye*. *Yeye*, a tall and well-spoken former village head, confirmed that he decided on all matters pertaining to his grandson while Taihe's grandmother provided daily care. Taihe missed his mother and felt hurt by her absence, but his grandfather was the most significant adult in his life.

6.2.2 Children's Perceptions of Their At-Home Fathers as Providers

Children's awareness that men should be *accountable* to their families as breadwinners informed their relationships with their fathers because they had a sense of how their fathers fared as providers. Research in other countries reveals that left-behind men's 'maintenance of their productive selves keeps them going' (Pingol, 2001 cited in Lam and Yeoh, 2015: 108). This chapter's child-oriented analysis builds on this insight by demonstrating that *the children realised* that a 'productive' identity was important to their fathers. Owing to their older ages, it was the daughters of lone migrant mothers we met who demonstrated their awareness of the impact of societal gender norms on their fathers' sense of self-worth and on their fathers' way of relating to them. For instance, Lanlan said:

In other families it is the mother at home and the father outside, so it is as if he thinks that he is useless. I never know what to say to him and he never knows what to say to me.

As Lanlan's, Caihong's and Jingjing's fathers did not have local off-farm jobs to bolster their provider identities, these girls tried to affirm their sense of worth.

6.2.2.1 Affirming Fathers Lanlan, Caihong and Jingjing tried to validate their fathers' worth by variously noting their economic contributions to the family, highlighting the off-farm aspects of their work, recognising the physical hardships that they endured in work, emphasising the non-work aspects of their

6.2 Perceptions When Only Mothers Have Migrated

efforts on behalf of the family and demonstrating their affection for their fathers in the face of their failed efforts to bring in money. The words and actions of Lanlan illustrate well her affirmation of her father's contribution to the family. On our visit to her home in 2014, the three of us – Lanlan, my research assistant and I – went back inside the house after standing on the porch to look out at the family's crops, at which point Lanlan told us in front of her father that he was the one who kept the family well-fed. Later, when her father was out of earshot, Lanlan told us:

I try to say things to make him feel better. Like the watermelons he planted, I said: 'Aye, these watermelons are much more delicious than any bought watermelons.' Then he said: 'If you like them, I'll plant more next year.' I could tell my words made him happy.

The girls also signalled their recognition of the physically demanding nature of their father's farm work through their gestures. For instance, when we first met Caihong in 2010, she told us that she felt happiest whenever she heated water for her father so he could drink hot tea and wash his feet after working all day in the fields. Gestures to recognise the physical toll of work on fathers may be more common among girls than boys: as discussed in Chapter 4, girls often used domestic work to build intimacy. But as is also mentioned in Chapter 4, boys recognised the toll that physically demanding work took on their mothers and grandparents and tried to help them.

A further way in which the girls affirmed their fathers' masculine identities was by seeing them as individuals who were busy 'outside' the home. In their conversations with my research assistant and me, Caihong talked about her father's obligations as a village committee accountant; Lanlan talked about the outside work her father did cutting wood for a neighbour; Jingjing talked about how her father often ran errands outside the home, especially when overseeing the construction of their new house. In explaining to us that their fathers were busy 'outside', they reflected an awareness of real demands on their fathers while portraying them in a positive light to us as outsiders.

The girls also empathised with their fathers' thwarted efforts to earn, recognising their hard work while blaming social complexity for their failure. This could be seen most clearly in Jingjing's relationship with her father. Jingjing's father had laboured in stone quarries since his late teens, later moving to factories. He had married in his early twenties and then migrated to Wenzhou with his wife. After several years, he had returned home to try to run a mini-van business but discovered that the routes within the county had all been purchased by well-connected individuals. He later returned to Wenzhou and tried to work in a foot massage parlour but found serving women and other men too demeaning, so he quit. Next, he migrated to Dongguan and worked as a security guard in a gated residential compound, but in 2012 he had an operation on his kidney and lost substantial weight. By 2014 he no longer had the stamina to

174   Children of Lone-Migrant Mothers and At-Home Fathers

endure night shifts, so he returned home for several months and then remigrated briefly, only to return home again in 2015.

When we visited him in Dongguan in 2013, he told us that his wife chastised him all the time for failing to bring in money, so much so he could not bear to answer her phone calls. In 2015, he told us that she had refused to lend him money to set up a shop in the village because she did not trust him to use the money wisely. By contrast, Jingjing never reproached him. Her face shone whenever he appeared, and he could see this. Unlike Lanlan and Caihong, and as noted in Chapter 3, Jingjing struggled academically. Like her father, she had endured successive setbacks and was filled with self-reproach. Hence, as noted in Chapter 4, the two found comfort in each other. In 2014, during her final year in junior high school, Jingjing said that her father had tried his best 'outside' and that she was glad that he was now home.

6.2.2.2 Ambivalence towards Fathers   While some children understood their fathers' status predicament and tried to affirm them, other children did not. Fangfang and Taihe did not mention their fathers' contributions to their families and even appeared ambivalent towards them. Our interviews with Fangfang yielded few responses, but on each occasion he said that he missed his mother, while at our second meeting he said: 'I won't speak to her on the phone, I'll only speak to her if she returns', additionally noting, 'the food is better when she is at home'. As discussed in Chapter 4, Fangfang mostly ignored his returnee father and preferred to spend his time at his grandmother's house. Taihe talked more than Fangfang but he too did not say much about his father. This may have been because it is shameful for a person to lose money gambling. Also, as noted previously, his father did not play a major role in his life while *Yeye* was his father-substitute. Therefore, unlike the girls, Fangfang and Taihe lived at an emotional distance from their fathers.

6.3   Striving in Lone-Migrant Mother Families

When mothers migrated alone, family strains could make the narrative of parents striving for their children's education less tenable. Notably, owing to a reversal in the parents' gender roles and to possible estrangement within the family, it was not always obvious that the fathers were working for the family or that the mothers were committed to the children's future. While most children wanted to advance through education regardless of who had migrated, when a mother had migrated alone, the striving narrative had to be adapted. Meanwhile the children also had to cope with the set of circumstances in their own family. This was especially so for children whose parents' capacity to support them had waned. Below, I discuss how children who had access to

6.3 Striving in Lone-Migrant Mother Families

different amounts of parental support varied in their perceptions of both their parents and their own educational prospects.

6.3.1 When Support for a Striving Team Endured

In five of the six 'migrant mother, at-home father' families, the members' aspirations mostly cohered around the children's education and future. Indeed, the members of these families explained the parents' work contributions in ways that were congruent with normative gendered divisions of labour. For instance, Lanlan's father said:

My wife needs to go outside because I can't. ... I'm used to her being outside. I don't wash clothes or cook. I farm 4 *mu* of land and I also farm the land of some other people in the village. I plant some vegetables and watermelons and raise some chickens too. **I *yangjia* (support the family) while my wife takes responsibility for the children's tuition fees.**

The children similarly saw their parents as making complementary gendered contributions to their well-being: the father provided sustenance while the mother took care of their education.

In Lanlan's and Caihong's families, the children's academic promise encouraged the parents to remain committed to the family's unconventional striving strategy while giving all the family members a sense of purpose. These family efforts received further encouragement in Spring 2015 when Lanlan and Caihong each received much coveted places at the only key-point public senior high school in Tranquil County, making their parents and grandmothers extremely proud. The two girls were thereafter urged on even more by their parents and grandmothers to follow in their elder sisters' footsteps.

Lanlan and Caihong also both realised that their fathers endured lonely and less comfortable lives because of their mothers' migration, for their sake. They reported sometimes overhearing their fathers on the phone asking their mothers when they were coming home or suggesting that they should return. They noted that their fathers appeared visibly happier when their mothers were about to visit. They said that they and their fathers both appreciated the extra-tasty meals that their mothers cooked on their visits home. The two girls also said that their mothers had told them and their fathers that they would work 'outside' for just a few more years to support the children through school. This accords with some scholars' observations of family members in rural Vietnam who stressed to each other the temporary nature of the mothers' migration in order to make the situation psychologically more bearable for the at-home fathers (Resurreccion and Ha, 2007; Thao, 2015). Certainly, Lanlan's and Caihong's mothers used a timeline for their migration and return linked to the children's educational progress to help the at-home men and children accept their migration.

Even though Lanlan's and Caihong's fathers each had physical infirmities that reduced their mobility, both men also demonstrated their support for their daughters' education. For instance, they attended parent–teacher meetings at the township junior high school. At these meetings the teachers told the parents and guardians to limit the children's television time, ensure that the children return straight home after school and keep the children on track so that they do not miss their chance in life. In previous years, these fathers had also attended such parent–teacher meetings on behalf of their eldest daughters, and they had subsequently accompanied their eldest daughters when they had gone to enrol at university.

Lanlan's and Caihong's fathers' attendance at the school meetings was compatible with their masculine identities because it involved them liaising with people outside the home. At the same time, though, both girls knew that their fathers' attendance at the meetings required them to make a special effort and move outside their comfort zone. Echoing research in other countries about how some poorer parents' *habitus* makes them feel 'out of place' in formal settings, including schools, both men felt self-conscious in the presence of teachers because of their poor-spoken Mandarin and their disabilities (Lareau, 2003; Morrow and Vennam, 2015). Moreover, the fathers' disabilities created practical obstacles for them in attending the meetings. Lanlan's father had lost his sight in one eye and had poor vision in the other, preventing him from riding a motorbike in the evening, so he had to pay a villager to take him to the township. Meanwhile, Caihong's father felt embarrassed walking slowly up the school stairs with his lame leg. The two girls appreciated their fathers' demonstration of their aspirations for their education and they wanted to bring honour to them through academic achievement.

In lone-migrant mother families where the marital relationship was strained or had ended, the parent–child striving team managed to function in a realigned form if the patrilineal family members had the economic resources to support the children's education and if the children showed some academic promise. For Mingming and Taihe, the father and *Yeye*, respectively, were the principal figures in the adult–child striving teams, while their mothers had receded from view. Mingming knew that it was her father who supported her studies financially. With his encouragement, she envisioned that her education would equip her for a future role in his business. When we met in 2015, she explained:

I want to study economics and English at a humanities university. I want a job in trade or languages, such as a translator. My dad has a company and if I specialise in foreign business then I can help him. He wants me to get into a first-rate university.

6.3 Striving in Lone-Migrant Mother Families 177

Taihe's family was less well off than Mingming's, but his grandfather had several sources of income. He received a state pension for his previous role as village head and he earned some money from sideline activities, in addition to farming. Taihe's grandfather explained that the boy's mother mostly just covered her own living expenses through her earnings, but she paid for the tutoring classes that Taihe attended for two to three weeks during the summer holidays held in the city where she worked. Furthermore, she had recently purchased a second-hand computer for him. Even as Taihe knew that his mother wanted him to do well at school, he spoke largely about his grandfather's support for him and his studies. His grandfather strictly supervised his homework, escorted him to and from school each day, told him to aim for Beijing University and promised to pay his university fees just so long as he got a place.

6.3.2 When Support for a Striving Team Wanes

In some lone-migrant mother families, because of a combination of external shocks and internal strains, the mothers' capacity or commitment to participate in a parent–child striving team could wane. This was the case for Shenyi and Kaili. These children's migrant mothers were both widowed and had remarried. Shenyi and Kaili recognised the importance of education but they each had to reconcile this with their own difficult family circumstances. In Shenyi's case, a dawning realisation that he was unlikely to advance academically had accelerated a decline in his mother's financial support for him. Few migration studies publications examine the lives of children affected by both parental migration and the loss of a parent, but limited evidence suggests that these children face added challenges (Luecke and Stoehr, 2012), which is consistent with the experiences of Shenyi and Kaili.

When we first met thirteen-year-old Shenyi in 2010, as noted in Chapter 3, he told us that his mother had migrated after his father had died from stomach cancer. The boy's bachelor uncle provided further insight into Shenyi's family circumstances, explaining that the boy's mother had remarried and then divorced because the man had mistreated her. In 2010, Shenyi boarded at school during the week, with his mother paying the tuition and boarding fees of 800 *yuan* per term. Shenyi missed both his parents terribly and longed for his mother's phone calls. At that time, Shenyi had wanted to study to become a doctor to help sick people. When we met again in 2014, Shenyi studied at a *minban* (people-run or private) 'ordinary' senior high school in the county seat. The school was a modest building that sat literally and figuratively in the shadow of the imposing building of the prestigious key-point public senior high school. At our second meeting, Shenyi was a tall, slim young man dressed from top to toe in black, with his fringe cut in the long triangular style of Korean pop idols. He was more talkative than when we had met him four years ago, and he attributed this change in temperament to the close friendship of classmates. He told us that he wanted to be an interior designer, but that his biggest obstacle in life was that he could not make himself study. This was because no matter how he tried, he could not find the material interesting or make it go into his head (*du bu jin*).

Shenyi told us that his mother had married for a third time and now had a child from that marriage. He said that she still phoned him from time to time, but that their relationship was becoming more distant. When I asked him why he thought that their relationship was becoming more distant, he explained:

She always finds fault with me. She always asks: 'Why do you need more money? Why do you waste money? Don't you have enough clothes?'

His mother had also let him know emphatically that he would need to support himself economically once he had finished senior high school, a prospect that worried him. His bachelor uncle and grandmother did not have the financial means to help him. His elder brother struggled to support himself, while his elder sister had married into another family where she had obligations of her own. Shenyi told us that not a day went by when he did not feel the pain of having grown up without his parents. But school was a sanctuary that delayed him from facing the world: he stayed at school not only during term-time but also during the school holidays. Even as Shenyi and his mother still cared about each other, they were ceasing to belong to the same parent–child striving team.

The circumstances of fifteen-year-old Kaili were challenging too. When Kaili was five years old and her brother was three years old, her migrant mother tried to escape the poverty of her marital family by leaving their father for another man. However, the biggest blow to the children came with the death of their father when Kaili was ten years old. Kaili clung to the memory of her father. Her happiest memory was of the time he had brought her a cake back from the county seat for her ninth birthday. It was the first time she had ever tasted cake.

Owing to her grandparents' frailty, Kaili did much of the heavy farm work alone. At the weekends she went to collect rattan canes in the mountains to sell in the township market. She usually went with another girl in the village, and they found the work arduous rather than fun. She earned just short of twenty *yuan* a month from selling the rattan and took two to three *yuan* for herself, handing over the rest to her *nainai* for household expenses. Her grandparents also received an old-age subsidy, and an allowance for the grandfather's service in the Korean War, which totalled nearly 700 *yuan* per month. Meanwhile, Kaili's family received an annual donation of 500 *yuan* for poor children from a Shenzhen charity, as well as a termly school subsidy. Kaili's mother did not

Conclusion   179

contribute anything to the upkeep of her children and had no contact with them: Kaili said that she could no longer remember her.

Kaili's test scores were twentieth in her year-grade, and she wished that her grades were better. She said that if there was any way she could make it to university, then – like Shenyi had once dreamt – she would study to become a doctor to help sick people. Pertinently, though, her priority was to raise (*yang*) her younger brother well. She supervised his homework, protected him from taking on farming and domestic chores, and felt responsible for making sure that he would have a route to a decent life. After the interview, my research assistant used a popular Chinese saying to descr be Kaili's relationship with her brother: 'Elder sister like a mother, elder brother like a father.' Even as Kaili's responsibility for her brother was undoubtedly a burden, as sociologists observe of older children in distressed families in other contexts (Abbey and Dallos, 2004; Elder, 1974 cited in Bronfenbrenner, 1979: 280), a feeling of being needed and responsible for someone else gave Kaili a sense of purpose that enhanced her resilience. Striving goals underpinned Kaili's daily efforts, but her aspirations were for her younger brother as she became the mother-figure.

Conclusion

This chapter explored how gendered expectations of parenting impacted on children's relationships with their mothers and fathers when their mothers had migrated alone. While research in other countries examines how migrant mothers 'do care' from afar or how left-behind fathers contend with their workloads and buttress their masculine identities, this chapter's use of a child-oriented lens revealed that the children knew their families' configuration contravened prevailing gender norms and signalled to other people their families' vulnerability. At the same time, the children also realised that societal gendered expectations affected how the parents saw themselves and how they related to them as their children (West and Zimmerman, 1987). Hence, the children contended with pre-existing family vulnerabilities, the absence of their mothers as primary caregivers, and strains within their families arising from a reversal in the parents' gendered roles.

During their younger years some children wanted to forget about their mothers because they blamed them for their hurt and loneliness, and they bonded with their grandmothers instead. But as some children grew older, they felt better able to understand their mothers and tried to communicate with them more. Children's efforts to understand their mothers were most pronounced in the cases of the two girls whose parents' commitment to their education was buoyed by their promising grades. By contrast, when parents' marriages floundered, mothers could become sidelined in the parent–child striking team. The children of discordant parents still cared about their migrant mothers, but they formed stronger bonds with their fathers and grandparents who more clearly belonged to the same striving team as them.

When the families of lone migrant mothers incurred economic hardship, men were at the gravest risk of negative gender assessment because their failure as providers was laid bare (West and Zimmerman, 1987). In some families where a father was either unwilling or unable to migrate, the children's academic potential offered hope that a 'weak' family could strengthen over time through the acquisition of cultural capital and distinction. In these families, a father's and a child's shared commitment to the child's education could deepen the emotional bond between the two (Obendiek, 2017). But when a child struggled academically, mutual solace could still provide an alternative basis for emotional closeness between father and child, as was the case with Jingjing and her father. Meanwhile, some older children understood their father's feelings about their left-behind circumstances given societal expectations of men, so they affirmed their father's worth as producer, provider, representative of the family 'outside' the home and fighter in a complex world. They thereby used their tacit understanding of gender norms in proactively shaping their relationship with their fathers.

In other cases, though, the lone migration of a mother corresponded with a severe shock that compromised the mother's capacity to participate in the parent–child striving team. As mentioned, some mothers were pushed out to the edge of the striving team by marital discord. Meanwhile, other mothers' positions in their children's families became tenuous after divorce or widowhood, thereby exposing the children to even more vulnerability. In such circumstances, a child's lack of obvious academic potential could also demotivate a mother from investing in her child, especially if poverty and the demands of a new family reduced what she could contribute. The children still wanted to strive, but cumulative setbacks thwarted their efforts to produce high test scores. They therefore had to find alternative ways of coping by using the few supports they had to rely on. In summary, children of lone-migrant mothers experienced different kinds of family circumstances, but they all had to contend with striving pressures and with trying to manage their relationships with significant adults in a family configuration that appeared anomalous both to the family members and to outsiders.

7 Children in Skipped Generation Families

> My heart lacks some warmth. Grandparents cannot compensate me because they are after all not my parents. My parents also cannot compensate me because I have only one month out of twelve when I am with them and it is absolutely not enough.
>
> – Yaping, an eleven-year-old girl from Jade County, Jiangxi, who had lived with her grandparents for three years following her return from Shanghai to her village
>
> *Nainai* is too feudal. She doesn't understand anything. She thinks that the internet is bad. When I was in Shenzhen I went online to chat with some of my friends. *Nainai* does not even know that you can go online to look at the news.
>
> – Hanhan, a twelve-year-old boy from Jade County, Jiangxi,
>
> (first introduced in Chapter 5)

By the twenty-first century, childcare by grandparents had become widespread in China's rural and urban areas because of an increase in women's participation in the labour force alongside a decline in public childcare institutions. Meanwhile, life expectancy increased, so many more children had surviving grandparents (Chen, Liu and Mair, 2011; He and Ye, 2013; Santos, 2017). In the countryside, against a background of unprecedented levels of two-parent migration, the proportion of 'skipped generation' households burgeoned. In 2012, over one-quarter of rural households nationwide counted as skipped generation (Chen and Sun, 2015: 45). In parts of Jiangxi province in the early 2010s, up to 90 per cent of rural households were skipped generation (Xu, Silverstein and Chi, 2014). But even as childcare by grandparents has become prevalent in China, research on the topic remains sparse (Chen, Liu and Mair, 2011: 572; Chen and Sun, 2015: 14; Santos, 2017: 93).

The sociologist Ester Goh (2009; 2011) draws on ethnographic research in China's coastal city of Xiamen to suggest that urban grandparents and parents together form 'intergenerational parenting coalitions', the dynamics of which affect children's lives. In this chapter, I adapt Goh's (2009; 2011) idea of 'intergenerational parenting coalitions' to see the migrant parents and the grandparent caregivers as forming 'multi-local intergenerational parenting

182   Children in Skipped Generation Families

coalitions' as a variant of the adult–child striving teams. Certainly, in a way that was consistent with Dreby's observation of grandmothers in Mexican transnational families, the grandparents we met in rural Anhui and Jiangxi did not seek to replace the migrant parents in the children's lives. Rather, they supported the migrants' efforts to build a better life for the children and encouraged the children to recognise their parents' sacrifices (Dreby, 2010: 205–206). Nevertheless, owing to the parents' absence, the grandparents performed many parental functions in the children's lives.

It is not new for rural Chinese children to spend much time in the care of their grandparents. Santos (2017) highlights historical continuity in 'surrogate parenting' by grandmothers in rural China. He explains that during the socialist era, despite campaigns encouraging men to help with domestic chores, the 'work of childrearing remained in the hands of *a female-centred intergenerational body* supervised by the mother under the guidance of the mother-in-law' – the latter retaining her authority because of her seniority and child-raising experience (Santos, 2017: 94). Santos states that the division of labour among the members of this *intergenerational body* helped mothers to balance their productive work – earning work points redeemable as a share of the collective harvest – with their domestic responsibilities (Santos, 2017: 95). Santos further observes that even as the traditional structure of 'multiple mothering' has continued, it has been reconfigured because of the migration of adult daughters and daughters-in-law (Santos, 2017: 99; see also He and Ye, 2013: 358–359).

Other research investigates the implications of raising grandchildren for the well-being of the grandparents, highlighting the effects of financial support and the integrity of reciprocal relationships (He and Ye, 2013; Liu, 2014; Dong, 2019). To this Cong and Silverstein (2008a) contribute the noteworthy finding that when rural Chinese elders receive remittances their depressive symptoms reduce, while both Cong and Silverstein (2008a) and Dong (2019) find that elders' psychological well-being is enhanced if they also care for grandchildren. Meanwhile, Baker and Silverstein (2012: 66) observe that grandparent caregivers in China enjoy better psychological well-being than grandparent caregivers in the United States because in the United States fostering by grandparent is mostly a 'reactionary' arrangement oriented to a past event – a crisis in the middle generation, while in China it is an arrangement oriented towards the *future of the family*. So, Chinese grandparents' emotional well-being improves because of a sense of belonging to and contributing to the family collective (Dong, 2019). Other research, mentioned in Chapter 1, quantitatively evaluates the impact of parental migration and grandparents' care on different dimensions of rural Chinese children's well-being, drawing mostly negative conclusions (e.g. Li, 2004; Chen and Sun, 2015; Yue et al., 2017).

Children in Skipped Generation Families 183

This research notwithstanding, few studies explore how rural Chinese *children* – such as Hanhan and Yaping, from whom we heard earlier – perceive their relationships with migrant parents and grandparents in skipped generation families. Scarcer still is research on how children and grandparents adapt their 'linked lives' to the circumstances created by the parents' migration. This chapter aims to address these gaps by exploring how *children* in Anhui and Jiangxi perceived and navigated their lives in the interstices of their spatially dispersed skipped generation families. The chapter draws on the interviews my research assistants and I conducted in 2010 and 2011 with forty-four children whose parents had both migrated without them – forty of them lived with grandparents, two of them had previously lived with their grandparents before living with relatives or else alone, and two of them used to live with grandparents but at the time of interview lived with aunts and uncles. I also draw on our interviews with the caregivers of forty-two of these children, and my interviews with the migrant parents of eight of the children. Additionally, I refer to my follow-up interviews with twelve of the forty-four children and their family members in 2013, 2014 and/or 2015, two of whom went on to live with relatives after a grandparent had become ill or died.

Most of the children and grandparents we met who lived in skipped generation families had spent months, or more commonly years, in each other's company, with this shared time generating mutual affection even as both sides sometimes also felt dissatisfied with aspects of the arrangement. For instance, as Hanhan's aforementioned comment illustrates, some children thought that their grandparents did not understand topics relevant to their lives. Meanwhile, grandparents frequently said of the children: 'When they're with me I'm tired and fed up, but when they're away from me I miss them.' At the same time, though, as can be seen in Yaping's previously mentioned comment, the children thought about their migrant parents, loving them, worrying about them, missing them, blaming them, wanting to see them or feeling ambivalent towards them, depending on the frequency and quality of their contact with them. Like grandchildren–grandparent relationships in other countries including the United States, the relationships between children and their grandparents in China were also simultaneously influenced by the quality of the relationship between the grandparents and the middle generation, which in turn impacted on the former's access to material and emotional support (King and Elder, 1995 cited in Xu, Silverstein and Chi, 2014: 223; Xu, Silverstein and Chi, 2014).

Yet even though children's conditions were affected by the grandparents' access to material and emotional support, the familial and societal contexts within which the children and grandparents co-resided were shaped also by the contradictory effects of a contemporary striving ethos. Specifically, the imperatives of the prevailing striving ethos devalued rurality and elderly people, and disproportionately channelled resources towards the younger generations and urban futures. This devaluation of rurality and of elderly people was reinforced

184   Children in Skipped Generation Families

by two dynamics. One was a state-endorsed marketisation discourse that impelled individuals to 'keep up with the times' and 'get ahead'. The other was the impetus for nuclear families to divide out from the elderly to accumulate capital for themselves in circumstances where the migrants often struggled financially. In view of these dynamics, internal power relations changed within the reconfigured intergenerational parenting coalitions (He and Ye, 2013; Santos, 2017): as noted in Chapter 1, grandparents became the least powerful members of intergenerational parenting coalitions (Santos, 2017).

The following discussion examines how children's relationships with grandparents and migrant parents varied by their family's demographic composition, the family's socio-economic status, the quality of the intergenerational relationships, the time that the children had spent with different adults, the children's ages and the children's views about their prospects. The discussion proceeds in five sections. Section 7.1 examines elites', rural adults' and children's perceptions of the quality of rural grandparents' care in an era where children's education was the cornerstone of striving. Section 7.2 discusses how patrilineal familialism informed understandings of intergenerational obligations such that most children lived with *paternal* grandparents while the middle generation strived for its own upward mobility. Section 7.3 discusses family circumstances when children lived with their maternal grandparents and the implications of these circumstances for the children's relationship with their caregivers. Section 7.4 teases out how children's relationships with grandparents and parents varied by their *care histories* and *age*. Section 7.5 explores children's visits to see their migrant parents in the cities during the summer holidays as a final aspect of how their linked lives spanned both generations and space.

7.1   Views about Grandparents' Care

With the increase in ageing parents' contribution to childcare, academics and policymakers in China have grown ever more perturbed about the implications of grandparents' 'unscientific' and 'old-fashioned' child-rearing techniques for children's development (Binah-Pollak, 2014; Naftali, 2016). Elites' concerns pertain to both urban and rural children, but as many scholars observe, the anxieties of pedagogues and policymakers are most pronounced for children left behind in the care of poorly educated rural grandparents (Li, 2004; Xiang, 2007; Nie, Li and Li, 2008; Li and Song, 2009: 71; Wang and Dai, 2009: 126; Ye and Pan, 2011; He and Ye, 2013; Hansen, 2015: 166; Yue et al., 2017). In the fieldwork counties, local elites – including county and township officials, school principals and teachers – echoed this wider national narrative that rural grandparents are ill-equipped to raise children in the contemporary era. Officials and teachers lamented the grandparents' lack of education and their preoccupation with 'life' matters (food, clothing and warmth) to the exclusion of discipline and

7.1 Views about Grandparents' Care

homework supervision. Several officials and teachers said that grandparents paid attention to *yang* but not to education/instruction (*zhong yang bu zhong jiao*), a view that overlooks the cultural importance of food in expressing a wish to nourish another person physically and emotionally (Jiang et al., 2007; Jankowiak, 2011). The officials and teachers also talked about how the 'low quality' of grandparents increased the schools' work burdens because the teachers had to give the children support that was not forthcoming at home (see also Hansen, 2015; Kim, 2018). Officials and teachers made these complaints about the quality of grandparents' care even as they also recognised that this care enabled the middle generation to earn two migrant wages for the family rather than just one.

The pragmatic focus of rural elderly caregivers on provision – a source of concern in the elite narratives noted earlier – appeared in a different form in some grandparents' own accounts of their childcare priorities. For instance, a seventy-six-year-old grandfather in Western County, Anhui, explained: 'If you compare children in my time and now, one was heaven and one hell. We had to beg for food.' A pragmatic attitude to child-raising was likewise manifest in some grandparents' comments that whereas they had raised several children, now having just one or two children 'eat at my place' feels relaxed. This emphasis on material provisioning and 'life' makes sense if we consider that in 2010 and 2011 the age of the grandparents who cared for the subset of forty children ranged from fifty-three to eighty-eight years – the average ages of the grandmothers and the grandfathers were sixty-seven and sixty-nine, respectively – so some of these grandparents would have been teenagers during the Great Famine of 1959–1961 and all of them would have endured the scarcity years of state socialism.

Nevertheless, elderly caregivers knew well that times had changed and often expressed anxieties about the quality of their own caregiving. Many of them regretted not being able to help their grandchildren with school work and they worried about their charges' school grades. Several grandparents told us that the grandchildren were naughty and would not listen to them, let alone do their homework, so they feared that the children could 'go to waste' or 'turn fallow' (*feidiao* or *huangdiao*) under their watch. Alternatively, some grandparents stated proudly that a grandchild's academic achievement had led the migrants to tell them: 'This is thanks to your hard work (*gonglao*)' or 'You did a good job of raising this child (*dai de hao*)'.

Ideas about deficiencies in the quality of grandparents' care were not only expressed by grown-ups. Children also mentioned inadequacies in elders' child-raising, including children who lived with both parents and with one parent, as well as 'fully' left-behind children. For instance, in 2011 a thirteen-year-old girl – also a classroom monitor – who lived on the main road of a rural township in Eastern County with her home-maker mother and truck driver father, explained to us how her daily life differed from that of her left-behind classmates. She said:

186   Children in Skipped Generation Families

Parents are notified of exam grades with a slip that they must sign and then the students must bring it back to school. But some left-behind kids live with illiterate grandparents so they cannot bring back the slips signed, and the teachers tell them off, so I can see that these kids have difficulties.

For their part, children from skipped generation families described deficiencies in their grandparents' child-raising. Hanhan, quoted at the start of this chapter, felt extremely frustrated that his grandmother insisted on sleeping alongside him at night to prevent him from creeping off to the internet bar, a place where some teenagers tried to escape from the competitive pressures of a striving life. Meanwhile, at age fifteen, Wang Delun was one of several children who said that a grandparent watched him while he did his homework and made him write out characters a hundred times if they looked ugly. Admittedly, some children who lived with both their parents also reported being subjected to these same kinds of *guan* practices. But when children came from skipped generation families, they saw such *guan* efforts as evidence of their grandparents' limitations and wished that their parents would return home to give them more enlightened care.

In contrast, a handful of children said that grandparents were kinder, more lenient and more tolerant than parents. These children's impression of the grandparents' softer discipline echoes Goh's (2011) observation that Chinese grandparents usually want to protect the emotional bond with their grandchildren so refrain from disciplining them severely. In Anhui and Jiangxi, children's reports of grandparents' leniency stood out most among ten- and eleven-year-olds, most likely because children of this age were subjected to more stringent discipline than teenagers. Two girls and two boys aged ten and eleven, who each lived with both their parents, said that they envied their classmates who lived with grandparents because they enjoyed a more relaxed life. Meanwhile, a handful of children in skipped generation families said that one good thing about living with grandparents was that they were not scolded or hit. An eleven-year-old-boy said: 'It is good that my parents are out and busy because if they are at home they are often fierce with me (*xiong wo*)', while a twelve-year-old boy said, 'It is better that they are out earning money because if they are at home they only tell me off, they don't play with me.' Similarly, when I asked another eleven-year-old boy, 'What is the best thing about living with grandparents?' he said, 'There is no one to *guan* me.'

7.2   Patrilineal Striving and Paternal Grandparents' Childcare

7.2.1   *Expectations of Paternal Grandparents' Childcare Provisioning*

Consistent with a wider national pattern (Chen, Liu and Mair, 2011; He and Ye, 2013; Xu, Silverstein and Chi, 2014; Zhang et al., 2016), most children we met in 2010–2011 from rural skipped generation families lived with their *paternal*

7.2 Patrilineal Striving and Grandparents' Childcare

grandparents ($n = 36$). As mentioned, two further children had once lived with paternal grandparents but at the time of our interviews with them in 2010 and 2011 one girl lived with an aunt while a fifteen-year-old boy lived alone. Also, two out of thirty-six children who lived with *paternal* grandparents had once lived with a maternal grandmother. In our set of cases, a cultural emphasis on patrilineal rather than matrilineal obligation thereby overrode other gender and family norms to configure family care after parents migrated. Indeed, four children we met had maternal grandmothers who were in good health, but they still lived with their widowed paternal grandfathers.

Chinese-language appellations for paternal and maternal kin reveal why skipped generation childcare mostly relied on patrilineal family. The terms for the sons and daughters of adult sons are *sunzi* and *sunnü*, respectively. However, the terms for maternal grandparents and maternal grandchildren carry the prefix *wai*, meaning 'outside', with maternal grandmother called *waipo*, maternal grandfather called *waigong* and an adult daughter's sons and daughters called *waisun* and *waisunnü*, respectively. The terminology thereby demonstrates that paternal grandparents and grandchildren belong to the same patrilineal family while maternal grandparents and grandchildren are outsiders.

When I asked elderly people why they had agreed to provide childcare, most of them indicated that it was inevitable for them to look after their *own* family. Responses included the following:

> 'Even if I'm unwilling, I have to raise (*dai*) them, for as long as I can physically move, I have to raise (*dai*) them.'
> 'They gave him to me when he was eight-months-old and it is the natural course of things (*lisuodangran*) for me to look after my grandson (*sunzi*).'
> 'I'm busy every day on his behalf, but he is my descendent (*houdai*) so this is what I ought to do (*yinggai de*). He needs to study.'
> 'If another family asked me to raise (*dai*) their child I wouldn't do it for any amount of money, but this child is my next generation (*xia yi dai*).'
> 'Looking after grandchildren is my responsibility. I don't have any thoughts about it because it is an essential obligation (*yiwu biyao de*). They *dagong*, so who will *dai*?'

Children also thought that given their parents' migration it was inevitable for them to live with their paternal grandparents. Indeed, owing to patrilocal marriage patterns, many children had lived near to their paternal grandparents or else in the same household as them before their parents' departures.

However, the influence of patrilineal norms notwithstanding, we met several families where one or both members of the middle generation could not migrate because the paternal grandparents refused to provide childcare. Typically, these ageing parents had two or three married adult sons and the constituent nuclear households were all poor. Echoing the account of Puhua's mother in Chapter 5,

188   Children in Skipped Generation Families

the elderly people in these families said that if they helped out one couple, then the other couples would expect help too, causing them to become overwhelmed in a situation where they still needed to work to ensure their own survival. When ageing parents declined to provide childcare, the middle generation usually felt deprived of an entitlement. As discussed in Chapter 5, some children overheard the conversations between their mothers and paternal grandmothers about migration and childcare, and they begged their mothers to stay at home.

7.2.2 'Fenjia' and Relationships in Patrilineal Skipped Generation Families

The expectation that children would be cared for by paternal grandparents co-existed with a countervailing expectation that the middle generation would divide from the older generation to strive for itself. The middle generation's reliance on the older generation's help with social reproduction on the one hand and the middle generation's imperative to accumulate capital for itself on the other caused tension within many extended families. Meanwhile, if and how this tension played out both affected and reflected the quality of intergenerational relationships, with implications for the material and relational micro-worlds the children inhabited.

'Dividing the family' or 'fenjia' customarily involves married sons taking a share of the family property with them such that, at a certain point in the family's demographic cycle, the elders end up with their property divided out from under them while relying on adult sons for old-age support (Croll, 1987 cited in Judd, 1994: 173–187; Cohen, 1993; Murphy, 2002: 64–65). There are, though, cases where married sons do not divide from their parents, for example when a man is an only son, when a man's brother or brothers have not married or have not had a child, or when a man's only brother has secured property and income outside the village. Even so, division remains a stage in the lifecycle of most rural families. Meanwhile, owing to a rise in labour migration, the practical significance of whether a family has formally divided has declined because sons no longer need a share of their parents' property to marry; the migrants manage their own budgets and savings; and the migrants live away from their ageing parents for consecutive years (Jacka, 2018).

Societal change notwithstanding, fenjia has retained a psychological significance for many people, including for their understanding of intergenerational obligations when the middle generation migrates. Elderly people varied in how cohesive they thought that the generations in their families were in the light of migration. One grandmother echoed a common view, saying: 'There is no way for us to fen (divide) because we look after the children.' Other elderly people expressed a more equivocal view about whether they had fen. They said that the

7.2 Patrilineal Striving and Grandparents' Childcare

money had *fen* but the *jia* (family) had not *fen*, or that the budgets had *fen* but they had not *fen* from the grandchildren, because otherwise, 'how would the children live?' Meanwhile, yet other grandparents stressed that even though they had *fenjia*, the intergenerational relationships remained mutually supportive. Some elderly people illustrated this mutual support by explaining that the migrants always helped them when medical costs arose because the middle generation realised that the elders needed to be in good health in order to provide childcare.

Children could tell when the relationships between their grandparent caregivers and migrant parents were good. They noted their migrant parents' frequent phone instructions to them to obey and help their grandparents, for instance, 'Help *nainai* carry water from the well', 'Don't let *nainai* get too tired' and 'Make sure *yeye* takes his medicine'. Four girls had even been told by their parents that they needed to stay with their grandparents to keep them company and to ensure that they were okay This resonates with research showing that left-behind children provided care to their grandparents even as they received care (Ye and Pan, 2011; He and Ye, 2013). Children also noted that their migrant parents sent or brought back gifts for their grandparents, with items such as vests, socks, shoes, nutrition supplements and medicines signalling their concern for them (He and Ye, 2013).[1] Meanwhile, grandparents encouraged their grandchildren to talk with their migrant parents on the phone, to appreciate their parents' sacrifices for them and to understand their parents' point of view. Noticeably, many of these children described their families as 'warm' (*wennuan*), 'happy' (*xingfu*) and 'harmonious' (*hemu*).

By contrast, eight of the thirty-six children cared for by paternal grandparents came from families afflicted by palpable discord, with money being a key source of tension. In five of these families, the migrants remitted little because they had not fared well in the city, with gambling sometimes exacerbating the difficulties. A corroborating picture comes from He and Ye's (2013) study of left-behind elders. Of the 226 left-behind elders in their survey who provided childcare, 25.7 per cent said that caring for children was a heavy economic burden while 16.8 per cent had to provide all or part of the children's tuition fees, with migrants' gambling being an added concern for some elders (He and Ye, 2013: 357).[2] In Anhui and Jiangxi, the elderly caregivers who did not receive adequate remittances relied on their own cash and in-kind farm income and an old-age pension from the government, which in 2015 was

---

[1] He and Ye (2013) report that 76.9 per cent of the 400 left-behind elders in their survey received gifts from migrants, indicating that gifts are commonly used in maintaining intergenerational relations.

[2] In a survey of 400 left-behind rural elders, 11.3 per cent identified the migrant children's gambling as a worry to them (He and Ye, 2013: 361).

190   Children in Skipped Generation Families

approximately 70 *yuan* per month. This income ensured the left-behind family members' survival but they still worried about their livelihoods.

In the other three of these families, though, the migrants provided enough for the left-behind children's and elders' subsistence and for the children's school fees, but not enough for contingencies. For instance, when we first met Zhangyong's grandfather in 2011, he told us that he had asked Zhangyong's mother for money to repair a leak in the roof, but she had referred him to his eldest son who lived in the village. When we met *Yeye* in 2013 and 2015, he confirmed that the roof still leaked. In 2013, when answering my question about his wishes in life, Zhangyong said he wished that his parents would repair *Yeye*'s roof. At our third meeting, though, Zhangyong's loyalties wavered: even as he sympathised with his grandfather, he could increasingly see the fruits of his parents' labours. He thought that his parents must have a good reason for not giving *Yeye* money for the roof, but he did not know what it was.

In a few families, elders responded to tensions with the middle generation by itemising how they had spent every *fen* of remittances. Younger children never made comments to us that indicated their awareness of family conflict over money, but a couple of teenagers had become aware of such tension over time. When we met Fengmian of Tranquil County, Jiangxi (discussed in Chapter 6), for a second time in 2014 at fifteen years old, she told us that her life with *Yeye* had been austere, not only because he had been strict with her but also because he had never given her money to buy ice lollies or sweet bread from the school yard vendor. It was only when Fengmian was a few years older that she realised that her grandfather had endured hardships and injustices (*weiqu*) of his own. But she was still not able to reach out to him, not even after his house had burnt down in an accident, for fear of offending her returnee mother. In Jade County, Jiangxi, another fifteen-year-old girl's realisation that her grandmother was not well-treated by her migrant parents resonated with her own sense of abandonment, such that she felt that she and her *nainai* needed to stick together.

7.2.3   Chinese New Year

Children's experiences of intergenerational family dynamics – including the family members' understandings of *fenjia* – can be further explored with reference to families' eating and living arrangements at Chinese New Year. Eating and living arrangements after the migrant parents returned to the village for Chinese New Year both affected and reflected the children's relationships with their parents and grandparents. On the one hand, the Chinese New Year celebrations helped people to sustain their relationships, while reminding everyone of family striving values. For instance, on New Year's Eve family members ate a reunion meal (*tuanyuan fan*) consisting of round foods like cakes and dumplings to symbolise the family's unity, as well as foods to

7.2 Patrilineal Striving and Grandparents' Childcare

represent 'hard work' – like celery which in Chinese is a homonym for 'industriousness', 'social mobility' – that the ladder-like structure of sugar cane represents, and 'prosperity' denoted by the Chinese homonym for fish (Oxfeld, 2017: 78–79, 93). On the other hand, eating and living arrangements during Chinese New Year also revealed to the family members that some aspects of affective bonds had changed during the migrants' absence.

If a family had not divided, then typically the different generations ate and lived together during the migrants' return visits. Meanwhile, in families where *fenjia* had occurred, either de facto because of the middle generation's migration or else following a verbal or written agreement among family members, the different generations still often ate together and sometimes lived together over the festive period.[3] This was because the visiting migrants did not have cooking utensils or food stores in their own houses and it was not worth them buying these items for a short stay. Importantly too, people of all ages shared meals because they enjoyed the conviviality of spending precious time together. Most children recalled Chinese New Year as being a 'happy' (*kuaile*) and 'lively' (*renao*) occasion that reunited all the members of the 'family', which in the eyes of the children included their grandparents and migrant parents. Many children also said that ordinary life was 'dull' (*kuzao*), 'boring' (*wuwei*) and 'cold and lonely' (*lengmo*) by comparison. Poignantly, though, several children recalled past Chinese New Years when they had felt especially lonely because their migrant parents had not returned home.

Yet even as many families enjoyed shared meals at Chinese New Year, intergenerational relationships still revealed some distance or strain. Notably, a few elders said that their adult sons and daughters-in-law were 'like guests' in their house (*zuoke yiyang*) because their manner was distant and polite, and their stay was fleeting. No young children and only a few teenagers mentioned noticing a distance between their grandparents and parents at these times, possibly because their focus was on their own relationships with the adults and because their families' circumstances would seem 'normal' to them. In a handful of families though, the elderly people ate separately from other family members, with three grandparents saying something like: 'I need to eat soft food because of my teeth so it is better that I cook and eat my own food.' Zhangyong saw his grandfather eating separately at Chinese New Year in pragmatic terms. He was tired of eating the softened food that his grandfather cooked, and which he used to teasingly tell him was like 'pig swill', and he relished the chance to eat more appetising fare with his parents, aunt, uncle and cousins and to enjoy their livelier company.

---

[3] This differs from Oxfeld's (2017: 56) observation in her village in Guangdong that: 'One does not share a New Year's meal with a family that has a ready divided economically.'

In families where *fenjia* had occurred unambiguously, the parents' return at Chinese New Year also prompted changes in sleeping arrangements. In some instances, the grandparents moved out of the migrants' newer houses where they lived with the grandchildren during most of the year and went to stay in their own older houses. Alternatively, some grandchildren moved from their grandparents' house to stay with their parents in their parents' newer house. The exception was in villages in Eastern County, Anhui, where the younger generation seldom built new houses in the village, though people sometimes changed the rooms in which they slept during the migrants' visits. Children's responses to changes in living arrangements over the Chinese New Year depended on their closeness to different adults. Some children were delighted to stay with their migrant parents, while other children wanted to stay with their grandparents even as they felt happy that their parents were visiting. Additionally, four children recounted how their younger siblings had resisted sleeping alongside their visiting mothers, preferring instead to stay close to their grandmothers.

7.3   Maternal Grandparents and Childcare

As noted earlier, children seldom lived with their maternal grandparents when their parents had migrated without them (Chen, Liu and Mair, 2011; Xu, Silverstein and Chi, 2014; Santos, 2017). Indeed, in 2010 and 2011 only four children in our set of cases lived with their maternal grandparents, two in Anhui and two in Jiangxi. A fifth child from Jiangxi, Liwei (discussed in the following text), lived with his paternal grandparents at the time of our 2010–2011 round of interviews, but he had previously lived with his maternal grandmother, and, at the time of a follow-up interview with him three years later, he had returned to live with his maternal grandmother. Another child was cared for by his paternal grandparents alongside his maternal aunt's son. Additionally, we learnt about four children who had once been cared for by maternal grandparents but who did not live with their maternal grandparents at the time of our 2010 and 2011 interviews: two of these children were our respondents, while another two children were the cousins of two other of our 109 child respondents, and had been mentioned in passing by grandparent interviewees. In the four cases, we learnt about where a child had previously lived with maternal grandparents, a daughter-in-law's childbirth had led to the child moving to a different household: one girl's migrant parents returned home to look after her, while the other three children went to live with a widowed paternal grandparent.

The unconventional nature of childcare by maternal grandparents could be seen not only in the rarity of the arrangement, but also in the caregivers' accounts of their family members' and neighbours' reactions to it. For instance,

7.3 Maternal Grandparents and Childcare

three elderly women told us that their married sons and daughters-in-law had objected to them looking after their *waisun* or *wainü*. Even so, these elderly women had stuck to their guns telling their sons and daughters-in-law that they had no choice but to help their daughters and that they would still help look after any patrilineal grandchildren. Furthermore, grandparents who looked after their migrant daughter's children at the time we interviewed them and grandparents who had previously looked after their 'outside' grandchildren told us that neighbours sometimes remarked to them that raising an 'outside' grandchild was to *bai dai*, that is, to 'raise in vain'. Additionally, some couples whose paternal in-laws were not available to help them with childcare reported that when they had asked the wife's parents to look after their children so that they could migrate, they had been told: 'We can't *dai*. Your brother has children who we need to look after.'

The five children we met who lived with maternal grandparents came from families characterised by poverty or the paternal grandparents' unavailability or both. Meanwhile, the five families also enjoyed close emotional ties along the matrilineal line. These three factors of poverty, lack of paternal grandparents, and close matrilineal ties could all be discerned in the account of one sixty-five-year-old woman from Tranquil County, Jiangxi, who told us that when her daughter-in-law had objected to her looking after her *waisun*, she had replied: 'There is no other way. Their family has much hardship. My daughter doesn't have a *nainai* or a *yeye* to *dai* for her.' She continued:

The children [who I look after] board at school during the week, but there is no food for them at school at the weekend, so they have to come back here to eat and I wash their clothes. My daughter doesn't give me much money because she has her own family and her own husband. She gives me six hundred *yuan* for school fees, but that does not cover [her child's] medicines and school items. But [my daughter's family] would be very wretched if I did not help them. I am her mother.

The close ties in these families existed not only between the migrant daughters and their ageing parents but also between the elderly caregivers and their grandchildren. The closeness can be seen in the example of Liwei's family, which although having a unique history and circumstances, nevertheless exemplified more broadly the role of emotional closeness in dampening the influence of patrilineal norms. In 2015, Liwei's *waipo* told us that when her migrant daughter fell pregnant to a migrant co-worker – a pauper with a lame leg – she had urged her to have an abortion and to leave the man to escape a lifetime of suffering. But the daughter did not follow her mother's advice. The *waipo* began to care for her grandson when he was only one month old, at which time she had just undergone two operations on her stomach so she could barely hold him. Furthermore, her husband was working in Shenzhen. A few years later, Liwei's mother bore a second boy who at age two she also entrusted to the *waipo*. Thereafter, the *waipo* reluctantly transferred Liwei to live with his paternal grandparents who were already caring for three grandchildren. Indeed, when we first met Liwei in 2011 at age eleven, he had been living at his paternal grandparents' house for over three years. At that time, he told us that he missed his *waipo* every day and phoned her weekly. Meanwhile, the boy's paternal grandmother told us that Liwei's *waipo* had raised him to be close to her (*dai de qin*) so he only ever wanted to be with her.

In 2015, nearly a year after Liwei had been boarding at the esteemed Jade County Senior High School, the boy's mother had phoned the *waipo* to say that owing to inadequate nutrition he had come out in white marks across his face. Thereafter, Liwei's *waipo* moved from her hometown to Jade County to look after Liwei and his younger brother. At the time of our meeting, the three of them lived in a flat which had been bought for their use by the *waipo*'s only son, the captain of a ship in Shenzhen, who at age thirty-four had no child of his own, so there was no *sunzi* or *sunnü* to compete for the *waipo*'s attentions. Because of the strong affection between Liwei and his *waipo*, and the *waipo*'s guilt about having left him in the past, she agreed to *peidu* her two grandsons in a heavily polluted city where she felt uncomfortable, consoling herself that it would all be worthwhile if they grew up to be 'useful people' (*you yong de ren*), meaning productive and hardworking. For his part, like many children who had been raised by their grandparents, Liwei resolved to repay the person who had raised him through hard work, loyalty and success.

Xu, Silverstein and Chi's (2014) study of intergenerational care helps us to position the five cases discussed here within a wider universe of cases of children cared for by maternal grandparents in rural China. Based on a sample of 928 older people in the 2009 wave of the Longitudinal Survey of Older Adults in Anhui Province, Xu, Silverstein and Chi (2014) compare rural grandparents' feelings of closeness to the children of their adult sons and the children of their adult daughters, finding that grandmothers felt closer to grandchildren who belonged to the patrilineage. But they found no difference in how close grandmothers felt to their adult sons and adult daughters. In other words, grandmothers felt closer to their adult sons' children, *but this was not because they felt closer to their adult sons than to their adult daughters* (Xu, Silverstein and Chi, 2014). Instead, it most likely reflects that because of patrilocal marriage patterns, the grandparents would have had more interaction with their sons' children than with their daughters' children.

Given these findings, the five families discussed earlier could be exceptional in terms of their emotional closeness. Indeed, the cases of childcare by maternal grandparents that we learnt about indirectly and directly could be conceptualised as sitting along a continuum. At one end of the continuum were children who were transient members of their maternal grandparents' families: – they would need to move on if or when a paternal uncle needed help with childcare.

At the other end of the continuum, though, were children, including the five children discussed here, who occupied a pivotal place in their maternal grandparents' affections and families. In these cases, emotional closeness underpinned a care arrangement from which the maternal grandparents received little economic gain and which custom did not obligate them to undertake. In other words, these grandparents were more motivated than other grandparents to take care of their daughters' children and owing to this self-selection effect, these children enjoyed more stability and emotional security in their relationships with their maternal grandparent caregivers than would ordinarily be the case. This conjecture coheres with Cong and Silverstein's (2012) other finding, derived from the same data set, that when ageing rural parents looked after their daughters' children, the middle generations' emotional support to the ageing parents was the most pronounced, generating deeper emotional closeness between the adult daughters and their own parents.

7.4 Children's Relationships with Grandparents and Parents

Children's relationships with their grandparent caregivers and migrant parents unfolded not only in a societal and family context characterised by patrilineal striving imperatives, but also in the context of lives linked by particular care histories. Sociologists have long observed that the life course is marked by life transitions after which point adult–child relationships and individuals' roles change (Bronfenbrenner, 1979), and that the impacts of life transitions on individuals and their relationships are contingent on their *timing* and *sequencing* in relation to other events (Elder, 1985). It is therefore not surprising that children's feelings about their relationships with their grandparents and migrant parents reflected their age on separation from their parents, prior and later shifts in the family's childcare arrangements, the length of time that the children had spent with given adults, the children's age at the time of interview, and the children's interpretation of their left-behind pasts in light of their view of the future (Parreñas, 2005; Dreby, 2010; Carling, Menjívar, and Schmalzbauer, 2012: 206–207).

In the following text, I discuss how children's relationships with their migrant parents and grandparents varied by their distinct care histories, by which I mean the length of time that they had spent with their parents and grandparents, especially during their formative years, and also by whether they had ever lived with their migrant parents in the city. Thereafter, I tease out younger children's (children of pre-school and primary school age) and teenagers' (children twelve years turning thirteen years, and older) feelings about their relationships with their migrant parents and grandparent caregivers in light of how their lives were linked to the lives of these significant adults within particular care histories.

196 Children in Skipped Generation Families

7.4.1 Children's Care Histories

The age at which children were separated from their parents, how parents pursued migration and who looked after the children at different stages of the life course all constituted the children's care histories. The care histories in turn affected the intimacy that children and adults built up with each other as their linked lives evolved. The perception of a connection between children's care histories and their closeness to a given adult resonates with sociologists' observation for China and other countries, which is that children's early relationships with their grandparents exert lingering effects (Xu, Silverstein and Chi, 2014: 229). Chiefly, sociologists note that when grandparents have taken more frequent care of children, the relationships later in life tend to be closer (Xu, Silverstein and Chi, 2014: 229). Moreover, research in one Chinese city observes that when children were looked after by their grandmothers for more than six years, they appeared to retain feelings of ambivalence towards their mothers that turned out to be life-long (Jankowiak, 2011). Even so, factors such as family economic circumstances and individuals' personalities also intersected with the children's care histories and shaped these care histories in ways both observable and unobservable to outsiders.

I divided the forty children who were cared for by their grandparents at the time of interview in 2010–2011 into two broad groups. Into group one I placed twelve children who had been raised by their grandparents since before the age of three – 30 per cent of the forty children. These children had spent nearly all their lives with their grandparents. Eight of them had been cared for by their grandparents since they had stopped suckling their mothers' milk. Into group two I put twenty-eight children who had lived with their parents until they were five years or older – 70 per cent of the forty children. These children had spent a few years or even several years living with their parents before their separation from them, and all could remember a time when they had lived with their parents. In fact, these children's parents had usually waited until the children could manage basic self-care such as dressing themselves and brushing their teeth before leaving them with their grandparents. The children in this second group could be further subdivided by *where* they had spent their earlier childhood. Eighteen of them had lived entirely in the countryside both before and after their parents' migration. The other ten had spent two or more years living with their migrant parents in the city and most had attended an urban-based migrant school before returning to the countryside to live with grandparents. Three of these ten 'returnee' children had only recently transferred from the city to their grandparents' care in the countryside at the time we met them in 2010 and 2011, and had to adjust to the totally new environment of the countryside having grown up in the city.

7.4 Relationships with Grandparents and Parents

Table 7.1 presents a breakdown of the children by their care histories – so their allocation to either group one or to group two – and the adult(s) to whom they felt closest. The table shows that two-thirds of the twelve children in group one – the children who were raised largely by their grandparents – felt closest to their grandparents. Additionally, a fifteen-year-old boy who lived alone at the time we met him had lived with his grandfather since he was a few months old until his grandfather had died the previous year. I did not count this boy formally among the children in 'group one' but he represents a further instance of a child who felt closer to his grandfather than to his migrant parents even though it was now only the memory of his grandfather that accompanied him. Conversely, approximately 60 per cent of children from group two felt closer to their migrant parents than to their grandparents. Meanwhile, a quarter of the children in each group felt equally close to their migrant parents and their grandparents. A Fisher's exact test ($p = 0.001$) confirmed that the identity of the adult(s) to whom the children felt closest differed significantly by who they had spent time with prior to their separation from their parents. Importantly, though, the pattern of association observed here cannot necessarily be extended beyond the forty cases to a wider population. Even so, the finding for these forty cases is consistent with a picture of greater closeness between children and their long-term caregivers observed elsewhere in the migration studies literature (Carling, Menjívar and Schmalzbauer, 2012: 206–207) as well as in research on child-raising in Chinese families (Jankowiak, 2011).

Table 7.1 *Count of children by care history and adult(s) to whom they felt closest*

		Adult(s) to whom the child feels closest			
		Feels closest to migrant parents	Feels closest to grandparents	Feels equally close to migrant parents and grandparents	Total
Group by Child's Care History	Group 1: spent most time with grandparents	1	8	3	12
	Group 2: spent much time with parents	17	4	7	28
Total		18	12	10	40

198 Children in Skipped Generation Families

7.4.2 Children's Age

Even as the children's relative closeness to their grandparents and their migrant parents was influenced by the amount of time that they had spent with each, these various adult–child relationships nevertheless evolved, changing as the children grew older. Variation among the children by their age brings to the fore the importance of change over the life course in the feelings that the children expressed about their grandparents and their migrant parents (Parreñas, 2005; Dreby, 2010). At the same time, the children's age also intersected with their unique care histories to shape their relationships with their grandparents and migrant parents.

7.4.2.1 Younger Children The accounts of the adults I met in Anhui and Jiangxi indicated that younger children who had been raised largely by their grandparents displayed greater closeness to these caregivers than to their parents, mirroring the research noted earlier. A few migrant parents told my research assistants and me that on their return visits home, when their children had been of pre-school or early primary school age, they had barely recognised them. Some visiting migrants had witnessed their young children calling an uncle or an auntie 'dad' or 'mum' because they had wanted someone to call 'dad' or 'mum' like their friends or cousins did or else their young children had mimicked a cousin in calling the visiting migrant parents 'uncle' or 'auntie'. Even when younger children called their visiting parents 'dad' or 'mum', they still knew that the parents would disappear again soon, so the grandparents remained the adults to whom they stayed the closest during the migrants' visits.

Grandparents' accounts of younger children's reactions to migrant parents likewise indicated that younger children saw their migrant parents as somewhat peripheral to their lives. A grandmother in Western County, Anhui, told us that after she had given the parents of her eleven-year-old granddaughter some cooking oil, grain and a chicken to take back with them to the city one Chinese New Year, the girl had asked her: 'Why did you let those two take our good food away?' The grandmother explained to her: 'They are your parents. If I give to you, then surely I will give to them.' The girl then said, 'But they do not *yang* me', to which the grandmother answered, 'They work hard to *yang* us all.' Certainly, grandparents' work of *yang* was very visible to the children: grandparents grew the grain and vegetables that fed them, prepared their meals, helped them with personal care, and, as shown in Figure 7.1, accompanied them to and from school.

At the same time, though, other factors intersected with the grandparents' care to colour the child-grandparent relationship. One set of

7.4 Relationships with Grandparents and Parents 199

factors pertained to family composition, namely, whether the grandparent caregiver was widowed. Nine out of the forty children we met lived with a widowed grandparent – four grandfathers and five grandmothers. The children and grandparents in these families often felt that they had only each other to rely on. Indeed, two years before eight-month-old Zhangyong had been handed over to *Yeye*, his grandmother had drunk pesticide to spare the family medical costs. *Yeye* fondly recalled that when Zhangyong was first handed over to him, he had slept with the baby in his arms, while in his early childhood Zhangyong had felt closer to *Yeye* than to anyone. In 2011, *Yeye* said that when Zhangyong returned home from

Figure 7.1 Boy walking home with his grandmother after school on a Friday afternoon, Jade County, Jiangxi

school he would ask, 'Did you miss me?' and *Yeye* would say, 'No, you're too much trouble', to which Zhangyong would reply, 'Trickster'. Similarly, two other children – one of whom was Wenwen discussed in Chapter 2 – enjoyed close bonds with their widowed grandfathers, forged partly because of the grandfathers' provision of daily care to them (which these elderly men had seldom provided for their own grown-up children and which the left-behind children seldom received from their own fathers). Fengmian – discussed in Chapter 5 – was an exception because even as her grandfather was her sole caregiver, his severity had prevented the growth of emotional intimacy between them.

A further aspect of family composition that could affect children's lives in their skipped generation families was the presence of other co-resident children. In 2010–2011, fifteen of the forty children who lived in skipped generation families were the only children in the household; the average number of children cared for by the grandparents was 2.12, while the number of children in each skipped generation family ranged from 1 to 4. Lone children in skipped generation families felt close to their grandparents because there was no one else to keep them company, but some of these younger children also talked about feeling lonely or even scared when their grandparents worked in the fields before dawn or after dusk leaving them by themselves in a dark house. Children with co-resident siblings or cousins mostly liked having other children in the household to keep them company, but sometimes children would also tease each other more intensely in the migrant parents' absence. Also, grandparents who cared for three or four children could become overwhelmed, especially if the children fought.

Younger children's lives in their skipped generation families were also influenced by how much the schools supplemented the families' social reproduction. As noted in Chapter 2, one dimension of help from schools was whether the schools provided lunch. In the Anhui fieldwork counties, most primary school children ate three meals a day with their grandparents, though we also met five children, two of whom lived with caregivers in poor health, who ate steamed dumplings for breakfast and lunch bought for one *yuan* from vendors outside the school gates, such as shown in Figure 7.2. But these children often felt hungry during afternoon lessons.

In some families, because of a lack of school boarding facilities or else because of family concerns about the poor quality of the boarding facilities, children lived with their grandmothers in a rented room near to the school in the township, returning to the village at the weekends. We met four such children, two in each province. These children witnessed their grandparents lugging vegetables, oil and rice from the village to the township on Sunday afternoons, and saw their grandmothers' everyday domestic *peidu* work, so they could see

Figure 7.2 Students buying snacks outside school

that it was their grandparents who raised them. Some primary school children from skipped generation households who boarded in the Jiangxi counties said that they looked forward to returning to their grandparents' house at the weekends because they could enjoy comforts not available to them at school such as good food, warm water for washing and someone to tuck them into their quilts at night.

When younger children felt very close to their grandparents, separations from these familiar caregivers could cause them much distress, highlighting that separation from parents was only one kind of separation that children in multilocal families endured (Ye and Pan, 2011; Zhang, 2015). Liwei and three other children who had transferred to another caregiver's house after a beloved grandparent had become ill or died told us of their sadness at no longer living with their grandparent. For instance, in 2015 when we met a fifteen-year-old boy in Western County, Anhui, for a second time, he smiled only when he talked about his grandfather. He said that he did not feel that he was with his own people (*ziji de ren*) while living with his aunt. Like two other children we

202   Children in Skipped Generation Families

met who were cared for by aunts, the boy said that he felt he had to exercise restraint at mealtimes at his aunt's house. Another four children talked to us about a younger sibling's distress at being removed from their grandparents to live with their migrant parents. For instance, a twelve-year-old girl described how her four-year-old brother had fought desperately when her parents had come to take him to Shanghai. The boy had wanted to stay with his *nainai*, and in the end her father had dashed with the wailing boy in his arms to a waiting car, which then sped away.

Parental strictness could also reinforce some younger children's preference to stay with a grandparent caregiver. Jingjing, discussed in Chapters 3 and 6, explained that her younger brother only ever wanted *Yeye* to collect him from school even when her father visited home. This was because he was accustomed to *Yeye*. But it was also because once when the children and their mother had visited her father in Dongguan city, her father had severely beaten the boy for nagging for an expensive toy in a shop, and the boy had never forgiven him. As mentioned, parents' strictness over study could also intensify some children's preference to be with grandparents. A grandfather in Tranquil County, Jiangxi, explained that his ten-year-old grandson cried whenever he went to Fujian to visit his parents during the summer holidays, saying:

I told him to just phone me once a week, not every day. He prefers to be at home with us. His parents are stricter and hit or curse him about study but we don't. Also, he is used to it here. We have looked after him since he was a baby.

The boy confirmed that he preferred to stay with his grandparents during the holidays.

At the other end of the spectrum, though, were children who felt closest to their migrant parents. As noted earlier, many of these children had lived with their parents until they were at least due to start primary school so could remember their upset on their initial separation from their parents. Some recalled feeling 'unable to speak out' (*shuo bu chu lai*) as they watched their parents packing to leave. Others talked about crying under their quilts at missing their parents. Grandparents described scenes of younger children desperately running after their parents down the village path or else searching for them after they had gone. Older children said that they never mentioned their migrant parents for fear of making their younger siblings cry. A few older teenagers laughed at the wretchedness of their younger selves when recalling missing their parents, saying that they had made such a fuss sobbing because they 'did not understand' (*bu dongshi*).

Children whose closeness to their migrant parents had developed by virtue of spending some of their early childhood with them and then later having periodic positive contact with them said that they missed their parents, worried about their health and wanted them to come home. But a couple of children felt

7.4 Relationships with Grandparents and Parents

ambivalent towards their migrant parents even though they could remember the initial separations. In these cases, contact between the children and the migrant parents was infrequent, with unfamiliarity breeding ambivalence. These children's grades were also poor, reinforcing their sense of languishing. One child said that he did not feel anything when his parents phoned him. He also said that he had no one to talk with and he seldom talked with his grandparents.

A few children who had been raised by their parents for several years before moving to live with their grandparents had found themselves in conflicted relationships with caregivers. We met three children who reported frequent upsetting conflict with a grandparent. Yaping, who had returned from Shanghai to Jade County, Jiangxi, at the age of nine, sobbed, saying that her grandfather often hit her, an occurrence that she said also caused her grandmother to cry. The girl longed to return to her parents while also resenting them for sending her to live with her grandparents. Meanwhile, a twelve-year-old girl in Western County, Anhui, who had lived with her grandparents for four years, said that her grandmother often said unkind things to her. The girl wanted to go to Wuhan to personally care for her mother whose arthritic bones ached from standing in a restaurant for long hours. For her part, as noted in Chapter 4, this grandmother said that the eldest daughter-in-law was ungrateful and always found fault with her: she had accused her of only feeding the son of her second son properly while raising the girl, the child of her first son, to be thin.

In other cases, though, children who felt closest to their migrant parents still enjoyed close bonds with their grandparents. They felt familiar with their grandparents and described them as kind and gentle. This was especially so for three children we met who had been looked after by their grandmothers when living alongside their migrant parents in the city. One of these children, Hanhan (mentioned previously), had been looked after in Guangzhou by his grandmother, then when he reached seven years old, his grandmother brought him back to Jade County, Jiangxi, to start school. Even though he missed his parents, his affection for his grandmother helped to ease the separation from his parents and his transition to the countryside. Moreover, his grandmother accompanied him and his younger sister every summer holiday to visit his parents in Guangzhou.

7.4.2.2 Teenagers Teenagers who had spent most of their lives with their grandparents resembled younger children who had been raised largely by grandparents in that they felt closer to their grandparents. Importantly, though, mirroring Dreby's (2010) observations in Mexico, while some younger children displayed indifference towards their migrant parents, some teenagers displayed resentment. Specifically, when teenagers said that they felt closest to their grandparents, they were often signalling an emotion-laden judgement that their migrant parents had let them down. For instance, in 2015 Liwei's maternal grandmother echoed several other grandmothers who cared for teenagers when she wept at her grandchild's refusal to talk with his migrant parents because he felt angry at them for not having raised him. She also told us that Liwei had repeatedly said to her that she was the one who had 'raised' (*yang*) him.

The influence of teenagers' care histories on their feelings towards their grandparents and migrant parents can be illustrated with a comparison of the sentiments of an eleven-year-old girl and her fifteen-year-old sister. When we met the girl in 2011 in Western County, Anhui, she had lived with her parents in Beijing for eight years before moving to live with her grandmother for three years. She told us: 'I'm closest to mama, baba, elder sister, and then grandmother.' Meanwhile, the girl's grandmother told us:

Her older sister [15 years old] blames her parents for the past and she often says to them 'when I was eight months old you dropped (*diu*) me with *nainai*', but my younger granddaughter never says that.

A few children who had been raised by their grandparents felt close to both their migrant parents and grandparents. These teenagers had been able to spend quality time with their parents despite being raised by their grandparents. For example, even though one boy I met in Tranquil County, Jiangxi, had been raised by his grandparents since babyhood, his parents' line manager jobs had afforded them some flexibility to return home periodically, or to take time off when he and his younger sister visited them. When we met his mother in Guangdong in 2013, she told us that her son felt closest to his grandmother, a closeness that reassured her he was okay but also made her feel that she had not properly fulfilled her maternal duties. For his part, in the same year – at age thirteen – the boy said that on the one hand, wherever his grandparents lived felt like his 'home' but on the other hand, his mother was the person to whom he talked about matters on his mind because she was best able to understand him so he often phoned her.

Teenagers' feelings towards their parents because of long-term separation could not always be disentangled from what they felt about their parents because adolescence is a developmental phase when young people increasingly assert their own identities and deal with conflicting emotions (Youniss and Smollar, 1985; Duchnesne and Larose, 2007). Nevertheless, echoing sociologists' observations from other countries (Parreñas, 2005; Dreby, 2010), the testimonies of the teenagers and adults we met in Anhui and Jiangxi indicated that long-term separation affected how the developmental tensions associated with adolescence played out, and how both teenagers and parents interpreted these tensions. Specifically, teenagers and their parents often saw a growing distance and tensions as caused by or as exacerbated by parental migration even as some teenagers who lived with both their parents similarly reported feeling estranged from their parents, usually because of study-related pressures. For

7.4 Relationships with Grandparents and Parents

instance, a non-migrant father who worked in a township health station in Tranquil County, Jiangxi, complained to us: 'Even the left-behind children call their parents *ma* and *ba*, but our son has a rebellious heart (*yifan xintai*) at our strictness and he won't call us *ma* and *ba*.'

When teenagers openly expressed resentment towards their migrant parents, it was often in response to two kinds of triggers. One trigger was the migrant parents' efforts to exercise discipline, with such efforts also observed in other countries to be alienating if occurring in the absence of familiarity and intimacy (Parreñas, 2005). For example, in 2013 Liwei's paternal grandmother – who we interviewed in addition to his maternal grandmother – told us that one evening the then thirteen-year-old boy went to market in a neighbouring township to buy a jacket and returned home late. His mother was home to help with school enrolment. She worried that Liwei had gone to an internet bar, so she scolded him when he got home. Liwei retaliated by telling his mother that she had never been there to *guan* him, so why did she think that she needed to *guan* him now? This made Liwei's mother cry. Liwei's *Yeye* then said to her: 'Don't cry. You've come all this way for a short time. It should be a happy time.'

A further trigger for some teenagers to express resentment was when their migrant parents tried to solicit reassurance from them of their affection and future old-age care. In 2015, at sixteen years old, Xinhui, an only child who we met in Chapters 3 and 4, said:

I'm closest to *nainai*. My mother can see this. For instance, if my mother and *nainai* quarrel I always take *nainai*'s side. My mother has noticed this and commented on it. She said: 'You're not close (*qin*) to me. You're closer to *nainai*. You might not look after me when I am old. So I joked back: 'That's right. So you'd better *dagong* now to earn more money for later.'

Sometimes teenagers' resentment towards their migrant parents could also be intensified by a perception that their parents had failed to compensate them for their absence. In 2013, fifteen-year-old Wang Delun told us that he had grown up without maternal love (*mu'ai*) and that his maternal grandparents had not been able to substitute for this. He acknowledged that his mother had tried to make up for her absence by sending him money so that he could eat extra food at school and by telling him not to go hungry. But he identified his maternal grandfather as the one person to whom he felt closest because he was the one who had raised him and taught him to be a person. As noted in Chapter 3, when we met Wang Delun in 2015, he had transferred from the township junior high to a vocational school in Hefei city. Like several other young people who had not excelled academically, he said that he had underperformed in the *zhongkao* and had not managed to obtain scores high enough to go to a private senior high school because his parents had not been home to *peidu*. Moreover, he said that the disadvantage of not having had a *peidu* mother had been exacerbated because his parents had kept him in the low-quality township junior high school rather than sending him to a private junior high boarding school in the county seat, as he wished.

However, in 2015 I was surprised to learn that Wang Delun's family had bought a small flat on the outskirts of the county seat. The flat was located three hours away by bus from Wang Delun's vocational school. His married twenty-two-year-old sister joined us on a visit to the flat. It had three bedrooms, was tiled throughout in white and was sparsely furnished. Wang Delun told us that his main hardship in life was that the monthly allowance from his parents was inadequate and he often went hungry towards the end of each month, which was difficult to endure (*nanshou*). Although the flat represented a tangible economic and symbolic achievement for the family, it still did not compensate Wang Delun for the past. He told us that there remained a gap in his relationship with his parents, especially with his mother. His sister tearfully interjected that it had been hard for them to grow up without their mother while all the other children had a mother with them, most likely reflecting the dominance of the lone-migrant father and at-home mother family configuration in the Eastern County countryside.

But even though adolescence could be a phase when teenagers distanced themselves from their parents, some teenagers thought that they needed to demonstrate their maturity and understanding of circumstances (*dongshi*), reflecting that as children grow older, they often adopt more of the 'cultural repertoire' – the norms, beliefs and practices – of adults (Coe, 2012: 915). Indeed, some teenagers we met contrasted their younger selves, when they had felt abandoned by their parents, to their more mature present selves. Expressing customary ideas about the essence of filial piety and resembling the daughters of the lone-migrant mothers discussed in Chapter 6 – these teenagers explained that a better understanding of their migrant parents had helped them to develop more feeling (*ganqing*) for them.

The evolution of teenagers' sentiments over time is well illustrated by extracts from two of my conversations with Liwei. In 2014, at age fifteen, shortly after receiving notice of his place at a top public senior high school, he said:

Sometimes I feel rebellious towards them but then I realise that they love me but they're just a bit stupid. For instance, they ask me, have I got my ration tickets (*fanpiao*) for school. They don't realise we use a swipe card. And they think using a mobile phone to go online is taking the wrong path in life. So, we have conflicts but then I try to understand. I used to blame them for not being with me ... but I don't have time for conflict with them now because I need to study.

A year later, we then had the following exchange:

LW: I know my parents feel guilty for having left me.
RACHEL: How?

7.5 Children's Visits to Migrant Parents in the Cities   207

LW: My father overcame his self-consciousness about being a cripple to go to a parent-teacher meeting in my second year of senior high. He left a message for me at my desk saying that he knew he had not been there for me ... []

RACHEL: Overall, looking back, would you say that your parents' migration was worth it?

LW: On balance my parents' migration was worth it because otherwise I would not be at senior high school ... [Even so] I would never leave my own children behind because I know a kind of pain that words can't express ... but I have started to forgive them.

7.5   Children's Visits to Migrant Parents in the Cities

A final aspect of many children's lives in multilocal skipped generation families was their visits to see their migrant parents in the cities during the summer holidays. Even though some children who lived with one parent or both parents had visited their migrant parents in the city at least once in the past, visits to see migrant parents in the city were most common among the children whose mothers and fathers both worked away. Of the 434 children in the 2010 Summer Survey who reported ever having visited their parents in the city, 66.36 per cent had two migrant parents, 24.88 per cent had one migrant parent and 8.75 per cent lived with both parents, the latter being the children of returnees. Meanwhile, 65.9 per cent (288 out of 437) of the children of two migrant parents, 40.15 per cent (108 out of 269) of the children of lone-migrant parents, and 12.5 per cent (38 out of 304) of the children of two at-home parents had visited a parent in the city at least once. Also, the thirty-seven out of thirty-nine children we interviewed, who had ever visited their migrant parents in the city, had two migrant parents.

Children's experience of visits to see migrant parents were affected by several intertwined factors including who accompanied them during their visits, their migrant parents' work and living conditions, and study pressures. In 2010 and 2011, when recalling their most recent visit to the city, eighteen children said that they had travelled with their parents to the city and spent some of each day with them: five of these children also had an infant sibling in the city and so they spent most days with their mother and younger sibling, while ten of the children mentioned spending some time at their parents' workplace. Five other children had travelled with a migrant parent to the city but then spent most days locked in a room: four of the children spent their days alongside at least one other child, while one child spent most days alone. The parents locked their children in because they worried about them being kidnapped. Another six children travelled to the city with a parent or relative and thereafter spent most days with an aunt, older cousin or older sibling.

208   Children in Skipped Generation Families

Meanwhile, eight other children travelled to the city with a grandparent who then looked after them during the day.

Migrant parents' working and living conditions, which typically included low pay, long working hours and cramped accommodation, also affected the children's experiences of city visits. Most migrant parents' lowly social and economic status in the city limited the amount of resources and 'quality' time that they could give to the children on their visits. The implications of the parents' socio-economic marginalisation for these children's summer visits can be extrapolated from findings in the United States and the United Kingdom about school holidays and unequal childhoods – sociologists report that school holidays exacerbate class-based educational inequalities because children whose parents have few capital endowments miss out on the enrichment activities and interactions that middle-class children enjoy (Alexander, Entwisle and Olson, 2007; Stewart, Watson and Campbell, 2018).

Nevertheless, some migrant parents had better urban-based family networks, better jobs, more income and better accommodation than others, with implications for the children's experiences. In general, children of better-off parents enthused more about the city. For instance, at thirteen years old Zhangyong said:

There are swings near to where my parents live. It's really good. During the day I stay at the house of my uncle's wife (*xiao jiuma*) then return to my parents at night though sometimes a cousin stays with me at my parents. But I'm also happy to return home from Kunshan. I'd prefer everyone to be together, *baba*, *mama* and *yeye* . . . Kunshan is a fun place. There are lots of boats in Tingting Park.

Zhangyong also mentioned that when in Kunshan City, he most enjoyed playing computer games with his seventeen-year-old cousin.

By contrast, a fourteen-year-old girl from Western County, Anhui, spent her days in a small hot hut (*pengzi*) in Tianjin with her eight-year-old sister, and two younger cousins. Her parents and aunt and uncle worked from dawn till dusk each day, collecting and recycling refuse. She and her sister never saw anything of Tianjin except where their parents stayed. The girl spent most of each day doing housework, though she and the other children also helped sort the rubbish that their parents had brought back to the hut. Other children similarly mentioned that they helped their parents with work, partly to be closer to them and partly to occupy themselves. As examples, an eleven-year-old boy talked about picking up screws from his parents' workshop floor; another eleven-year-old boy mentioned helping his mother thread cables; and a fifteen-year-old girl said that she sometimes mixed and carried plaster but she also went daily to study for a few hours at a nearby public library.

7.5 Children's Visits to Migrant Parents in the Cities

The five children who spent long days in a room talked about intense loneliness and boredom. A thirteen-year-old boy from Tranquil County, Jiangxi, said:

I prefer home to Shenzhen because here I can climb the mountain and play with village friends and cousins. When I'm in Shenzhen I long to return home and when I'm at home I sometimes want to go to Shenzhen because I want to see my parents. When I'm in Shenzhen, they go to work every day returning at 8 or 9 p.m. We eat once my parents return. In Shenzhen I'm in the room all by myself . . . [he starts to cry].

Children also indicated that their relationships with their siblings could become fraught in these claustrophobic conditions. Three instances of acute conflict I heard about involved younger brothers who teased their elder sisters so mercilessly that their elder sisters took it upon themselves to severely *guan* them. For instance, a fifteen-year-old girl from Eastern County once became so frustrated with her seven-year-old brother that she locked him out on the small balcony of their parents' rented apartment in Shanghai for so long that he got sunstroke.

Younger children – namely, the nine- and ten-year-olds – offered uniquely poignant insights into how their experience of the city was defined by the constrained socio-economic niches of their migrant parents. Their accounts focused on a single concrete but defining aspect of their city visit, exemplifying both the narrowness and the blandness of their urban experience. This can be seen in the following extract of my exchange with a nine-year-old boy in Western County, Anhui, who together with his thirteen-year-old sister had just spent the two-month summer holiday in Tianjin with his duck-meat seller parents.

RACHEL: What is Tianjin like?
BOY: There is roast duck in Tianjin.
RACHEL: What did you do when you were in Tianjin?
BOY: I ate roast duck.
RACHEL: Is Tianjin better or home better?
BOY: Home is better.
RACHEL: Why?
BOY: Because I got fed up of roast duck. I can't stand to eat duck meat anymore.

The constraints on the migrant parents notwithstanding, nearly three-quarters of the children who had ever visited their parents in the city mentioned at least one outing with their parents that they had enjoyed during their last visit. Some of these outings appeared to me to be mundane, but they were obviously special to the children. For instance, at our first meeting, then twelve years old Jingjing said: 'In Dongguan we visited where my Dad works. It was great fun. We got to ride on the escalators.' Several children also talked about outings that were more obviously 'excursions', for instance, to shopping malls, parks, to

Guangdong zoo to see a white tiger and even to the seaside – memories that they treasured. For example, in 2014, Wenwen, a fourteen-year-old girl from Tranquil County, Jiangxi – mentioned at the end of Chapter 2 – recalled: 'I once went with my parents to a park in the suburbs. This memory makes all the sad things go away.'

But even when the children recalled fun outings during their city visits, they still mostly preferred for their parents to visit them in the countryside rather than go to the city themselves. This was because when their migrant parents visited them, their parents did not need to work, but when the children visited their parents in the city, the parents usually had to go to work, so time together was scarce. Some children from Tranquil County and Western County also told us that when they visited their migrant parents in the city, they missed the beautiful scenery, the clean air and the peacefulness of their home villages. Certainly, when children came from scenic villages, their exposure to their migrant parents' noisy, cramped and polluted accommodation and workplaces made them more appreciative of the good things about their otherwise 'boring' villages.

But some children did not refer to an outing when talking about their most recent visit to the city, reflecting the constraints and strains on their migrant parents. Like the girl mentioned earlier whose parents collected refuse, these children only ever stayed near to where their parents lived or worked. Moreover, a few children recalled only sad memories of time with their parents. The case of an eleven-year-old boy called Sanxin stands out. Sanxin's mother worked in a restaurant while his father did odd jobs on construction sites. When we met him in the playground of his school in Western County, Anhui, Sanxin said that on his last visit to Beijing, he had been for a walk with his father and had felt happy to be with him. But after a short distance his father spotted a casino and disappeared inside, leaving Sanxin outside for what seemed like ages. Sanxin's mother happened to walk past and on seeing him, she took him inside the casino to find his father, where his parents fought fiercely.

Sanxin's bad experiences did not end there. Sanxin told us that during holiday visits his mother would beat his buttocks and legs with brambles and rub salt into the wounds. Even though survey-based studies indicate that a high proportion of rural Chinese children, boys in particular, are subject to corporal punishment, especially when their parents have less income and less education (Chen and Liu, 2012; Li and Lau, 2012; Ni et al., 2018), the punishment described by Sanxin still alarmed my research assistant who also hailed from rural Anhui. The reasons for the beatings were always low grades or homework errors. Sanxin said that he thought that this was his mother's way of taking responsibility for him (*guan*) and that at least she tried to *guan* him, whereas his father only *guan*-ed gambling. His grandmother often pleaded for the boy's mother to return home. She said:

Conclusion 211

This child will 'turn fallow' (*huangdiao*) because he is being raised by illiterate grandparents who cannot make him study. We had an older granddaughter stay with us and she dropped out of the second year of junior high. We blame ourselves for letting her turn fallow instead of 'turning into useful talent' (*chengcai*). So, I want my daughter-in-law to return because just one look from her and he does as he is told.

Although Sanxin's visits to the city were unhappy, he still wanted to be with his mother. He also wanted to make his parents proud by becoming a scientist 'of use to the country'.

Certainly, Sanxin's experience was extreme. But study pressures nonetheless featured in most of the children's visits to see their migrant parents. Several children told us that on their summer holiday visits, their parents either punished or rewarded them for their end-of-term test scores. Most children also had to study during their holiday visits. Two children attended tuition classes in the city for two weeks of the summer vacation, but this was rare – these children's parents were senior high school and technical school graduates and worked in jobs such as managers and graphic designers. Instead, as was the case for Zhangyong (introduced in Chapter 1), most children were expected to do self-study, sometimes using additional workbooks bought for them by the migrant parents. Some children we met conflated the physical and economic constraints of where they stayed in the city with the study pressures on them. They simultaneously contrasted their feeling of being unfree in the city with a feeling of being more at ease in the countryside where the physical surroundings were usually more expansive, and their grandparents were more lenient. Children's urban visits were therefore a bitter-sweet dimension of their striving lives linked in limbo.

Conclusion

Children were the cornerstones of their spatially dispersed intergenerational striving teams. These spatially dispersed striving teams were created in the children's names, and for their sake, but not chosen by them. Indeed, as scholars note for China and other low-income countries, children are seldom consulted about the family's migration strategies and the care decisions that impact on their lives (Ye and Pan, 2011; Hoang and Yeoh, 2015). In Anhui and Jiangxi, children's lack of participation in their family's migration decisions could be seen in the children's recollections of feeling unable to speak as their parents were preparing to migrate without them. It was similarly evident in the handing over of children to their grandparents when they were too young to know what was happening.

The children we met in multilocal skipped generation families in Anhui and Jiangxi were profoundly affected by their relationships with both their migrant parents and grandparents, while also actively shaping these relationships. Many children longed for and reproached their migrant parents in equal

212 Children in Skipped Generation Families

measure while relying on their grandparents for practical and emotional support in the parents' absence and as much as family circumstances would allow. Differences in family circumstances notwithstanding, most children we met saw both their migrant parents and their grandparents as their 'family' members and envisioned an ideal life as one where all of them could reside together or at least in closer proximity.

The imperatives of multilocal striving affected families' economic conditions and emotional relationships in ways both consistent with and more complex than some sociologists' emphasis on Chinese families' intergenerational cohesiveness and adaptive solidarity might suggest (Chen, Liu and Mair, 2011), but also in ways consistent with while more cohesive than portraits of transnational families riven by conflict and 'structured by unequal power relations along gendered and generational lines' (Schmalzbauer, 2005:3). In Anhui and Jiangxi, skipped generation family configurations were underpinned by norms of reciprocity and a cycle of family division, both of which intersected with state and market endorsed discourses about the desirability of attaining social mobility through work, spatial mobility, self-improvement, capital accumulation and competition.

The resulting striving impetus generated contradictory impulses. On the one hand, people took for granted that their children would be cared for by grandparents, enabling the middle generation to earn two migrant wages rather than one. On the other hand, even as many elderly people received material support and a feeling of enhanced emotional belonging in their extended families because of their provisioning of childcare, they remained devalued and deprioritised in the allocation of family resources.

Most grandparents we met in the fieldwork counties in Anhui and Jiangxi received regular remittances and expressions of appreciation from the middle generation from which they drew psychological succour, confirming observations elsewhere in rural China (He and Ye, 2013; Dong, 2019). This money and emotional recognition helped these grandparents to create a home environment that the children felt to be 'warm' and 'harmonious'. By contrast, in nearly a quarter of the skipped generation families we visited economic adversity and palpable intergenerational tensions prevailed, which could affect children's relationships with their caregivers in two ways. On the one hand, adversity and tension could cause the children and grandparents to cling to each other for solace. On the other hand, contentious intergenerational relationships could impair grandparents' capacity to nurture the children materially and emotionally.

In line with research into transnational families (Parreñas, 2005; Dreby, 2010), children's relationships with their migrant parents and their grandparents in Anhui and Jiangxi also varied with the children's age and care histories. Younger children tended to display more emotional closeness to whoever they

Conclusion 213

had spent the most time with. Teenagers articulated considered statements about who they felt closest to and why, with the tensions of adolescence sometimes intersecting with complex emotions accumulated over many years of parent–child separation. In general, though, regardless of how close children felt towards their grandparents, children of all ages enjoyed better relationships with their migrant parents if they interacted regularly and positively with them, an impression consistent with findings from various quantitative studies discussed in Chapter 1.

Teenagers' views of their migrant parents were also mediated by their view of their future. This could be seen in the changing sentiments of Liwei, whose academic achievements enabled him to believe in the promises of the parent–child striving team. Similarly, Zhangyong's sentiments also evolved alongside his view of his future: at age eleven, he felt closer to his grandfather, and at age thirteen he felt equally close to his parents and his grandfather. The conjecture that teenagers' feelings about their parents encompassed their impressions of their parents' past support for them as well as their own prospects resonates with Gruijters's (2017) finding that in China young adults of rural origins are more likely to keep in contact with ageing parents in richer families, and with Pei and Cong's (2020) finding that in rural China the highest educated adult children provide the most financial support to their ageing parents. Nevertheless, we also encountered counterexamples. Chiefly, as discussed in Chapter 6, owing to deep mutual empathy, Jingjing's devotion to her father endured for the five years that I knew her, even as the promises of the striving team faded.

Children's relationships within their skipped generation families also varied depending on the identities of the caregivers. As discussed, children usually lived with their paternal grandparents while their paternal grandmothers provided the daily care. Nevertheless, interpersonal interactions in families with alternative care configurations could also generate emotional intimacy that transcended prevailing patrilineal and gender norms. Notably, Liwei loved his maternal grandmother more deeply than anyone else and Wang Delun felt closest to his maternal grandfather. Meanwhile, a few children enjoyed affectionate relationships with widowed grandfathers who did the cooking, cleaning and comforting that they had seldom performed for their own children and that the children's own fathers had seldom done for them. The presence of other children in a household also affected children's home environments, generating both burdens on grandparents and conflicts among children, but also providing children with companionship.

In summary, even as their circumstances varied, children in skipped generation families tried to sustain meaningful relationships with both their grandparent caregivers and their migrant parents. Many children helped their grandparents in daily life while relying on them practically and emotionally as parent substitutes. At the same time, most children tried to sustain their relationships with their migrant parents. They studied as best they could; they helped their parents during their visits to see them in the city; and as they grew older they dealt with their distanced, reproachful and conflicted feelings towards their migrant parents by trying to understand them better. Children also drew comfort from idealised memories of time spent with their migrant parents, for instance memories of past Chinese New Year celebrations and excursions during summer holiday visits to the cities. At the same time, as sociologists observe of children facing adversity more generally, these children also fixed their eyes on the future (James, Jenks and Prout, 1998: 74), anticipating reunions and dreaming of making their families proud of them through hard work and educational success, to try to displace pain in the present.

8 Left-Behind Children in Striving Teams

8.1 The Contribution

How has parental migration changed Chinese childhoods? Drawing on ethnographic materials, in-depth interviews with 109 children, matched interviews with the children's caregivers and teachers, and longitudinal interviews with twenty-five of the children and their caregivers, I explored the effects of rural–urban migration on children's lives and family relationships in China's rural interior. Specifically, I engaged with the following questions: (1) How do children interpret and adapt to the changes that parental migration brings to their families? (2) How do children participate in family migration projects aimed at investing in their education and in other aspects of their futures? (3) How do the objectives of the family migration project vary by the children's gender? How do boys' and girls' subjective experiences differ when their parents migrate without them? (4) How do children perceive and participate in their relationships with their parents and at-home caregivers when only fathers migrate, when only mothers migrate, and when both parents migrate while leaving them in the care of grandparents?

My approach to exploring the lives of 'left-behind' children living in rural China is unique in three respects. Firstly, I focus on the impacts of rural–urban migration on family relationships, rather than on quantifying the impacts of parents' migration on different dimensions of children's well-being, as so many other studies have done. Secondly, I view parental migration as motivated by family aspirations for the children's education, thereby identifying 'study' as integral to how the children interpret their parents' migration and their own obligations. My research thereby diversifies literature on childhood and cultural capital accumulation strategies from exploring families where parents and children co-reside, to exploring families where parental migration is pivotal to the child-raising strategy. Thirdly, my analysis privileges children's viewpoints rather than adults' viewpoints. In doing so I examine variation among children by their gender, age, and academic performance, situating their agency in the multiscalar context of 'linked lives', especially of parent–child and grandparent–child dyads; the families' gendered and generational configurations and socio-economic circumstances; features of place including local school regime characteristics; and wider institutional, economic and cultural structures.

Overall, my findings reveal that in a context of economic restructuring and the wider adaptive transformation of filial piety, parental migration profoundly changed children's relationships with the adults in their families. The children my research assistants and I met were all socialised in their homes and schools to see their parents' migration as generating an intergenerational debt for them to repay through study, while educational aspirations were articulated in relation to the family's migration project. At the same time, children's perceptions of their families' support and care for them were influenced by (1) a wider 'development'-oriented striving imperative that valorised youth and cities over elders and rural places, and (2) social constructions of motherhood and fatherhood that deemed certain family forms and certain caregivers to be more suitable than others in preparing children for decent urban futures. This book's findings further reveal that despite a contemporary striving ethos's promise of a 'sweet' future, the children themselves most longed for belonging, affection, security and a sense of self-worth in the present. Nevertheless, 'study' prevailed as the main way for them to try to realise these desires, with the possibilities for them to do so affected by the precise interaction of the many influences discussed earlier.

8.2 The Scholarly Conversation

Mirroring several pioneering studies – most pertaining to international migration – I find that parental migration alters childhood in often paradoxical ways (Parreñas, 2005; Dreby, 2010; Coe, 2014). Specifically, several studies demonstrate that parental migration is enacted in the name of the child to ensure the families' longer-term reproduction and security (Orellana et al., 2001; Pan and Ye, 2011; Hoang and Yeoh, 2015). At the same time, though, parental migration places immense strain on family relationships, especially on parent–child relationships (Parreñas, 2005; Dreby, 2010), with left-behind children disproportionately shouldering the emotional consequences (Parreñas, 2005; Dreby, 2010; Pan and Ye, 2011; Gardner, 2012; Hoang and Yeoh, 2015). Even so, the literature simultaneously reveals that children have their own perspectives and interests, influenced by but distinct from those of the adults, and that these change across their life course. Furthermore, children act on their perspectives, negotiating with their migrant parents, at-home parents, grandparent caregivers and siblings, influencing their families' migration projects and their own care arrangements in the process (Parreñas, 2005; Dreby, 2010; Graham et al., 2012; Hoang et al., 2015).

8.2 The Scholarly Conversation

The idea of the parents' migration as a 'sacrifice' undertaken for the children highlights that migration is aimed at facilitating capital accumulation in the next generation, a logic that binds together the parent–child striving teams discussed in this book. One strand of research on the theme of migration as a project undertaken for the children's education focuses on families where the children move accompanied by their mothers from countries and regions such as China, Hong Kong, South Korea and Taiwan to attend school in countries such as Australia, Canada, Singapore, New Zealand and the United States (Huang and Yeoh, 2005; Waters, 2005; Lee and Koo, 2006; Huang and Yeoh, 2011; Waters, 2015). Waters (2015) observes that the imperatives that drive this kind of education-oriented migration exemplify a neat fit between Bourdieu's (1986) idea of capital and Katz's (2008) idea of children as 'sites of accumulation'. However, Waters also points out that most of this research concentrates on the mothers while 'far too little research' looks at the children. She therefore argues that migration researchers need to go beyond seeing children as passive 'vessels of/for capital' by 'focusing in on the child him or herself' in relation to a wider social environment. As discussed in Chapter 1, such a critique of the migration studies literature applies also to research on left-behind children.

But the glass is not entirely empty. The transnational migration studies literature offers a number of rich insights into children's agency and experiences when their parents have migrated without them. As mentioned earlier, much of this literature highlights that the framing of parents' migration as a 'sacrifice' generates a debt, which left-behind children are obligated to repay through diligence in their studies, helpfulness at home, and good behaviour, as well as longer-term support for those who have raised and supported them (Parreñas, 2005; Dreby, 2010; Coe, 2014). In a Chinese cultural context this dynamic of intergenerational reciprocity is articulated through the idiom of filial piety. However, children's responses to the expectations that family striving places on them can be contradictory. Indeed, studies on transnational families draw attention to the emotional turmoil that children incur because their parents' migration can derail their efforts to study hard, leaving them feeling disillusioned (Parreñas, 2005; Dreby, 2010; Coe, 2014).

A further theme in research on both migration and childhood, which resonates with this book's findings, is the strong influence of a *future* orientation on individuals' identities and lives in the present (e.g. Qvortrup, 2009; Carling, Menjívar and Schmalzbauer, 2012). Some transnational migration studies research elucidates how children's experiences of moving between countries or of inhabiting a 'transnational social field' orient them towards a particular *habitus* such that they grow up envisioning their future in a distant place (Coe, 2012; Gardner, 2012; Zeitlyn and Mand, 2012). Meanwhile, studies of education highlight the significance of schools as institutions where children become socialised into an urban or cosmopolitan habitus, 'learning to leave' their hometowns (Corbett, 2007; Morrow and Vennam, 2015). The combined potency of migration and education in shaping left-behind children's aspirations and subjectivity becomes even more apparent if we invoke Xiang's (2014) idea of 'would-be migrants'. Xiang (2014) uses the term 'would-be' migrants to describe adults who think about and prepare to migrate overseas to the extent that their lives in the present are significantly changed. The left-behind children discussed in this book counted as 'would-be' migrants in that they derived much of the moral purpose for their present lives from the promise of the future: they were preparing themselves to migrate.

Over the past fifteen years, several landmark studies have provided further powerful insights into labour migration systems' appropriation and reworking of families' gendered and generational social relations, and the implications for children's lives (e.g. Parreñas, 2005; Dreby, 2010; Graham et al., 2012; Coe, 2014; Hoang et al., 2015). Meanwhile, a parallel literature on child-raising and education offers finely grained analyses of the gendering of families' capital accumulation strategies, even though children's experiences of these strategies have received less attention (e.g. Field, 1995; Reay, 2001; Lan, 2018). A recurring finding in all these literatures, confirmed also in this book's analysis, is that children's perceptions of their families' gendered and generational configurations are deeply affected by an intersection of social constructions of gender and hierarchical ideas about suitable caregivers, and by disturbances to the gendered order of families (e.g. Colen, 1995; Parreñas, 2005; Dreby, 2010; Graham and Jordan, 2011; Jordan and Graham, 2012; Hoang et al., 2015).

Existing research also emphasises how 'cultural context' mediates children's interpretations of their families' gendered and generational configurations. For instance, some research reveals that cultures vary in their historical antecedents for 'distributing children' across caregivers and in the flexibility of their family and gender norms, influencing children's understandings of their own parents' migration and care (Fog Olwig, 1999; Graham and Jordan, 2011; Jordan and Graham, 2012; Coe, 2014). But even as children in some cultures– for instance, in West Africa – see their parents' migration more positively and as less disruptive than children in some other cultures, parent–child separation still causes emotional dilemmas and feelings of loss for many (Coe, 2014). This is because migration removes a significant person from the children's home life while long-term separation prevents the sharing of daily life necessary for nurturing familiarity and intimacy. Through attention to familial obligations centred on education my findings confirm for rural China the salience of culture in imbuing children's experiences of multilocal family life with certain meanings. My findings also echo Hu's (2019) observation that two features of Chinese culture – familialism and an emphasis on education – serve as sources of resilience for some left-behind children (Hu, 2019), while leading to other teenagers' self-denigration.

In summary, previous literature finds that children participate in the capital accumulation projects that their families envision for them, while adapting themselves to the challenges that their parents' migration poses for them practically and emotionally. The literature also demonstrates that children draw on the cultural resources at their disposal in interpreting their parents' migration. The literature concurrently demonstrates that children rely on the care available to them in trying to meet their parents' expectations of them, the hardships and strains notwithstanding. These findings resonate with my observations in Anhui and Jiangxi. Specifically, even as left-behind children are depicted in China's public discourse as vulnerable, powerless and miserable, they nevertheless participated in family relationships and gave meaning to these relationships. At the same time, though, some children rebelled against, withdrew from or reproached their migrant parents, with their responses varying by their circumstances and life course stage, as well as varying from one moment to the next. The heterogeneity and contradictions of left-behind children's agency and subjective experiences led me to grapple with how best to interpret them. The approach of seeing the children as participants in multilocal parent–child striving teams helped me in doing so.

8.3 Children as Participants in Multilocal Parent–Child Striving Teams

How does a view of left-behind children as participants in multilocal parent–child striving teams shed light on their agency and lived experiences? Four themes to emerge from this book's use of a 'striving team' lens are as follows: the importance of ideological parameters and cultural context in shaping the children's agency; children's perceptions and practices in light of their family members' gendered and generational obligations to each other; the temporal dimensions of migration and childhood in family, national and global capital accumulation agendas; and the problem of children's agency given real-world constraints, inequalities and injustices. I discuss each of these four themes in turn.

Firstly, a lens of family 'striving' heightens the visibility of the ideological parameters of the lives of people in multilocal families, including those of children's lives. Recalling the concept of cultural 'repertoires', noted in Chapter 1, the impetus to strive was so potent among the people I met from Anhui and Jiangxi because it was inherent in the cultural values, beliefs and practices that so pervaded 'ordinary experience as to blend imperceptibly about what is true' (Swidler, 1986: 281). These values, beliefs and practices included family, gender, motherhood, fatherhood, filial piety, sacrifice, love, care, morality, work, school, self-improvement and modernisation. Indeed, striving struck at the heart of the rural family, with pathways to 'recognition' within and beyond the family cohering such that failure at school, in the labour market, or in the marriage market was not just a personal failure but failure as a child, parent or spouse. My analysis especially highlights that migration and education – each enabled by social reproduction – were the twin pillars of the rural family members' struggle for recognition. The *children studying in the rural areas* participated in this struggle for recognition as much as the adults. Striving – and the wider social structures that fused with striving family culture (Swidler, 1986: 281) – permeated the everyday micro-worlds in which the children learned through the 'goals, control, permission and affection (and anger) of adults' that 'other people's happiness depended on their input' (Mayall, 2000: 248), shaping their agency.

Secondly, my lens of 'parent–child striving teams' highlights the complex influences of families' gendered and generational relationships on the children's multilocal family fields, and on their subjectivity and agency within these fields. Confirming the scholarly observations discussed previously, I found that social constructions of gender intersected with generational inequalities to affect different family members' experiences of migration, including children's experiences of migration. But this book also echoes Dreby's (2010) observation for Mexico in finding that, at least for pre-teens, many aspects of boys' and girls' experiences of parental migration were similar. Nevertheless, my findings depart from Dreby's (2010) by revealing that the *children's gender* itself motivated different trajectories of family striving, affecting what the parents aimed to provide for their children, how the children viewed their parents' migration, and the children's responses to differential treatment vis-à-vis opposite-gender siblings.

My relational emphasis on *teams* also yields fresh insights. I highlight not only that 'left-behind' children viewed their relationships with their families as the cornerstone of their lives but also that they related to their families differently depending on the gender of the parent(s) who had migrated – a topic that has so far received little attention in the literature. Mirroring Parreñas's (2005) and Dreby's (2010) observations for the Philippines and Mexico, respectively, I found that in rural China 'nurturer mother and breadwinner father' sat at the top of a notional hierarchy of family configurations such that the children were less accepting of a mother's migration than a father's migration. Nevertheless, I also demonstrate that children in differently configured families drew on gendered expectations of parenting when managing their relationships with their parents. For instance, some children echoed mainstream public discourses' as well as their grandmothers' views about the superiority of maternal care when urging their own mothers to stay at home. Some children used their migrant mother's failure to provide direct maternal love (*mu'ai*) when lobbying

8.3 Children as Participants in Multilocal Teams 221

their parents for certain forms of support, for instance to attend a private school. Meanwhile, as discussed in Chapter 6, a handful of children also subtly affirmed their left-behind fathers' masculine worth as producers, providers and fighters in an unfair and complex world.

My lens of multilocal striving further draws out the relational dimension of children's agency within skipped generation families, notably their interactions with their migrant parents and grandparent caregivers. It demonstrates that some children forged close emotional ties with their grandparents, particularly if the parents had migrated when the children were still infants. Conversely, many children whose parents had left them when they were older felt closer to their migrant parents even as they made the best of the care that their grandparents offered them. Children living in skipped generation families also calibrated their emotional responses to the complex relational dynamics that could arise between their grandparents and migrant parents because of the latter's quest to accumulate funds for their own nuclear families; this could impact both the grandparents' care of the children and the children's relationships with their grandparent caregivers.

Thirdly, a striving lens reveals the temporal dimensions of the children's subjectivity and agency by highlighting the future orientation of the family migration project. Although, as noted in the previous section, the future orientation of migration and the future orientation of childhood have each been discussed in separate scholarly literatures, this book's view of children as participants in multilocal striving teams casts fresh light on how migration responds to, harnesses and intensifies the future orientation inherent in childhood (James, Jenks and Prout, 1998; Katz, 2004; Qvortrup, 2009; Coe, 2014; Xiang, 2014). Indeed, the subject position of 'would-be migrants' as individuals 'in the process of becoming' Xiang (2014) is also the subject position that society requires children to occupy (Qvortrup, 2009; Tisdal and Punch, 2012).

In Anhui and Jiangxi, some of the temporal quality of children's and adults' linked lives can be conceptualised as lived in *abeyance*. 'Abeyance' has at least two overlapping meanings. It can mean 'a state of suspension, being put aside or up in the air', and it is also a legal term describing a title or property that is promised. The word 'abeyance' derives from the late sixteen-century old French term '*abeance*', which – pertinent to the concerns of this book – comprises the word '*abeer*,' meaning 'to aspire after' or 'to expect', with '*a*' meaning 'towards' and '*beer*' meaning 'to gape'.[1] A state of abeyance aptly expresses the idea that the members of multilocal families lived their lives while waiting for promised 'recognition' and economic security to arrive. The problem, though, is that recognition and economic security were always 'yet to come'. Indeed, owing to endless inflation in the absolute value of the capital

---

[1] www.lexico.com/en/definition/abeyance

that people needed to be 'recognised' as worthy in the *vital* competitions of education, employment and marriage, and owing to the 'adverse terms of recognition by which the poor must negotiate the norms that frame their social lives,' rural people typically found themselves trying simply to not fall behind even as they yearned to get ahead (Rao and Walton, 2004: 24; citing Appadurai, 2004). The point at which life was 'sweet' enough to enjoy was therefore postponed indefinitely, and not just within one lifetime but across generations.

Sociologists observe that a future orientation can be a source of both pressure and resilience for children (James, Jenks and Prout, 1998: 74). This was so for the left-behind children I met because an intensified future orientation placed high expectations on them whilst also giving them a focus with which to displace their suffering in the present. Crucially, though, the future-oriented positioning of children – amplified by the multilocal striving ethos – was 'at odds with the children's own experiences of time passing' (James, Jenks and Prout, 1998: 74).[2] Indeed, to borrow terminology from the Marxist philosopher, Martin Hägglund (2019), multilocal family striving required that ever more of children's and adults' time be devoted to work in the 'realm of necessity' – work oriented towards the accumulation of 'numeric capital' (e.g. exam scores, money) (Woronov, 2016) necessary for the family's survival and reproduction – which differs from work in the 'realm of freedom' whereby people pursue their interests, passions and commitments. This book's findings thereby invite critical reflection on the implications of both parental migration and intense study pressures for children's possibilities to live more contemporaneously and to enjoy a happy childhood as a value in its own right.

Finally, in seeing the children as participants in multilocal striving teams I engage with conundrums raised in the sociology of childhood about researching children's viewpoints and agency. Pertinently, sociologists Tisdall and Punch (2012) ask: With an emphasis on children's agency, empowerment and capacity to live meaningful lives – even in the face of extreme deprivation – what becomes of children's vulnerability? In probing this question, they note that many excellent studies fully document the structural constraints to children's agency, but they find that this is inadequate. They therefore suggest that researchers do more to explore the ambiguity of children's agency and propose that attention to children's relationships offers one way to do this. This suggestion resonates well with recognition of migration as relational. Indeed, seeing children as participants in intergenerational teams brings their relationships to the centre of an understanding of their agency, elucidating ambiguities and contradictions in this agency.

---

[2] As Dreby (2010) observes for transnational families in Mexico, time passed more slowly for left-behind children than for migrant adults.

8.3 Children as Participants in Multilocal Teams 223

Even so, studying children's agency in circumstances of suffering, deprivation and relative powerlessness is controversial. Attention to how children give meaning to their lives is liable to be criticised by some commentators for downplaying or even 'normalising' the sources of the children's adversity, in this case long-term parent–child separation because of parental migration. For instance, Wei (2018) sees an exploration of how left-behind children exercise agency within the context of family relationships as akin to disregarding (1) the harm and misery that migration's disturbance to parent–child attachment inflicts on children and (2) the need for policy reforms to end discrimination against rural migrants. This line of argument stems from good intentions and has merits, but also flaws. One problem is that it wrongly attributes all left-behind children's suffering to their separation from their parents. As Parreñas (2005) observes for the Philippines and as Xiang (2007) observes for China, some children come from families too poor to have even the luxury of mourning the emotional costs of parental migration. These children's parents usually have immobility imposed on them, and their poverty inflicts its own emotional toll on the family members.

As observed in Chapter 5, children who lived with both their parents often wanted one parent to migrate. This was the case for a thirteen-year-old boy from Eastern County, Anhui, who lived with his parents and older sister in a house with an earthen floor and crumbling mud walls. The boy's father worked part-time as a postman and farmed the land of his migrant brother to bring in extra income. The father explained that he could not migrate because he needed to look after his ill wife. The boy showed me detailed weekly self-study plans that he had drawn up. When I asked him about his views on parental migration and left-behind children, he replied:

Many of those children waste their parents' hard-earned money on sweets and electronic games. And when their note books are not even finished, they buy new ones. I think that left-behind children are not pitiful at all. They have grandparents who spoil them and parents who give them money. And they also feel entitled to care, but every family has its difficulties. I would like my parents to go out and earn money. If they were not by my side, I would be self-reliant. I have learned from extra-curricular books that it is necessary to forge one's own path in life. I want to go to university, but my family's resources are limited. Even though I can talk easily to my parents I do not think that I have an advantage over other classmates whose parents have migrated. I can see that they have economic advantages, which are necessary for further study.

Another problem with Wei's (2018) view that recognising 'left-behind' children's agency 'normalises' split families is that multiple dynamics precipitate and 'normalise' parent–child separation in contemporary China, and parental migration interacts with these other dynamics. China's authoritarian political system has long required people to subordinate family interests to national interests and to various 'development' agendas. In 1950s–1970s, family members were often separated from each other because individuals were expected to go wherever socialist construction most needed them, reflected in the slogan 'sacrifice the small family for the nation' or literally, the 'nation-family' (*wei guojia xisheng xiaojia*[3]).

More recently, in the twenty-first century, vast numbers of primary school children in China have been compelled by a vigorous school consolidation programme and compulsory boarding policies to live separated from their parents during the week. In China, boarding disproportionately affects those children who come from poor families and have less well-educated parents, many of whom live in rural regions: Young and Hannum discover that the predicted probability of boarding at school is 63 per cent for children of parents who have not progressed beyond primary school, 43 per cent for children with at least one parent who has progressed beyond primary school but not post-secondary education, and only 12 per cent for children with at least one parent who has post-secondary education (Young and Hannum, 2018: 1077). Some ethnic minority children also find themselves disproportionately affected by school consolidation programmes and boarding. For instance, many Tibetan primary and junior high school children board for weeks and months at a time without seeing their parents, generating distress for them (Wright, 2018). Meanwhile, in 2019 the state's use of schools to separate Uyghur children from their parents and to socialise them in state-approved secular Han culture was widely reported in the Western media (Sudworth, 2019). At the same time, the adverse impacts of boarding, especially at the primary school stage, on rural left-behind children's emotional well-being, sense of school belonging and academic achievement notwithstanding (Mei et al., 2015; Wang and Mao, 2018), Chinese policymakers have continued to advocate for an expansion of boarding schools to address left-behind children's much lamented care deficits (Yan and Zhu, 2006; Zhou, 2007; Xie, 2009; Yao and She, 2009; Ministry of Education, 2013). Indeed, in 2016 at an executive meeting of the State Council convened by the Premier Li Keqiang, the delegates 'vowed to make more efforts to establish boarding schools' in response to the 'problem' of left-behind children (China Daily, 2016).

Importantly too, an emphasis on children's misery takes us only so far. If, by contrast, we listen to children and see them as social actors rather than just document their vulnerability and misery, we highlight their right to be heard even if we also emphasise a need for their lives – including their right to a family life – to be protected (Tisdall and Punch, 2012). This recalls a question raised by the sociologist, Jingzhong Ye and his collaborators who on reporting that they have 'become increasingly dissatisfied with ... description[s] of the miserable conditions of migrant workers and their left

---

[3] This slogan is often used in forcible dam relocation projects.

8.3 Children as Participants in Multilocal Teams

behind family members attached with some policy recommendations,' ask: What is the step beyond recognising misery (Ye, Wang, Wu et al., 2013: 1138)? In exploring the lives of children left behind in Anhui and Jiangxi, I hope that this book contributes in some small way to documenting how multilocal striving becomes normalised, and to highlighting that it is not inevitable for everyone – young and old – to endure lifetimes of 'aggregated competitive pressures' whereby they must 'strive ever harder,' feeling so physically tired and emotionally depleted all the time (Yan 2012 cited in Hansen, 2015: 142), while irretrievably forfeiting time spent with loved ones. Indeed, Ye and his co-authors call for a paradigm shift in how 'development' is understood (Ye et al., 2013: 1138). But what is the alternative to a development model whereby rural families' social reproduction serves urbanisation and capital accumulation in a globalising market (Day, 2013)? Are the logic of market competition and the disempowerment of rural people too entrenched in economic, cultural and institutional structures for radical alternatives to be thinkable, let alone viable (Day, 2013)?

A corresponding question is: How can a paradigm shift occur? With an emphasis on rendering power relations *visible*, the sociologist Atkinson (2015) cites Bourdieu (1999: 629) in urging scholars to 'raise awareness as widely as possible . . . that the problems, worries, suffering, stresses and pains in people's lives are not inevitable or freely chosen but are produced by what society has set up, and that 'what society has done, it can, armed with this knowledge, undo' (Atkinson, 2015: 184). In a similar vein, Katz (2004; 2008) and Coe (2014) argue that when the ideological assumptions, power relations and cultural repertoires that underpin mundane decisions and practices around social reproduction become *visible*, they can be talked about and critiqued. Likewise, Hägglund highlights that the capitalist social order appropriates the *time* of precious finite human life in ways that people do not recognise, saying: 'To cast off our chains and seize our *time* we must grasp that all we have – who we are is inseparable from the material and social practices through which we transform our lives' (Hägglund, 2019: 331).

Importantly, though, toil, insecurity and strain are not unique to China. Rather this book documents a *locally and historically situated* manifestation of *wider global processes* whereby 'social relations and material bases of capitalism are forever renewed' in ways that obscure the costs of capital accumulation imperatives, placeless capital and state divestment from public welfare (Katz, 2008). Specifically, this book explores how in the second decade of twenty-first-century China rural people's attentions were absorbed in particular ways by domestic routines, the demands of reproduction and anxieties about their children's futures, such that they were largely distracted from the wider structures that unhinged production from social reproduction, and compelled them to ceaseless striving (Katz, 2004; Katz, 2008; see also Hansen,

226 Left-Behind Children in Striving Teams

2015). Micro-studies of childhood in rural China – including this book – reveal that, as in many other parts of the world, children disproportionately bear the emotional costs of the unhinging of social reproduction from production and the competitive pressures of capital accumulation (see also Ye, 2011; Ye and Pan, 2011). In searching for alternatives, Katz (2004) contends that children's play can help to reveal the constructed nature of the social world and therefore that it could be made differently.

Some authors also argue that people could look to children's voices for inspiration for a paradigm shift, or at least for generating awareness about a need to order society differently (Gilligan, 2011; see also Ye, 2011). Carol Gilligan (2011) observes that in a patriarchal society, care prepares people for competition in a world in which men dominate women and other men. She further contends that care is a relational ethic but one that is subordinate to competition. She refers to her research team's longitudinal interviews with children in the United States to explain that as the children grew older and adapted to the world of competitive patriarchy, they learned to disconnect themselves from others and to silence their own inner authentic voices to meet gendered expectations and to preserve relationships (Gilligan, 2011: 26–39; 106–109). In this way, competition required 'a loss of voice and a sacrifice of relationship' (Gilligan, 2011: 33). In looking for alternatives to a dehumanising competitive social order, she contends that in a true democracy care would be a humanist ethic rather than a feminist ethic. Moreover, such an ethic would recognise all human beings' interdependence and need for emotional connection. This recalls the sociologist Mayall's observation that children, with their 'natural emphasis [on] interdependence and reciprocity as central values' if truly heard could inspire and shape an ethic of care (Mayall, 2000: 248).

Certainly, as described in this book, we met young children who 'could not speak out' as their parents prepared to migrate without them; children who stifled their crying under their bed quilts at night; children who wished that their migrant fathers would show them affection; children who longed for their parents to return home; and teenagers who laughed when looking back on the wretchedness of their younger selves before they 'grew up' and came to 'understand things'. We heard about children who said that their migrant parents were dead as a way to let off steam and to convey their longing for companionship. I also witnessed several teenagers knock their foreheads with the base of their hand as they expressed frustration that they could not master their study materials, letting their families down and closing off the only route to a worthwhile future. While national development and school agendas forever reminded the children that they needed to advance upwards, the children themselves most longed for time to spend with their mothers and fathers, and for time to rest and play, alongside time to learn. Children's voices, if heard,

8.4 The Future of Migrants' Children

could inspire different values by which to organise society, thereby unsettling the subordination of basic human needs for social protection, intimacy, interdependence and shared time with loved ones to the relentless competitive pursuit of capital accumulation under patriarchy.

8.4 The Future of Migrants' Children

China's Party-state frames the existence of a large population of left-behind children as a side effect of the country's incomplete urbanisation, thereby casting it as a transitional problem. But as mentioned in Chapter 1, such framing elides the reality that a rural–urban labour migration system based on protracted family separation is integral to rather than incidental to a national strategy of rapid capital accumulation in a globalising market. Even so, during the 2010s the Party-state has felt under mounting pressure to address the 'problem' of left-behind children. In 2016, at the State Council meeting that followed the second tragedy involving left-behind children in Bijie County, Guizhou Province, Premier Li Keqiang vowed to 'protect the welfare of left-behind children, reduce the size of their population and not let the left behind problem become a pain to the family and a tragedy to society' (China Daily, 2016). In February 2016, a State Council directive that emanated from this meeting banned migrant parents from leaving children alone while advising that, 'parents should do their best to take their children with them' or else make appropriate care arrangements in their hometowns (China Daily, 2016; Su, 2016; see also Yin, 2016).

Certainly, one might assume that with an increase in China's urbanisation rate from 36.22 per cent in 2000 to 57.35 per cent in 2016 to a predicted 70 per cent in 2030 the proportion of rural migrant workers' children who were 'left behind' would decrease (China Statistical Yearbook Data Base, 2018). So far, though, this does not appear to have been happening. As noted in Chapter 1, during the 2010s, migrants' access to public services worsened in many major cities. Hence, even as the numbers of rural children affected by parental migration increased and the numbers of rural children who migrated to the cities also increased, the proportion of the children of migrants who migrated to the cities declined after 2010: in 2000, 60 per cent of the children of migrants were left behind, rising to 67 per cent in 2015 (Chan and Ren, 2018: 139).

A shift in the proportion of rural versus urban left-behind children also indicates that urbanisation does not inevitably mitigate the left-behind children problem. As mentioned, in Chapter 1, between 2010 and 2015 the number of rural left-behind children in China fell from 61 million to 41 million, while the number of urban left-behind children rose from 7.7 million to 28.3 million (Chan and Ren, 2018: 139). These changing proportions represent an increase in the share of urban-to-urban migration within China's overall internal migration, but they mostly reflect a reclassification of rural regions as urban without any meaningful change in the children's circumstances (Chan and Ren, 2018: 139). Importantly, too, as discussed in Chapter 7, many children resemble their parents in living in limbo between rural and urban worlds, such that they are migrants at some points in their life and left-behinds at others (Zhang, 2015; Chan and Ren, 2018).

Many commentators in China envision that the size of the left-behind children population will reduce alongside urbanisation and industrialisation in the interior provinces. In the late 2010s, the volume of China's inter-provincial migration declined and the volume of intra-provincial migration increased. Moreover, in 2018 the volume of migrants to the Pearl River Delta fell by 3.9 per cent, while the volume of migrants to China's interior and the west grew by 4.2 per cent (Bugarin, 2019). Return migration also increased and China's policymakers talked ever more about the possibilities for return migration and returnee business creation to resolve the left-behind children problem (State Council, 2016). Over the same period, articles in Party newspapers claimed that industrial and commercial development in the interior provinces enabled returnee parents to both earn money and take care of their at-school children (e.g. Guizhou Daily, 2017; Anhui Federation of Trade Unions, 2018; Huang et al., 2019), with some commentaries commending returnee parents for alleviating labour shortages in the interior's manufacturing sector (Du, 2013). Media reports also praised local government efforts to help returnee *peidu* mothers find work in township and county factories such that these 'left-behind' rural women no longer needed to choose between *dagong* and *peidu* (e.g. Anhui Daily, 2013; Dong, 2018).

The optimism notwithstanding, given a wider 'race to the bottom' in the global competition for capital investment, factory jobs in China's interior provinces have often entailed repetitive tasks, low pay, and exposure to poor environmental health conditions that are even worse than in coastal provinces, such that many younger migrants prefer to look for other options, for instance service-sector jobs in coastal cities. More positively, though, factories in interior regions can offer locally based workers greater flexibility to attend to family matters than would be the case if they were migrants, for instance a longer lunch break to go home and cook for their children (Anhui Daily, 2013). Sociologists Chan and Selden (2014) also see sources of hope for improvements in working conditions in interior provinces. They suggest that if people can work in or near their hometowns, they can use their local kinship and social networks to mobilise for improved working conditions. They further suggest that labour shortages arising from demographic changes may strengthen workers' leverage for better conditions.

8.4 The Future of Migrants' Children

If such improvements in workers' conditions were to materialise, this could significantly affect parent–child relationships because as Bronfenbrener says, the conditions of parents' work are 'among the most powerful influences' on the 'development of young children in the industrialised world' (Bronfenbrenner, 1979: 3–4), with migrant employment representing an extreme instance of monitored labour and long working hours – both characteristics of work inimical to nurturing parenting practices. Chiefly, when parents work long inflexible hours and are subjected to close supervision – usually in jobs that require little education – this carries over into their parenting practices, manifest in high levels of stress and a world view whereby people must conform to the dictates of others. However, when parents have more flexibility and self-direction in their work – usually in jobs that require more education – they can bequeath to their children a more empowered world view and give their children more of their time (Bronfenbrenner, 1979: 245–249). Bronfenbrenner's thesis is consistent with Lareau's (2003) observation that poor and working-class children in the United States tend to develop an emerging sense of constraint while middle-class children learn to negotiate with authority.[4]

Although most policy discussions in China pin hopes for the resolution of the 'transitional problem' of 'left-behind children' on urbanisation and development, different levels of the Party-state apparatus have nevertheless also responded to State Council directives by intensifying their efforts to safeguard the well-being of left-behind children and prevent more tragedies from occurring. As noted in Chapter 3, in the 2010s the formal requirements on local governments, schools and other agencies to monitor the welfare of left-behind children increased, with policy attention after 2016 concentrating on the children of two migrant parents. Certainly, such interventions can be expected to help some children, but they cannot be expected to properly meet the children's emotional and developmental needs.

China's policy commentators clearly recognise that rural schools struggle to provide emotional care for left-behind children. They acknowledge, as noted in Chapter 3, that teachers are under immense pressure to reach progression and attainment targets and to manage with limited resources (Wang and Wu, 2016: 46). Moreover, even when resources are available to support dedicated interventions for left-behind children, the limitations of such interventions are evident. For instance, in several regions with high rates of parental out-migration, an organisation called Growing Home organises for teachers and volunteers to read out bedtime stories to the children over the dormitory

---

[4] Lareau's analysis (2003) draws on the insights of Bourdieu (e.g. Bourdieu and Passeron, 1990; Bourdieu, 2000; Bourdieu, 2010) and Kohn, with Kohn having built on Urie Bronfenbrenner's early research (e.g. Kohn, 1963).

loudspeakers. The Chinese organiser initiated this bedtime stories programme after learning about an intervention in the United States whereby volunteers read healing stories to young offenders in prison, leading to improvements in their behaviour and emotional well-being (China Daily, 2018). But while laudable, this intervention poignantly reveals the intimacy gap in these children's everyday lives.

The 2010s also saw a proliferation of village-based outreach schemes run by social organisations and community volunteers in partnership with local government agencies or with local government endorsement. Indeed, in the 2010s the Chinese media carried many reports about weekend and summer holiday activities targeting left-behind children and their families. These activities were run mostly by retired teachers, local-educated young people or university students. In 2018, I saw a news item on Jiangxi Television Station about such an initiative. It told the story of a retired teacher in his seventies called Yan Yanxiang who set up a club for left-behind children in his village. He spent 2,000 *yuan* of his own money to buy a television, a CD player and CDs about Chinese history for the children. One of the children featured in the news bulletin told the reporter: 'He is very kind. He teaches us what we can't learn in class or by ourselves. We would just be outside passing time by ourselves. We can learn more things from him.' Meanwhile, Yan Yanxiang explained that he felt supported by the local Party branch and he felt happy when he was with the children.[5]

In 2016, 2017 and 2018, Anhui provincial news similarly featured reports about interventions for left-behind children. A few of these items referred to a summer holiday intervention carried out in Western County, Anhui, co-ordinated by the prefectural Women's Federation, Education Bureau and Communist Youth League. The media reports showed local officials visiting rural families to check on the safety of 'fully' left-behind children. The media reports also showed teams of female university students referred to as volunteer *aixin mama* or 'compassionate mothers' tutoring the children as well as groups of male and female university students running military style activity camps (*junying*) for them. The 2010s additionally saw a rise in interventions aimed at improving the parenting skills of rural caregivers and migrant parents, with an emphasis on encouraging these adults to interact with the children warmly and to refrain from using corporal punishment.[6]

---

[5] Xinwen Yehang [Evening News] Jiangxi Television Station, November 20, 2018, 22.55hrs.

[6] Visit to a social work centre for migrants in an 'urban village' in Guangdong Province, August 28, 2017. I am grateful to Bin Wu of Nottingham University for giving me the opportunity to join him on the visit to this centre. Also, personal communication (June and July 2019) with Professor Zhenning Xu of the Department of Sociology, Shanghai Academy of Social Sciences who has participated in such outreach activities among left-behind children and their families in rural communities.

8.4 The Future of Migrants' Children

While such interventions can be expected to help some children, as Wang and Wu (2016) observe in their review of policies towards left-behind children, the measures remain ad hoc and mostly express good intentions. Furthermore, such interventions endorse the logic of multilocal striving in several respects. For instance, the language of 'care' (*guanai*) and 'compassion' (*aixin*) used to deliver these interventions reinforces wider discursive hierarchies that marginalise rural people while impelling them to strive (Sun, 2009a). These interventions also contribute to the social reproduction of the next generation of hard-working and emotionally resilient labourers and citizens while keeping social reproduction activities contained in the countryside. At the same time, echoing Hansen's (2015) observations about 'authoritarian individualisation' in China's schools, these activities and the discourses surrounding them encourage left-behind children to work hard, to use their time productively, to concentrate on their private striving goals and to take responsibility for their own well-being without referring to the wider institutional context or the processes of class reproduction that shape their circumstances.

While left-behind children are one constituency evidently affected by multilocal striving, another is the tens of millions of former left-behind children who have reached and will reach adulthood in the late 2010s and 2020s: What is the likely legacy of this generation of former left-behind children on Chinese society? As noted in Chapter 1, research on young migrants in the 2010s finds that individuals who were 'left behind' in their childhood incurred a wage penalty independently of their years of education, while left-behind histories also correlated negatively with their years of education (Lyu and Chen, 2019). Other research reports that many rural young people feel deep despair when they leave school and migrate only to discover that the good urban jobs promised to them as rewards for hard work and sacrifice are elusive (Chan and Selden, 2014; Koo, 2016; Pun and Koo, 2019). Such disappointment can be especially bitter for former left-behind children who have endured not only gruelling study regimes but also long-term family separation for the sake of future social mobility.

A child psychology literature finds that when people are raised without secure emotional attachments and without feeling in control of their circumstances and outcomes, they are at greater risk of forming negative views of their own traits and abilities, which become manifest as a sense of helplessness and lower self-worth (Chorpita and Barlow, 1998). These negative views tend to emerge substantively in middle childhood, and correlate with individuals' poorer psycho-emotional health (Chorpita and Barlow, 1998). Indeed, in Chapter 3 we saw how junior high school students with low grades described themselves as 'useless' and 'without ability'. Meanwhile, as discussed in Chapter 1, worse outcomes feature as a recurring theme in much survey-based research on the psycho-emotional well-being of 'left-behind' children in rural China. A generation of former left-behind youth could therefore be less resilient while facing greater adversity and more intense disappointment than other young people.

On the flipside, though, many children we met in Anhui and Jiangxi enjoyed close bonds with their family members. Specifically, they had formed warm relationships with their caregivers, and they sustained connections with their migrant parents. All of the children also wanted secure and happy family lives: when asked about their three wishes in life, a desire for family members to live together or for a happy and peaceful family life featured in the open responses of over 90 per cent of the left-behind children surveyed in the 2010 Summer Survey, and it also featured in the responses of most left-behind children we interviewed. But unlike Pan (2018) who reports that the former left-behind children she met were not terribly perturbed about the idea of leaving their own children behind because they were accustomed to the practice, nearly all the left-behind children I followed over five years and later interviewed as teenagers stated emphatically that when they became parents they would never leave their own children behind because they knew first-hand of the emotional pain. The exceptions were three boys, including Wang Delun (discussed in Chapter 7), who felt that as men they would do whatever was required to support their families.

If my respondents' sentiments are more widely shared among former left-behind young people, then many of China's next generation of migrants are likely to want to live with their children – a legacy of their past that sits alongside other influences, including that they have been socialised to expect an urban future. Certainly, these young people did not see the city as a place of temporary sacrifice, as their own migrant parents did, but as a place where they would settle. At the same time, many long-term migrant parents had invested their years of hard-earned wages in their children rather than in old-age savings for themselves. Unless they could live with their adult children in the cities, many of these parents would face a precarious old age in their rural hometowns. Policy blueprints since 2014 have successively indicated that changes are planned that would enable rural families to settle in the cities, with the former director of China's National Development and Reform Commission, Xin Liu, stating in 2019: 'In the future the main driving force of China's urbanisation will be conferring the benefits of urban citizenship on rural migrant workers,' starting in the lower-tier cities (Ouyang, 2019).

But this glance to an urbanised future inevitably leaves us with many more questions than it answers. These questions include: What class position will the children of the former left-behind generation occupy in China's cities? Will they be able to realise their aspirations for material and emotional security in the cities? If not, how will they cope with the thwarting of their aspirations and the denial of their perceived entitlements? Will they support their parents once

8.4 The Future of Migrants' Children

their parents reach old age, even as long-term separation may have weakened some parent–child bonds? Will the children of the former left-behind generation pursue educational mobility or will urban class-based countercultures emerge (Pun and Koo, 2019)? Will China's model of development ever transform to recognise the centrality of affective well-being to human flourishing? Will ideas about human worth and success, and routes for educational progression and towards success ever become more plural (to include, for instance, viable alternative learning paths and rural identities)? And much more broadly, can humankind ever collectively contemplate democratic alternatives to a world dominated by the competitive imperatives of capital accumulation under patriarchy?

Appendix: Field Research on Left-Behind Children in China

This book is based on the fieldwork that I conducted over the course of twenty-four weeks between 2010 and 2015, namely my matched interviews with 109 rural children and their at-home parents and grandparent caregivers in four counties located in two provinces, Anhui and Jiangxi, in China's southeast interior, as well as my intermittent follow-up interviews with twenty-five of the children and their families. All the names of people and places referred to in this book are pseudonyms, except for the names of provinces and major cities. In this Appendix, I explain the child-centred approach to data collection and the analysis of the data on which the book draws.

In researching this book, I worked through primary schools and junior high schools situated in two counties in each province, and then I moved out to the children's homes in their villages. In each of the four fieldwork counties, which I have given pseudonyms: – 'Tranquil County' and 'Jade County' in Jiangxi, and 'Eastern County' and 'Western County' in Anhui – I based myself in two townships, so eight townships in total. For reference, a township is a rural administrative subdivision of a county. Its administrative centre incorporates several streets where a visitor will see township government offices, schools, a medical clinic, banks, a mobile phone agency, shops and a farmers' market open on days set by the lunar calendar, serving the surrounding villages.

The eight townships were the sites of an earlier related research project: a multistage randomised survey to investigate the impact of parents' labour migration on children's educational performance, which my collaborators and I implemented in Summer 2010. As mentioned in Chapter 1, details of this survey, the stratified random sampling procedure and the sample characteristics can be found in Zhou, Murphy and Tao (2014). As also stated in Chapter 1, the survey had a final sample of 1,010 children in grades 4, 6 and 8. Because some of these children started school earlier than required while others were delayed in enrolling or else repeated years of study, these children were aged between eight and seventeen years with an average age of twelve years. The survey project also collected matching data for 1,000 of the children from a survey of at-home caregivers. Of these surveyed children, 69.9 per cent ($n=$ 706) had at

234

least one migrant parent, which is seventeen percentage points higher than the 2010 averages for Anhui and Jiangxi provinces.

Foreign-based social scientists often experience difficulties in gaining sustained access to fieldwork sites in China. I therefore selected the fieldwork sites pragmatically. Owing to previous introductions from when I helped to implement the 2010 Summer Survey, the education bureau officials, headteachers and teachers in the four counties and eight townships already knew about my research interests, and they agreed to accommodate my project. As members of their county's middle class, they saw 'left-behind children' as a social problem that warranted attention. Indeed, on learning about my topic, the wife of a teacher in one township school clasped my hands and said with much feeling: 'You really have compassion' (*ni hen you aixin*). Her kindness notwithstanding, I did not feel I deserved praise because research is a self-indulgent and privileged undertaking. Even so, her words indicated more generally that the 'gatekeepers' thought it was understandable for an outsider to want to investigate the topic of left-behind children, a factor that helped to create trust. Additionally, since my research explored migration and family life rather than school management, these 'gatekeepers' did not see me as posing a threat to them professionally.

Nevertheless, some officials and headteachers still worried about my identity as a foreign researcher. Firstly, hosting an outsider who will write about what she learns presents some risk. In a worst-case scenario, I could uncover a negative circumstance or write a distorted picture that could affect their reputations and work evaluations. More practically, the officials, headteachers and teachers in my fieldwork sites were extremely busy and had their own work and family responsibilities. Yet I needed their time and help in answering questions and in arranging introductions to research participants. I therefore decided to visit several schools across four counties rather than just one school or one county. In common with some other foreign sociologists working in China, I found that a strategy of spreading fieldwork across various locations helped to reassure gatekeepers that the risks associated with helping me were low (Eklund, 2010). The strategy of doing fieldwork in several places also spread the burden of my requests for help more thinly across localities, schools and individuals.

I adopted a 'maximum variation selection' strategy whereby I aimed to recruit respondents who covered the full spectrum of positions relevant to the phenomenon under study (Patton, 1990): rural children with at least one parent who had migrated without them. As the homeroom teachers understood the students' circumstances well, their help was indispensable to implementing this recruitment strategy. In constructing my initial set of cases, I chose children in grades 4, 6 and 8. In doing so, I aimed to target children who were aged between ten and fifteen years, though the actual ages of the children in my set of 109

236 Appendix: Field Research on Left-Behind Children in China

cases turned out to range from nine to seventeen years, again reflecting earlier enrolments as well as delays in enrolment or progression. As noted in Chapter 1, the median age of the 109 children the first time I interviewed them in 2010 and 2011 was twelve years, with a mean age of 12.71 years. I selected children in this age range because while studies based on the recollections of young adults offer valuable insights into their experience of having been left behind (e.g. Parreñas, 2005; Smith, Lalonde and Johnson, 2004), I wanted to explore children's thoughts at the time of their parents' migration. I also thought that children aged ten to fifteen years would be old enough to handle my questions. Furthermore, because children's age influences their agency and relationships (Thorne, 2004; Dreby, 2010; Carling, Menjívar and Schmalzbauer, 2012), I hoped that interviewing children in mid-childhood and adolescence would give me insight into the impact of their life course stage on their perspectives. I interviewed boys ($n= 60$) and girls ($n= 49$) because, as discussed in Chapter 4, children's gender influenced family migration strategies and childcare practices. Children's gender also corresponds with variations in subjective well-being (Leng and Park, 2010). I asked the teachers to introduce me to children who differed in their academic performance, which in China means school test scores (Kipnis, 2011), with academic performance potentially both affecting and reflecting the quality of the parent–child relationship, the children's subjective well-being (Roeser, Eccles and Sameroff, 2000; Schoon, 2006) and the parents' migration decision-making (Connelly, Roberts and Zheng, 2012). I also asked the teachers to introduce me to children from richer, middling and poorer families.

As I wanted to understand the experiences of children who lived in families differently configured by parental migration, I requested introductions to children with only the mother out, with only the father out, and with both parents out. I recruited children from these three family configurations until interviews with subsequent respondents yielded no new insights (Small, 2009). The exception was in the recruitment of children whose mothers had migrated alone. I would have liked to recruit more of these children to probe further the variation in their circumstances. However, as I discussed in Chapters 2 and 6, lone-mother migration from the fieldwork sites was rare. Even so, the migration status of some parents changed over time, giving me a few additional cases for understanding children's experiences when their mothers migrated alone. But the overall number of children I encountered in this family configuration between 2010 and 2015 remained small. These cases have nevertheless permitted me to offer preliminary insights into these children's circumstances, corroborated by data from other sources, which may provide useful leads for other researchers.

I also asked the teachers for introductions to the 'negative case' of children who lived with both their parents. This is because in highly migratory regions

Appendix: Field Research on Left-Behind Children in China

all children are affected by social norms that endorse migration as a route to a better life. Importantly, the inclusion of children who lived with both their parents into the overall set of respondents helped me to discern which aspects of children's perceptions and aspirations could be attributed to parental migration and which aspects resulted from dynamics operating alongside but independently of parental migration: for instance, declining family size, rising educational competition, increasing intra-rural and rural–urban inequality, and urbanisation. Interviewing children who lived with both parents also alerted me to the reality that many of these children's parents had been migrants at some point: sixteen children lived with parents who had both been at home ever since the children had started school, while thirteen children had a least one parent who had once been a migrant for a period of time after the children had started school. A breakdown of the 109 children by their parents' migration status at the time of my first interview with them in 2010–2011 is presented in Table A.1 below.

I interviewed the children in the company of one of my Chinese research assistants. Five of my research assistants were female post-graduate students from a provincial university or prefectural technical college. The children called them 'big sister', and their presence helped to lessen the distance between the children and me, a mature-aged foreign researcher with messy yellow hair. Two of these research assistants had grown up in the countryside, and their insights on the interviews were especially helpful. Another research

Table A.1 *Distribution of 109 children interviewees by parents' migration status*

	Total		Anhui	Jiangxi
Parents' Status	No. of cases	Per cent	No. of cases	No. of cases
Both parents have migrated	44	40.4	24	20
Both parents are at home	29	26.6	14	15
(at least one parent is a returnee)	(13)	(44.8)	(2)	(11)
Only mother has migrated	5	4.6	0	5
(father is a returnee)	(3)	(60)	0	(3)
Only father has migrated	28	25.7	21	7
(mother is a returnee)	(14)	(50)	(9*)	(5)
A parent died; a parent is a migrant	2[+]	1.8	0	2
A parent died; a parent is a returnee	1	0.9	0	1
Total	109		59	50

* Includes four mothers who shuttle between their husbands' urban stalls and the village spending at least three-quarters of the year in the village. Previously, they had been out with their husbands long-term. [+] One migrant mother abandoned her children, and they did not know where she was. Another migrant mother remarried, then divorced and remarried again.

assistant was an older urban woman who the children saw as a reassuring auntie figure. Meanwhile, one other research assistant was a young male researcher from a rural background who had himself been 'left behind' as a child. His presence helped because he could introduce himself to the children in ways that let them know he understood them. He also tactfully left the interview in a couple of instances when teenage girls alluded to the start of menstruation as a time when they had particularly wished that their mothers had been there for them. Who accompanied me during an interview depended on the location of the fieldwork and who was available at the time of my visit – so it was not necessarily the same person who accompanied me on repeated visits to the same family or to all the interviews in one location.

My research assistants and I talked with the children in Mandarin in the schools. As sociologists of childhood caution, though, interviewing children in a school setting could affect what they say because schools are places where adult–child hierarchies prevail, where children are subject to certain discourses and where they may feel that they need to give the expected answers (Clark, 2011; Punch, 2002a). Indeed, in one school when we went to do interviews, the teacher had written on the blackboard in large characters, 'even though we are left-behind we are self-reliant (*ziqiang*)', thereby indicating an approved narrative for the children. Certainly, the school setting may have contributed to the children's overwhelming emphasis on the importance of study in their accounts of their daily lives and their relationships with their parents and grandparent caregivers. But this emphasis is also likely to have arisen because study is a salient aspect of all at-school children's lives. Indeed, as the sociologist Qvortrup (2009) observes, in many rapidly urbanising societies, owing to children's identities as the bearers of a modern future, preparing children through education is integral to how they are treated and therefore to how they evaluate their own obligations, performance and worth. Meanwhile, research on rural China highlights the dominance of education in families' aspirations for their children (Thøgersen, 2002; Hannum, Kong and Zhang, 2009; Kipnis, 2011; Hansen, 2015).

To mitigate the potential constraints of the school setting on the children and to create space for them to feel freer while expressing themselves, my research assistants and I interviewed the children in a corner of the school playground or else in a vacant office out of the earshot of teachers or other students. We kept the questions deliberately open, inviting the children to talk about memories of their parents' migration and return visits; their views about their migrant parents' lives; their relationships with parents, non-parent caregivers, and other children in the household; happy memories and sad memories; typical weekdays and weekends; memories of holidays; involvement in housework; perceptions of the countryside and the city; and possibilities and aspirations for the future. I also invited children to elaborate on impressions or anecdotes that

Appendix: Field Research on Left-Behind Children in China   239

they volunteered. Prior to carrying out the interviews, my research assistants and I spent a few days in each school playing English-language games with the children such as Simon Says and 'guess what is in the bag'. This helped to build a rapport between the teachers and me, and to increase the children's familiarity with me and my research assistants. Children were also given notebooks and pens at the end of each interview to thank them for talking with us. As noted in Chapter 1, to recognise the attributes, help, and skills of my research assistants in the interviews, I mostly refer to who 'we' interviewed and what they told 'us' in 'our' conversations.

Although much academic and media discourse about rural Chinese left-behind children rightly emphasises their vulnerability, suffering and 'misery', I also want to highlight that even though some children cried during our interviews with them, especially when they talked about missing their parents, they were also humorous and playful in their interactions with us. I do not wish to downplay the children's adversity but to acknowledge the nuance and creativity with which they dealt with circumstances, including with my presence and questions. For instance, when I asked an eleven-year-old boy who had poor grades and came from a poor family about his three wishes in life, he said: 'To grow gigantic feet and to go around asking people what their three wishes are, and if they can't answer to squash them with my big foot.' As another example, one lunchtime a group of four girls whom we had interviewed earlier in the morning came over to me in the playground, flapping their arms, and saying that they wished that they were 'not left behind', *fei liu shou*, with the word *fei* meaning 'not' being a homonym for 'flying'. Children also often imitated my incorrect Chinese pronunciation by dropping tones or repeating my use of non-idiomatic language.

A subset of children seemed to especially want to spend time with my research assistant and me, especially the 'big sister' research assistants, possibly because we were adults who gave them attention. Most research participants asked me to sign my name in their school textbooks for good luck. Several children gave me pictures they had drawn, often of scenery. Some children taught me clapping games. Three girls tried to give me gifts, including in one instance a jade stone necklace on a red string, which I understood to be an expression of a wish for connection. In these instances, my research assistants helped me in returning the gifts and in talking with the girls so that they would feel that their kind gesture had been warmly received though I could not keep the item. The children also loved posing for photos. I include Figure A.1 to show that these were vibrant multidimensional children.

As discussed in Chapter 1, this book draws not only on the interviews with the 109 children but also on matching interviews with at least one adult caregiver for each of the children, as per Figure A.2. In two cases, though, we were not able to interview adult caregivers: these included a fifteen-year-old

Figure A.1 Children playing with an improvised slide at a township primary school in Jade County, Jiangxi

boy who lived alone after the death of his grandfather and a twelve-year-old girl who lived alone in a mud house next to her aunt's house. We interviewed the children's caregivers in their village homes to glimpse insight into their living conditions. Where possible, my research assistants and I also spent whole days or half days in the villages with the at-home family members.

The questions to the adults covered their own childhoods and biographies, their families' migration histories, children's responses to their parents' migration and return visits, their own and the children's contact with the migrants; the children's and caregivers' relationships with the migrants; their interactions with the schools; daily life; sources of hardship and happiness in caregiving; and possibilities and aspirations for the future. Adult respondents were paid 30 *yuan* for their time in the interview, calculated on the basis that they could earn up to 70 *yuan* doing a day of casual labouring. This was enough to offset the costs of their time in talking with us, but it was not enough to create incentives

Appendix: Field Research on Left-Behind Children in China   241

Figure A.2 To the rural homes to interview caregivers

for them to participate unwillingly or to distort the interview process. In any event, we stressed to all respondents that they could stop the conversation at any point without explanation to us and without any loss of either the token gift in the case of the children or the 30 *yuan* in the case of the adults.

This book also draws on my follow-up interviews with twenty-five children, twenty-two of whom had at least one migrant parent in 2010–2011, and twenty-three of whom had at least one migrant parent by 2014–2015. It further refers to my interviews with at least one of their caregivers. Unfortunately, though, the visiting parents of a fifteen-year-old-girl refused when we asked to interview them. I followed this subset of children over time to pursue greater depth in my interactions with them because my own work and family responsibilities meant that I could not spend several consecutive months in the field as I had done in my younger years. The follow-up interviews enabled me to trace some children's transitions from primary to junior high school, including sixteen children's transitions from junior high to senior high school or to a vocational school. These follow-up interviews also provided me with valuable insights into changes in the children's and family's circumstances over time and into the evolution of their sentiments, relationships and aspirations.

I selected the children for follow-up interview by their availability at the time of my return visits. By 'availability' I mean that the school or local education bureau had a phone number for the children's caregivers, and my research assistants and I could locate the child during the time that we were visiting the county. Twelve of the children recruited for follow-up interviews were girls while thirteen were boys. The method of recruiting the children for follow-up interviews may have biased the set of cases. Of the sixteen children who were old enough to go to senior high school at the time of my last visit to see them in 2015, thirteen had made it from junior high school to some form of academic-track school in the county seat, which represents a high level of success for rural children. Meanwhile, working through schools to recruit research participants meant that I missed out left-behind children who had dropped out of junior high school or senior high school to earn money in the cities (Gong, 2005; Normille, 2017; Pan, 2018). Nevertheless, the logic of qualitative research differs from quantitative research in that it aims at conceptual extrapolation from a set of cases rather than at generalisation from a sample to a population. Hence, the analysis remains valid so long as the findings are contextualised (Small, 2009).

I also interviewed the migrant parents of fourteen children when they had returned briefly to the village and I followed the parents of a further six children to the cities of Kunshan, Shanghai, Dongguan and Shenzhen, interviewing them in their places of residence there. I was accompanied in my interviews in the Pearl River Delta by a doctoral student from the Social Policy School at Zhongshan University, whose help was essential to finding the migrant parents. Additionally, I gained supplementary insights by interviewing twenty rural primary and junior high school teachers and headteachers. Hence, in total, accompanied by research assistants, I formally interviewed over 250 individuals, including children and adults, and had informal conversations with many others.

In advance of the interviews, my research assistants and I gave all the respondents age-appropriate verbal and written information about the project and asked permission to digitally record the interviews. I explained to the respondents that I needed to record because owing to my poor Chinese I would need to listen to the conversation again. All but three children and three adults agreed to be recorded but they nevertheless permitted me to write notes during the interviews. The interviews with the children lasted from fifteen minutes to one hour and twenty minutes, with an average duration approaching forty minutes. Many interviews with younger children, those aged nine or ten years, were punctuated by long silences such that I felt a need to check with them intermittently if they were happy to stay and talk, which they all said they

Appendix: Field Research on Left-Behind Children in China   243

were. The interviews generally flowed better and lasted longer with older children, those aged thirteen years and older. Meanwhile, interviews with adults ranged from thirty minutes to two hours with the average interview lasting fifty-five minutes. However, some interviews with elderly respondents were lengthened by my research assistants' interpreting of the content between Mandarin and local dialect or the interjections of other family members.

In interviewing children and adults in matched sets, I was guided by childhood and family sociologists. Childhood studies scholars highlight that children's relationships with adults define the experience of childhood (Dobson, 2009; Tisdall and Punch, 2012; Alanen, Brooker and Mayall, 2015: 3) such that researchers need to acquire a 'double vision' to see both the children's and the adults' vantage points (Clark, 2011). Meanwhile, family sociologists explain that children and adults are in role relationships, and there can be no role relationships without role partners. Specifically, by interacting with their parents or their grandparents and by interpreting the adults' behaviour, children actively construct their caregivers' roles and the adult–child relationships in collaboration with the adults. Hence, any holistic understanding of children's experiences of their relationships with parents or non-parent caregivers requires the perspectives of both children and the relevant significant adult (Milkie, Simon and Powell, 1997; Kuczynski, 2003; Goh, 2011). Additionally, as observed by Dreby (2010), interviewing adults as well as children gives the researcher insight into dynamics and situations that a child cannot or does not articulate.

Conducting matched interviews with children and adults sometimes threw up inconsistencies, but these inconsistencies could be illuminating. Some inconsistencies highlighted the influence of social norms on how individuals wanted to present their families to outsiders, as well as children's and adults' different perceptions of these norms. For example, one thirteen-year-old girl from a poor family whose father was disabled told me in a follow-up interview that her mother had migrated to a biscuit factory to support her education before returning home. However, in my interview with her parents at their house one weekend, they stated that they had never migrated. The girl later came to find me in the vegetable garden and told me that her mother had not migrated, but that she really wished her mother would value her studies enough to do so. She then added that a cousin – the son of her father's half-brother – had made it to university funded by his fathers' migration but his family so looked down on her family that they had refused to accept a red envelope of congratulatory money from them. This incident made her long to attend university to vindicate her parents.

Inconsistencies in children's and adults' accounts could also elucidate aspects of children's experiences because even though their accounts might not convey actual circumstances, they nevertheless reflected aspects of an emotional truth. For instance, the 2017 White Paper by the NGO On the Road to School reports that in their survey 11.4 per cent of the left-behind children marked down that a migrant parent was dead even though that year China's annual death rate was 0.7 per cent. The NGO's representatives concluded that some children had deliberately filled in incorrect information to make fun or let off steam, as well as to convey that they wanted more companionship and care (Li, 2017). Inconsistencies in children's and adults' accounts further indicated intergenerational power and information asymmetries, in that adults do not share all information with children while children do not necessarily tell adults what is going on, either to protect the adults from worry or so that the children can protect themselves from adults' judgement. To be sure, complexities exist in all families, but labour migration exacerbates the messiness (Dreby, 2010).

In analysing the interview material, I adopted a version of grounded theory that takes seriously peoples' *perceptions* in constructing their social worlds (Charmaz, 2006). Importantly, a construction-oriented version of grounded theory does not see an objective world out there to be discovered through inductive analysis, as some positivist grounded theory scholars do (Glaser, 1992), but instead recognises that the interviewees and the researcher are implicated in co-constructing a representation of the social world. Interviewees' *perceptions* shape aspects of their reality and are given meaning in conversation with the interviewer, something that is true of both children and adults (Bronfenbenner, 1979: 4). Meanwhile, the researcher recruits respondents with particular characteristics or experiences, asks certain questions on the basis of emerging understanding and imposes categories on the data during the processes of data collection and analysis (Charmaz, 2006). Research is thereby both inductive and deductive (Charmaz, 2006).

I transcribed the interviews from Chinese into English while listening out for recurring themes, formalising a process that I had commenced in the field after the very first interview. I started by thematically coding the transcripts of the interviews with the children, using subject headings and an extended Excel log to index key features of the circumstances, attributes and experiences of each child. Through the coding of children's subjective accounts, I identified 'work' as an umbrella concept that incorporated the themes of 'study and education', alongside 'migrant work and earning money', and 'domestic work and care'. Thereafter, other subthemes to emerge included the experiences of boys and girls; the relationships between children and different adults, including the gendered and generational dimensions of these relationships; and children's and adults' feelings about the past, the present and the future. I then examined the matched interviews with the adults to contextualise the children's accounts and to elaborate on the recurring themes. Finally, I selectively integrated the themes and subthemes into an overarching axial concept of 'striving teams', referring repeatedly to the literature discussed in Chapter 1 in the process. The

Appendix: Field Research on Left-Behind Children in China 245

axial concept of 'striving teams' enabled me to articulate the connections among the core themes in the data. In repeated rounds of coding, I both refined and thickened the analysis by teasing out variations among the children by their geographic and social locations, and by their families' circumstances.

I have presented the fieldwork data in the book in two ways. Firstly, I have presented excerpts from the interviews to illustrate patterns and variations among the different categories of respondents – with a given category of respondent providing the analytical focus for each of the core empirical chapters: namely, all at-school left-behind children in Chapter 3, boys and girls in Chapter 4, and children in families differentiated by their gendered and generational configuration in Chapters 5 to 7 At the same time, I have presented longitudinal case studies of individual children whom I selected to represent either a wider type of experience or an unusual experience, thereby harnessing the analytical value of coherence and context, which the thematic coding of interview transcripts fragments (Coffey and Atkinson, 1996).

In contextualising the analysis, I also consulted information and insights derived from my observations in schools and villages, from informal conversations with officials, teachers and villagers, and from watching local and national television programmes, all of which I documented in approximately 300 pages of handwritten field notes. I collated a portfolio of more than 300 photos of people and places to help me recognise details that escaped my attention at the time and to refresh my memory of certain people and places. Finally, I consulted Chinese-language documents from schools, local and national government bureaus, local and national newspapers, and academic reports.

Bibliography

Abbey, Caroline and Rudi Dallos. 2004. 'The Experience of the Impact of Divorce on Sibling Relationships: A Qualitative Study'. *Clinical Child Psychology and Psychiatry* 9 (2): 241–259.

Alanen, Leena, Liz Brooker and Berry Mayall. 2015. 'Introduction'. In *Childhood with Bourdieu*, edited by Leena Alanen, Liz Brooker and Berry Mayall, 1–13. London: Palgrave Macmillan.

Alexander, Karl L., Doris Entwisle and Linda Steffel Olson. 2007. 'Lasting Consequences of the Summer Learning Gap'. *American Sociological Review* 72(2): 167–180.

All China Women's Federation Research Group (ACWF). 2008. 'Research Report on the Situation on Rural Left-Behind Children Nationwide' [Quanguo nongcun liushou ertong zhuangkuang yanjiu baogao]. *China Women's Movement [Zhongguo funyun]* 6: 34–37. www.wsic.ac.cn/academicnews/63814.htm

All China Women's Federation Research Group (ACWF). 2013. 'Research Report into the Situation of Rural Left-Behind Children and Rural to Urban Migrant Children' [Woguo nongcun liushou ertong, chengxiang liudong zhuangkuang yanjiu baogao]. *China Women's Movement [Zhongguo fuyun]* 6: 30–34. http://mall.cnki.net/magazine/Article/ZFYZ201306009.htm

Anagnost, Ann. 2004. 'The Corporal Politics of Quality (Suzhi)'. *Public Culture* 16 (2): 189–208.

Anderson, Thomas M. and Hans Peter Kohler. 2013. 'Education Fever and the East Asian Fertility Puzzle: A Case Study of South Korea'. *Asian Journal of Population Studies* 9 (3): 196–215.

Andreas, Joel and Shaohua Zhan. 2015. '*Hukou* and Land: Market Reform and Rural Displacement in China'. *Journal of Peasant Studies* 43 (4): 798–827.

Anhui Daily [Anhui Ribao]. 2013. 'Neglect Neither "Peidu" – Accompanying Studying Children – Nor "Dagong" – Working for Money' [Peidu dagong liang bu wu], *Anhui Daily*, 26 June. http://roll.sohu.com/20130626/n379889785.shtml

Anhui Federation of Trade Unions. 2018. 'The Wave of Migrant Workers Returning Home: Anhui's Phenomenon of People Returning for Five Successive Years' [Nongminggong fanxiangchao lai le: Anhuisheng lianxu 5 nian chuxian renkou hui liu], 14 August. www.ahghw.org/DocHtml/1/18/08/00140196.html

Anhui People's Government (Anhui Renmin Zhengfu). 2017. 'Thirteenth Five-Year Plan for the Development of the Population of Anhui Province' [Anhuisheng renkou fazhan 'shisan wu' guihua], 5 June. http://xxgk.ah.gov.cn/UserData/DocHtml/731/2017/6/21/700893996254.html

Bibliography

Anhui Survey Group of National Statistical Bureau. 2018. 'New Phenomenon of Migrant Workers' Mobility in Our Province in 2017'. www.ahdc.gov.cn/Google Scholar

Anon. 2008. 'Eastern County's Army of One Hundred Thousand Pans for Gold in the Construction Industry'. *Provincial News*, 5 March (publication name changed to prevent place being identified).

Anon. 2016. 'More than Thirteen Thousand People from Eastern County Work Overseas'. *Municipal News*, 3 February (publication name changed to prevent place being identified).

Appadurai, Arjun. 2004. 'The Capacity to Aspire: Culture and the Terms of Recognition'. In *Culture and Public Action*, edited by Vijayayendra Rao and Michael Walton, 59–84. Stanford: Stanford University Press.

Archambault, Caroline S. 2010. 'Women Left Behind? Migration, Spousal Separation, and the Autonomy of Rural Women in Ugweno, Tanzania'. *Signs* 35 (4): 919–942.

Arguillas, Marie Joy B. and Lindy Williams. 2010. 'The Impacts of Parents' Overseas Employment on Educational Outcomes of Filipino Children'. *International Migration Review* 44 (2): 300–319.

Ariès, Philippe. 1965. *Centuries of Childhood: A Social History of Family Life*. Translated by Robert Baldick. Oxford: Vintage Books.

Asis, Maruja M. B. 2006. 'Living with Migration: Experiences of Left-Behind Children in the Philippines'. *Asian Population Studies* 2 (1): 45–67.

Astone, Nan M. and Sara S. McLanahan. 1991. 'Family Structure, Parental Practices, and High School Completion'. *American Sociological Review* 56 (3): 309–320.

Atkinson, Will. 2015. *Class*. Cambridge: Polity Press.

Attané, Isabelle. 2009. 'The Determinants of Discrimination against Daughters in China: Evidence from a Provincial Level Analysis'. *Population Studies* 63 (1): 87–102.

Awaworyi Churchill, Sefa and Vinrod Mishra. 2018. 'Returns to Education in China: A Meta-Analysis'. *Applied Economics* 50 (54): 5903–5919.

Baker, Hugh. 1979. *Chinese Family and Kinship*. New York: Columbia University Press.

Baker, Lindsey and Merril Silverstein. 2012. 'The Wellbeing of Grandparents Caring for Grandchildren in China and the United States'. In *Contemporary Grandparenting: Changing Family Relationships in Global Contexts*, edited by Sara Arber and Virpi Timonen, 51–70. Bristol: Polity Press.

Barbalet, Jack. 2014. 'Self-Interest in Chinese Discourse and Practice: Temporal Distinctions of Self'. *Sociological Review* 61 (4): 649–666.

Basten, Stuart. 2012. 'Family Planning Restrictions and a Generation of Excess Males: Analysis of National and Provincial Data from the 2010 Census'. Department of Social Policy and Intervention, University of Oxford, Oxford Centre for Population Research, Working Paper 59, December. https://papers.ssrn.com/sol3/papers.cfm?abstract_id=2202738

Batistella, Graziano and Ma Cecilia Conaco. 1998. 'The Impact of Labour Migration on the Children Left Behind: A Study of Elementary School Children in the Philippines'. *Sojourn: A Journal of Social Issues in Southeast Asia* 13 (2) (October): 220–241.

Ben-Porath, Sigal R. 2010. *Tough Choices: Structured Paternalism and the Landscape of Choice*. Princeton: Princeton University Press.

248 Bibliography

Bertrand, Marianne and Jessica Pan. 2013. 'The Trouble with Boys: Social Influences and Gender Gap in Disruptive Behavior'. *American Economic Journal: Applied Economics* 5 (1): 32–64.

Bi, Congzheng and Daphna Oyserman. 2015. 'Left-Behind or Moving Forward? Effects of Possible Selves and Strategies to Attain Them among Rural Chinese Children'. *Journal of Adolescence* 44 (October): 245–258.

Binah-Pollak, Avital. 2014. 'Discourses and Practices of Child-Rearing in China: The Biopower of Parenting in Beijing'. *China Information* 28 (1): 27–45.

Bo, Shaoling. 2016. 'Why the Nationwide Number of Rural-Left Behind Children Has 'Dropped' by over 50 Million' [Quanguo nongcun liushou ertong weihe 'ruijian' wuqian duo wan]. *China Youth Daily* [*Zhongguo qiannian bao*], 10 November, p. 1. http://society.people.com.cn/n1/2016/1110/c1008-28849226.html

Boehm, Deborah A. 2008. 'For My Children: Constructing Family and Navigating the State in the US-Mexico Transnation'. *Anthropology Quarterly* 81 (4): 777–804.

Boehm, Deborah A., Julia Meredith Hess, Cati Coe, Heather Rae-Espinoza and Rachel R. Reynolds. 2011. *Everyday Ruptures: Children, Youth, and Migration in Global Perspective*. Nashville, TN: Vanderbilt University Press.

Bond, Michael H. 1991. *Beyond the Chinese Face: Insights from Psychology*. Oxford: Oxford University Press.

Booth, Margaret Zoller. 2003. 'The Impact of Parental Availability on Swazi Students' School Achievement: A Nine-Year Longitudinal Study'. *International Journal of Educational Development* 23 (3): 257–274.

Bourdieu, Pierre. 1986. 'The Forms of Capital'. In *A Handbook of Theory and Research for the Sociology of Education*, edited by John G. Richardson, 241–258. New York: Greenwood.

Bourdieu, Pierre. 1999. 'Postscript'. In Pierre Bourdieu et al. *The Weight of the World: Social Suffering in Contemporary Society*, translated by Priscilla Parkhurst Fergeson, Susan Emanuel, Joe Johnson and Shoggy T. Waryn, 627–629. Cambridge: Polity Press.

Bourdieu, Pierre. 2010. *Distinction*. London: Routledge.

Bourdieu, Pierre and Jean Claude Passeron. 1979. *The Inheritors*. Chicago: University of Chicago Press.

Bourdieu, Pierre and Jean Claude Passeron. 2000. *Reproduction in Education, Society and Culture*. 2nd edition. London: Sage.

Bossen, Laurel. 2002. *Chinese Women and Rural Development: Sixty Years of Change in Lu Village, Yunnan*. Lanham, MD: Rowan and Littlefield.

Brandtstädter, Susanne. 2009. 'The Gender of Work and the Production of Kinship Value in Taiwan and China'. In *Chinese Kinship: Contemporary Anthropological Perspectives*, edited by Susanne Brandtstädter and Gonçalo D. Santos, 154–178. London: Routledge.

Bronfenbrenner, Urie. 1979. *The Ecology of Human Development: Experiments by Nature and Design*. Cambridge, MA: Harvard University Press.

Brooks-Gunn, Jeanne, Greg J. Duncan and Nancy Maritato. 1997. 'Poor Families, Poor Outcomes: The Wellbeing of Children and Youth'. In *Consequences of Growing Up Poor*, edited by Greg J. Duncan and Jeanne Brooks-Gunn, 1–17. New York: Russell Sage.

Bibliography

Brooks-Gunn, Jeanne, Wen-Jui Han and Jane Waldfogel. 2002. 'Maternal Employment and Child Cognitive Outcomes in the First Three Years of Life: The NICHD Study and of Early Childcare'. *Child Development* 73 (4) (July/ August): 1052–1072.

Brown, Philip H. and Albert Park. 2002. 'Education and Poverty in Rural China'. *Economics of Education Review* 21 (6) (December): 523–541.

Bryant, John. 2005. 'Children of International Migrants in Indonesia, Thailand and the Philippines: A Review of Evidence and Policies'. *Innocenti Working Paper* No 05–2005, Florence, UNICEF Innocenti Research Centre. www.unicef-irc.org/publica tions/pdf/iwp2005_05.pdf

Bugarin, Janvier Castro. 2019. 'Chinese Workers Move Back to Interiors as Migration to Cities Slows Down'. *EFE News Agency*, English edition, 13 July. www.efecom/ efe/english/world/chinese-workers-move-back-to-interiors-as-migration-cities-slows-down/50000262–4022042

Caldwell, John C. and Bruce K. Caldwell. 2005. 'The Causes of the Asian Fertility Decline: Macro and Micro Approaches'. *Asian Population Studies* 1 (1): 31–46.

Carling, Jorgen, Cecilia Menjívar and Leah Schmalzbauer 2012. 'Central Themes in the Study of Transnational Parenthood'. *Journal of Ethnic and Migration Studies* 38 (2): 191–217.

Carlson, Marcia J., Sara McLanahan and Jeanne Brooks-Gunn. 2008. 'Coparenting and Nonresident Fathers' Involvement with Young Children After a Nonmarital Birth'. *Demography* 45 (2) (May): 461–488.

Chan, Chris King-Chi. 2014. 'Constrained Labour Agency and the Changing Regulatory Regime in China'. *Development and Change* 45 (4) (July): 685–709.

Chan, Jenny. 2017. 'Intern Labor in China'. *Rural China: An International Journal of History and Social Science* 14: 82–100.

Chan, Jenny and Mark Selden. 2014. 'China's Rural Migrant Workers, the State and Labor Politics'. *Critical Asian Studies* 46 (4): 599–620.

Chan, Jenny, Pun Ngai and Mark Selden. 2015. 'Interns or Workers? China's Student Labor Regime'. *Asian Studies* 1 (1): 69–98.

Chan, Kam Wing. 1994. *Cities with Invisible Walls: Reinterpreting Urbanisation in Post 1949 China*. New York: Oxford University Press.

Chan, Kam Wing. 2009. 'The Chinese *Hukou* System at 50'. *Eurasian Geography and Economics* 50 (2): 197–221.

Chan, Kam Wing and Will Buckingham. 2008. 'Is China Abolishing the *Hukou* System?' *The China Quarterly* 195: 776–828.

Chan, Kam Wing and Yuan Ren. 2018. 'Children of Migrants in China in the 21st Century: Trends, Living Arrangements, Age-Gender Structure, and Geography'. *Eurasian Geography and Economics* 59 (2): 133–163.

Chan, Ko Ling. 2015. *Chinese Migration and Families-at-Risk*. Newcastle: Cambridge Scholars Publishing.

Chang, Hongqin, Xiao-yuan Dong and Fiona MacFail. 2011. 'Labor Migration and Time Use Patterns of the Left-Behind Children and Elderly in Rural China'. *World Development* 39 (12): 2199–2210.

Chant, Sylvia and Sarah Radcliffe. 1992. 'Migration and Development: The Importance of Gender'. In *Gender and Migration in Developing Countries*, edited by Sylvia Chant and Sarah Radcliffe, 1–12. New York: Belhaven Press.

250   Bibliography

Chao, Ruth and Vivian Tseng. 2002. 'Parenting of Asians'. In *Handbook of Parenting: Social Conditions and Applied Parenting, volume 4*, edited by Marc H. Bornstein, 59–94. Mahwah, NJ: Laurence Earlbaum Associates Publishers.

Chao, Ruth, 1994. 'Beyond Parental Control and Authoritarian Parenting Style: Understanding Chinese Parenting through the Notion of Training'. *Child Development* 65 (4) (August): 1111–1119.

Charmaz, Kathy. 2006. *Constructing Grounded Theory: A Practical Guide Through Qualitative Analysis*. Newbury Park, CA: Pine Forge Press.

Chen, Feinian, Guangya Liu and Christine A. Mair. 2011. 'Intergenerational Ties in Context: Grandparents Caring for Grandchildren in China'. *Social Forces* 90 (2): 571–594.

Chen, Hanyu. 2014. *When Migrant Women Return Home: Their Life Experiences in a Fast-Growing Chinese Hinterland*. PhD Dissertation. Department of Applied Social Sciences. Hong Kong Polytechnic University. http://ira.lib.polyu.edu.hk/handle/10397/7416

Chen, Jennifer Jun-Li. and Xiaodong Liu. 2012. 'The Mediating Role of Perceived Parental Warmth and Parental Punishment in the Psychological Wellbeing of Children in Rural China'. *Social Indicators Research* 107 (3) (July): 483–508.

Chen, Mengtong and Xiaoyue Sun. 2015. 'Parenting and Grandparenting of Left-Behind Children in Rural China'. In *Chinese Migration and Families-At-Risk*, edited by Ko Ling Chan, 37–52. Newcastle: Cambridge Scholars Publishing.

Chen, Wen-jing and Qing-fei Chen. 2009. 'Research on the Related Factors of Mental Health of Parent-Absent Middle School Students'. [15–18 sui liushou zinü xinli jiankang zhuangkuang de yingxiang yinsu fenxi]. *Journal of Southwest Jiaotong University (Social Sciences) [Xinan jiaotong daxue xuebao – shehui kexue ban]* 10 (4) (August): 97–101.

Chen, W. S. 2007. 'Survey Report on the Situation of the Compulsory Education of Migrants' Children'. *Education Policy Reference [Jiaoyu juece cankao]* 7 (2). Jiangxi Provincial Education Office, Jiangxi Education Online (in Chinese). www.jxedu.gov.cn/info/1124/39940.htm

Chen, Xiaojin, Ningxin Liang and Stephen F. Ostertag. 2017. 'Victimisation of Left Behind Children in Rural China'. *Journal of Research in Crime and Delinquency* 54 (4): 515–543.

Chen, Xinxin, Qiuqiong Huang, Scott Rozelle, Yaojiang Shi and Linxiu Zhang. 2009. 'Effect of Migration on Children's Academic Performance in Rural China'. *Comparative Economic Studies* 51 (3): 323–343.

Chen, Yixin. 2011. 'Under the Same Maoist Sky: The Disparity in Death Rates between Anhui and Jiangxi during the Great Leap Forward Famine'. In *Eating Bitterness: New Perspectives on China's Great Leap Forward and Famine*, edited by Kimberly Manning and Felix Wemheuer, 197–225. Vancouver: University of British Colombia University Press.

China Daily. 2013a. 'China's Left-Behind Children Face Multiple Challenges'. 11 August. http://womenofchina.cn/html/womenofchina/report/152656-1htm (last accessed 4 December 2013).

China Daily. 2013b. 'Care for Kids Left Behind', *China Daily*, 12 August. http://eur ope.chinadaily.com.cn/opinion/2013–08/12/content_16886444.htm (last accessed 4 December 2013).

Bibliography 251

China Daily. 2013c. 'Sex Offenders Prey on Chi dren Left Behind'. *China Daily*, 14 August. http://usa.chinadaily.com.cn/epaper/2013–08/14/content_1689345.htm (last accessed 4 December 2013).

China Daily. 2013d. Number of Left Behind Children Surpasses 60 m. *China Daily*, 13 May. http://china.org.cn/china/2013–05/13/content_28806092.htm (accessed 25 June 2013).

China Daily. 2016. 'A Solution to the Problem of Left-Behind Kids'. *China Daily*, 8 February. www.chinadaily.com.cn/opinion/2016–02/06/content_23413919.htm (last accessed 3 December 2018).

China Daily. 2018. 'Psychotherapist Uses Stories to Encourage 'Left-behind' Children'. *China Daily*, 24 October, reproduced on All-China Women's Federation Net, www .womenofchina.cn/womenofchina/html1/people/newsmakers/1810/5621–1.htm (last accessed 10 November 2019).

China Development Brief. 2015a. 'Road to School Releases White Paper on the Mental Issues Facing Left-Behind Children'. 24 June. www.chinadevelopmentbrief.cn/news/ road-to-school-releases-white-paper-on-chinese-left-behind-childrens-mental-condition

China Development Brief. 2015b. 'Yuan En Space Round Table on China's Left-Behind Children'. 1 July. www.chinadevelopmentbrief.cn/articles/yuan-en-space-roundtable -on-chinas-left-behind-children/ (last accessed 6 December 2018).

China Development Brief. 2017. 'Stanford Professor Scott Rozelle's Talk on Rural Education Causes a Stir in China'. 22 September. www.chinadevelopmentbrief.cn/n ews/stanford-professor-scott-rozelles-talk-on-rural-education-causes-a-stir-in-china/ (last accessed 6 December 2018).

China Education Online [Zhongguo jiaoyu zaixian]. 2016. 'The Number of Rural Left Behind Children Has Precipitously Fallen but the Magnitude is Still Enormous' [Nongcun liushou ertong shuliang duanyanshi xiajiang dan guimo reng juda]. Zhongguo jiaoyu wang]. *China Education Net [Zhongguo jiaoyu wang]* http://xiaox ue.eol.cn/news/201612/t20161206_1473369.shtml

China International Labour Net (CILN). 2013. 'China's Rural Workers Head Overseas to Work'. www.ciwork.net/news/view.asp?id=8163, downloaded 15 August 2016. In Chinese.

China Labor Bulletin (CLB). 2008. 'Those Left Behind'. September. https://clb.org.hk /en/content/those-left-behind

China Labor Bulletin (CLB). 2018. 'Migrant Workers and Their Children'. May. https:// clb.org.hk/content/migrant-workers-and-their-children (updated version of 2010 report).

China Net (Zhongguo wang). 2012. 'Ministry of Education: Nationwide There are 22 Million Rural Left-Behind Children in the Compulsory Education Phase'. [Jiaoyubu: Quanguo yiwu jiaoyu jieduan nongcun liushou ertong 2200 wan] http://jiangsu .china.com.cn/html/jsnews/bwzg/1347_1.html (last accessed 12 August 2014).

China News [Zhongguo xinxi bao]. 2014. 'Jiangxi's Rural Migrant Workers Exceed 10 Million for the First Time'. [Jiangxi nongmingong shouci tupo qianwan] *Zhongguo xinxi bao*, 28 March. www.zgxxb.com.cn/tjdk/201403280012.shtml

China Statistical Yearbook Database. 2019. online at cnki.net.

Choi, Susanne Y. P. and Yinni Peng. 2016. *Masculine Compromise: Migration, Family and Gender in China*. Berkeley, CA: University of California Press.

Bibliography

Choi, Susanne Y. P., Brenda S. A. Yeoh and Theodora Lam. 2018. 'Editorial Introduction: Situated Agency in the Context of Research on Children, Migration and Family in Asia'. *Population, Space and Place*. April.

Chorpita, Bruce F. and David H. Barlow. 1998. 'The Development of Anxiety: The Role of Control in the Early Environment'. *Psychological Bulletin* 124 (1): 3–21.

Christopher, Karen. 2013. 'African American and Latina's Mothering Scripts: An Intersectional Analysis'. In *Notions of Family: Intersectional Perspectives*, edited by M Kohlman, D Kreig and B. Dickerson, 187–208. Bingley: Emerald Group Publishing.

Chuang, Julia. 2016. 'Factory Girls after the Factory: Female Return Migrations in Rural China'. *Gender and Society* 30 (3): 467–489.

Chyi, Hau and Bo Zhou. 2014. 'The Effects of Tuition Reforms on School Enrollment in Rural China'. *Economics of Education Review* 38 (C) (February): 104–123.

Cunha, Flavio, James J. Heckman, Lance Lochner and Dimitriy V. Masterov. 2005. 'Interpreting the Evidence on Lifecycle Skill Formation', Working Paper 11331 (May), National Bureau of Economic Research, Cambridge, Massachusetts.

Clark, Cindy Dell. 2011. *In a Younger Voice: Doing Child-Centred Qualitative Research*. New York: Oxford University Press.

Coe, Cati. 2011. 'How Children Feel about Their Parents' Migration: A History of the Reciprocity of Care in Ghana'. In *Everyday Ruptures: Children, Youth, and Migration*. In *Global Perspective*, edited by Deborah A. Boehm, Julia Meredith Hess, Cati Coe, Heather Rae-Espinoza and Rachel R. Reynolds, 97–114. Nashville, TN: Vanderbilt University Press.

Coe, Cati. 2012. 'Growing Up and Going Abroad: How Ghanaian Children Imagine Transnational Migration'. *Journal of Ethnic and Migration Studies* 38 (6): 913–931.

Coe, Cati. 2014. *The Scattered Family: Parenting, African Migrants and Global Inequality*. Chicago: University of Chicago Press.

Coffey, Amanda and Paul Atkinson. 1996. *Making Sense of Qualitative Data: Complementary Research Strategies*. California and London: Sage Publications.

Cohen, David. 2012. 'The Curious Case of Zhan Haite'. *The Diplomat*, 19 December.

Cohen, Myron L. 1992. 'Family Management and Family Division in Contemporary China'. *China Quarterly* 130: 357–377.

Cohen, Myron L. 1993. 'Cultural and Political Inventions in Modern China: The Case of the Chinese "Peasant"'. *Daedalus* 122 (2): 151–170.

Coleman, James S. 1988. 'Social Capital in the Creation of Human Capital'. *American Journal of Sociology* 94 (supplement 1): S95–S120.

Coleman, James S., Earnest Q. Campbell, Carol J. Hobson, James McPartland, Alexander M. Mood, Frederick D. Weinfeld and Robert L. York. 1966. *Equality of Educational Opportunity*. Washington, DC: US Government Printing Services.

Colen, Shellee. 1995. '"Like a Mother to Them': Stratified Reproduction and West Indian Childcare Workers and Employees in New York'. In *Conceiving a New World Order: The Global Politics of Reproduction*, edited by Faye D. Ginsburg and Rayna Rapp, 78–102. Berkeley, CA: University of California Press.

Cong, Zeng and Merril Siverstein. 2012. 'Caring for Grandchildren and Intergenerational Support in Rural China'. *Ageing and Society* 32 (3): 425–450.

Bibliography

Cong, Zeng and Merril Silverstein. 2008a. 'Intergenerational Time-for-Money Exchanges in Rural China: Does Reciprocity Reduce Depressive Symptoms in Older Adults?' *Research in Human Development* 5 (1): 6–25.

Cong, Zeng and Merril Siverstein. 2008b. 'Intergenerational Support and Depression among Elders in Rural China: Do Daughters-in-Law Matter?' *Journal of Marriage and Family* 70 (3) (August): 599–612.

Congressional-Executive Commission on China. 2005. 'China's Household Registration System: Sustained Effort Needed to Protect China's Rural Migrants'. Congressional-Executive Commission on China, 7 October. www.cecc.gov

Connell, R. W. and James W. Messerschmidt. 2005. 'Hegemonic Masculinity: Rethinking the Concept'. *Gender and Society* 19 (6): 829–859.

Connelly, Rachel, Kenneth Roberts and Zhenzher Zheng. 2011. 'The Settlement of Rural Migrants in Urban China – Some of China's Migrants Are Not Floating Anymore'. *Journal of Chinese Economic and Business Studies* 9 (3) (August): 283–300.

Connelly, Rachel, Kenneth Roberts and Zhenzhen Zheng. 2012. 'The Role that Children's Education Plays in the Migration Decisions of Chinese Rural Women', *Journal of Contemporary China* 21 (73) (January): 93–111.

Connelly, Rachel and Zhenzhen Zheng. 2007. 'Educational Access for China's Post-Cultural Revolution Generation: Enrolment Patterns in the 1990s'. In *Education and Reform in China*, edited by Emily Hannum and Albert Park, 81–92. London: Routledge.

Corbett, Michael. 2007. *Learning to Leave: The Irony of Schooling in a Coastal Community*. Blackpoint, NS: Fernwood Publishing Co.

Croll, Elisabeth. 1983. *Chinese Women since Mao* London: Zed Books.

Croll, Elisabeth. 1994. *From Heaven to Earth: Images and Experiences of Development in China*. London: Routledge.

Croll, Elisabeth. 1987. 'New Peasant Forms in Rural China'. *Journal of Peasant Studies* 14 (4) (July): 469–499.

Croll, Elisabeth. 2006. 'The Intergenerational Contract in the Changing Asian Family'. *Oxford Development Studies* 34 (4): 473–491.

Croll, Elisabeth and Ping Huang. 1997. 'Migration for and Against Agriculture in Eight Chinese Villages'. *The China Quarterly* 149 (March): 128–146.

Day, Alexander, F. 2013. *The Peasant in Post-Socialist China: History, Politics and Capitalism*. Cambridge: Cambridge University Press.

De Brauw, Alan and Scott Rozelle. 2007. 'Returns to Education in Rural China'. In *Education and Reform in China*, edited by Emily Hannum and Albert Park, 207–223. London: Routledge.

Démurger, Sylvie and Hui Xu. 2013. 'Left-Behind Children and Return Decisions of Rural Migrant in China'. IZA Discussion Papers, No. 7727, Institute for the Study of Labor (IZA), Bonn.

Ding, Tongfang and Duyu Sun. 2009. 'Status-Investigation on Family Education of Children Left in Quanjiao Anhui'. [Anhuisheng Quanjiaoxian nongcun liushou youer jiating jiaoyu xianzhuang diaocha]. *Journal of Chuzhou University [Chuzhou xueyuan xuebao]* 11 (4) (August): 75–77.

Dobson, Madeleine E. 2009. 'Unpacking Children in Migration Research'. *Children's Geographies* 7 (3) (August): 355–360.

254   Bibliography

Dodson, Lisa and Jullian Dickert. 2004. 'Girls' Family Labor in Low Income Households: A Decade of Qualitative Research'. *Journal of Marriage and Family* 66 (2) (May): 318–332.

Dong, Mingsheng. 2018. 'Anhui Quanshu County: The Neighbourhood Government Helps Mothers Accompanying Studying Children to Work Where They Reside' [Anhui Quanshuxian: shequ zhuli 'peidu mama' juzhu jiuye], China News Net, 18 August, reposted on The State Council Leading Group Office of Poverty Alleviation and Development website, www.cpad.gov.cn/art/2018/8/16/art_5_87906.html

Dong, Weizhen. 2019. 'Self-Rated Health among Elders in Different Out-Migration Areas: A Case Study of Rural Anhui, China'. *Chinese Journal of Sociology* 6 (9) https://doi.org/10.1186/s40711-019–0096-y

Douglass, Mike. 2006. 'Global Householding in Pacific Asia'. *International Planning Development Review* 28 (4): 421–446.

Douglass, Mike. 2014. 'Afterword: Global Householding and Social Reproduction in Asia'. *Geoforum* 51 (January): 313–315.

Dreby, Joanna. 2010. *Divided By Borders: Mexican Migrants and Their Children.* Berkeley, CA: University of California Press.

Dreby, Joanna and Leah Schmalzbauer. 2013. 'The Relational Contexts of Migration: Mexican Women in New Destination Sites'. *Sociological Forum* 28 (1): 1–26.

Du, Jincun. 2013. [Jianxian 2000 duoming zai wai wugong jiazhang huixiang peidu: dangdi zhongshi jiaoyu yijuliangde: bang le nongcun haizi jie le yonggong nanti] [Over 2000 Migrant Worker Parents Return to Jian County to *peidu* – Accompany Studying Children – The Two Birds and One Stone of Local Attention to Education: Help Rural Children and Alleivate the Difficulty of the Local Labour Shortage] *Jiangxi Ribao [Jiangxi Daily]*, 23 February.

Du, Xiao. 2009. 'Survey of Rural Boarding Schools in Central and West China: The Students Have Many Emotional Problems'. [Zhongxibu nongcu jisu xuexiao diaocha: xuesheng duo cunzai xinli wenti] *Legal Daily[Fazhi ribao]*, 3 March. http://news.sina.com.cn/c/2009–03-075717324108.shtml (last downloaded 28 April 2013).

Du, Xiao. 2012. 'Survey of Crime by Left-Behind Youths and Children: Trend Towards Younger Ages' [Liushou shaonian ertong fanzui diaocha: cheng duo fa dilinghua qushi]. Bi-Monthly Forum [Banyue Tan] 3 July. www.china.com.cn/news/law/2012–07/04/content_25801190_2.htm (last accessed 5 December 2018).

Duan, Chengrong. 2016. 'The Heart of Resolving the Problem of Left-Behind Children Lies at Stopping the Source' [Jiejue liushou ertong wenti de genben zaiyu zhizhu yuantou]. *Journal of Wuhan University [Wuhan daxue xuebao]* 69 (2): 15–18.

Duan, Chengrong, Lidan Lü, Jing Guo and Zong-ping Wang. 2013. 'Survival and Development of Left-Behind Children in Rural China: Based on the Analysis of Sixth Census Data' [Woguo nongcun liushou ertong shengcun he fazhan jiben zhuangkuang – jiyu di liu ci renkou pucha shuju de fenxi]. *Population Journal [Renkou xuekan]* 35 (3): 37–49.

Duan, Chengrong, Yan Yuan and Jing Guo. 2013. 'The Latest Features of China's Floating Population' [Woguo liudong renkou de zuixin zhuangkuang]. *Northwest Population [Xibei Renkou]* 34 (6): 1–12.

Duan, Chengrong and Lili Wu. 2009. 'The Status Quo of Rural Left Behind Children in China and its Analysis'. [Woguo nongcun liushou ertong zuixin zhuangkuang yu

Bibliography 255

fenxi]. *Journal of Chongqing Technology and Business University [Chongqing gongshang daxue xuebao]* 26 (1) (February): 24–30.

Duan, Chengrong and Ge Yang. 2008. 'Study of the Situation of Left-Behind Girls in China's Countryside'. [Zhongguo liushou nütong zhuangkuang yanjiu]. *Collection of Women's Studies [Funü yanjiu lunzong]* 6 (November) (overall series number 89): 18–25.

Duan, Chengrong and Ge Yang. 2009. 'Trends in Destination Distribution of Floating Population in China'. [Woguo liudong renkou de liuru di fenbu biandong qushi yanjiu]. *Population Research [Renkou yanjiu]* 33 (6) (November): 1–12.

Duan, Chengrong, Ge Yang, Ai Zhang and Xuehe Lu. 2008. 'Nine Big Trends in Changes in China's Floating Population Since the Reform and Opening' [Gaige kaifang yilai woguo liudong renkou biandong de jiu da qushi]. *Population Research [Renkou yanjiu]* 32 (6) (November): 30–43.

Duan, Chengrong and Fulin Zhou. 2005. 'A Study on Left Behind Children'. [Woguo liushou ertong zhuangkuang yanjiu]. *Population Research [Renkou yanjiu]* 29 (1) (January): 29–36.

Duchnesne, Stephane and Simon Larose. 2007. 'Adolescent Parental Attachment and Academic Performance and Motivation in Early Adolescence'. *Journal of Applied Social Psychology*, 37 (7) (July): 1501–1521.

Eastern County Education Bureau. 2008. *Eastern County Primary and Junior High School Care for Left-Behind Children Compilation – Edited Collection of Morality Education Material [Xian zhongxiaoxue guana liushou haizi pian – Deyu cailiao huibian]*. Eastern County: Anhui Province.

Eastern County Government. 2009. *Report on the Development Situation of the Construction Industry of Eastern County* [Guanyu Dongxian jianzhu fazhan qingkuang baogao] Speech by the Head of the County Construction Bureau at the 21st Meeting of the 15th People's Representative Meeting of Eastern County, 30 October.

Eklund, Lisa. 2010. 'Cadres as Gatekeepers? The Art of Opening the Right Doors'. In *Research Realities in the Social Sciences: Negotiating Fieldwork Dilemmas*, edited by George Szarycz, 129–148. Amherst, NY: Cambia Press.

Elder, Jnr., Glen H. 1974. *Children of the Great Depression*. Chicago: University of Chicago Press.

Elder, Jnr., Glen H. 1985. *Life Course Dynamics*. Ithaca, NY: Cornell University Press.

Elder, Jnr., Glen H. 1998. 'The Life Course as Developmental Theory'. *Child Development* 69 (1): 1–12.

Elder, Glen. Jr, Monica Kirkpatrick Johnson and Robert Crosnoe. 2003. 'The Emergence and Development of Life Course Theory', In *Handbook of the Life Course*, edited by Jeylan T. Mortimer and Michael J. Shanahan, 3–19. New York: Plenum.

Elder, Jnr., Glen H. and R. C. Rockwell. 1978. 'Economic Depression and Post-War Opportunity in Men's Lives: A Study of Life Patterns and Health'. In *Research in Community and Mental Health*, edited by R. A. Simmons, 240–303. Greenwich, CT: JAI Press.

Epstein, J. L. 1983. 'Longitudinal Effects of Family-School-Person Interactions on Student Outcomes'. *Research in the Sociology of Education and Socialisation* 4: 101–128.

Bibliography

Epstein, J. L. 2001. *School, Family and Community Partnerships: Preparing Educators and Improving Schools*. Boulder, CO: Westview Press.

Escobar, Arturo. 1995. *Encountering Development: The Making and Unmaking of the Third World*. Princeton: Princeton University Press.

Evans, Harriet. 2010. 'The Gender of Communication: Changing Expectations of Mothers and Daughters in Urban China'. *China Quarterly* 204 (December): 980–1000.

Fan, Cindy. 2003. 'Rural-Urban Migration and Gender Division of Labor in Transitional China'. *International Journal of Urban and Regional Research* 27 (1): 24–47.

Fan, Cindy C. 2008. *China on the Move: Migration, the State and the Household*. London: Routledge.

Fan, Fang, Linyan Su, Mary Kay Gill and Boris Birmaher. 2010. 'Emotional and Behavioural Problems of Chinese Left-Behind Children: A Preliminary Study'. *Social Psychiatry and Psychiatric Epidemiology* 45 (6): 655–664.

Fang, I-Chieh. 2015. 'Family Dynamics after Migration in Post-Mao China'. *Anthropology of This Century* 12 (January): http://aotcpress.com/articles/family-dynamics-migration-postmao-rural-china/

Fei, Xiaotong. 1992. *From the Soil: The Foundations of Chinese Society [Xiangtu Zhongguo]*. Translated by Gary G. Hamilton and Wang Zheng. Berkeley, CA: University of California Press.

Feng, Chongyi. 1999. 'Jiangxi in Reform: The Fear of Exclusion and the Search for a New Identity'. In *The Political Economy of China's Provinces*, edited by Hans Hendrischke and Chongyi Feng, 249–277. London: Routledge.

Field, Norma. 1995. 'The Child as Laborer and Consumer: The Disappearance of Childhood in Contemporary Japan'. In *Children and the Politics of Culture*, edited by Sharon Stephens, 51–78. New Jersey, NJ: Princeton University Press.

Feinberg, Mark E., Janae M. Neiderhiser, Sam Simmens, David Reiss and E. Mavis Hetherington. 2003. 'Sibling Comparison of Differential Parental Treatment in Adolescence: Gender, Self-Esteem, and Emotionality as Mediators of the Parenting-Adjustment Association'. *Child Development* 71 (6): 1611–1628.

Fincher, Leta Hong. 2018. *Betraying Big Brother: The Feminist Awakening in China*. London: Verso.

Fog Olwig, Karen. 1999. 'Narratives of Children Left Behind: Home and Identity in Globalised Caribbean Families'. *Journal of Ethnic and Migration Studies* 25 (2): 267–84.

Fong, Vanessa L. 2002. 'China's One-Child Policy and the Empowerment of Urban Daughters'. *American Anthropologist* 104 (4): 1098–1109.

Fong, Vanessa. 2004. *Only Hope: Coming of Age Under China's One-Child Policy*. Stanford: Stanford University Press.

Gaetano, Arianne M. 2015. *Out to Work: Migration, Gender and the Changing Lives of Rural Women in Contemporary China*. Honolulu, HI: University of Hawaii Press.

Gaetano, Arianne M. and Tamara Jacka, eds. 2004. *On the Move: Women and Rural-to-Urban Migration in Contemporary China*. New York: Columbia University Press.

Gao, Yang, Liping Li, Jean Hee Kim, Nathan Congdon, Joseph Lau and Sian Griffiths. 2010. 'The Impact of Parental Migration on Health Status and Health Behaviours among Left Behind Adolescent School Children in China'. *BMC Public Health* 10: 56. www.biomedcentral.com/1471–2458/10/56

Bibliography

Gardner, Katy. 2012. 'Transnational Migration and the Study of Children: An Introduction'. *Journal of Ethnic and Migration Studies* 38 (6): 889–912.

Garfinkel, Irwin and Sara S. McLanahan. 1986. *Single Mothers and Their Children: A New American Dilemma*. Washington, DC: Urban Institute Press.

Gibson, Jennifer E. 2012. 'Interviews and Focus Group Discussions: Methods that Match Children's Developing Competencies'. *Journal of Family Theory and Review* 4 (2): 149–159.

Gilligan, Carol. 2011. *Joining the Resistance*. Cambridge: Policy Press.

Ginsburg, Faye D and Rayna Rapp. 1995. 'Introduction: Conceiving the New World Order'. In *Conceiving a New World Order: The Global Politics of Reproduction*, edited by Faye D. Ginsburg and Rayna Rapp, 1–18. Berkeley, CA: University of California Press.

Glaser, Barney G. 1992. *Emergence Versus Forcing: Basics of Grounded Theory Analysis*. Mill Valley: Sociology Press.

Goh, Ester. 2009. 'Grandparents as Childcare Providers: An In-Depth Analysis of the Case of Xiamen, China'. *Journal of Aging Studies* 23 (1): 60–68.

Goh, Ester. 2011. *China's One-Child Policy and Multiple-Caregiving: Raising Little Suns in Xiamen*. Abingdon: Routledge.

Goh, Ester and Leon Kuczynski. 2014. 'She is Too Young for These Chores – Is Housework Taking a Back Seat in Urban Chinese Childhood?' *Children and Society*, 28 (4) (August): 280–291.

Gong, Hong-lian. 2005. 'Analysis and Thoughts on the Problem of the Education of China's Rural Migrant Workers: Impressions of the Survey on the Education of Migrant Children in Shenzhen's 'Yaoxu Street''. [Zhongguo nongmingong zinü jiaoyu wenti de fenxi yu sikao: Shenzhen Yaoxu jie nongmingong zinü jiaoyu zhuangkuang diaocha you gan]. *Lanzhou Scholarly Journal [Lanzhou xuekan]* 143 (2): 232–234.

Goodburn, Charlotte. 2009. 'Learning from Migrant Education: A Case Study of the Schooling of Rural Migrant Children in Beijing'. *International Journal of Educational Development* 29 (3): 495–504.

Goodburn, Charlotte. 2014. 'Rural-Urban Disparities and Gender Differences in Child Health Care in China and India'. *Development and Change* 45 (4): 631–655.

Graham, Elspeth and Lucy P. Jordan. 2011. 'Migrant Parents and the Psychological Wellbeing of Left Behind Children in Southeast Asia'. *Journal of Marriage and Family* 73 (4): 763–787.

Graham, Elspeth, Lucy P. Jordan, Brenda Yeoh, Theodora Lam, Maruja Asis and Sukamadi. 2012. 'Transnational Family and the Family Nexus: Perspectives of Indonesia and Filipino Children Left Behind by Migrant Parent(s)'. *Environment and Planning A* 44 (4): 793–815.

Greenhalgh, Susan and Jiali Li. 1995. 'Engendering Reproductive Policy and Practice in Peasant China: For a Feminist Demography of Reproduction'. *Signs* 20 (3) (Spring): 601–641.

Greenhalgh, Susan and Edwin. A. Winkler. 2005. *Governing China's Population*: From Leninist to Neoliberal Biopolitics. Palo Alto, CA: Stanford University Press.

Gruijters, Rob J. 2017. 'Intergenerational Contract in Chinese Families: Structural and Cultural Explanations'. *Journal of Marriage and Family* 79 (3): 758–768.

258 Bibliography

Guizhou Daily [Guizhou Ribao]. 2017. 'The Return of Rural Migrant Workers to the Local Area has Much Value' [Nongminggong huiliu bendi juyou duozhong jiazhi], 8 April, reproduced on China Youth Net http://news.youth.cn/jsxw/201705/t201705 08_9692688.htm (last accessed 10 November 2019).

Hägglund, Martin. 2019. *This Life: Why Mortality Makes Us Free*. London: Profile Books.

Han, Qing. 2016. 'Solving the Problem of Left-Behind Children Cannot Rely on Statistics: Requiring Parents to Return is Not as Good as Letting Children Enter the City'. [Jiejue liushou ertong wenti bu neng kao tongji: rang fumu fanxiang buru rang haizi jincheng], *Caixin Net [Caixin wang]* 11 November. http://nanduguancha .blog.caixin.com/archives/153612

Hannum, Emily. 2005. 'Market Transition, Educational Disparities, and Family Strategies in Rural China: New Evidence on Gender Stratification and Development'. *Demography* 42: 275–99.

Hannum, Emily and Jennifer Adams. 2009. 'Beyond Cost: Rural Perspectives on Barriers to Education'. In *Creating Wealth and Poverty in Postsocialist China*, edited by Deborah S. David and Feng Wang, 156–171. Stanford: Stanford University Press.

Hannum, Emily, Peggy Kong and Yuping Zhang. 2009. 'Family Sources of Educational Inequality in Rural China: A Critical Assessment'. *International Journal of Educational Development* 29 (5) (September): 474–486.

Hannum, Emily and Albert Park, eds. 2007. *Education and Reform in China*. London: Routledge.

Hannum, Emily and Albert Park. 2007. 'Academic Achievement and Engagement in Rural China'. In *Education and Reform in China*, edited by Emily Hannum and Albert Park, 154–172. London: Routledge.

Hannum, Emily, Albert Park and Kai-ming Chen. 2007. 'Introduction: Market Reforms and Educational Opportunity in China'. In *Education and Reform in China*, edited by Emily Hannum and Albert Park, 1–14. London: Routledge.

Hannum, Emily and Meiyan Wang. 2006. 'Geography and Educational Inequality in China'. *China Economic Review* 17 (3): 253–265.

Hannum, Emily, Meiyan Wang and Jennifer Adams. 2010. 'Rural–Urban Disparities in Access to Primary and Secondary Education under Market Reform'. In *One Country, Two Societies?: Rural–Urban Inequality in Contemporary China*, edited by Martin King Whyte, 125–146. Cambridge, MA: Harvard University Press.

Hansen, Mette Halskov. 2013. 'Recent Trends in Chinese Rural Education'. In *Towards a New Development Paradigm in Twenty-First Century China*, edited by Eric Florence and Pierre Defraigne, 165–178. London: Routledge.

Hansen, Mette Halskov. 2015. *Educating the Chinese Individual: Life in a Rural Boarding School*. Seattle, WA: University of Washington Press.

Hansen, Mette Halskov and Terry Woronov. 2013. 'Demanding and Resisting Education: A Comparative Study of Schools in Rural and Urban China'. *Comparative Education* 49 (2): 242–259.

Hao, Lingxin, Alfred Hu and Jamie Lo. 2014. 'Two Aspects of the Rural-Urban Divide and Educational Stratification in China: A Trajectory Analysis'. *Comparative Education Review* 58 (3) (August): 509–536.

Harrell, Steven and Gonçalo Santos. 2017. 'Introduction'. In *Transforming Patriarchy: Chinese Families in the Twenty-First Century*, edited by Gonçalo Santo and Steven Harrell, 3–38. Seattle, WA: University of Washington Press.

Bibliography

Hart, Caroline Sarojini. 2012. *Aspirations, Education and Social Justice—Applying Sen and* Bourdieu. London: Bloomsbury.

Hart, Caroline Sarojini. 2016. 'How Do Aspirations Matter?' *Journal of Human Development and Capabilities* 17 (3): 324–341.

Hays, Sharon. 1996. *The Cultural Contradictions of Motherhood*. New Haven and London: Yale University Press.

He, Congzhi and Ye. Jingzhong 2013. 'Lonely Sunsets: Impacts of Rural-Urban Migration on the Left Behind Elderly in Rural China'. *Population, Place and Space* 20 (4) (May): 352–369.

Heckman, James, Jora Stixrud and Sergio Urzua. 2006. 'The Effects of Cognitive and Non-Cognitive Abilities on Labor Market Outcomes and Social Behaviour', Working Paper 12006 (January), National Bureau of Economic Research, Cambridge, MA.

Ho, David Y. F. 1987. 'Fatherhood in Chinese Society'. In *The Father's Role: Cross-Cultural Perspectives*, edited by Michael Lamb, 227–246. Hillsdale, NJ: Lawrence Erlbaum Associates.

Hoang, Lan Anh, Theodora Lam, Brenda Yeoh and Elspeth Graham. 2015. 'Transnational Migration, Changing Care Arrangements and Left-behind Children's Responses in Southeast Asia'. *Children's Geographies* 13 (3): 263–277.

Hoang, Lan Anh and Brenda S. H. Yeoh. 2011. 'Breadwinning Wives and Left-Behind Husbands: Men and Masculinities in the Vietnamese Transnational Family'. *Gender and Society* 25 (6): 717–739.

Hoang, Lan Anh and Brenda S. H. Yeoh. 2015. 'Children's Agency and Its Contradictions in the Context of Transnational Labour Migration from Vietnam'. *Global Networks* 15 (2): 180–197.

Hoang, Lan Anh, Brenda S. H. Yeoh and Anna M. Wattie. 2012. 'Transnational Migration and the Politics of Care in the Southeast Asian Family'. *Geoforum* 43 (4): 733–740.

Hondagneu-Sotelo, Pierrette and Ernestine Avila. 1997. "'I'm Here, but I'm There': The Meanings of Latina Transnational Motherhood'. *Gender and Society* 11 (5): 548–571.

Hochschild, Arlie Russell. 2002. 'Love and Gold' In *Global Woman: Nannies, Maids and Sex Workers in the New Economy*, edited by Barbara Ehrenreich and Arlie Russell Hochschild, 15–30. London: Granta Books.

Hsieh, Chiao-min and Jean Kan. Hsieh 1995. *China: A Provincial Atlas*. New York: Macmillan Library Reference Publishers.

Hu, Anning. 2017. 'Providing More but Receiving Less: Daughters in Intergenerational Exchange in Mainland China'. *Journal of Marriage and Family* 79 (3): 739–757.

Hu, Feng. 2012. 'Migration, Remittances and Children's High School Attendance'. *International Journal of Education Development* 32 (3): 401–411.

Hu, Shu. 2019. 'It's for Our Education: Perception of Parental Migration and Resilience among Left-Behind Children in Rural China'. *Social Indicators Research* 145 (2): 641–661.

Hu, Yang. 2015. 'Gender and Children's Housework Time in China: Examining Behavior Modelling in Context'. *Journal of Marriage and Family* 77 (5): 1126–1143.

Huang, Shirlena and Brenda Yeoh. 2011. 'Navigating the Terrains of Transnational Education: Children of Chinese 'Study Mothers' in Singapore'. *Geoforum* 42: 394–403.

Bibliography

Huang, Shirlena and Brenda S. A. Yeoh. 2005. 'Transnational Families and Their Children's Education: China's 'Study Mothers' in Singapore'. *Global Networks* 5 (4): 379–400.

Huang, Pin and Chengrong Duan. 2012. 'Discussion of the Interaction Rituals of Rural Left Behind Wives in the Family'. [Lun nongcun liushou qizi jiating zhong de hudong yishi]. *Guangdong Social Sciences [Guangdong Shehui Kexue]* 4: 209–214.

Huang, Xing, Jian Chen, Chi Jin, Linyue Li. 2019. 'Working Outside Does Not Compare to o Working at Home, the Return of Rural Migrant Workers Boosts Development in the Centre West'. [Zai wai dagong bu ru zai jia jiuye, nongmingong huiliu licu zhongxibu fazhan]. *Economic Reference News [Jingji cankao bao]* 29 October. www.xinhuanet.com /fortune/2019–10/29/c_1125164214.htm (last accessed 10 November 2019).

Huang, Yuqin. 2012. 'Jumping Out of the Agricultural Gate: Social Mobility and Gendered Intra-household Resource Distribution among Children in a Central Chinese Village, 1950–2012'. *China Perspectives* 4: 25–33.

Jacka, Tamara. 1997. *Women's Work in Rural China: Change and Continuity in an Era of Reform*. Cambridge: Cambridge University Press.

Jacka, Tamara and Arianne M. Gaetano. 2004. 'Introduction: Focusing on Migrant Women'. In *On the Move: Women in Rural-to-Urban Migration in Contemporary China*, edited by Arianne M. Gaetano and Tamara Jacka, 1–40. New York: Columbia University Press.

Jacka, Tamara. 2012. 'Migration, Householding and the Well-Being of Left-Behind Women in Rural Ningxia'. *The China Journal* 67: 1–21.

Jacka, Tamara. 2014. 'Left-Behind and Vulnerable? Conceptualising Development and Older Women's Agency in Rural China'. *Asian Studies Review* 38 (2): 186–204.

Jacka, Tamara. 2018. 'Translocal Family Reproduction and Agrarian Change in China: A New Analytical Framework'. *Journal of Peasant Studies* 45 (7): 341–1359.

Jacka, Tamara, Andrew B. Kipnis and Sally Sargeson. 2013. *Contemporary China: Society and Social Change*. Melbourne: Cambridge University Press.

James, Alison, Chris Jenks and Alan Prout. 1998. *Theorizing Childhood*. Cambridge: Polity Press.

Jampaklay, Aree. 2006. 'Parental Absence and Children's School Enrolment: Evidence from a Longitudinal Study in Kanchanaburi, Thailand'. *Asian Population Studies* 2 (1): 93–110.

Jankowiak, William. 2011. 'The Han Chinese Family: The Realignment of Parenting Ideals, Sentiments and Practices'. In *Women and Gender in Contemporary Chinese Societies: Beyond Han Patriarchy*, edited by Shanshan Du and Ya-chen Chen, 109–132. Lantham, MD: Lexington.

Jess, Pat and Doreen Massey. 1995. 'The Contestation of Place'. In *A Place in the World? Places, Culture and Globalization*, edited by Doreen Massey and Pat Jess, 133–176. Oxford: Oxford University Press.

Jiangxi Province Bureau of Statistics [Jiangxi Sheng Tongjiju]. 2016. *Jiangxi Province 1 % Population Survey Sample, 2015* [Jiangxisheng 1% renkou chouyang diaocha ziliao, 2015]. Beijing: National Bureau of Statistics, cnki.net online.

Jiangxi Province Bureau of Statistics [Jiangxi Sheng Tongjjiju]. 2017. 'Jiangxi Province Citizens' Economic and Social Development Statistical Report for 2016'. [2016 nian Jiangxi sheng guomin jingji he shehui fazhan tongji baogao], 30 March. www.ha .stats.gov.cn/sitesources/hntj/page_pc/tjfw/tjgb/gjhgsgb/arti cle3938a3df7805444d95648b91aef89549.html

Bibliography 261

Jiangxi Provincial Government Education Supervision Office [Jiangxi Sheng Zhengfu Jiaoyu Jianduweiyuanhui Bangongshi]. 2018. 'Educational Ecology – Looking at Jiangxi – Insights on Advancing the Balanced Development of Education in Jiangxi Province' [Jiaoyu shengtai kan Jiangxi – Jiangxi sheng tuijin yiwu jiaoyu junheng fazhan de qishi] *Jiangxi Daily* [*Jiangxi ribao*], 27 October. www.jxedu.gov.cn/info/3291/140725.htm

Ji, Yingchun. 2015. 'Between Tradition and Modernity: Left Over Women in Shanghai'. *Journal of Marriage and Family* 77 (5): 1057–1073.

Ji, Yingchun. 2017. 'A Mosaic Temporality: New Dynamics of Marriage and Gender Systems in Contemporary Urban China'. *Temporalitiés: Revue de Sciences Sociales et Humaines* 27 online URL: http://journals.openedition.org/temporalites/3773; DOI:10.4000/temporalites.3773

Jia, Zhaobao, Lizheng Shi, Yang Cao, James Delancy and Wenhua Tian. 2010. 'Health-Related Quality of Life of 'Left-Behind Children' A Cross-Sectional Survey in Rural China'. *Quality of Life Research* 19 (6): 775–780.

Jia, Zhaobao and Wenhua Tian. 2010. 'Loneliness of Left-Behind Children: A Cross-Sectional Survey Sample of Rural China'. *Child: Care, Health and Development* 36 (6): 812–817.

Jiang, Jingxiong, Urban Rosenqvist, Huishan Wang, Ted Greiner, Guanli Lian and Anna Sarkadi. 2007. 'Influence of Grandparents on Eating Behaviors of Young Children in Chinese Three-Generation Families'. *Appetite* 48 (3) (May): 377–383.

Jiang, Quanbao, Marcus W. Feldman and Shuzhuo Li. 2014. 'Marriage Squeeze, Never-Married Portion and Mean Age at First Marriage in China'. *Population Research Policy Review* 33 (2) (April): 189–203.

Jiang, Shan, Jie Chu, Cuicui Li, Alexis Medina, Qiongwei Hu, Jing Liu and Chengchao Zhou. 2015. 'Alcohol Consumption is Higher among Left-Behind Chinese Children Whose Parents Leave Rural Areas to Work'. *Acta Pediatrica* 104 (12) (December): 1298–1304.

Jordan, Lucy P. and Elspeth Graham. 2012. 'Resilience and Wellbeing among Children of Migrant Parents in Southeast Asia'. *Child Development* 83 (5): 1672–1688.

Judd, Ellen. 1994. *Gender and Power in Rural North China*. Stanford: Stanford University Press.

Kanaiaupuni, Shawn Malia. 2000. *Sustaining Families and Communities: Nonmigrant Women and Mexico-U.S. Migration*. Center for Demography and Ecology Working Paper. Madison, WI: University of Wisconsin–Madison.

Kandel, William and Grace Kao. 2001. 'The Impact of Temporary Labor Migration on Mexican Children's Educational Aspirations and Performance'. *International Migration Review* 35 (4): 1205–31.

Kandel, William and Douglass Massey. 2002. 'The Culture of Mexican Migration: A Theoretical and Empirical Analysis'. *Social Forces* 80 (3): 981–1004.

Katz, Cindi. 2001. 'Vagabond Capitalism and the Necessity of Social Reproduction'. *Antipode* 33 (4): 708–727.

Katz, Cindi. 2004. *Growing up Global: Economic Restructuring and Children's Everyday Lives*. Minneapolis, MN: University of Minnesota Press.

Katz, Cindi. 2008. 'Childhood as Spectacle: Relays of Anxiety and the Reconfiguration of the Child'. *Cultural Geographies* 15 (1): 5–17.

Kaufmann, Vincent and Betrand Montulet. 2008. 'Between Social and Spatial Mobilities: The Issue of Social Fluidity'. In *Tracing Mobilities: Towards a Cosmopolitan Perspective*, edited by Weert Canzler, Vincent Kaufmann and Sven Kesserlring, 37–56. Aldershot: Ashgate Publishing.

Kennedy, John James and Yaojiang Shi. 2019. *Lost and Found: The "Missing Girls" in Rural China*. Oxford: Oxford University Press.

Kim, Sung Won. 2018. 'Left Behind Children: Teachers' Perceptions of Family-School Relations in Rural China'. *Compare: A Journal of Comparative and International Education* 49 (4): 584–601.

King, Valerie and Glen H. Elder. 1995. 'American Children View Their Grandparents: Linked Lives Across Three Rural Generations'. *Journal of Marriage and Family* 57 (1) (February): 165–178.

Kipnis, Andrew. 2006. 'Suzhi: A Keyword Approach'. *China Quarterly* 186: 295–313.

Kipnis, Andrew. 2009. 'Education and the Governing of Child-Centred Relatedness'. In *Chinese Kinship: Contemporary Anthropological Perspectives*, edited by Susanne Brandtstädter and Gonçalo D. Santos, 154–178. London: Routledge.

Kipnis, Andrew. 2011. *Governing Educational Desire: Culture, Politics and Schooling in China*. Chicago: University of Chicago Press.

Klocker, Natascha. 2007. 'An Example of Thin Agency: Child Domestic Workers in Tanzania'. In *Global Perspectives on Rural Childhood and Youth: Young Rural Lives*, edited by Ruth Panelli, Samantha Punch and Elsbeth Robson, 81–148. London: Routledge.

Knight, John, Quheng Deng and Shi Li. 2017. 'China's Expansion of Higher Education: The Labor Market Consequences of a Supply Shock'. *China Economic Review* 43 (April): 127–141.

Knight, John and Shi Li. 1996. 'Educational Attainment and the Rural-Urban Divide in China'. *Oxford Bulletin of Economics and Statistics* 58 (1): 83–117.

Knight, John, Shi Li and Quheng Deng. 2010. 'Son Preference and Household Income in Rural China'. *Journal of Development Studies* 40 (10): 1786–1805.

Kohn, Melvin. 1963. 'Social Class and Parent-Child Relationships: An Interpretation'. *American Journal of Sociology* 68 (4): 471–480.

Kohrman, Matthew. 2005. *Bodies of Difference: Experiences of Disability and Institutional Advocacy in the Making of Modern China*. Berkeley, CA: University of California Press.

Koo, Anita. 2012. 'Is There Any Chance to Get Ahead? Education Aspirations and Expectations of Migrant Families in China'. *British Journal of Sociology of Education* 33 (4) (July): 547–564.

Koo, Anita. 2016. 'Expansion of Vocational Education in Neoliberal China: Hope and Despair among Rural Youth'. *Journal of Education Policy* 31 (1): 46–59.

Koo, Anita, Holly Ming and Bill Tsang. 2014. 'The Doubly Disadvantaged: How Return Migrant Children Fail to Access and Deploy Capitals for Academic Success in Rural Schools'. *Sociology* 48 (4): 795–811.

Kowal, Amanada and Laurie Kramer. 1997. 'Children's Understanding of Parental Differential Treatment'. *Child Development* 68 (1): 113–126.

Bibliography

Kowal, Amanda, Laurie Kramer, Jennifer L. Krull and Nicki R. Crick. 2002. 'Children's Perceptions of the Fairness of Parental Preferential Treatment and their Socioemotional Well-being'. *Journal of Family Psychology* 16 (3): 297–306.

Kramer, Karen Z. and Amit Kramer. 2016. 'At-Home Father Families in the United States: Gender Ideology, Human Capital and Unemployment'. *Journal of Marriage and Family* 78 (5) (October): 1315–1331.

Krien, Sheila Fitzgerald and Andrea H. Beller. 1988. 'Educational Attainment of Children from Single Parent Families: Differences by Exposure, Gender and Race'. *Demography* 25 (2): 221–234.

Kuczynski, Leon. 2003. 'Beyond Bidirectionality: Bilateral Conceptual Frameworks for Understanding Dynamics in Parent-child Relations'. In *Handbook of Dynamics in Parent-Child Relations*, edited by Leon Kuczynski, 1–24. Thousand Oaks, CA: Sage.

Lahaie, Claudia, Jeffrey A. Hayes, Tinka Markham Piper and Jody Heymann. 2009. 'Work and Family Divided across Borders: The Impact of Parental Migration on Mexican Children in Transnational families'. *Community, Work and Family* 12 (3): 299–312.

Lam, Theodora and Brenda S. A. Yeoh. 2015. 'Long-Distance Fathers, Left-Behind Fathers, and Returnee Fathers: Changing Fathering Practices in Indonesia and the Philippines'. In *Globalized Fatherhood*, edited by Marcia C. Inhorn, Wendy Chavkin and José-Alberto Navarro, 103–128. New York and Oxford: Berghahn Books.

Lam, Theodora and Brenda S. A. Yeoh. 2018. 'Migrant Mothers, Left Behind Fathers: The Negotiation of Gender Subjectivities in Indonesia and the Philippines'. *Gender, Place and Culture* 25 (1): 104–117.

Lan, Pei-Chia. 2018. *Raising Global Families: Parenting, Immigration, and Class in Taiwan and the US*. Stanford: Stanford University Press.

Lauby, Jennifer and Oded Stark. 1988. 'Individual Migration as a Family Strategy: Young Women in the Philippines'. *Population Studies* 42 (November): 473–486.

Lareau, Annette. 2003. *Unequal Childhoods: Class, Race and Family Life*. Berkeley, CA: University of California Press.

Lee, Ching Kwan. 1998. *Gender and the South China Miracle: Two World of Factory Women*. Berkeley, CA: University of California Press.

Lee, Ming-Hsuan. 2011. 'Migration and Children's Welfare in China: The Schooling and Health of Left-Behind Children'. *The Journal of Developing Areas* 44 (2): 165–182.

Lee, Yean-Ju and Hagen Koo. 2006. "Wild Geese Fathers' and a Globalised Family Strategy for Education in Korea'. *International Development Planning Review* 28 (4): 533–553.

Lei, Lianlian, Feng Liu and Elaine Hill. 2018. 'Labour Migration and the Health of Left-Behind Children in China'. *Journal of Development Studies* 54 (1): 93–110.

Leng, Lee and Albert Park. 2010. '*Parental Migration and Child Development in China*'. Working Paper, *Gansu Survey of Children and Families*.

Lerner, Melvin J. 1974. 'The Justice Motive: 'Equity' and 'Parity' among Children'. *Journal of Personality and Social Psychology* 29 (4): 539–550.

264   Bibliography

Levitt, Peggy and Nina Glick Schiller. 2004. 'Conceptualizing Simultaneity: Transnational Perspectives on Migration'. *International Migration Review* 38 (3): 595–629.

Li, Amy. 2013. 'School Place for Migrant Pupil Sparks 'Locust' Row in Shanghai'. *South China Morning Post*, 10 September. www.scmp.com/news/china-insider/arti cle/1307570/school-place-migrant-pupil-sparks-locust-row-shanghai (last accessed 3 December 2018).

Li, Eva. 2017. 'Reports of Parents' Deaths by China's Left-Behind Children Prompt a Closer Look at the Family Dynamic'. *South China Morning Post*, 27 July. www.scmp.com/news/china/society/article/2104255/reports-parents-deaths-chinas-left-behind-children-prompt-closer (last accessed 7 December 2018).

Li, Shi, Hiroshi Sato and Terry Sicular. 2019. 'Rising Inequality in China: Key Issues and Findings'. In *Rising Inequality in China*, edited by Shi Li, Hiroshi Sato and Terry Sicular, 1–43. Cambridge: Cambridge University Press.

Li, Wanxin and Maggie Lau. 2012. 'Interpersonal Relationships and Subjective Wellbeing among Preadolescents in China'. *Child Indicators Research*. 5 (4) (December): 587–608.

Li, Wen, Albert Park and Sanggui Wang. 2007. 'School Equity in Rural China'. In *Education and Reform in China*, edited by Emily Hannum and Albert Park, 27–44. London: Routledge.

Li, Xiangmei. 2016. 'Holding Up Half the Sky? The Continuity and Change of Visual Gender Representation in Elementary Language Textbooks in Post-Mao China'. *Asian Journal of Women's Studies* 22 (4): 477–496.

Li, Wenxin. 2013. *Chinese Internal Rural Migrant Children and Their Access to Compulsory Education*. Doctoral Dissertation, Department of Law, Queen Mary, University of London.

Li, Xuan. 2016. 'The 'Nursing Dad'? Constructs of Fatherhood in Chinese Popular Culture'. *Intersections: Gender and Sexuality in Asia and the Pacific*. 39 (July). http://intersections.anu.edu.au/issue39/li.pdf (last accessed 5 December 2018).

Li, Xuan and William Jankowiak. 2016. 'The Chinese Father: Masculinity, Conjugal Love and Parental Involvement'. In *Changing Chinese Masculinities: From Imperial Pillars of the State to Global Men*, edited by Kam Louie, 186–203. Hong Kong: Hong Kong University Press.

Li, Xuan and Michael E. Lamb. 2015. 'Fathers in Chinese Culture: Traditions and Transitions'. In *Fathers Across Cultures: The Importance, Roles, and Diverse Practices of Dads*, edited by Jaipaul Roopnarine, 273–306. New York: Praeger.

Li, Guangyou and Fangbiao Tao. 2009. 'Survey on Mental Health Status and Suicidal Ideation among Rural Left Behind Children 14–16 Years'. [14–16 sui liushou ertong xinli zhuangkuang ji zisha qingxiang fenxi]. *Chinese Journal of Public Health [Zhongguo gonggong weisheng]* 25 (8) (August): 905–907.

Li, Qiang. 2015. *Vast Country, Vacant Village: Left-Behind Children, Women and the Elderly* [Daguo kongcun: nongcun liushou ertong, funü yu laoren]. Beijing: China Economic Press.

Li, Quan-mian. 2004. 'Study on Households of Grandparents with Grandchildren at the Stage of Social Transformation'. [Nongcun laodongli wailiu Beijing xia gedai jiating chutan]. *Market and Demographic Analysis [Shichang yu renkou fenxi]* 10 (6): 31–36.

Li, Rui and Nan Song. 2009. 'A Study of the Protection of Rights and Interests of Rural Left Behind Children'. [Nongcun liushou ertong quanyi baozhang chutan]. *Journal of Beijing University of Agriculture [Beijing nongxueyuan xuebao]* 24 (2) (April): 70–73.

Li, Song. 2009. 'Analysis of the Family Environment, Emotional Health and Academic Grades of Rural Left-Behind Children'. [Nongcun liushou ertong jiating huanjing, xinli jiankang ji xueye chengji de fenxi]. *Hubei Social Sciences [Hubei shehui kexue]* 9: 182–185.

Li Zeying, Yingzhi Liang and Heng Liu. 2009. 'Women Who Walk on the Edge of Marriage – An Investigation and Suggestion about the Marriage Issues of Women Left in Rural Areas in Sichuan Province'. [Xingzou zai hunyin yuanbian de nürenmen – Sichuansheng nongcun liushou funü jiating wenti diaocha yu jianyi]. *Journal of China Women's University [Zhonghua nüzi xueyuan xuebao]* 21 (4) (August): 75–78.

Liao, Yunsheng, Shujuan Song and Bo Chen. 2009. 'Research on Emotional Communication between Rural Left-Behind Children and Their Parents'. [Nongcun liushou ertong yu fume qinggan goutong de yanjiu]. *Cutting Edge [Qianyan]* 8: 155–157.

Lin, Justin Yifu. 1988. 'The Household Responsibility System in China's Agricultural Reform: A Theoretical and Empirical Study'. *Economic Development and Cultural Change* 36 (S3) (April): S119–S224.

Lin, Ping and Yuting Mu. 2016. 'Diaocha cheng liushou ertong yinian jian bu dao fumu zhan 7.7%, zhi haizi quefa zizun' [Survey states 7.7% of left behind children do not see their parents all year, causing the children to lack self-respect]. *Rule of Law in China [Fazhi Zhongguo]* 25 June, p. 1. http://m.thepaper.cn/newsDetail_forward_1489122

Ling, Minhua. 2015. 'Bad Students Go to Vocational Schools: Education, Social Reproduction and Migrant Youth in Urban China', *China Journal* 73 (January): 108–131.

Ling, Minhua. 2017. 'Precious Son, Reliable Daughter: Redefining Son Preference and Parent-Child Relations in Migrant Households in Urban China'. *The China Quarterly* 229: 150–171.

Liu, Chengfang, Linxiu Zhang, Renfu Luo, Scott Rozelle, Brian Sharbono and Yaojiang Shi. 2009. 'Development Challenges, Tuition Barriers, and High School Education in China'. *Asia Pacific Journal of Education* 29 (4): 503–520.

Liu, Fengshu. 2015. 'The 'Rise' of the Priceless Child in China'. *Comparative Education Review* 60 (1): 105–130.

Liu, Fengshu. 2019. 'Chinese Young Men's Construction of Exemplary Masculinity: The Hegemony of Chengong'. *Men and Masculinities* 22 (2): 294–316.

Liu, Jieyu. 2014. 'Aging, Migration and Family Support in Rural China'. *Geoforum* 51 (January): 305–312.

Liu, Jieyu. 2016. 'Intimacy and Intergenerational Relations in Rural China'. *Sociology* 51 (5): 1034–1049.

Liu, Li-Juan, Xun Sun, Chun-Li Zhang, Yue Wang and Qiang Guo. 2010. 'A Survey in Rural China of Parent-Absence through Migrant Working: The Impact on Their Children's Self-Concept and Loneliness'. *BMC Public Health* 10 (32). https://bmcpublichealth.biomedcentral.com/articles/10.1186/1471–2458-10-32

Liu, Xiao-hui, Xiao-juan Wang, Yu-yan Yang, Lina He, Qiuli Li and Xiuying Dai. 2012. 'Comparison of the Mental Health Status between Left-Behind Children Under Different Guardianship Arrangements and Non Left-Behind Children'. [Butong jianhu leixing liushou ertong yu yiban ertong xinli jiankang zhuangkuang de bijiao yanjiu]. *Chinese General Practice* 15 (5a) (May): 1507–1509.

Liu, Xin. 2000. *In One's Own Shadow: An Ethnographic Account of the Condition of Post-Reform Rural China*. Berkeley, CA: University of California Press.

Liu, Xuelian. 2017. *The Top Performer' of China's Property Market and Its Driving Factors: A Case Study of Hefei*. MSc Dissertation, Contemporary Chinese Studies, Oxford School of Global and Area Studies, supervised by Kyle Jaros.

Liu, Zhengkui, Xinying Li and Xiaojia. Ge 2009. 'Left Too Early: The Effects of Age at Separation from Parents on Chinese Rural Children's Symptoms of Anxiety and Depression'. *American Journal of Public Health* 99 (11): 2049–2054.

Liu, Zhiqiang, Li Yu and Xiang Zheng. 2017. *No Longer Left-Behind: The Impact of Return Migrant Parents on Children's Performance*, ADBI Working Paper No. 716, Tokyo: Asian Development Bank Institute.

Locke, Catherine, Nguyen Thi Ngan Hoa and Nguyen Thi Thanh Tam. 2012. 'Visiting Marriage and Remote Parenting: The Changing Strategies of Rural-Urban Migrants to Hanoi, Vietnam'. *Journal of Development Studies* 48 (1): 10–25.

Locke, Catherine and Peter Lloyd-Sherlock. 2011. 'Qualitative Life Course Methodologies: Critical Reflections from Development Studies'. *Development and Change* 42 (5): 1131–1151.

Locke, Catherine, Janet Seeley and Nitya Rao. 2013. 'Migration and Social Reproduction at Critical Junctures in the Family Life Course'. *Third World Quarterly* 34 (10): 1881–1895.

Lou, Binbin, Zhenzhen Zheng, Rachel Connelly and Kenneth D Roberts. 2004. 'The Migration Experiences of Young Women from Four Counties in Sichuan and Anhui'. In *On the Move: Women in Rural-to-Urban Migration in Contemporary China*, edited by Arianne M. Gaetano and Tamara Jacka, 207–242. New York: Columbia University Press.

Lou, Binbin. 2004. 'Impacts of Husbands' Migration on Women'. In *Migration and the Development of Rural Women*, edited by Zhenzhen Zheng and Z Xie, 114–128. Beijing: Chinese Social Science Academic Press. (in Chinese, cited in Biao Xiang 2003).

Lou, Jiayou, Rong Zong, Kuanbao Yao, Rushan Hu, Qiyun Du, Junqun Fang and Mingyuan Zhu. 2008. 'The Status of Care and Nutrition of 774 Left-Behind Children in Rural Areas in China'. *Public Health Report* 123 (3): 382–389.

Lu, Yao. 2012. 'Education of Children Left Behind in Rural China'. *Journal of Marriage and Family* 74 (2): 328–341.

Lu, Yao and Donald J. Treiman. 2008. 'The Effect of Family Size on Educational Attainment in China: Period Variations'. *American Sociological Review* 73 (5): 813–834.

Lu, Yao and Donald Treiman. 2011. 'Migration, Remittances and Educational Stratification among Blacks in Apartheid and Post-Apartheid South Africa'. *Social Forces* 89 (4): 1119–1144.

Lu, Zhen. 2019. *The Implementation of China's New-Type Urbanisation Plan to Reduce Educational Inequality among Migrant Children in Changsha*, Doctoral thesis in Department of Urban Studies and Planning, University of Sheffield.

Lucas, Robert E. B. and Oded Stark. 1985. 'Motivations to Remit: Evidence from Botwana'. *Journal of Political Economy* 93: 901–918.

Bibliography 267

Luecke, Mattias and Tobias Stoehr. 2012. 'The Effects of Migration in Moldovia and Georgia on the Children and Elderly Left Behind'. Europe Aid Project DCI-MIGR /210/229–604. The Kiel Institute for the World Economy (mimeo) http://mgsog .merit.unu.edu/research/docs/moldova_georgia_researchpaper03.pdf

Luo, Chuliang and Terry Sicular. 2019. 'Inequality and Poverty in Rural China'. In *Rising Inequality in China*, edited by Shi Li, Hiroshi Sato and Terry Sicular, 197–229. Cambridge: Cambridge University Press.

Luo, Ruiyao. 2017. 'Survey: Ten Million out of Twenty Three Million Left-Behind Children See Their Parents Less than Twice a Year'. [Diaocha: liushou ertong 2300 wan shubaiwan yi nian jian fumu budao liang ci] Caixin Net (Caixin wang), 24 December. www.360doc.com/content/17/0724/09/10170615_673683678.shtml (last accessed 7 December 2018).

Lyu, Lidan and Yu Chen. 2019. 'Parental Migration and Young Migrants' Wages in Urban China'. *Urban Studies* 56 (10): 1968–1987.

Magnani, Elisabetta and Rong Zhu. 2012. 'Gender Wage Differentials among Rural-Urban Migrants in China'. *Regional Science and Urban Economics* 42 (5) (September): 779–793.

Mahler, Sarah J. and Patricia R. Pessar. 2001. 'Gendered Geographies of Power: Analysing Gender across Transnational Spaces'. *Identities: Global Studies in Culture and Power* 7 (4): 441–459.

Mallee, Hein. 1995a. 'China's Household Registration System under Reform'. *Development and Change* 26 (1) (January): 1–29.

Mallee, Hein. 1995b. 'In Defence of Migration: Recent Chinese Studies on Rural Population Mobility'. *China Information* 10 (3–4): 108–140.

Massey, Doreen. 1993. 'Power-Geometry and a Progressive Sense of Place'. In *Mapping the Futures: Local Cultures, Global Change*, edited by John Bird, Barry Curtis, Tim Putnam and Lisa Tickner, 60–70. London: Routledge.

Massey, Doreen. 1994. *Space, Place and Gender*. Cambridge: Polity Press.

Mayall, Berry. 2000. 'The Sociology of Childhood in Relation to Children's Rights'. *International Journal of Children's Rights* 8 (3): 243–259.

Mazzucato, Valentina and Djamila Schans. 2011. 'Transnational Families and the Wellbeing of Children: Conceptual and Methodological Challenges'. *Journal of Marriage and Family* 73 (August): 704–712.

McHale, Susan M., Kimberly A. Updegraff, Lily Shanahan, Ann A. Crouter and Sarah E. Killoren. 2005. 'Siblings' Differential Treatment in Mexican American Families'. *Journal of Marriage and Family* 67 (December): 1259–1274.

McHale, Susan M. and Terese M. Pawletko. 1992. 'Differential Treatment of Siblings in Two Family Contexts'. *Child Development* 63 (1): 68–81.

McKenzie, David and Hillel Rapoport. 2006. *Can Migration Reduce Educational Attainment?: Evidence from Mexico*. Washington, DC: The World Bank.

McLanahan, Sara and Gary Sandefur. 1994. *Growing Up with a Single Parent*. Cambridge, MA: Harvard University Press.

McLoyd, Vonnie C. 1998. 'Socioeconomic Disadvantage and Child Development'. *American Psychologist* 53 (2): 185–204.

Mei, Hong, Quanbao Jiang, Yuanyuan Xiang and Xiaoping Song. 2015. 'School Consolidation: Wither China's Rural Education?' *Asian Social Work and Policy Review* 9 (2): 138–150.

268 Bibliography

Meisner, Maurice. 1986. *Mao's China and After: A History of the People's Republic of China*. New York: The Free Press.

Meng, Xin and Chikako Yamauchi. 2015. 'Children of Migrants: The Impact of Parental Migration on Their Children's Education and Health Outcomes'. Institute for the Study of Labour, IZA Discussion Paper No. 9165 http://ftp.iza.org/dp9165.pdf

Menjívar, Cecilia and Victor Agadjanian. 2007. 'Men's Migration and Women's Lives: Views from Rural Armenia and Guatemala'. *Social Science Quarterly* 88 (5): 1243–1262.

Milkie, Melissa A., Robin W. Simon and Brian Powell. 1997. 'Through the Eyes of Children: Youths' Perceptions and Evaluations of Maternal and Paternal Roles'. *Social Psychology Quarterly* 60: 218–37.

Miller, Eric T. 2004. 'Filial Daughters, Filial Sons: Comparisons from Rural North China'. In *Filial Piety: Practice and Discourse in Contemporary East Asia*, edited by Charlotte Ikels, 34–52. Stanford: Stanford University Press.

Milwertz, Cecelia. 1997. *Accepting Population Control: Urban Chinese Women and the One Child Family Policy*. Surrey: Curzon.

Ming, Holly H. 2013. *The Education of Migrant Children and China's Future: The Urban Left-Behind*. New York: Routledge.

Ministry of Education (MOE). 2012. 'The Ministry of Education's 2011 Statistical Report on the Development of Education in China' [Jiaoyubu 2011 nian quanguo jiaoyu shiye fazhan tongji gongbao] *China Education Daily* [*Zhongguo jiaoyu bao*] 31 August. http://paper.jyb.cn/zgjyb/html/2012–08/31/content_77122.htm (last accessed 5 December 2018).

Ministry of Education (MOE). 2013. 'Responsible Persons from the Five Ministries Including the Ministry of Education Hold a Press Conference on Strengthening the Care and Education Work of Rural Left Behind Children During the Compulsory Education Phase'. [Jiaoyubu deng 5 bumen you guan fuzeren jiu jiaqiang yiwu jiaoyu jieduan nongcun liushou ertong guanai he jiaoyu gongzuo da jizhe wen]. Website of the Ministry of Education of the People's Republic of China, 1 October. www.moe.edu.cn/publicfiles/business/htmlfiles/moe/s271/201301/146675.html (last accessed 12 August 2014).

Montes, Veronica. 2013. 'The Role of Emotions in the Construction of Masculinity: Guatemalan Migrant Men, Transnational Migration, and Family Relations'. *Gender and Society* 27 (4): 469–490.

Morrow, Virginia and Uma Vennam. 2015. "Those Who Are Good to Us, We Call Them Friends.' Social Support and Social Networks for Children Growing Up in Poverty in Rural Andhra Pradesh, India'. In *Childhood with Bourdieu*, edited by Leena Alanem, Liz Brooker and Berry Mayall, 142–165. London: Palgrave Macmillan.

Moser, Leo J. 1985. *The Chinese Mosaic: The People's and Provinces of China*. Boulder, CO: Westview Press.

Murphy, Rachel. 2002. *How Migrant Labor is Changing Rural China*. Cambridge: Cambridge University Press.

Murphy, Rachel. 2004a. 'Turning Peasants into Modern Chinese Citizens: "Population Quality" Discourse, Demographic Transition and Primary Education'. *China Quarterly* 177: 1–20.

Murphy, Rachel. 2004b. 'The Impact of Labor Migration on the Well-Being and Agency of Rural Chinese Women: Cultural and Economic Contexts and the Life Course'. In

Bibliography

On the Move: Women in Rural-to-Urban Migration in Contemporary China, edited by Arianne M. Gaetano and Tamara Jacka, 243–278. New York: Columbia University Press.

Murphy, Rachel. 2007. 'Paying for Education in Rural China'. In *Paying for Progress in China: Public Finance, Human Welfare and Changing Patterns of Inequality*, edited by Vivienne Shue and Christine Wong, 69–95. Abingdon: Routledge.

Murphy, Rachel. 2009. 'Introduction: Labour Migration and Social Development in China'. In *Labour Migration and Social Development in Contemporary China*, edited by Rachel Murphy, 1–17. Abingdon: Routledge.

Murphy, Rachel. 2010. 'The Narrowing Digital Divide: A View from Rural China'. In *One Country, Two Societies: Rural-Urban Inequality in Contemporary China*, edited by Martin King Whyte, 168–187. Cambridge, MA: Harvard University Press.

Murphy, Rachel. 2014a. 'School and Study in the Lives of Children in Migrant Families: A View from Rural Jiangxi, China'. *Development and Change* 45 (1): 29–51.

Murphy, Rachel. 2014b. 'Sex Ratio Imbalances and China's Care for Girls Programme: A Case Study of a Social Problem'. *China Quarterly* 129 (September): 781–807.

Murphy, Rachel, Ran Tao and Xi Lu. 2011. 'Son Preference in Rural China: Patrilineal Families and Socio-Economic Change'. *Population and Development Review* 37 (4): 665–690.

Murphy, Rachel, Minhui Zhou and Ran Tao. 2016. 'Parents' Migration and Children's Subjective Wellbeing and Health: Evidence from Rural China'. *Population, Space and Place*, 22 (8): 766–780.

Naftali, Orna. 2016. *Children in China*. Cambridge: Polity Press.

National Bureau of Statistics Research Office [Gucjia Tongji Ju Diaocha Bangongshe]. 2011. *The Numbers, Composition and Special Characteristics of the New Generation Rural Workers*. [Xinshengdai nongmingong de shuliang, jiegou he tedian]. Beijing: National Bureau of Statistics, released 11 March.

National Bureau of Statistics [Guojia Tongji Ju]. 2015. *The 2014 Report of the Nationwide Monitoring Survey of Rural Workers*. [2014 nian quanguo nongmingong jiance diaocha baogao]. Beijing: National Bureau of Statistics.

National Bureau of Statistics [National Bureau of Statistics]. 2016. *The 2015 Report of the Nationwide Monitoring Survey of Rural Workers* [2015 nian nongmingong jiance diaocha baogao]. Beijing: National Bureau of Statistics, released 28 April.

Nelson, Nici. 1992. 'The Women Who Have Left and Those Who Have Stayed Behind: Rural-Urban Migration in Central and Western Kenya'. In *Gender and Migration in Developing Countries*, edited by Sylvia Chant and Sarah Radcliffe, 109–138. London: Belhaven.

Nguyen, Mint T. N. 2014. 'Translocal Householding: Care and Migrant Livelihoods in a Waste-Trading Community of Vietnam's Red River Delta'. *Development and Change* 45 (6): 1385–1408.

Nguyen, Minh T. N. and Catherine Locke. 2014. 'Rural-Urban Migration in Vietnam and China: Gendered Householding, Production of Space and the State'. *Journal of Peasant Studies* 41 (5): 855–876.

Ni, Y. X Zhou, L.M. Li and T. Hesketh. 2018. 'Child Maltreatment in Zhejiang Province of China: Role of Parental Aggressive Tendency and History of Maltreatment in Childhood'. *Child Abuse Review* 27 (5): 389–403.

270 Bibliography

Nie, Mao, Lei Li and Huajun Li. 2008. *Wounded Village: A Record of Worries of Rural China's Left-Behind Children* [Shangcun: Zhongguo nongun liushou ertong yousi lu]. Beijing: Renmin Ribao Chubanshe [People's Daily Publisher].

Nobles, Jenna. 2011. 'Parenting from Abroad: Migration, Non-Resident Father Involvement, and Children's Education in Mexico'. *Journal of Marriage and Family* 73 (4): 729–746.

Normille, Denis. 2017. 'One in Three Chinese Children Faces an Education Apocalypse'. *Science*. 21 September. www.sciencemag.org/news/2017/09/one-three-chinese-children-faces-education-apocalypse-ambitious-experiment-hopes-save (last accessed 5 December 2018).

Obendiek, Helena. 2017. 'Higher Education, Gender, and Elder Support in Rural Northwest China'. In *Transforming Patriarchy: Chinese Families in the Twenty-First Century*, edited by Gonçalo Santo and Steven Harrell, 74–90. Seattle, WA: University of Washington Press.

Obermeyer, Carla Makhlouf and Rosario Cardenas. 1997. 'Son Preference and Differential Treatment in Morocco and Tunisia'. *Studies in Family Planning* 28 (3): 235–244.

O'Brien, Maeve. 2007. 'Mothers' Emotional Care Work in Education and its Moral Imperative'. *Gender and Education* 19 (2): 159–177.

Oi, Jean. 1989. *State and Peasant in Contemporary China: The Political Economy of Village Government*. Berkeley, CA: University of California Press.

On the Road to School. 2015. *2015 White Paper on the Emotional Situation of China's Left-Behind Children* [Zhongguo liushou ertong xinling zhuangkuang baipi shu 2015 nian]. Beijing: On the Road to School NGO (Shangxue lushang) and Renmin University. China White Paper Net [*Zhongguo baipi wang*] www.docin.com/p-1949 801458.html (last accessed 3 December 2018).

On the Road to School. 2016. *2016 White Paper on the Emotional Situation of China's Left Behind Children* [Zhongguo liushou ertong zhuangkuang baipi shu 2016 nian]. Beijing: On the Road to School NGO (Shangxue lushang) and Renmin University. China White Paper Net [Zhongguo baipi shu wang] www.doc88.com/p-608780078 7771.html (last accessed 3 December 2018).

On the Road to School. 2017. *2017 White Paper on the Emotional Situation of China's Left Behind Children* [Zhongguoo liushou ertong zhuangkuang baipi shu 2017 nian]: Beijing: On the Road to School NGO (Shangxue lushang) and Renmin University.

Orellana, Majorie F. Barrie Thorne, Anna Chee and Wan Shun Eva Lam. 2001. 'Transnational Childhoods: The Participation of Children in Processes of Family Migration'. *Social Problems* 48 (4): 572–591.

Oster, Emily. 2009. 'Does Increased Access Increase Equality? Gender and Child Health Investments in India'. *Journal of Development Economics* 89 (1): 62–76.

Ouyang, Shijia. 2019. 'Residency Shift Part of Plan to Boost Urban Base'. *China Daily*, 9 April. www.chinadaily.com.cn/a/201904/09/WS5cab92b7a3104842260b5049 .html

Oxfeld, Ellen. 2017. *Bitter and Sweet: Food, Meaning and Modernity in Rural China*. Berkeley, CA: University of California Press.

Oyserman, Daphna and Hazel Rose Markus. 1990. 'Possible Selves and Delinquency'. *Journal of Personality and Social Psychology* 59 (1): 112–125.

Bibliography

Pan, Lu. 2018. 'From Left-Behind Children to Young Migrants: The Intergenerational Social Reproduction of Migrant Labor'. *Eurasian Geography and Economics* 59 (2): 184–203.

Pande, Rohini P. 2003. 'Selective Gender Differences in Childhood Nutrition and Immunization in Rural India: The Role of Siblings'. *Demography* 40 (3): 395–418.

Pang, Lihua, Alan de Brauw and Scott Rozelle. 2004. 'Working Until You Drop: The Elderly of Rural China'. *The China Journal* 52 (July): 73–94.

Patton, Michael Quinn. 1990. 'Purposeful Sampling'. In *Qualitative Evaluation and Research Methods*, edited by Michael Quinn Patton, 169–186. Beverley Hills:Sage.

Parreñas, Rhacel Salazar. 2005. *Children of Global Migration: Transnational Families and Gendered Woes*. Stanford: Stanford University Press.

Parreñas, Rhacel Salazar. 2008. 'Transnational Fathering: Gendered Conflicts, Distant Discipline and Emotional Gaps'. *Journal of Ethnic and Migration Studies* 34 (7): 1057–1072.

Pei, Yaolin and Zhen Cong. 2020. 'Children's Education and Their Financial Transfers to Ageing Parents in Rural China: Mothers' and Fathers' Strategic Advantages in Enforcing Reciprocity'. *Ageing and Society* 40 (4): 896–920.

Peng, Yinni and Odalia M. H. Wong. 2013. 'Diversified Transnational Mothering via Telecommunication: Intensive, Collaborative, and Passive'. *Gender and Society* 27 (4): 491–513.

Pessar, Patricia R. and Sarah J. Mahler. 2003. 'Transnational Migration: Bringing Gender In.' *International Migration Review* 37 (3) (Fall): 812–846.

Pepper, Suzanne. 1996. *Radicalism and Education in Twentieth Century China: The Search for an Ideal Development Model*. Cambridge: Cambridge University Press.

Pingol, Alicia. 2001. *Remaking Masculinities: Identity, Power and Gender Dynamics in Families with Migrant Wives and Househusbands*. Philippines: University Centre for Women's Studies.

Ping, Tu. 2000. 'Trends and Regional Differences in Fertility Transition'. In *The Changing Population of China*, edited by Xizhe Peng and Zhigang Guo, 22–29. Oxford: Blackwell.

Pissin, Annika. 2013. 'The Global Left-Behind Child in China: Unintended Consequences in Capitalism'. Centre for East Asian and South East Asian Studies Working Paper 39, Lund University, Sweden.

Potter, Sulamith Heins and Jack M. Potter. 1990. *China's Peasants: An Anthropology of a Revolution*. Cambridge: Cambridge University Press.

Pottinger, Audrey M. 2005. 'Children's Experience of Loss by Parental Migration in Inner City Jamaica'. *American Journal of Orthopsychiatry* 75 (4): 485–496.

Prefectural People's Government. 2017. 'Western County Establishes A Care for Left-Behind Children Foundation', 6 September. Prefectural people's government website (in Chinese).

Prout, Alan and Alison James. 1997. 'A New Paradigm for the Sociology of Childhood'. In *Constructing and Reconstructing Childhood: Contemporary Issues in the Sociological Study of Childhood*, edited by Alison James and Alan Prout, 7–33. New York: Routledge Farmer.

Pun, Ngai. 2005. *Made in China: Women Factory Workers in a Global Factory Workplace*. Durham, NC: Duke University Press.

Pun, Ngai and Jenny Chan. 2013. 'The Spatial Politics of Labour in China: Life, Labour and a New Generation of Migrant Workers'. *The South Atlantic Quarterly* 112 (1): 179–190.

Pun, Ngai and Anita Koo. 2019. 'Double Contradiction of Schooling: Class Reproduction and Working-Class Agency at Vocational Schools in China'. *British Journal of Sociology of Education* 40 (1): 50–64.

Pun, Ngai and Huilin Lu. 2010. 'Neoliberalism, Urbanism and the Plight of Construction Workers in China'. *World Review of Political Economy* 1 (1): 127–141.

Punch, Samantha. 2002a. 'Research with Children: The Same or Different from Research with Adults?' *Childhood* 9 (3): 321–341.

Punch, Samantha. 2002b. 'Youth Transitions and Interdependent Adult-Child Relations in Rural Bolivia'. *Journal of Rural Studies* 18 (2): 123–133.

Punch, Samantha. 2012. 'Studying Transnational Children: A Multi-Sited, Longitudinal, Ethnographic Approach'. *Journal of Ethnic and Migration Studies* 38 (6): 1007–1023.

Putnam, Robert D. 2015. *Our Kids: The American Dream in Crisis*. New York: Simon and Schuster.

Qin, Desirée B. 2009. 'Gendered Processes of Adaptation: Understanding Parent-Child Relations in Chinese Immigrant Families'. *Sex Roles* 60 (7/8): 467–481.

Qin, Jiang and Björn Albin. 2010. 'The Mental Health of Children Left Behind in Rural China by Migrating Parents: A Literature Review'. *Journal of Public Mental Health* 9 (3): 4–16.

Qvortrup, Jens. 1994. 'Childhood Matters: An Introduction'. In *Childhood Matters: Social Theory, Practice and Politics*, edited by Jens Qvortrup, Marjatta Bardy, Giovanni Sgritta and Helmut Wintersberger, 1–24. Aldershot: Avebury.

Qvortrup, Jens. 1995. 'From Useful to Useful: The Historical Continuity of Children's Constructive Participation'. In *Sociological Studies of Children, Volume 7*, edited by Nancy Mandell, 49–76. Bingley: Emerald Group Publishing.

Qvortrup, Jens. 2009. 'Childhood as a Structural Form'. In *The Palgrave Handbook of Childhood Studies*, edited by Jens Qvortrup, William Cosaro and Michael Sebastian Honing, 21–33. Basingstoke: Palgrave Macmillan.

Rae-Espinoza, Heather. 2011. 'The Children of Émigrés in Ecuador: Narratives of Cultural Production and Emotion in Transnational Social Fields', In *Global Perspective*, edited by Deborah A. Boehm, Julia Meredith Hess, Cati Coe, Heather Rae-Espinoza and Rachel R. Reynolds, 114–140. Nashville: Vanderbilt University Press.

Raghuram, Parvati. 2012. 'Global Care, Local Configurations: Challenges to Conceptualisations of Care'. *Global Networks* 12 (2): 155–174.

Rao, Vijayendra and Michael Walton. 2004. 'Culture and Public Action: Relationality, Equality of Agency, and Development'. In *Culture and Public Action*, edited by Vijayendra Rao and Michael Walton, 3–36. Stanford: Stanford University Press.

Razavi, Sharhra. 2011. 'Rethinking Care in a Development Context: An Introduction'. *Development and Change* 42 (4): 873–903.

Reay, Diane. 1998. *Class Work: Mothers' Involvement in Their Children's Primary Schooling*. London: University of London Press.

Reay, Diane. 2000. 'A Useful Extension of Bourdieu's Conceptual Framework? Emotional Capital as a Way of Understanding Mothers' Involvement in their Children's Education?' *Sociological Review* 48 (4): 568–585.

Bibliography

Reay, Diane. 2001. 'Finding or Losing Yourself: Working Class Relationships to Education'. *Journal of Education Policy* 16 (4): 333–346.

Reay, Diane, Miriam David and Stephen Ball. 2005. *Degrees of Choice: Social Class, Race and Gender in Higher Education*. Stoke-on-Trent: Trentham Books.

Ressureccion, Bernadette P. and Thi Van Khanh Ha. 2007. 'Able to Come and Go: Reproducing Gender in Female Rural-Urban Migration in the Red River Delta'. *Population, Space and Place* 13 (3): 211–224.

Risman, Barbara. 2004. 'Gender as Social Structure: Theory Wrestling with Activism'. *Gender and Society* 18 (4): 429–450.

Roberts, Kenneth, Rachel Connelly, Zhenming Xie and Zhenzhen Zheng. 2004. 'Patterns of Temporary Labor Migration of Rural Women from Anhui and Sichuan'. *The China Journal* 52: 49–70.

Robson, Elsbeth, Stephen Bell and Natascha Klocker. 2007. 'Conceptualizing Agency in the Lives and Actions of Rural Young People'. In *Global Perspectives on Rural Childhood and Youth: Young Rural Lives*, edited by Ruth Panelli, Samantha Punch and Elsbeth Robson, 135–148. London: Routledge.

Roeser, Robert W., Jacquelynne S. Eccles and Arnold J. Sameroff. 2000. 'School as a Context of Early Adolescents' Academic and Social-Emotional Development: A Summary of Research Findings'. *The Elementary School Journal* 100 (5): 443–471.

Ross, Heidi. 2006. 'Challenging the Gendered Dimensions of Schooling: The State, NGOs and Transnational Alliances'. In *Education and Social Change in China*, edited by Gerald Postiglione, 53–74. Armonk: ME Sharpe.

Ruddick, Sara. 1998. 'Care as Labor and Relationship'. In *Norms and Values: Essays on the Work of Virginia Held*, edited by Mark S. Halfon and Joram C. Haber, 3–25. Lanham, MD: Rowan and Littlefield.

Ruhm, Christopher J. 2008. 'Maternal Employment and Adolescent Development'. *Labour Economics* 15 (5): 958–983.

Santos, Gonçalo. 2017. 'Multiple Mothering and Labor Migration in Rural South China'. In *Transforming Patriarchy: Chinese Families in the Twenty-First Century*, edited by Gonçalo Santo and Steven Harrell, 91–112. Seattle, WA: University of Washington Press.

Santos, Gonçalo and Steven Harrell, eds. 2017. *Transforming Patriarchy: Chinese Families in the Twenty-First Century*. Seattle, WA: University of Washington Press.

Schiavenza, Matt. 2013. 'Mapping China's Income Inequality'. *The Atlantic*, 13 September. www.theatlantic.com/china/archive/2013/09/mapping-chinas-income -inequality/279637/ (last accessed 16 January 2019).

Schmalzbauer, Leah. 2004. 'Searching for Wages and Mothering from Afar: The Case of Honduran Transnational Families'. *Journal of Marriage and Family* 66 (5): 1317–1331.

Schmalzbauer, Leah. 2005. *Surviving and Striving: A Daily Life Analysis of Honduran Families*. London and New York: Routledge.

Schmalzbauer, Leah. 2008. 'Family Divided: The Class Formation of Honduran Transnational Families'. *Global Networks* 8 (3): 29–46.

Schoon, Ingrid. 2006. *Risk and Resilience: Adaptations in Changing Times*. Cambridge: Cambridge University Press.

Scheider, Helen M. 2010. *Keeping the Nation's House: Domestic Management and the Making of Modern China*. Vancouver: University of British Columbia Press.

Seltzer, Judith A. 1994. 'Consequences of Marital Dissolution for Children'. *Annual Review of Sociology* 20: 235–266.

Settersen, Richard A Jnr. 2015. 'Relationships in Time and the Life Course: The Significance of Linked Lives'. *Research in Human Development* 12 (3/4): 217–223.

Shen, Ke and Yuan Zhang. 2018. 'The Impacts of Parental Migration on Children's Subjective Well-being in Rural China: A Double-Edged Sword'. *Eurasian Geography and Economics* 59 (2): 267–289.

Shen, M., S. Yang, J. Shi, R. Yang, Y. Du and L. Stallones. 2009. 'Non-Fatal Injury Rates among the Left-Behind Children of Rural China'. *Injury Prevention* 15 (4): 244–247.

Shen, Yifei. 2011. 'China in the 'post-patriarchal era': Changes in the Power Relationships in Urban Households and an Analysis of the Course of Gender Inequality in Society'. *Chinese Sociology and Anthropology* 43 (4): 5–23.

Shi, Lihong. 2017a. *Choosing Daughters: Family Change in Rural China*. Stanford: Stanford University Press.

Shi, Lihong. 2017b. 'From Care Providers to Financial Burdens: The Changing Role of Sons and Reproductive Choice in Rural Northeast China'. In *Transforming Patriarchy: Chinese Families in the Twenty-First Century*, edited by Gonçalo Santo and Steven Harrell, 59–73. Seattle, WA: University of Washington Press.

Shi, Xingzheng. 2016. 'The Impact of Educational Fee Reduction Reform on School Enrollment in Rural China'. *Journal of Development Studies* 52 (12): 1791–1809.

Shi, Yaojing, Linxiu Zhang, Yue Ma, Hongmei Yi, Chengfang Liu, Nathalie Johnson, James Chu, Prashant Loyalka and Scott Rozelle. 2015. 'Dropping Out of Rural China's Secondary Schools: A Mixed-Methods Analysis'. *China Quarterly* 224 (December): 1048–1069.

Short, Susan E., Fengying Zhai, Xu Siyuan and Mingliang Yang. 2001. 'China's One Child Policy and the Care of Children: An Analysis of Qualitative and Quantitative Data'. *Social Forces* 79 (3): 913–943.

Silverstein, Louise B. 1991. 'Transforming the Debate about Child Care and Maternal Employment'. *American Psychologist* 46 (10): 1025–1032.

Siu, Kaxton. 2015. 'Continuity and Change in the Everyday Lives of Chinese Migrant Factory Workers'. *The China Journal* 74 (July): 43–65.

Small, Mario Luis. 2009. 'How Many Cases Do I Need? On Science and the Logic of Case Selection in Field-Based Research'. *Ethnography* 10 (1): 5–38.

Smith, Andrea, Richard N. Lalonde and Simone Johnson. 2004. 'Serial Migration and its Implications for the Parent-Child Relationship: A Retrospective Analysis of the Experiences of the Children of Caribbean Immigrants'. *Cultural Diversity and Ethnic Minority Psychology* 10 (2): 107–122.

Smith, Chris and Jenny Chan. 2015. 'Working for Two Bosses: Student Interns as Constrained Labour in China'. *Human Relations* 68 (2): 305–326.

Solinger, Dorothy J. 1999. *Contesting Citizenship in Urban China: Peasant Migrants, the State and the Logic of the Market*. Berkeley, CA: University of California Press.

Song, Jing. 2017. *Gender and Employment in Rural China*. London and New York: Routledge.

Song, Shige and Sarah A. Burgard. 2008. 'Does Son Preference Influence Children's Growth in Height? A Comparative study of Chinese and Filipino Children'. *Population Studies* 62 (3): 302–320.

Bibliography 275

Song, Yue. 2018. *Children of Migrant Workers in Urban High Schools: An Analysis of the Dual Role of Education*, Doctoral Thesis, School of Education, University of Glasgow.

Stafford, Charles. 2000. 'Chinese Patriliny and the Cycles of Yang and Laiwang'. In *Cultures of Relatedness: New Approaches to the Study of Kinship*, edited by Janet Carsten, 35–54. Cambridge: Cambridge University Press.

Stafford, Charles. 2013. 'Ordinary Ethics in China Today'. In *Ordinary Ethics in China*, edited by Charles Stafford, 2–27. London: Bloomsbury Academic Publishing.

Stark, Oded and Robert E. B. Lucas. 1988. 'Migration, Remittances and the Family'. *Economic Development and Cultural Change* 36 (April): 465–482.

Stark, Oded. 1991. *The Migration of Labour*. Cambridge: Blackwell.

State Council. 2016. 'State Council to Safeguard 'Left-Behind' Children'. 14 February, http://english.www.gov.cn/policies/latest_releases/2016/02/14/content_281475289683304.htm (last accessed 9 January 2017).

Stewart, Hilary, Nick Watson and Mhairi Campbell. 2018. 'The Cost of School Holidays for Children from Low Income Families'. *Childhood* 25 (4) (November): 516–529.

Su, S., X. Li, D. Lin and M. Zhu. 2013. 'Psychological Adjustment among Left Behind Children in Rural China: The Role of Parental Migration and Parent-Child Communication'. *Child: Care, Health and Development* 39 (2): 162–170.

Su, Wang. 2016. 'Cabinet Bans Younger 'Left-Behind' Children From Living Alone'. *Caixin Online*, 16 February. www.caixinglobal.com/2016–02-16/cabinet-bans-younger-left-behind-children-from-living-alone-101011862.html (last accessed 3 December 2018).

Suárez-Orozco, Carola, Irina L. G. Todorova and Josephine Louie. 2002. 'Making Up for Lost Time: The Experience of Separation and Reunification among Immigrant Families'. *Family Process* 41 (4): 625–643.

Sudworth, John. 2019. 'China's Muslims: Xinjiang Schools Used to Separate Children from Families'. 4 July. www.bbc.co.uk/news/world-asia-china-48825090

Sun, Dan. 2012. 'The Influence of the Rural Gender Imbalance on Farmers' Intentions to Enter the Cities for Work' [Nongcun nanü bili shiheng dui nongmin jincheng wugong yiyuan de yingxiang]. *Renkou yanjiu [Population research]* 36 (6): 57–70.

Sun, Wanning. 2002. 'Discourse of Poverty: Weakness, Potential and Provincial Identity in Anhui'. In *Rethinking China's Provinces*, edited by John Fitzgerald, 153–177. London: Routledge.

Sun, Wanning. 2005. 'Anhui *Baomu* in Shanghai: Gender, Class and a Sense of Place'. In *Locating China*, edited by Jing Wang, 171–189. London: Routledge.

Sun, Wanning. 2009a. *Maid in China*. London: Routledge.

Sun, Wanning. 2009b. '*Suzhi* on the Move: Body, Place and Power'. *Positions: East Asia Cultures Critique* 17 (3): 617–642.

Swider, Sarah. 2015. 'Building China: Precarious Employment among Migrant Construction Workers'. *Work, Employment and Society* 29 (1): 41–59.

Swidler, Ann. 1986. 'Culture in Action: Symbols and Strategies'. *American Sociological Review* 51 (2) (April): 273–286.

Tan, Li, Yufang Zhao and Jing Liang. 2009. 'Interpersonal Trust of Rural Left-Behind Junior Students in Liangping County'. [Liangping xian nongcun liushou chuzhongseng renji xinren zhuangkuang fenxi]. *Chinese Journal of School Health [Zhongguo xuexiao weisheng]* 30 (8) (August): 725–727.

276 Bibliography

Tang, Junchao. 2016. 'Lost at the Starting Line: A Reconsideration of Educational Inequality in China 1978–2008'. *The Journal of Chinese Sociology* 3 (8): 1–18.

Tang, Zongli and Ming Cheng. 2014. 'Changes in Clan Culture in Rural Areas of Southern Anhui'. *Rural China: An International Journal of History and Social Sciences* 11 (1): 88–118.

Tao, Lin. 2009. 'Research into the Facilities of Rural Primary and Middle Boarding Schools and Counter Measures'. [Nongcun zhongxiaoxue jisuzhi shishi ji duice yanjiu]. *Journal of Hubei University of Education [Hubei dier shifan xueyuan xuebao]* 26 (7) (July): 101–103.

Tao, Ran. 2009. 'Hukou Reform and Social Security for Migrant Workers in China'. In *Labour Migration and Social Development in Contemporary China*, edited by Rachel Murphy, 73–75. Abingdon: Routledge.

Thao, Vu Thi. 2013. 'Making a Living in Rural Vietnam from (Im)mobile Livelihoods: A Case of Women's Migration'. *Population, Place and Space* 19 (1): 87–102.

Thao, Vu Thi. 2015. 'When the Pillar of the Home is Shaking: Female Labor Migration and Stay-at-Home Fathers in Vietnam'. In *Globalized Fatherhood*, edited by Marcia C. Inhorn, Wendy Chavkin and José-Alberto Navarro, 129–151. New York and Oxford: Berghahn Books.

Thøgersen, Stig. 2002. *A County of Culture: Twentieth Century China Seen from the Village Schools of Zouping, Shandong*. Ann Arbor, MI: University of Michigan Press.

Thorne, Barrie. 1987. 'Re-Visioning Women and Social Change: Where are the Children?' *Gender and Society* 1 (1) (March): 85–109.

Thorne, Barrie. 2004. 'Theorizing Age and Other Differences'. *Childhood* 11 (4): 403–408.

Tisdall, E. Kay M. and Samantha Punch. 2012. 'Not So 'New': Looking Critically at Childhood Studies'. *Children's Geographies* 10 (3): 249–264.

Toyota, Mika, Brenda S. A. Yeoh and Liem Nguyen. 2007. 'Editorial Introduction: Bringing the Left Behind Back into View in Asia'. *Population, Space and Place* 13 (3): 157–161.

UNICEF. 2016. *Harnessing the Power of Data for Girls: Taking Stock and Looking Ahead to 2030, October*. New York: UNICEF Data and Analytics Section, Division of Data, Research and Policy.

Wan, Meng. 2009. 'Statistical Analysis of Survey of Left-Behind Children in Rural Areas in Jiangxi province'. [Jiangxi nongcun liushou ertong diaocha tongji fenxi]. *Technological Forum [Keji guangchang]* 6: 31–33.

Wang, Fan-en. 2009. 'Study on the Emotional Cost During the Transfer of China's Rural Surplus Rural Labor'. [Woguo nongcun shengyu laodongli zhuanyi zhong de qinggan chengben yanjiu]. *Journal of Suzhou University [Suzhou xueyuan xuebao]* 24 (4) (August): 12–14+43.

Wang, Jing and Zhao Shaoming. 2016. 'Seeking to Explain the Puzzle of the Sharp Fall in the Numbers of Left Behind Children from 61 Million and Twenty Thousand to 9 Million and Twenty Thousand'. [Cong 6102 wan dao 902 wan qiu jie liushou ertong shuju ruijian zhi mi]. *China Society News [Zhongguo shehui bao]*, 22 November. http://mzzt.mca.gov.cn/article/nxlsrtbjlxhy/mtgz/201611/20161100 887683.shtml (last accessed 5 December 2018).

Bibliography

Wang, Kaiyu. 2007. *A Different Childhood: Survey Investigation Report of the Children of China's Migrant Workers* [Bu yiyang de tongnian: Zhongguo nongmingong zinü diaocha baogao]. Hefei: Hefei Technology University Press.

Wang, Lamei and Judi Mesman. 2015. 'Child Development in the Face of Rural-to-Urban Migration in China: A Meta-Analytic Review'. *Perspectives on Psychological Science* 10 (6): 813–831.

Wang, Qiang. 2014. 'Rural Students Are Being Left Behind in China'. *Nature* 510, 26 June: 445.

Wang, Shutao and Yaqing Mao. 2018. 'The Effect of Boarding on Campus on Left-Behind Children's Sense of School Belonging and Academic Achievement: Chinese Evidence from Propensity Score Matching Analysis'. *Asia Pacific Journal of Education* 38 (3): 378–393.

Wang, Yuxiang and Lizhong Wu. 2016. 'Study of the Evolutionary Progress and Special Characteristics of China's Policy on Left-Behind Children'. [Woguo liushou ertong zhengce de yanjin guocheng yu tedian yanjiu]. *Youth Exploration [Qingnian tansuo]* 5 (204): 42–50.

Wang, Zhanghua and Lichao Dai. 2009. 'Education of the Rural Left-Behind Children and the Intervention of Social Work'. [Nongcun liushou ertong jaioyu wenti yu shehui gongzuo jieru]. *Journal of Hebei Normal University [Hebei shifan daxue xuebao]* 11 (7) (July): 125–129.

Waters, Johanna L. 2005. 'Transnational Family Strategies and Education in the Chinese Diaspora'. *Global Networks* 5 (4): 359–377.

Waters, Johanna. 2015. 'Educational Imperatives and the Compulsion for Credentials: Family Migration and Children's Education in East Asia'. *Children's Geographies* 13 (3): 280–293.

Weale, Sally. 2017. 'Gender Pay Gap Starts Early with 20% Disparity in Pocket Money – Study'. *The Guardian*, 24 January. www.theguardian.com/world/2017/jan/24/gender-pay-gap-starts-early-20-disparity-pocket-money-study (last downloaded 23 December 2018).

Wei, Shang-Jin and Xiaobo Zhang. 2011a. 'The Competitive Savings Motive: Evidence from Rising Sex Ratios and Savings Rates in China'. *Journal of Political Economy*, 119 (3): 511–564.

Wei, Shang-Jin and Xiaobo Zhang. 2011b. 'Sex Ratios, Entrepreneurship and Economic Growth in the People's Republic of China'. National Bureau of Economic Research, Working Paper No. 16800: www.nber.org/papers/w16800

Wei, Yanning. 2018. 'Leaving Children Behind: A Win-Win Household Strategy or a Path to Pauperization?' *Eurasian Geography and Economics* 59 (2): 164–183.

Wen, Ming and Danhua Lin. 2012. 'Child Development in Rural China: Children Left Behind by Their Migrant Parents and Children of Non-Migrant Families'. *Child Development* 83 (1): 120–136.

West, Candace and Don H. Zimmerman. 1987. 'Doing Gender'. *Gender and Society* 1 (2): 125–151.

Wikipedia. 2016. 'List of Chinese Administrative Regions by GDP Per Capita'. https://en.wikipedia.org/wiki/List_of_Chinese_administrative_divisions_by_GDP_per_capita#Historical_data (last accessed January 2019).

Woon, Yuen-Fong. 1983/84. 'The Voluntary Sojourner among Overseas Chinese: Myth or Reality'. *Pacific Affairs* 56 (Winter): 673–690.

278   Bibliography

Wolf, Margery. 1972. *Women and the Family in Rural Taiwan*. Stanford: Stanford University Press.

Wolf, Margery. 1985. *Revolution Postponed: Women in Contemporary China*. Stanford: Stanford University Press.

World Bank. 2009. *From Poor Areas to Poor People: China's Evolving Poverty Reduction Agenda*. Beijing: World Bank. www.worldbank.org.cn/china

Woronov, Terry. 2009. 'Migrant Children and Migrant Schooling: Policies, Problems and Possibilities'. In *Migration and Social Development in China*, edited by Rachel Murphy, 96–114. Abingdon: Routledge.

Woronov, Terry. 2016. *Class Work: Vocational Schools and China's Urban Youth*. Stanford: Stanford University Press.

Wright, Stuart. 2018. *Governing Social Change in Amdo: Tibetans in the Era of Compulsory Education and School Consolidation*, July, Doctoral Thesis, University of Sheffield.

Wu, Bebei, Jingdong Luan and Kaiyu Lü. 2009. 'Investigation and Analysis on the Health Status of Left-Behind Children in Rural Anhui' [Anhuisheng nongcun liushou ertong jiankang zhuangkuang de diaocha yu fenxi]. *Technology Economics [Jishu jingji]* 28 (7): 121–127.

Wu, Huifang and Jingzhong Ye. 2016. 'Hollow Lives: Women Left Behind in Rural China'. *Journal of Agrarian Change* 16 (1): 50–69.

Wu, Qiaobing, Deping Lu and Mi Kang. 2015. 'Social Capital and the Mental Health of Children in Rural China with Different Experiences of Parental Migration'. *Social Science and Medicine* 132: 270–277.

Wu, Xiaogang and Donald J. Treiman. 2007. 'Inequality and Equality Under Chinese Socialism: The Hukou System and Intergenerational Occupational Mobility'. *American Journal of Sociology* 113 (2): 415–445.

Wu, Zhihui and Li Jingmei. 2015. 'The Investigation Report of Survival Status for Left Behind Children in Rural Areas' [Zhonggup nongcun liushou ertong shengcun xianzhuang diaocha baogao]. *Journal of China Agricultural University [Zhongguo nongye daxue xuebao]* 32 (1): 65–74.

Xiang, Biao. 2007. 'How Far Are the Left-Behind Left Behind? A Preliminary Study in Rural China'. *Population, Space and Place* 13 (3): 179–191.

Xiang, Biao. 2014. 'The Would-Be Migrant: Post-Socialist Primitive Accumulation, Potential Transnational Mobility, and the Displacement of the Present in Northeast China'. *TRaNS: Trans-Regional and National Studies of Southeast Asia* 2 (2) (July): 183–199.

Xiao, Lina. 2014. *The Experiences of Left-Behind Children in Rural China – A Qualitative Study*, Doctoral Thesis, Department of Social and Policy Sciences, University of Bath, UK.

Xie, Ailei. 2016. *Family Strategies, Guanxi and School Success in Rural China*. Abingdon: Routledge.

Xie, Jianwu. 2009. 'Problems and Countermeasures for the Education of Left Behind Children'. [Liushou xinü de jiaoyu wenti yu duice]. *Education Research Monthly [Jiaoyu xuemu yuekan]* 8: 79–81.

Xu, Hongwei and Yu Xie. 2013. 'The Causal Effects of Rural-to-Urban Migration on Children's Wellbeing in China'. *Population Studies Centre Research Report*, Report

Bibliography 279

Number 13–798, August, Population Studies Research Centre, University of Michigan Institute of Social Research.

Xu, Ling, Merril Silverstein and Iris Chi. 2014. 'Emotional Closeness between Grandparents and Grandchildren in Rural China: The Mediating Role of the Middle Generation'. *Journal of Intergenerational Relationships* 12 (3): 226–240.

Xu, Minglei and Chen Fukuan. 2016. 'The Precipitous Decline in the Numbers of Left Behind Children' [Liushou ertong shuliang zhen duanyashi xiajiang qushi]. *Guangming Ribao [Guangming Ribao]*, 1 December, accessed on People's Consultative Net [Renmin zhengxie wang] http://csgy.rmzxb.com.cn/c/2016–12-01/1185073.shtml (last accessed 4 December 2018).

Xu, Wenjuan and Tang Jianfan. 2011. Jiangxisheng nongcun liushou ertong jiaoyu zhuangkuang diaocha. *Jiaoyuxue [Education Studies]*, 14 September. https://wenku.baidu.com/view/5ec72b1514791711cc7917dd.html (last accessed 4 December 2018).

Xu, Yiyuan, Jo Ann M. Farver, Zengxiu Zhang, Qiang Zeng, Lidong Yu and Beiying Cai. 2005. 'Mainland Chinese Parenting Styles and Parent-Child Interaction'. *International Journal of Behavioral Development* 29 (6): 524–531.

Yan, Hairong. 2008. *New Masters, New Servants: Migration, Development and Women Workers in China*. Durham: Duke University Press.

Yan, Honghe and Xiatao Zhu. 2006. 'Survey of the Influence of the Boarding School System on the Education of Left Behind Children in the Countryside'. [Jisuzhi xuexiao dui nongcun liushou ertong jiaoyu yingxiang de diaocha]. *Modern Middle School and Primary School Education [Xiandai zhongxiaoxue jiaoyu]* 1 (143): 4–6.

Yan, Yunxiang. 2003. *Private Life Under Socialism: Love, Intimacy and Family Change in a Chinese Village*. Stanford: Stanford University Press.

Yan, Yunxiang. 2010. 'The Chinese Path to Individualization'. *British Journal of Sociology* 61 (3): 489–512.

Yan, Yunxiang. 2011. 'The Individualization of the Family in Rural China'. *Boundary 2* 38 (1): 204–229.

Yan, Yunxiang. 2012. 'Of the Individual and Individualisation: The Striving Individual in China and the Theoretical Implications'. In *Futures of Modernity: Challenges for Cosmopolitan Thought and Practice*, edited by Michael Heinlein, Cordula Kropp, Judith Neumer, Angelika Poferi and Regina Römhild, 177–195. Bielefield: Transcript-Verlag.

Yan, Yunxiang. 2013. 'Afterword: The Drive for Success and the Ethics of the Striving Individual'. In *Ordinary Ethics in China Today*, edited by Charles Stafford, 263–292. London: Bloomsbury Academic Publishing.

Yang, Jing. 2009. 'Brief Analysis of Bias in the Socialization of Rural Left-Behind Children'. [Qiantan nongcun liushou ertong de shejuihua piancha]. *Knowledge Economy [Zhishi jingji]* 14: 83–84.

Yao, Bianfang and Ya She. 2009. 'Analysis on the Management Policy of Left-Behind Children's Education'. [Touxi nongcun liushouo ertong jiaoyu guanli zhengce]. *Education and Teaching Research [Jiaoyu yu jiaoxue yanjiu]* 23 (8) (August): 18–22.

Ye, Jingzhong. 2011. 'Left-Behind Children: The Social Price of China's Economic Boom'. *Journal of Peasant Studies* 38 (3): 613–650.

Ye, Jingzhong, Chunyu Wang, Huifang Wu, Congze He and Juan Liu. 2013. 'Internal Migration and Left-Behind Populations in China'. *Journal of Peasant Studies* 40 (6): 1119–1146.

Ye, Jingzhong and Lu Pan. 2011. 'Differentiated Childhoods: Impacts of Rural Migration on Left Behind Children in China'. *Journal of Peasant Studies* 38 (2): 355–377.

Yeoh, Brenda. 2019. 'Global Householding, Care Migration and the Question of Gender Inequality'. Seminar in Dept. of Social Anthropology, University of Oxford, 11 March.

Yeoh, Brenda and Theodora Lam. 2006. 'The Costs of (Im)mobility: Children Left Behind and Children Who Migrate with A Parent', In *Perspectives on Gender and Migration*, 120–149. Bangkok: United Nations Economic and Social Commission for Asia and the Pacific.

Yeung, Wei-Jun Jean and Xiaorong Gu. 2016. 'Left Behind by Parents in China: Internal Migration and Adolescents' Well-Being'. *Marriage and Family Review* 52 (1–2): 127–161.

Yi, Hongmei, Guirong Li, Liying Li, Prashant Loyalka, Linxiu Zhang, Jiajia Xu, Elena Kardanova, Henry Shi and James Chu. 2018. 'Assessing the Quality of Upper-Secondary Vocational Education and Training: Evidence from China'. *Comparative Education Review* 62 (2) (May): 199–230.

Yin, Pumin. 2016. 'Caring for Left-Behind Children'. *Beijing Review* 13, 31 March. www.bjreview.com/Nation/201603/t20160329_800053309.html (last accessed 3 December 2018).

Youniss, James and Jacqueline Smollar. 1985. *Adolescent Relations with Mothers, Fathers and Friends*. Chicago: University of Chicago Press.

Young, Nathalie A. E. and Emily Hannum. 2018. 'Childhood Inequality in China: Evidence from Recent Survey Data (2012–2014)'. *China Quarterly* 236 (December): 1063–1087.

Yu, Ning. 2015. 'A New Wave of the "Study is No Use" Theory Exists in the Countryside – Does the Countryside Not Love Study Anymore?' [Xinyibo dushu wuyong lun cunzaiyu zhongguo xiangcun – nongmen bu zai ai dushu?]. *Jingji ribao [Economic Daily]*, 15 November: 1. www.gywb.cn/content/2015–11/15/content_4148820.htm

Yue, Ai, Yaojiang Shi, Renfu Luo, Jamie Chen, James Garth, Jimmy Zhang, Alexis Medina, Sarah Kotb and Scott Rozelle. 2017. 'China's Invisible Crisis: Cognitive Delays among Rural Toddlers and the Absence of Modern Parenting'. *China Journal*, 78 (July): 50–80.

Zeitlyn, Benjamin and Kanwal Mand. 2012. 'Researching Transnational Childhoods'. *Journal of Ethnic and Migration Studies* 38 (6): 987–1006.

Zelizer, Viviana A. 1994. *Pricing the Priceless Child: The Changing Social Value of Children*. Princeton, NJ: Princeton University Press.

Zeng, Cuigu. 2005. 'Substitute Mother 'Zhong Wenhua' – The Story of Teacher Zhong Wenhua who Cares for Rural Left Behind Children in Yushan County Nanshan Township'. [Daili mama Zhong Wenhua – Yushanxian Nanshanxiang jiaoshi Zhong Wenhua guanai nongcun liushou ertong jishi]. *Jiangxi Education [Jiangxi jiaoyu]* 10A: 16–17.

Zhan, Shaohua. 2017. '*Hukou* Reform and Land Politics in China: The Rise of a Tripartite Alliance'. *The China Journal* 78 (1): 25–49.

Bibliography

Zhang, Hong. 2007. 'China's New Rural Daughters Coming of Age: Downsizing the Family and Firing up Cash-Earning Power in the New Economy'. *Signs* 32(3): 671–698.

Zhang, Li. 2001. *Strangers in the City: Reconfigurations of Space, Power, and Social Networks Within China's Floating Population*. Stanford: Stanford University Press.

Zhang, Li. 2012. 'Economic Migration and Urban Citizenship in China: The Role of Points Systems'. *Population and Development Review* 38 (3) (September): 503–533.

Zhang, Nan, Laia Bécares and Tarani Chandola. 2015. 'Does the Timing of Parental Migration Matter for Child Growth? A Life Course Study on Left-Behind Children in Rural China'. *BMC Public Health* 15 (1): 966.

Zhang, Nan, Tarani Chandola, Liai Bécares and Peter Callery. 2016. 'Paternal Migration, Intergenerational Obligations and the Paradox for Left-Behind Boys in Rural China', *Asian Population Studies* 12 (1): 68–89.

Zhang, Nana. 2013. 'Rural Women Migrant Returnees in Contemporary China'. *Journal of Peasant Studies* 40 (1): 171–188.

Zhang, Nana. 2015. 'Home Divided, Home Reconstructed: Children in Rural-Urban Migration in Contemporary China'. *Children's Geographies* 13 (4): 381–397.

Zhang, Ran. 2007. 'Changing Constructions of the Right to Education in China'. Paper presented at the Annual Meeting of the American Research Association, Chicago, 9–13 April.

Zhang, Sufeng. 2009. 'Legal Relationship and Legal Liability in Substitute Management of Left-Behind Children'. [Nongcun liushou ertong daiguan de falü guanxi ji falü zeren]. *Journal of Anhui Normal University [Anhui shifan daxue xuebao]* 37 (7) (July): 420–425.

Zhou, Chengchao, Sean Sylvia, Linxiu Zhang, Renfu Luo, Hongmei Yi, Chengfang Liu, Yaojiang Shi, Prashant Loyalka, James Chu, Alexis Medina and Scott Rozelle. 2015. 'China's Left-Behind Children: Impact of Parental Migration on Health, Nutrition and Educational Outcomes'. *Health Affairs* 34 (11): 1–8.

Zhou, Minhui, Rachel Murphy and Ran Tao. 2014. 'Effects of Parents' Migration on the Education of Children Left Behind in Rural China'. *Population and Development Review* 40 (2): 273–292.

Zhou, Xianqian. 2007. 'Brief Discussion of How to Make Boarding Schools the Second Home of Left-Behind Children'. [Qiantan ruhe ba jisu xuexiao dazao cheng liushou ertong de di er ge jia]. *Research into Basic Education [Jichu Jiaoyu Yanjiu]* 7 (July): 15–17.

Index

2010 Summer Survey, 234

abeyance, 221–222
abuse
  physical abuse of a child, 210
  sexual abuse of left-behind children, 22
Africa, 50, 138–139, 153
age
  and children's relationships in skipped
    generation families, 198–207
  and children's views of parents' support, 110
  and life course, 4
  children's age at father's migration, 153, 160
agency
  and inequalities, 40
  and structure/context, 6–10
  definition, 4
  of children, 7, 10, 22, 36, 211, 216–225
agricultural mechanisation, 126
agricultural production. *See* farming
agricultural taxes, 42
alcohol, 29
ambiguous loss, 156
ambivalence, 156, 170, 174, 196, 203
Anagnost, Ann, 32
Anhui
  economic conditions, 40–53
  migration patterns, 49
  percentage of rural children left behind, 51
Ariès, Philippe, 4
aspiration
  for education, 67–70
aspirations
  and expectations, 85
  and striving, 5
  definition of, 9
  for education, 66
  of parents for children's education, 45,
    70–73
  to buy urban housing, 59
  urbanisation of, 17, 59
Atkinson, Will, 7–9, 95, 225

attachment
  mother–child, 29, 136
  parent–child, 26

Bijie county, Guizhou province, 22, 77, 227
boarding school, 20, 53–64, 93, 98, 123–126,
  194, 224
Bourdieu, Pierre, 7–9, 25, 31, 217
boys
  and behavioural problems, 121, 130
  impact of parental migration on, 27–28
  poor nutrition of left-behind boys, 29, 105
  teachers' view of, 60
Brandtstädter, Susanne, 33
Bronfenbrenner, Urie, 6, 36, 229
bullying, 28

Caihong, 168–170, 172–176
capital, 152
  accumulation of, 22, 184, 225, 227
  definition of, 8
  numeric, 44, 222
  placeless, 225
capitalism
  global, 13, 15
  renewal of, 225
  Western neoliberal, 30
care
  across distance, 19, 36
  as provisioning, 185
  children's wish to care for migrant
    parents, 203
  definition of, 18–19
  ethic of, 18–19, 226
  idiom of, 24, 231
  of left-behind children, 18–20, 207
Care for Left-Behind Children
  activities to, 229–231
  official calls to, 77
  slogans, 25
care histories of children, 196–197
Chao, Ruth K., 35

Index

child development, 26, 35
child, as a relational category, 33–34
childhood, new social studies of, 4
child-raising, intensive, 10
children
  and play, 39, 61, 226, 240
  as emotionally precious/rising scarcity
    value, 36, 99, 132
  as sites of accumulation, 217
  encouraging mothers to stay at home, 140
  go to 'waste', 185, 211
  living alone, 20, 83
  perceptions of gender inequality, 115–120
  perceptions of grandparents' care, 185–186
  perceptions of parental support, 84, 138
  relationship with migrant parents, 191–192,
    195–214
children, young, 192, 198–203
children's outings, with migrant parents,
  209–210
children's viewpoints, 4, 22, 183, 216, 222
children's voices, 33, 224–227
Chinese New Year, 72, 155, 158, 190–192
Choi, Susanne and Yinni Peng, 133–134, 166
cities
  concentration of educational resources in, 59
  inland, 103
  left-behind children's experiences of,
    207–211
  low status of migrants in, 17–18, 133
class, 9, 23–25
classmates/friends, 63, 83, 84, 93, 152, 178,
  181, 209
Coe, Cati, 19, 20, 138, 160, 206, 217–218, 225
communes, 11, 30, 44
communication technologies, 19, see phone
  calls
communication, parent–child, 19, 28, 36, 82
Compulsory Education Law, 15–16, 46
Connell, Raewyn W. and James
    W. Messerschmidt, 133
construction workers, 49–50, 138–139, 154,
  158–159
cousins, 119, 128, 191, 198–200, 208, 209
crime, by left-behind children, 23
cultural capital
  accumulation of, 9, 132
  definition of, 8
cultural context, 30–37, 98–100, 219–221
Cultural Revolution, 45
culture of migration, 9, 137
curriculum
  regional differences in, 17
  rural–urban differences in, 45, 67
  urbanisation of, 75

dagong, 18, 39, 69, 73–74, 228
daughters, 98
  and closeness to parents, 107
  housing for, 106–107, 111
  study pressures on, 110
death
  of a grandparent caregiver, 83, 197, 201
  of a parent, 64, 177–179
delinquency, of left-behind children, 23
disability, 139, 159, 167, 170, 176
discrimination, against migrants, 17
divorce, 26, 171
domestic chores
  of children, 122–126, 127–128, 179
  of grandmothers, 165–166
  of grandparents, 35, 198, 201
  of men, 166, 182
  of women, 60, 133, 139, 165
Douglass, Mike, 7
Dreby, Joanna, 40, 71, 73, 95, 182, 203, 212,
  220, 244
drop-outs, 44, 46
Duan Chenrong, 12, 14, 17

education
  and children's gender, 69, 107–110
  gender gap in, 48
  returns to, 69–70
  rural–urban gap in, 46, 56–59, 67–69
education migration, 217
education, compulsory, 53
educational progression, 46, 67
educational well-being
  of left-behind children, 26–30
elder care, reliance on children, 99
Elder, Glen, 6, 195
emotional well-being
  of children of lone-migrant mothers,
    167–168
  of left-behind children, 26–29
exams, 17, 32, 75
  gaokao, 45, 53, 59, 70
  zhongkao, 53, 67, 68, 91, 205

factories
  interns in, 88–89
  migrants' work in, 50–51
  recruitment tests, 48
  working conditions, 43, 74, 228–229
familialism, 110, 129, 218
  mosaic familialism, 34–35
family bargains, 93
family conflict, 170–172, 189–190, 203, 212
family dissolution, 26
family division (fenjia), 11, 184, 188–192

284   Index

family fragmentation, 26
family nuclearisation, 34, 132, 184
family, ideal image of, 136
Fan, Cindy, 163
Fangfang, 121, 126, 164–166, 174
farming
  and gender, 12
  and subsistence, 20
  by at-home fathers, 175
  by at-home mothers, 142–143
  by grandparents, 20, 140, 189, 198, 200
  children's involvement in, 122, 126, 178
  income from, 42
  migrant fathers' return to help with, 157
fatherhood, 7, 133, 153, 166, 216, 219
  urban middle-class models of, 134, 137
fathers
  and discipline of children, 134, 156, 166
  children's relationships with migrant fathers,
    153–159
  children's view of migrant fathers as
    providers, 153–161
  Jingjing's father, 86–88
  lone migration of, 25–29, 49
  migrant fathers' emotions for children, 134
  migrant fathers' provisioning, 133–134
Fei Xiaotong, 35, 77
Fengmian, 149–152, 190, 200
fertility decline, 13, 34, 36, 53, 69, 115
fertility limitation policies, 24
Field, Norma, 9, 30
fieldwork counties
  economic conditions, 42–43
  farm crops, 42
  gender gap in parents' education, 48
  industrial sectors, 43
  percentage of children by parents' migration
    status, 53
  research access to, 234–235
filial piety, 33–37, 71, 75, 76–77, 93, 97, 169,
    206, 216, 217, 219
fiscal decentralisation, 45
food, 36, 155, 185, 190, 200–201
future, the, 9, 182, 217–218, 221–222, 225

gambling, 139, 141, 143, 159, 172, 174,
    189, 210
gatekeepers, in fieldwork access, 235
gender
  and filial obligation, 98
  and resource distribution to children, 95–120
  definition of, 95
  division of labour, 12, 127–128,
    164–166, 175
  doing gender, 95

social construction of, 7, 218
gender beliefs, 23, 96, 138
gender equality
  children's perceptions of, 119
  in parents' education investments, 107–111
gender substitution effect, 122
gendered bargain, in farmer-migrant
    families, 145
geographic location, 40
Ghana, 163
gifts, 115, 189
Gilligan, Carol, 226
global house-holding, 7
Goh, Ester, 21, 181, 186
gongzuo, 18
grandfathers
  as father substitute, 174
grandmothers, 119
  as mother substitute, 165–166
  encouraging daughters-in-law to stay
    home, 140
grandparent caregivers' well-being, 182
grandparents, 73, 125
  children's care of, 83, 189
  children's relationships with, 181–207
  children's separations from grandparent
    caregivers, 201–202
  education of, 45, 47
  leniency of, 186
  maternal grandparent caregivers, 192–195
  paternal grandparent caregivers, 186–192
  perceived inadequacies of, 23, 182, 184–186
  unavailable for childcare, 147, 187–188
Great Famine of 1959–1961, 44
Great Leap Forward of 1958, 44
Gross Domestic Product, 41
grounded theory, 244
Growing Home, 229
Gruijters, Rob, 213
guan, 2, 35, 36, 138, 148, 205

habitus, 8, 9, 31, 47, 95, 176, 217
Hägglund, Martin, 225
Hanhan, 149–152, 181–184, 186, 203
Hannum, Emily, 70
Hansen, Mette Halskov, 32, 69, 231
health
  of grandparent caregivers, 83, 189
  of left-behind children, 26, 29
hegemonic masculinity, 133
hierarchies, 31, 32
higher education
  admissions discrimination, 68
  aspirations for, 66, 68–70, 176–177
  expansion of, 69

Index

internal stratification of, 68, 70
hobbies, 67
holidays, 202, 207–211, 230
homework, 1, 10, 23, 28, 72, 145, 148, 150, 155, 177, 185, 186, 210
household registration system. *See hukou*
household responsibility farming system, 11, 44
household, definition of, 11
housing
    and marriage, 101–102
    and school admissions, 59, 103
    buying in the county seat, 103–106
    house-building in villages, 101–103
    improvements to, 103
    prices in county seat, 104
hukou, 11, 12, 15–17, 49, 59, 64, 145, 150
    conversion of, 17, 104
    points-based system, 17

immobility, 21, 40, 137, 167, 223
imperial governing complex, 32
individualisation, 35, 231
Indonesia, 155, 163
industrial zones, 42
industrialisation, 11
industrialisation, in interior provinces, 228–229
industries, relocation inland, 49
injuries
    of left-behind children, 29
    of migrants, 15
intensive mothering, 132–133, 160
intergenerational comparison, 46–47
intergenerational debt, 34
internet, 88
    addiction, 28
    bars, 3
interviews, 3, 234–244
    analysis of interview data, 244–245
    children's playfulness in, 239
    follow-up interviews, 242
    inconsistencies, 243
    influence of school setting on, 238–239
    matching interviews with adult caregivers, 239–244
    maximum variation selection, 235
    selection of research participants, 235–238
intimacy
    children and at-home fathers, 170
    children and at-home mothers, 144
    children and grandparents, 169–170, 192–195, 196–207
    children and migrant fathers, 153–157
    children and parents, 36–37

children and returnee mothers, 152
feminisation of, 132
gap in children's lives, 230
girls and grandmothers, 128

Jacka, Tamara, 7, 11, 12, 165, 188
Jankowiak, William, 36, 134, 198
Japan, 70
Ji Yingzhun, 34
Jiangxi
    economic conditions, 40–53
    migration patterns, 49
    percentage of rural children left behind, 51
jiedufe, 59
Jingjing, 85–89, 119, 164, 172–174, 180, 202, 209, 213

Kaili, 64, 178–179
Katz, Cindi, 5, 14, 22, 37, 217, 225, 226
Kipnis, Andrew, 8, 33, 34, 43, 67–70, 99, 135
Kohrman, Matthew, 167
Koo, Anita, 85

labour shortages, 228
land
    and subsistence, 19
    transfers of farmland usage rights, 42
Lanlan, 169–176
left-behind
    critique of framework, 21–22
left-behind children
    behavioural problems, 28
    policies towards, 79, 227–231
    representation of, 22–25
    school activity rooms for, 78–82
    school support for, 77–84
    statistics on, 13–14, 227–228
Lele, 109–110, 119, 155
Libya, 154
life course, 4, 6–7, 195–207, 216
linked lives, 6–10, 34, 183, 184, 195, 196, 215
Liu, Fengshu, 165
Liwei, 192–194, 203–204, 206–207, 213
loneliness, 28, 29, 103, 142, 169, 200

majority world, 1, 4
manual work, 46
market economy, 9, 18, 165
marriage, 46, 99, 107, 111, 163–165
    discord, 170–172, 176–177
Massey, Doreen, 39
maternal migration, negative view of, 24, 140
Mayall, Berry, 45, 220, 226
medical debts, 163
mega-cities, 17

286   Index

Menjívar, Cecilia and Victor Agadjanian,
   132
meritocracy, 70, 75
Mexico, 96, 134, 137, 158, 167, 203, 220
middle-class, 10, 24, 31, 92, 133, 137, 160,
   208, 235
migrant children
   schools for, 15–17, 25, 68, 121
   well-being of, 27
migrant parents, criticism of, 23
migrants
   age of, 13
   census definition, 12
   destinations, 49, 50
   gender of, 12–13, 49–53
   generational change, 18
   permanently temporary, 156
   statistics on, 12
migration
   transnational, 49
Mingming, 171–172, 176–177
Ministry of Civil Affairs, 14
Ministry of Education, 15, 16, 56, 78
motherhood, 7, 24, 132, 152, 216, 219
mothers
   and children's studies, 144–145
   as gatekeepers between migrant fathers and
     children, 158–159
   as homemakers, 135–138
   children's relationships with at-home
     mothers, 140–146
   children's relationships with migrant
     mothers, 168–172
   children's relationships with returnee
     mothers, 146–152
   educational disadvantages of, 133
   lone migration of, 26–29, 49, 162–173
multilocal families
   definition, 5
   literature on, 7–8
multilocal intergenerational parenting
   coalitions, 182
multiple mothering, 182

neglect, of left-behind children, 23
new migrants, former left-behinds,
   231–233
normalisation, of parental migration, 39,
   223–226
nutrition, 29, 96, 189, 194

off-farm employment, local, 42–43
On the Road to School, 14, 27, 28, 29, 85, 134,
   163, 167
One Child policy, 24

Pan, Lu, 232
paradigm shift, 225–227
parent–child relationships, 36
parent-child striving teams, 10, 30, 38,
   171–179, 217, 219–227
parenting
   gendered models of, 132, 135–138,
     159–161, 168, 218
   impact of stress on, 26
   impact of working conditions on, 229
   interventions, 230
parents' departures, 71–73, 86, 157, 202
Parents' Differential Treatment (PDT) of
   siblings, 97, 110
parents, education of, 46
parent–teacher meetings, 176
Parreñas, Rhacel Salazar, 23, 134, 156, 220
patriarchy, 13, 34, 64, 145, 165, 226
peidu, 56, 105, 148–152, 165, 194, 200,
   228
pension, old age, 15, 177, 189
people-centred development, 16
Philippines, 134, 155, 163
phone calls, 19, 27, 72–73, 82, 125, 153, 156,
   159, 174, 178, 189
   from lone-migrant fathers, 134
place
   idea of, 39
   in children's lives, 61–62
pocket money, 46, 190
pollution, 104
population aging, 13
price scissors, 11
production, and forms of work, 5
production, ceaseless, 10
Production, definition of, 14
Public Security Bureau, 15
Puhua, 126, 141–142, 152, 157
punishment, corporal, 91, 145, 155, 202,
   210, 230

qin (close), 137, 153, 170

real–estate, 16
recognition, 7–8, 66, 95, 127, 130, 173, 212,
   220–221
relatives as caregivers, 202
remittances, 96, 132, 139, 153–159, 167, 182,
   189–190, 193
repertoires, 8, 34, 36, 96, 206, 219, 225
research assistants, 237–239
resentment
   of teenagers towards migrant parents,
     204–206
resilience, 84, 219, 232

Index

return migration
  of children, 17, 60, 196
  of fathers, 137–138, 154–155, 164, 167
  of mothers, 136, 146–152, 163
  of parents, 228
Risman, Barbara J., 95
Rozelle, Scott, 27, 136
rural status
  devalued, 11, 24, 45, 64, 183

sacrifice
  migration as, 71, 84, 94, 189, 217
  mothers' non-migration as, 142–146
  of left-behind fathers, 175
Santos, Gonçalo, 182
Sanxin, 210–211
Schmalzbauer, Leah, 40, 212
school fees, 3, 17, 20, 45, 54, 68
school progression rates, 27
schools
  admissions, 59, 105
  and care of children, 20
  and children's daily lives, 62–64
  and family care routines, 60
  and meals, 53–56
  as institutions, 8
  as social services infrastructure, 40
  mergers and consolidation, 53–56
  private, 59, 61
  senior high, 53
service sector, 50–51, 164, 228
sex ratio imbalance, 98–100, 120
Shenyi, 71, 164, 177–178
siblings, 27, 72, 83, 101, 111–122, 125, 128, 192, 200, 207–209
  separated by parental migration, 120–122
skill, learning a, 89–91
skipped generation families, 181–207
smoking, 29
social and spatial mobility, 17, 33
social capital, 8, 71
social field
  and recognition, 8–9
  market economy as a, 9
  translocal, 22
  transnational, 217
social location, 40, 48
social reproduction, 225
  definition, 14
  schools' contribution to, 53–62, 200–201
social services infrastructure, 40
socialisation, 21, 71
  and gender, 95, 107
  in school, 75–84
  in the family, 71–74

of children, 8
to expect an urban future, 217, 232
sons
  housing for, 101–106, 110
  preference for, 98, 163
spectacle, childhood as, 22
Stafford, Charles, 35
State Council, 15, 78, 224, 227
strategies, definition of, 8
stratified reproduction, 20
striving, 30–33
  definition, 5–10
  objectives, 44
  slogans, 75
striving ethos, 183
study
  pressures, 110
  as work, 5
  children's inner conflicts about, 84–89
  pressures, 93, 211
Summer Survey, 4, 43, 46, 48, 49, 51, 56, 66, 125, 126, 162, 163, 167, 207, 232, 235
Sun Zhigang, 12
Sun, Wanning, 24, 41, 43
suzhi, 32, 43, 68, 124
suzhi education reforms, 67
Swider, Sarah, 156

Taihe, 164, 172, 174, 176–177
teachers
  as substitute parents, 63, 76
  boarding with, 58
  during the Cultural Revolution, 45
  numbers of, 53
  pressures on, 76, 81
  support to children from, 83
  view of grandparent caregivers, 185
  view of migrant parents, 23
teenagers, 84, 144, 203–207
television, 18, 23, 84, 111, 135, 137, 157
Tianming, 148, 158
time-space compression, 39
tragedies, involving left-behind children, 22, 227
travel, costs for migrants, 19, 155
travel, to school, 53, 56, 62, 198
tutoring, 63, 66, 87, 145, 160, 177, 230
two basics, 69
two exemptions and one subsidy, 17
two-parent migration, 25–29, 49

underdevelopment
  as identity, 43
  rural, 24
urban bias, 18

288   Index

urbanisation
  exclusionary, 27
  in interior provinces, 49
  policies, 16, 232
urbanisation rates, 49, 227
uterine family, 146

victimisation, 28
Vietnam, 164, 166, 175
visits
  of children to *see* parents, 2, 19, 73, 84, 123,
    202, 207–211
  of lone-migrant mothers, 175
  of migrant fathers, 154–157
  of parents to *see* children, 19, 72, 84,
    125, 198
vocational schools
  and internships, 89
  low status of, 69, 89
  migrants' access to, 16
  regional differences in, 89–91

wages, 31
  gender gap in, 137
  in Africa, 139
  of migrants, 15
  wage penality of former left-behinds, 231
Wang Delun, 48, 63–64, 90, 123, 186,
    205–206, 213

Waters, Joanna, 217
Wenwen, 62–63
West, Candace and Don H. Zimmerman, 95,
    168, 179–180
widowed grandparents, 199
Wolf, Margery, 36, 132
work
  and affective value/emotions, 33
  and masculinity, 133, 166–167, 172–174
  children helping migrant parents with, 208
  Chinese terms for, 18
  conceptualisation of, 5–8, 33–34
  working hours, 15
work points, 11
work unit, 30, 70
Woronov, Terry, 44
would-be migrants, 218

Xiang, Biao, 21, 24, 218
Xinhao, 144–145, 155–156
Xinhui, 90, 106–107, 111

Yan, Yunxiang, 31, 32, 225
yang, 1, 35, 157, 185, 198, 204
Yaping, 181–183
Ye Jingzhong, 18, 224
Yulin, 140–141, 154–155

Zhangyong, 1–3, 127, 190, 199, 208, 213

Printed in the United States
by Baker & Taylor Publisher Services